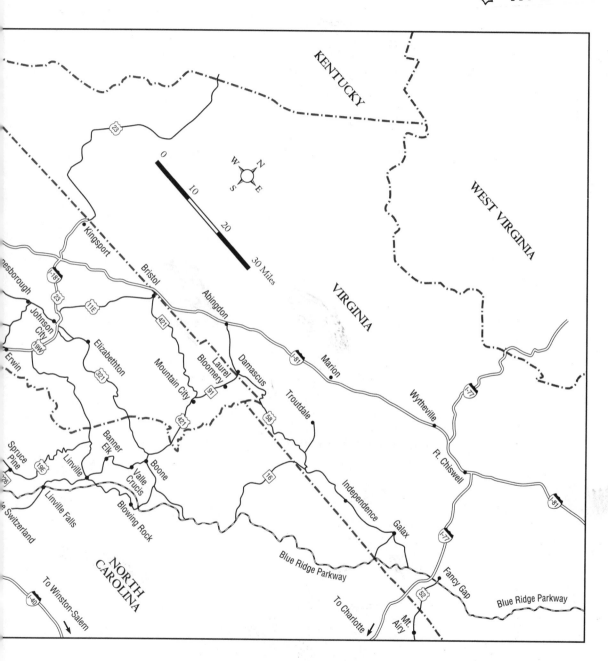

Traveling the
SOUTHERN HIGHLANDS

A COMPLETE TOUR GUIDE TO THE MOUNTAINS OF NORTHEAST GEORGIA,
EAST TENNESSEE, WESTERN NORTH CAROLINA, AND SOUTHWEST VIRGINIA

CATHY AND VERNON SUMMERLIN

RUTLEDGE HILL PRESS ■ *Nashville, Tennessee*

Published in Nashville, Tennessee, by Rutledge Hill Press®, 211 Seventh Avenue North, Nashville, Tennessee 37219. Distributed in Australia by The Five Mile Press Pty., Ltd., 22 Summit Road, Nobel Park, Victoria 3174. Distributed in Canada by H. B. Fenn & Company, Ltd., 34 Nixon Road, Bolton, Ontario L7E 1W2. Distributed in New Zealand by Tandem Press, 2 Rugby Road, Birkenhead, Auckland 10. Distributed in the United Kingdom by Verulam Publishing, Ltd., 152a Park Street Lane, Park Street, St. Albans, Hertfordshire AL2 2AU.

Typography by Compass Communications, Inc., Nashville, Tennessee
Design by Bruce Gore, Gore Studio, Inc., Nashville, Tennessee
Maps by Parrot Graphics

All photographs are by the authors unless otherwise indicated.

Library of Congress Cataloging-in-Publication Data

Summerlin, Vernon, 1943–
    Traveling the Southern Highlands / Vernon and Cathy Summerlin.
        p.   cm.
    Includes index.
    ISBN 1-55853-484-9
    I. Appalachian Region, Southern—Guidebooks.   I. Summerlin,
Cathy, 1953–   . II. Title.
F217.A65S88   1997
917.504'43—dc21   97-9487
                                                                                              CIP

Printed in the United States of America

10 9 8 7 6 5 4 3 2 — 01 00 99 98

For Bobbie McAllister, for all the love through all the years.

For Bud and Carolyn Tipton, for making so many of my earliest adventures such fun.

CSS

For Conrad and June Summerlin, who have shown me warmth and kindness all my life.

For Carolyn Collier, who gave me gifts and told me stories from exotic lands that created a yearning to see what's over the horizon.

VSS

Contents

21   Fontana: Best Kept Secret in the Smokies   175
22   Franklin: Where the Beauty Never Ends   179
23   Highlands: High Altitude and Attitude   187
24   Cashiers and Lake Toxaway   193
25   Hendersonville, Flat Rock, and Lake Lure   199
26   Waynesville: Fashionably Old-Fashioned   207
27   Maggie Valley: The Playground   213
28   Dillsboro: A New Spirit Springs from the Past   220
29   Blue Ridge Parkway: The Best of Then Is Now   228
30   Cherokee: Home of the Eastern Band of the Cherokee   238
31   Balsam: Comfort Among the Mountains   247
32   Asheville: An Uptown Downtown   250
33   Weaverville: Rustic and Cozy   266
34   Banner Elk, Linville, Little Switzerland, Spruce Pine, Valle Crucis:
       The Higher Highlands   269
35   Boone: Coolest Town in the South   276
36   Blowing Rock: Crown Jewel of the Blue Ridge   281
37   Mount Airy: A Great Place for a Day or a Lifetime   289
38   North Carolina Outdoor Recreation   293

Virginia   308

39   Abingdon: Living History   309
40   Damascus: Friendliest Town on the Appalachian Trail   317
41   Troutdale: In the Shadow of Mount Rogers   320
42   Independence: Legacy Preserved   322
43   Galax: Virginia's Rising Star   325
44   Virginia Outdoor Recreation   329

     Suggested Readings   339
     Index   341

Acknowledgments

There were as many people involved in making this book possible as there are pages in it. Although we can't mention each one by name, we must acknowledge Larry Stone, president of Rutledge Hill Press, for his faith in this book and willingness to support it; Amy Lyles Wilson, this book's champion and editor; and Kath Hansen, our persistent publicist.

We thank all who have opened their inns and businesses to us and graciously shared their time and knowledge: Kay Powell, Bob Easton, Steve Galyean, Judy Watson, Dave Redman, Daniel Jeanette, Alan Wray, George and Rita Sivess, Cobb and Cindy Milner, Marilyn Bateman, Merrily Teasley, Caroline Logie, Martin and Tesa Burson, Rebecca Ogle, Frank Kraft, Joey Barnes, Ben Collins, Ginger and Bud Shinn, Sharon Hartbarger, Kathy Price, Ham Schwartz, Richard and Hazel Ramos-Cano, Mark and Janet Holmes, Peggy Palmer, and Christopher Welch.

The Convention and Visitor's Bureaus and Chambers of Commerce in Tennessee, Georgia, North Carolina, and Virginia provided us with invaluable local information, and rangers in the Great Smoky Mountains National Park and the Blue Ridge Parkway gave us the benefit of their immense knowledge.

A special thanks to Anita Duck, John Maxwell, and Libby Oldfield for sharing their love of the mountain places; to Kim Sory and Charlie Rush for their encouragement and support; and to Nelson Parks for sharing his Blue Ridge biking experiences.

As always we are grateful to Kathie German for giving us peace of mind while we're traveling.

Most of all perhaps, we appreciate the kindness of all those of you who talked with us on the streets and trails of the Southern Highlands and shared with us your favorite places to visit.

Introduction

Although most of you are familiar with the alluring Great Smoky Mountains National Park, a few of you may not realize that the southern Appalachian Mountains, also known as the Southern Highlands, extend through portions of northern Georgia, western North Carolina, and western Virginia, as well as East Tennessee.

We would like to acquaint you with these regions and the equally lovely mountain resorts and retreats in them, while giving you a more intimate view of the Great Smoky Mountains.

In order to do so, we explain the geologic events that led to the formation of the Southern Highlands; the history of the Indian presence; early colonization by the Scots-Irish during the 1700s; and visit significant cultural and historic sites.

The North Georgia section includes the site of our nation's first gold rush in Dahlonega, wonderful old mountain resorts from the 1800s, hiking along the southern terminus of the Appalachian Trail, and whitewater sports on the famous Chattooga River.

In the Tennessee section, we have included information about remarkable learning opportunities for those of you with special interests ranging from Wilderness Week in Pigeon Forge to the Smoky Mountain Field School, Arrowmont School in Gatlinburg, wildflower pilgrimages, fiddle festivals, and sacred harp singings.

North Carolina contains the longest segment of the Blue Ridge Parkway taking you along the oldest mountains in the world from Cherokee to Asheville's Biltmore Estate and fine dining, to golf and skiing resort communities in the higher Highlands, to natural and manmade wonders, and to the "shoppingest" city in western North Carolina.

In the far western tip of the state, we take you to old cities grown new again, water falls and hiking trails, and a multitude of places you'll love. The air in western North Carolina is contagious—you'll want to breathe it forever.

The small area of Virginia we cover is host to a great variety of sensory stimulations. You can take in the vistas from Mount Rogers and the Grayson Highlands; enjoy plays at Abingdon's Barter Theatre; listen to the oldest fiddle festival in the United States; sample the cooking coming from splendid B&B kitchens; and feel the cool waters of the world's second oldest stream. There is much to delight you in southwestern Virginia.

Of course, no book about the Southern Highlands would be complete without directions to waterfalls, scenic hikes, swinging bridges, mountain vistas, and locales with abundant wildflowers, so we've included enough of these to keep you coming back for years.

You'll also find descriptions of museums, campgrounds, bed and breakfasts, historic inns, antiques and specialty shops, outdoor recreation opportunities, and our favorite restaurants in each area.

Traveling the Southern Highlands is designed to direct you to adventures in a series of loop tours through each of the four states that will allow you to return to your point of origin or venture into the next state via the routes we believe most worthy of travel. The majority of roads are US and state highways, but occasionally we direct you to especially scenic backroads as an alternate, should you have the time and inclination.

For those of you taking a series of weekend trips, look in each section's prelude for directions via interstates to favored destinations.

We urge you to enjoy these natural and cultural resources, and to gain a deeper appreciation of the importance of protecting these sites for the enjoyment of future generations.

We didn't write about every single wonderful hidden mountain paradise because we haven't yet found them all, but we plan to enjoy all the years we're going to spend trying to do so. We believe you will too!

The mountains are not only places of majesty, but as Karen Wade, superintendent of the Great Smoky Mountains National Park, says, they are places that restore the spirit.

We hope you enjoy your travels in the Southern Highlands.

(Photo by Alan Buck)

Traveling the
SOUTHERN HIGHLANDS

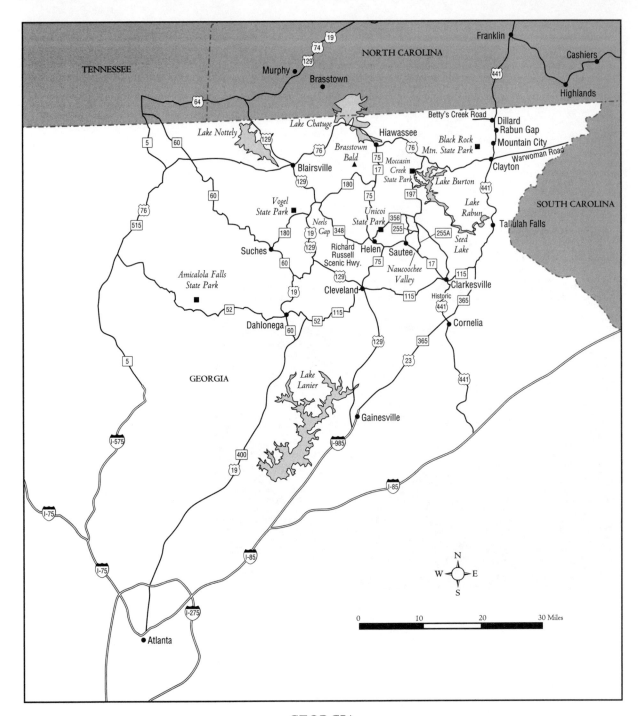

GEORGIA

Georgia

Georgia

Many of you may already realize that the northeast Georgia mountains are much like the Great Smoky Mountains. As well they should be, for both are part of the southern Appalachians (most of us say "ap-ah-latch-uns") we know as the Southern Highlands. The north Georgia chapters are arranged as a loop tour. In other words, an itinerary that will return you to your starting point via a wide circle.

We begin at historic Dahlonega, the site of our nation's first major gold rush. The Appalachian Trail begins its 2,100-mile trek to Mount Katadin, Maine, outside Dahlonega at Amicalola Falls State Park at the foot of Springer Mountain. The circuit continues through Alpine Helen, a very popular resort town, and the lovely Sautee Nacoochee Valley on the way to Clarkesville on US 441, a major north-south thoroughfare.

Leaving Clarkesville and heading north on US 441, we visit the scenic Tallulah Gorge; the Chattooga, a Wild and Scenic River outside Clayton; and Rabun Gap, the home of Foxfire, a center of Appalachian culture popularized by the series of Foxfire books published by Doubleday in the 1970s.

The Chattahoochee National Forest (CNF) is part of the largest wilderness in the eastern United States, and you can travel much of north Georgia in or near its boundaries. Within its vast acreage, visitors will find waterfalls, archaeological sites, tremendous gorges, scenic vistas, hundreds of miles of hiking trails, and plentiful sites for fishing, hunting, and camping. This area is breathtaking when the seasons change. Our northern terminus on US 441 is Dillard.

Our path returns west across the mountains to Hiawassee and Blairsville, or along the mountain lakes of Rabun, Seed, and Burton before returning to Dahlonega. This tour is designed for entrance anywhere along "the loop."

A favorite trip of ours is Rabun County, Georgia, in late spring or early summer. Stay at the York House, go antiquing and dining in Dillard, tour the Foxfire museum in Mountain City, hike the historic Bartram Trail in Warwoman Dell, canoe at Lake Rabun or Seed Lake, and fish on Lake Burton (and in mountain streams). Highlands and Asheville in North Carolina are convenient day trips. In fact, Rabun County is a very good jumping-off point for several trips into the Great Smoky Mountains and the high country of the Blue Ridge to the north.

Georgia offers short hikes to scenic waterfalls like the twin cascades at Helton Creek Falls.

 DIRECTIONS

From north Atlanta—US 129/GA 400 to Dahlonega.

From Atlanta—I-85/I-985 to US 129 to Helen or US 365 to US 441N to Clarkesville.

From the Blue Ridge Parkway or I-40 at Asheville—via US 441S to Dillard.

I Dahlonega:

After the Gold Rush

Northeast Georgia was the site of the first major gold rush in the United States.

Dahlonega (pronounced "da-lawn-a-ga"), nestled in the north Georgia mountains about 75 miles northeast of Atlanta, was the site of America's first major gold rush. One day in 1828, Benjamin Parks discovered a gold-streaked rock while deer hunting. Within four years the population in nearby Auraria had swelled to 10,000 gold-hungry prospectors.

Therein lies a tale of tragedy for the "Ani-Yun-Wiya," the "Principal People," as the Cherokee called themselves. No one knows exactly where they came from, but they inhabited more than four million acres, including the area that was to become north Georgia.

Shifting allegiances were formed as the Cherokee sought to protect their lands from neighboring tribes and then from invading colonists. They were caught up in various European intrigues and made a fateful choice to side with the British against the colonists during the American Revolution.

A series of treaties with the United States ceded lands to the Federal government and created political and philosophical divisions within the Cherokee Nation.

The Georgia legislature passed a series of acts prohibiting the Cherokee from mining on their own property or testifying against whites in court on matters ranging from theft to murder. The crowning blow came in 1831 when the legislature enacted a provision to divide Cherokee lands into tracts that would be awarded by lottery to Georgians.

Factions for and against joining the Cherokee who had already moved west debated the issues, but a clandestine group of pro-removal supporters negotiated a treaty for removal on Dec. 29, 1835, and the deadline for removal was established as May 28, 1838. This series of events paved the way for the gold rush in north Georgia. For more information, see the Cherokee, NC, section.

Between 1828 and 1848, north Georgia produced $35 million in gold coins. In 1838, the United States opened a Federal Branch Mint and the boom continued. In 1848, gold was discovered in California, and Dahlonega was left behind by the hordes of prospectors heading west.

The last large gold mining company, Georgia Consolidated, closed in 1906 when it was determined that the cost of mining the gold remaining in the Georgia mountains exceeded the value of the gold itself. The mine, located on US 19, has been restored and renovated and is on the National Register of Historic Places. Fifty-four pounds of gold were removed from this mine on a single day in 1901.

While you wait for the next guided underground tour to begin, try your hand at panning for gold by swirling the water and dirt to wash off the lighter weight rock. Repeated washings reveal a layer of iron oxide known as black sand. Hidden within this layer you'll find flecks the color of egg yolks—gold! Those really bitten by the gold bug, like Consolidated miner and guide Ronnie Gaddis, compete in the World Open Gold Panning Championships held each year in Dahlonega.

At Crisson Mine, a family operation just 2.5 miles outside Dahlonega on US 19 connector, we learned that Fool's Gold, iron pyrite, is shinier and more lightweight than gold. Gold is 50 percent heavier than lead and 19 times heavier than anything else you're likely to find in the pan.

Crisson was an operating mine from 1847 to 1987, and much of the stamp milling equipment is still present. (Stamps were used to crush rock in the process of ore extraction.) You'll also find buckets of soil containing gemstones like rubies, emeralds, garnets, and sapphires that are great for younger children and impatient adults, because they're easier to work with than the gold pans. Although our

Gold is found hidden within a layer of iron oxide known as black sand.

expert advisor could "work" a gold pan in three or four minutes (she's been doing this for years), it took us around 20 minutes. Either way be prepared to get muddy—and to have lots of fun.

There's more than gold and gemstones in these hills. Dahlonega has a very attractive downtown historic district because the citizens were wise enough to support ordinances that limited urban sprawl and maintained architectural integrity. Rather than the ever common McDonald's arches, the only gold reaching to the skyline here is the dome of the former U.S. Mint building on the campus of North Georgia College.

The storefronts haven't changed much since the days of the 1820s, although the specialty shops today are filled with great selections of new, old, and handmade items. Wander around the square and unearth some of Dahlonega's charm.

Stop at the Welcome Center on the square at South Park Street from 9:00 A.M. to 5:30 P.M. Monday through Saturday, and 12:00 to 5:30 P.M. Sunday, for maps, brochures, restrooms, and directions.

In the center of the square you'll see the old Lumpkin County Courthouse, which is now the Dahlonega Gold Museum. The story of mining in the area is told with slide shows, photos, displays of artifacts, and, of course, gold. There are many choices for shopping

Stamp mills were used at Crisson Mine to crush tons of rock in the search for gold.

The Dahlonega Gold Museum tells the story of Georgia's gold rush.

The preservation of historic buildings along the courthouse square adds to the charm of downtown Dahlonega's shopping district.

on the square. Antiques and Things, at the South Chestatee corner of the square, had several nice quilts and some depression glass. Next door, Mountain Tyme Antiques displayed copper, glassware, silver, and furniture.

The Dahlonega General Store had everything from weather vanes to marbles, including knives, hats, moccasins, kerosene lamps, a large collection of reproduction tin advertising signs, honey, and preserves. Antiques and Gifts of Dahlonega had fishing and hunting collectibles and several very nice pieces of antique furniture, including sofas, china cabinets, beds, and many smaller items. Cabin Fever offered antiques, collectibles, and jewelry.

Studio Jewelers had handmade custom designed jewelry in addition to antique estate jewelry, including rings, lockets, bracelets, and earrings. The Country Cottage featured old-fashioned porch brackets, rag rugs, wood carvings, and welcome signs. Several shops have placed "husband benches" in strategic locations.

The most unusual shop we visited is one of the few "upstairs shops" in town. Just a short trek up the stairs, Hummingbird Lane's selection of local and regional products was quite extraordinary. The gallery included a broad selection of twig furniture, Adirondack chairs, pottery, birdhouses, paintings, walking sticks, stone lamps, and bronze sculptures.

The Corner House and Quigley's Rare Books round out the tour on North Chestatee. Specialties include classics, Civil War and history books, Blue Ridge china, trunks, and American primitive and European antique furniture.

You'll find several restaurants sprinkled around and near the square. One of our favorites is also part of the downtown accommodation we recommend, the Smith House on South Chestatee.

The Smith House was built on top of a gold vein by Capt. Frank Hall in 1884 that has remained untouched because ordinances prevent mining within the city limits. What is now the lobby was the old carriage house, and the restaurant housed the stables.

Today you'll find 16 rooms with private baths, including 2 handicapped accessible rooms on the first floor. Our room had been nicely modernized, but retained its high ceilings and long win-

The Smith House is a local tradition for lunch, dinner, and overnight accommodations.

dows. There were two double beds, wingback chairs, cable TV, and a coffeemaker in the room.

If the accommodations alone don't entice you, consider the fact that the restaurant draws diners from Atlanta. You can choose a "lighter" lunch from the menu, or you can sit down to a family-style meal that is guaranteed to leave you stuffed and satisfied. The freshly prepared vegetables and meats vary, but selections like green beans, potatoes, squash, slaw, corn, broccoli, fried chicken, roast beef, and ham are often featured. The biscuits are delicious, and we bet you'll be hard pressed to save room for dessert.

We were surprised to find a good Italian restaurant in town. Caruso's Italian Restaurant and Curly's Pizza are two sides of the same establishment. If one side is filled (and it may well be), just slip over to the other side for the same menu. The meatballs are the size of tennis balls, the chicken parmigiana is excellent, and the pizza is popular, so you can't go wrong.

The Antique Rose Emporium draws gardeners seeking old garden roses, herbs, and perennials in display gardens open to the public daily. One of our Nashville friends visits every year—quite a recommendation.

If gold, great shopping, and good food aren't enough to get you on the road to Dahlonega, remember that it's situated at the southern edge of the Appalachian Mountains, which means the scenery is gorgeous. Many visitors creep along the two-lane winding roads just to view intense fall foliage that is east, west, and north of town. The southern terminus of the Appalachian Trail is only 18 miles west of town at Amicalola State Park on GA 52 West. On the way to visit Amicalola Falls, we suggest you stay at the Forest Hills Mountain Hideaway, especially if you're in the mood for a romantic getaway. Honeymooners from 19 to 91 have delighted in the accommodations, as have couples celebrating 50-year anniversaries. Featured in magazines like *Modern Bride*, the resort has access to a wedding coordinator, a minister, licensing information, and even a horsedrawn carriage.

The very private cabins appear rustic, but some have architectural details like crown molding, marble fireplaces, a glass-enclosed Jacuzzi room, and amenities like CD/tape player, large-screen

The southern terminus of the Appalachian Trail begins 18 miles west of Dahlonega at Amicalola Falls State Park.

The Forest Hills Mountain Hideaway has romantic cabins ranging from rustic to ritzy.

TV/VCR, refrigerator, and microwave. Others have rustic interiors with canopy beds and fireplaces.

Also part of the same resort are three Victorian houses with fully equipped kitchens, hot tubs, and fireplaces; the Rose Garden Restaurant (open to the public on weekends only and guests daily); the Gold City Corral (they'll give horseback riding lessons to guests who are novices); two lodges to accommodate families; and the newest facility, the Mountain Laurel Inn, which has twelve 1,200-square-foot bilevel suites and a new restaurant serving breakfast and dinner entrees like Chateaubriand, mahi mahi, prime rib. and escargot.

Amicalola Falls State Park has cottages, tent and trailer camping, mountain bike trails, hiking trails, and a fishing pond at the base of the falls. At the top of the falls, you'll find a lodge with a restaurant, and breathtaking views of the countryside. A rustic lodge, the Len Foote Walk-In, is planned for Appalachian Trail hikers. Scheduled for completion in 1997, it will require an approximately 5-mile hike to reach it, and it's designed for minimal environmental impact (including solar power and composting toilets). Although owned by the state park, it will be operated by the Appalachian Trail club. As you might imagine, the changing seasons here are exquisite.

The following are Dahlonega, GA 30533 and area code 706 except where noted.

ACCOMMODATIONS

Amicalola Falls State Park—Star Route, Box 215, Dawsonville, 30534;
    Reservations 800-864-PARK; From Metro Atlanta 770-389-PARK,
    265-8888.
Blood Mountain Cabins—US Hwy. 19/129; 800-284-6866.
Days Inn:—US 60/19, south of town square; 864-2338.
EconoLodge:—US 19 North; 864-6191.
Forest Hills Mountain Hideaway—Rt. 3, Box 510, 800-654-6313, 800-
    94CUPID or 864-6456; From Atlanta, toll free, 770-534-3244.
HoJo—US 60 South; 864-4343.
Mountain Top Lodge—Old Ellijay Road; Rt. 3, Box 510; 864-5257.
The Smith House Hotel and Restaurant—202 South Chestatee: 867-7000.
Stanton Storehouse Bed and Breakfast—202 N. Meaders Street: 864-6114.
Worley Homestead Bed and Breakfast—W. Main St.; 864-7002.

ATTRACTIONS

Appalachian Outfitters—POB 793; 800-426-7117, 864-7117.
Consolidated Gold Mine—Hwy. 19 North; 864-8473.
Crisson's Gold Mine—Hwy. 19 North; 864-6363.
Gold Museum—Town Square; 864-2257.
Holly Theater—101 S. Park; 864-2257; Vintage movies, plays, bluegrass
    shows.

DINING

Caruso's/Curly's Italian Restaurant—E. Main; 864-4664.
Coffee House—867-6324.
Front Porch—864-0124.

The Gold City Corral offers riding
lessons for beginners.

Robyn's Nest—Courthouse Square; 864-9169.
The Smith House—202 S. Chestatee; 864-7000.

✱ SHOPPING

Antiques and Gifts of Dahlonega—N. Park St.; 864-3637.
Antique Rose Emporium—Rt. 10, Box 2220; Cavendar Creek Rd.; 864-5884.
Country Cottage—Town Square; 864-7557.
Dahlonega General Store—Town Square; 864-2005.
Golden Memories Antiques—Town Square; 864-7222.
Hummingbird Lane—Town Square; 864-5991.
Rockhouse Antique Marketplace—Hwy. 52 East; 864-0305.
Quigley's Antiques, Conner Storehouse—Town Square; 864-0161.
Studio Jewelers—Town Square; 864-4234.

✱ SPECIAL EVENTS

April—*World Championship Gold Panning Competition*
May—*Wildflower Festival of the Arts*
June—*Bluegrass Festival*
October—*Gold Rush Days*

✱ CAMPING

Amicalola Falls State Park—GA 52, Star Route, Box 215; 800-864-PARK;
    Metro Atlanta, 770-389-PARK, 265-8888.
Blackburn Park—Camping, full hook-ups; 864-4050.
Dockery Lake Recreation Area, Chattahoochee National Forest—745-6928.

✱ FOR MORE INFORMATION

Dahlonega/Lumpkin County Chamber of Commerce and Welcome Center—13 S. Park
    St.; 864-3711; 9:00 A.M. to 5:30 P.M., Mon. through Sat., and 12:00
    to 5:30 P.M., Sun.; Maps, brochures, restroom, and directions.

✱ DIRECTIONS

From Atlanta—I-985 or US 19/GA 400 to GA 60 and turn north; town
    square is 5 miles from the intersection of US 19/GA 400 and GA 60.
From I-75 south of Chattanooga—US 76 to GA 52.

2 Helen:

Georgia's Alpine Village and Sautee Nacoochee Valley

The Nacoochee Valley is unusually beautiful, even by Georgia mountain standards. It is another of our favorite areas because it offers bed and breakfasts, historical and cultural enrichment, and opportunities to enjoy the outdoors. The area is usually referred to as the Sautee-Nacoochee Valley because the two valleys connect near the Old Sautee Store at the intersection of GA 17 and GA 255.

Clovis arrowheads, or points as they are called, dating to 15,000-9,000 BC found in the valley indicate an early Indian presence. Archaic points dating from 8,000-1,000 BC are plentiful signifying increased occupation. By the 1700s the Cherokee had established a "lower" settlement town, Chota, in the Nacoochee Valley.

The Unicoi Turnpike passed through the Nacoochee Valley and brought the first white settlers into the valley in 1822. Ten years later the Georgia Legislature made preparations for a land lottery to redistribute seized Cherokee lands to Georgians. The first gold in north Georgia was actually found in White County rather than at Dahlonega in Lumpkin County. You can still see placer pits used in digging for gold in the fields on the eastern side of GA 75 south of Helen. (Placer pits were usually situated along creeks or on flood plains to collect the gold that washed downstream.)

In 1838, Cherokee gathered in the Nacoochee Valley to begin the Trail of Tears (for more information, see Dahlonega, GA, and Cherokee, NC, sections). The area still has the feel of ancient

Alpine Helen is a popular vacation spot for visitors to the North Georgia mountains.

The Nacoochee Indian mound is the subject of legends of star-crossed lovers.

Crescent Hill Baptist Church was built in the mid-1800s.

Indian lands. When we first saw the area more than twenty years ago, we felt it was one of the most beautiful places we'd ever seen. And today it remains remarkably unchanged.

We'll begin the tour of the Sautee Nacoochee Valley at the intersection of GA 75 and GA 17 about 2 miles south of Helen. The Nacoochee Indian mound stands in a privately owned pasture at this intersection. Excavations in 1915 indicated that it is a traditional Indian burial mound. Since the early 1900s, the top of the mound has been graced with an often-photographed gazebo built by the Hardeman family. The beautiful house across GA 17 from the mound was the home of a former Georgia governor named Hardeman and is privately owned. We hope that both these areas will eventually become public lands.

The pretty little church next door to the Hardeman house was built by slaves in the 1840s or 1850s. It is now home to the Crescent Hill Baptist Church, which leaves its doors open to a respectful public. The parking lot is a good place to park and walk across the road to view the mound.

As you continue along GA 17, you'll come to the intersection with the Sautee Valley at GA 255 North. The Old Sautee Store sits overlooking the junction of the Sautee Valley to the north and the Nacoochee Valley to the east and west. It's on the National Register of Historic Places and is another frequently photographed site. Inside you'll see lots of interesting country store memorabilia (not for sale) and a Scandinavian gift shop that sells beautiful sweaters, crystal, and imported foods.

Across the road from the Old Sautee Store, Van Gogh's in the Valley has an art gallery in the front and a good restaurant in back. Chef Bryant Withers' menu includes appetizers like crab cakes, baked brie and escargot, apple blue cheese walnut romaine salad with raspberry vinaigrette, and entrees ranging from North Georgia trout with cheese grits soufflé to rack of lamb. Reservations are accepted, set-up services provided, and there are burgers, chicken, and pasta for children. It lacks a romantic atmosphere, but the food is excellent.

For picnic fare, there's a sandwich shop tucked in the basement toward the side of the building that houses Van Gogh's. There's a picnic area at the covered bridge up 255 North in the Sautee Valley if dining in the great outdoors appeals to you. And the Chattahoochee Riding Stables next door to Van Gogh's offer hour-long rides through the valley.

There are several bed and breakfast establishments near this point. Across the road from the Old Sautee Store you'll find the Nacoochee Valley Guesthouse which has three rooms with private baths and a country French dining room that seats 35 and is open to the public for lunch and dinner.

Lumpsden Homeplace Bed and Breakfast Inn is located in the 1890 home of former state senator Jessie Richardson Lumsden. It is listed on the National Register of Historic Places, and is open yearround.

A short drive up the Sautee valley is one of the oldest houses in the area, the Stovall House, which now is a country inn. The house was built in 1837, according to Hamilton "Ham" Schwartz, the current owner.

Ham was chief engineer for a hospital in Atlanta and had been vacationing at area bed and breakfasts for several years. On his 1982 trip, he discovered that the Stovall House was for sale. He bought it December 1982 and opened the inn on Labor Day 1983. The restaurant opened in 1984.

The house sits on a hill amid the property's 26 acres. Inside you'll find original heart-of-pine floors downstairs and doors of

The landmark Old Sautee Store marks the intersection of the Sautee and Nacoochee Valleys.

The Stovall House Bed and Breakfast welcomes visitors to the beautiful Sautee Valley.

Bedroom skylights at the Stovall House are strategically situated for a delightful view of the night sky.

black walut, including the double front doors, that were handmade on the property. We were appreciative of Ham's minimal disturbances in the home's original structure, but must admit we loved the addition of a skylight over the bed that looked up to the Big Dipper and individual thermostat controls for heat and air. Transoms over the doors with stained-glass panels, Victorian furniture, the absence of television or telephone, and a nice fireplace downstairs that invites you to sit and relax all contribute to a profound feeling of peace and quiet. Five rooms are available yearround. Guests are served a Continental breakfast.

The area that was once a back porch has been converted to an intimate summer dining room that looks out across green fields to the distant mountains, past a walnut tree that's more than 200 years old. There's also an attractive, larger dining room inside the house. Reservations are taken for dinner only.

While the delicious smells of dinner drifted to the front porch, we sat in wicker rockers and watched bluebirds defend their homes in the shadow of Mount Yonah, as we were kept company by Sunset, Ham's golden retriever.

As you drive up the Sautee Valley on the way to the Stovall House, keep your eye out for the Sautee Nacoochee Arts and Community Center on your left on the grounds of a school building and cannery built in 1920. It is open six days a week yearround, and on Sundays as well in summer. Community volunteers enthusiastically acquaint you with the area they so love. All labor, furniture, and equipment have been donated by members of the very active community association.

The Sautee Nacoochee Arts and Community Center includes a gallery and a museum with displays about Spanish explorers searching for gold, as well as Indian history.

Inside you'll find the small but interesting museum filled with artifacts and personal treasures loaned by residents who want to share the history of the area and the legend of Sautee, the man, and his love for Nacoochee, the evening star.

There's an art gallery that features works by skilled artists and craftsmen within a 50-mile radius. There is a long tradition of crafts in the area and the gallery supports the work of the best local artists.

What do you do when you live 60 miles from the closest cultural center? If you're in Sautee Nacoochee, you create your own entertainment in a well-equipped 120-seat auditorium that offers award-winning regional theater. In addition to featuring one Shakespeare and one original production each year, the Echota Performing Arts Festival in June promises song, dance, and visual arts. When we visited, the stage was being prepared in the Old Gym for the Atlanta Ballet.

The driving tour offers several choices at this point. Continue up GA 255 to the covered bridge, west on Skylake Road, and west on GA 356 to visit Unicoi State Park, Anna Ruby Falls, and return via Helen.

You may also continue east on GA 255 to its intersection with GA 197 and visit Lake Burton and LaPrade's Restaurant. A southerly (right if you're heading east on GA 255) turn at the GA 197/255 intersection will take you past the Mark of the Potter on the Soque River (pronounced "sew-kwee" and "soak," depending on whom you ask), a tributary of the Chattahoochee, as you head for Clarkesville.

You can also return to the Nacoochee Valley via GA ALT 255 by turning west on GA 17 to complete the loop you began at the intersection of GA 75 and GA 17, south of Helen.

HELEN

Helen was established in 1913 as a lumber town and was named after one of the lumbermen's daughters. As you enter Helen from the south, you'll pass Nora Mill Granary and Store, which has been in business since 1876. The water-powered turbine wheels turn out buckwheat and rye flour, grits, and cornmeal. Special gift orders can be packaged and shipped. Homestead Antiques and Collectibles, across the road from Nora Mill, is worth a stop. Here you'll find two floors of antiques and collectibles.

The old Byrd-Matthews Lumber Company was off to the right on the big flat as you approach Helen. The houses on the left were the homes of the managers and superintendents of the lumber company. They eventually milled out all the timber, and by the 1940s Helen was a dying lumber town.

In the late 1960s, Helen basically consisted of a few houses, a garage, a gas station and Orbit Manufacturing (makers of Argyle

Nora Mill has produced flour, grits, and cornmeal since 1876.

A dying lumber town in the 1960s, Helen revitalized itself into an Alpine village with more than 150 gift shops and restaurants.

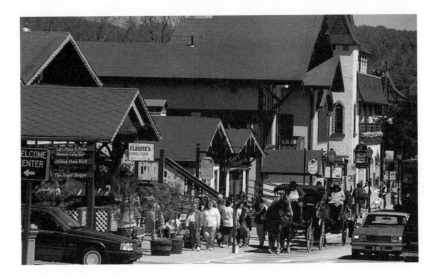

socks), the only sizable employer in the area. In 1969, area businessmen got together over lunch trying to think of what to do to revive their town. John Kollock, a local watercolor artist, came up with the concept of attracting tourists while on their way to the lakes and national forests near Helen by transforming rows of cinderblock structures to look like buildings he'd seen in the villages of alpine Bavaria while stationed in the army during WWII.

Jim Wilkins, president of Orbit Manufacturing, offered Orbit for the first renovation. Ray L. Sims and J.S. Chastain translated sketches into balconies, stucco, and trim. Each shop owner paid for his own renovation, the city paid for the street lights and planters, local power and phone companies ran underground wiring at their own expense, and citizen volunteers planted trees.

The result is "Alpine" Helen, a collection of more than 150 import gift shops with Alpine murals and gingerbread trim. There are funnel cake shops and ice cream shops sprinkled up and down Main Street. The Museum of the Hills uses wax figures to depict what life in and around Helen was like at the turn of the century.

Helen used ingenuity in dealing with its particular set of circumstances and it is a thriving mountain town today as a result of its appeal to visitors. We found a neverending stream of tourists

riding a horsedrawn carriage around town, shopping, eating knock-
wurst, and drinking beer. On summer days, tubing down the Chattahoochee River ("place of marked" or "flowered rocks"), which
runs through the middle of town, is always popular.

There are three public parking lots in town, accessed by (driving from south to north on GA 75) a right turn on Chattahoochee Street, left onto Dye Street, right onto White Street, and
left onto Spring Street. The handicapped parking is on Main
Street. Public restrooms with handicapped access are found at the
Welcome Center on Chattahoochee and the southern intersection
of Main Street and River Street.

Nearly at the northern end of town, Betty's Country Store had
evolved since we saw it 1987 in the older building across the street.
That structure houses the Appalachian Design Shop, which sells
bird feeders, outdoor furniture, twig furniture, and dried flowers.

The "new" Betty's has gleaming, wide aisles displaying jerky,
nuts, dried fruit, preserves, fresh produce and meats, Octagon soap,
freshly baked breads, pies, and cookies, cartons of goat milk, and
cans of Eight o'clock Coffee Beans, amid thousands of other items.

One of the best restaurants in Helen is Paul's Steak House, by
the Chattahoochee. The parking lot is packed on weekends, especially during fall foliage season. Paul's specializes in steaks and
seafood and has handicapped access. Many area restaurants offer
full-bodied beers, schnitzels, wursts, and bratens, "northeast Georgia Style," including the Alt Heidelberg Restaurant and Lounge and
the Wurst Haus, which serves wurst, kraut, and German potato
salad. Many visitors choose the restaurant at Unicoi State Park for
its breakfast buffet or evening mountain trout specialty.

You'll find a wide variety of accommodations in and near
Helen, including Georgia Mountain Madness Cabins, the 98-unit
Helendorf Inn on the Chattahoochee River, the Hilltop House
Bed and Breakfast, and Innsbruck Resort.

As you depart Helen to the north on GA 75, you'll pass one of
the area's largest flea markets at Robertstown. GA 75 continues north,
climbing into the mountains. The Appalachian Trail crosses the road
at Unicoi Gap before GA 75 drops into the Hiawassee valley.

The gleaming aisles of Betty's
Country Store are filled with
thousands of interesting items.

Unicoi State Park is 4 miles north of Helen. After you make the turn on GA 356 to go to Unicoi, you'll pass the road to the twin Anna Ruby Falls 1.5 miles on the left just before you cross the bridge.

After the Civil War, the falls were named for Anna Ruby, the beloved daughter of owner Col. John H. "Captain" Nichols. Drive 3.6 miles to the parking area of the most visited waterfall in Georgia. A paved 0.4-mile hiking trail to the base of the twin falls is steep, but classified as easy to moderate. It has benches along the way for resting. You'll need about 30 minutes to walk the path. On the left, Curtis Creek drops 150 feet in two stages, and on the right, York Creek plummets 50 feet in a single column. They join to form Smith Creek, a tributary of the Chattahoochee that forms the lake at Unicoi. The Lion's Eye Trail along Smith Creek is wheelchair accessble and has Braille signs along the route.

During the early 1900s, this area was logged by Byrd-Matthews Lumber Company, and a narrow gauge railroad transported the logs to Helen. Today you'll find picnic sites with tables and grills amid a predominantly hardwood forest. The 1,600-acre Anna Ruby Falls Scenic Area is deep within land that has been part of the Chattahoochee National Forest since 1925. Spring wildflowers, summer shade, fall colors, and unobstructed winter views make the falls popular in all seasons.

The Visitor's Center is a cooperative effort between the Forest Service and a nonprofit association, the Chattahoochee/Oconee

Unicoi State Park offers popular accommodations and delicious food.

Heritage Association. Inside you'll find bathrooms, snack and drink machines, and paintings, pottery, and crafts. Earnings support interpretive programs.

Some visitors choose to stay in Quonset-hut type cabins along the 53-acre mountain lake at Unicoi State Park, but many more stay at the attractive 100-room lodge uphill. All lodge rooms have two double beds and do not have phones or TVs. Most are non-smoking, and some are handicapped accessible.

Contained within the park's 1,081 acres are 30 cottages, 84 tent and trailer sites, and 4 lighted tennis courts. The Smith Creek Cottages have fireplaces. There are white sand beaches along the lake where you can swim, fish, or boat, along with hiking trails and picnic areas for day-use visitors.

The park's dining room is very popular with both visitors and locals. Special programs are offered on mountain heritage and traditional crafts.

Backtrack to Helen via GA 356 or turn on Skylake Road and head south on GA 255 for the longer, scenic tour of the Sautee-Nacoochee Valley before returning to GA 75.

The following are Helen, GA 30545 and area code 706 except where noted.

⮞ ACCOMMODATIONS

Alpine Best Western—800-435-3642; Outdoor pool.
Alpine Motel—800-535-1251, 898-2840; Indoor pool.
Comfort Inn—Box 1178; 878-8000 or 800-443-6488; Outdoor pool.
Georgia Mountain Madness Cabins—POB 308; 878-2851; From Metro
    Atlanta, 770-534-6452.
Helendorf River Inn and Conference Center—Box 305; 878-2271 or 800-445-
    2271; Pool.
Hilltop Haus Bed and Breakfast—362 Chattahoochee Strasse; 878-2388.
Innsbruck Resort and Golf Club—800-20-HELEN or 878-2400.
The Lumsden Homeplace—POB 388, Sautee, 30571; 878-2813.
Nacoochee Valley Guest House—2220 Hwy. 17, Sautee, 30571; 878-3830.
The Stovall House Inn/Restaurant—1526 Hwy. 255 North, Sautee, 30571;
    878-3355.
Tanglewood Cabins and Conference Center—GA 356; 878-1044.
Unicoi State Park—GA 356; 878-2201 or 800-864-PARK.

❧ ACTIVITIES

Alpine Bike Rental—878-1966.
Alpine Tubing—878-8823; May to Sept.
Chattahoochee Stables—Nacoochee Valley, 878-7000; Open daily yearround; $15 single, $20 double.
Chattooga Ranger District—Burton Road, GA 197, Clarkesville, 30523; 754-6221.
Helen Carriage Rides—878-3445.
Hornes Buggy Rides—878-3658.
Innsbruck Resort of Helen—878-2400, 800-20-HELEN; Eighteen-hole golf course; closed Mondays.
Scaly Mountain—Dillard, GA; 800-929-7669.
Sky Valley Ski Resort—Dillard, GA; 800-437-2416.
Sunburst Stables—947-7433; Closed Mondays.

❧ ATTRACTIONS

Anna Ruby Falls—GA 356; 878-3574.
Museum of the Hills—Castle Inn Bldg.; 878-3140; Wax museum with video about Helen.
Nacoochee Indian Mound—Nacoochee Valley, GA 17.
Nora Mill and Granary—GA 75 south of Helen; 878-2375.
Old Sautee Store—Sautee Nacoochee Valley, GA 17 and GA 255; 878-2281.
Sautee-Nacoochee Community Center—POB 66, Sautee, GA; 878-3300.

❧ DINING

Alt Heidelberg Restaurant and Lounge—878-2986; Lunch, dinner.
Chattahoochee Cafe—So. Main Street—878-1019; Breakfast, lunch, dinner.
The Courtyard Restaurant—River Level at the Castle Inn; 878-3117.
Hofbrauhaus Inn Restaurant and Lounge—N. Main St.; 878-2248.
LaPrade's—Lake Burton, east of Helen; 800-262-3313.
Nacoochee Valley Guest House—878-3830.
Paul's Steak House—Main St.; 878-2468.
The Stovall House—Sautee Valley; 878-3355.
Tanglewood Restaurant—Hwy. 356, 1 mile north of Unicoi State Park; 878-1044; Breakfast, lunch, dinner.
Unicoi State Park—GA 356, north of Helen; 878-2201.
Van Gogh's—Nacoochee Valley; 878-3275.
The Wurst House—878-2647.

❧ SHOPPING

Alpine Village Factory Outlets—878-3016.
Betty's Country Store—Main St.—878-2943.
Homestead Antiques & Collectibles—Historic Martin House across from Nora
    Granary; 898-1929.
Mark of the Potter—Rt. 3, Box 3164, Clarkesville, 30523; 947-3440; Daily.
The Old Sautee Store—Sautee Nacoochee; 878-2281.
Van Gogh's—Nacoochee Valley; 878-3275.

❧ SPECIAL EVENTS

February—*Sautee Nacoochee, Black History Festival*
March—*Sautee Nacoochee , Women's History Festival*
May—*Helen, Hot Air Balloon Race and Festival*
June—*Sautee Nacoochee, Arts and Crafts Fair*
June to August—*Helen, Bavarian Summer Nights*
July to August—*Sautee Nacoochee, Echota Performing Arts Festival*
September—*Sautee Nacoochee, Folk Festival*
September and October—*Nightly except Sundays, Helen, Octoberfest*
November—*Helen, Alpenstroll and Holiday Lighting*
November—*Sautee Nacoochee, Mountain Art Auction*

❧ CAMPING

Unicoi State Park—4 miles north of Helen; 878-2201, 800-864-PARK.

❧ FOR MORE INFORMATION

Alpine Helen/White County Convention and Visitors Bureau—POB 730, Helen,
    30545; 878-2181, 865-5356.
Sautee Nacoochee Arts and Community Center—878-3300.

❧ DIRECTIONS

From Atlanta—I-985 to US 129 north to Gainesville, Clermont, Cleveland
    and GA 75 to Helen.
From Asheville—Take US 441 south to Clarkesville and GA 17 west to
    Sautee Nacoochee.
Locally the Nacoochee Valley is bisected by GA 17 and the Sautee Valley is
    divided by GA 255.

3   *Clarkesville and Tallulah Falls:*
Out of the Hills of Habersham

Clarkesville was established in 1818 in what once was Cherokee Indian territory. It became the county seat of Habersham County in 1823. The climate produced bountiful crops of apples and grapes for winemaking and drew coastal dwellers trying to escape the heat and the threat of malaria. The railroad followed the route of present-day US 441 and the growth of the region accelerated with the influx of summer visitors during the late 1800s. The historic town square remains the focal point of the community and more than 40 structures have been nominated for the National Register of Historic

The Habersham Bank Hospitality Center welcomes visitors to the historic Clarkesville town square.

Places. It is still a small, sleepy southern town and may receive some protection from uncontrolled tourist development by the "new" US 441 route that bypasses the downtown area a mile or two east.

The Habersham Bank Hospitality Center welcomes tourists with directions, suggestions, cold drinks, and a vault full of brochures. The historic town square has several antiques shops, including Dixie Gallery Antiques, which had an outstanding half-tester bed, dining room suites, lots of occasional chairs, leaded glass, Blue Willow china, and an East Lake fainting couch. Wonders Antiques on Water Street featured English and American antiques. When we visited they had an especially nice loveseat, Blue Ridge pottery, brass and oak beds, and several dining room sets in a variety of styles. Once Upon a Time Antiques, on the square at North Washington, offered English furniture and collectibles, including Maxfield Parrish prints. Parker Place Antiques had an interesting assortment of American primitives, 1940s and 50s furniture and collectibles, and quilts and quilt tops. Specialty shops offer everything from books and crafts to soaps and fine art. The Tin Roof had an assortment that ranged from baskets and birdhouses to dolls made of quilt scraps or corn-shucks. The Habersham Arts Council Gallery on South Washington is open daily and represents regional artists and craftsmen.

The Last Train Restaurant has a lunch menu that includes chicken salad, soups, sandwiches, and a hot lunch buffet special. The Trolley Restaurant at the edge of the square on North Washington is an excellent choice for lunch or dinner daily, except Mondays. The 1907 building was once a drugstore and the combination of the cool, dim interior and the Southern and Italian cuisine is just the pre-scription for hungry travelers. Luncheon selections include creamy roasted red pepper soup, Caesar salad, fried green tomatoes, and iron skillet trout. Dinner selections offer new twists on old favorites, like Bourbon-barbequed shrimp over stone-ground cheese grits and vine ripe tomatoes topped with green onions and fried cold-water lobster tail over seasonal vegetables with horseradish honey-mustard sauce.

Mervis' Sports Grill specializes in beer and a variety of man-sized sandwiches like the Cuban, with salami, ham, roast pork, cheese, and special sauce on a sub roll, a well as grilled chicken salads and burgers.

Bill's Dish Barn on US 441 offers concrete lawn ornaments and reproduction Fiesta Ware.

Stoney's Family Restaurant at the intersection of GA 115 and GA 197 is well-known for its breakfasts. For lunch or dinner, the fried chicken is a local favorite.

The 1901 Burns-Sutton House Inn on South Washington Street is a three-story bed and breakfast listed on the National Register of Historic Places. Guest rooms with shared or private baths are available. The Charm House Bed and Breakfast is also on South Washington.

Along old US 441 north of Clarkesville, Bill's Dish Barn is a hodgepodge of concrete yard ornaments, reproduction Hull and Fiesta Ware dishes, pickle crocks, and flower pots.

To find truly outstanding accommodations, travel north 8.5 miles on US 441 and look for the sign for Glen-Ella Springs Inn at Orchard Road. The 100-year-old inn up the dirt road was named for Glen and Ella Davison, the builders. By the 1980s it was languishing when Barrie and Bobby Aycock decided to restore it.

Along the way it won a citation of Excellence from the Georgia Trust for Historic Preservation and was named one of *Travel and Leisure* magazine's Top Ten Getaways. Its 16 guest rooms are refined and rustic and each has its own bath, phone, air conditioner, and section of the porch for rocking. The 17-acre property has a 20x40 foot swimming pool. Some units have whirlpools and fireplaces.

Each of the rooms at Glen-Ella Springs has a private bath and air conditioning, although the inn is on the National Register of Historic Sites.

Did we mention that the restaurant was featured in *Great Cooking With Country Inn Chefs* (Rutledge Hill Press, 1996)? There are vegetable and herb gardens for the chef's inspiration and perennial gardens to inspire the rest of us. The dining room is open to the public for dinner Tuesday through Saturday and for Sunday brunch yearround. Lunch is added in the summer. From Glen-Ella Springs return to US 441 or continue along Bear Gap Road to reach Lake Rabun and visit the lovely Minnehaha Falls (see Mountain Lake Country section for directions and more information). Proceed along Burton Dam Road to GA 197. A right turn on 197 will take you to LaPrade's and Moccasin Creek State Park.

A left turn on 197 will take you back to Clarkesville along the Soque River, past Landmark Antiques and Pottery in a converted feed and seed store that's now filled with antiques, "oddities," and regional crafts.

If you missed lunch at LaPrade's, the Batesville General Store is at hand—a good stop for a sandwich from the grill. Continue on GA 197 to visit the Wood Duck, a small shop that's a worthwhile stop about one mile north of Mark of the Potter. If you have time, you can watch as Frank Brown carves his decoys. The Mark of the Potter is the oldest craft shop in northeast Georgia and displays crafts of 30 local artists in pottery, glass, weaving, and jewelry. Owner Jay Bucek can tell you about the building, which was converted from a grist mill, and the population of "pet" mountain trout waiting to be fed off the porch overlooking the Soque River.

Other choices for loop tours out of Clarkesville include GA 17 out of Clarkesville to the Sautee Nacoochee Valley and Helen; GA 115 to Cleveland, home of Cabbage Patch Dolls and Babyland General Hospital; or scenic US 441 toward Tallulah Falls and Clayton.

In Tallulah Falls, the Co-op Craft Store at the Old Train Depot displays quality crafts and gifts from the area. According to *The Life and Times of Tallulah...The Falls, The Gorge, The Town,* by John Saye, the Tallulah River created an impressive 1,000-foot deep, two-mile-long gorge on its way through the hills of Habersham County.

The Tallulah River dropped 650 feet in the first half-mile near the presentday dam site, plummeting over a series of six falls. The

Visitors journey to Babyland General Hospital to witness "births" every 45 minutes. Many adopt their very own Cabbage Patch "baby."

combined flowage of the falls, the cascades, and the river itself created a roar that travelers heard over a mile away. The roar of the turbulent water drowned out normal conversation in the gorge. The force was so tremendous that the Indians called the area "talulu," meaning "the terrible".

As you would expect, several Cherokee legends exist about the falls and the gorge. *Footsteps of the Cherokee*, by Vicki Rozema, tells us about a species of "little people" who lived in the area and lured hunters to their deaths in the gorge. Visitors are warned rather than lured these days. Several deaths occur from mishaps here every year, so be certain you heed the warnings and maintain the proper respect for this rugged, beautiful country.

Property was purchased for a dam just above the falls around 1905 by a hydroelectric company. A dam constructed on the site was placed in operation by the Georgia Railway and Power Company in 1913 to supply power for Atlanta. It was 126 feet high and 426 feet long, small by today's standards. The 72,000-kilowatt facility is a Historic Engineering Site and a monument to the men who braved the wilds to build it, armed with vision and determination. Tallulah is one of six dams built in a stairstep fashion from the highest at Burton Dam to the lowest at Yonah Dam. For more information, see Georgia Outdoor Recreation section.

Thousands of observers watched the Great Wallenda walk across Tallulah Gorge on a high wire on July 17, 1970, suspended between a tower on a rock cliff near lookout No. 4 on the North Rim Trail and south tower across the gorge. Wallenda made it across that day, but some who came could not bear to witness the heart-stopping walk across the breathtaking gorge. The gorge is now being managed by a cooperative partnership between Georgia Power and the Georgia Department of Natural Resources. The excellent facilities at the Tallulah Gorge State Conservation Park include a visitor's center and extensive hiking trails for those fond of heights and rugged beauty. There's a campground with 50 campsites and a bathhouse and 27 picnic sites at Terrora. Continue along US 441 to visit Clayton, Mountain City, Rabun Gap, and Dillard.

Terrora Campground offers the closest facilities to the Tallulah Gorge State Conservation Park.

The following are Clarkesville, GA 30523 and area code 706 except where noted.

ACCOMMODATIONS

Burns-Sutton House Inn—124 S. Washington St.; 754-5565.
Charm House B&B—S. Washington St.; 754-9347.
Glen-Ella Springs Inn and Restaurant—Bear Gap Rd., Rt. 3, Box 3304; 800-552-3479 or 754-7295.
Happy Valley Resort—Cabins with fireplaces and whirlpool tubs on 36 acres 7 miles outside Clarkesville; 754-3377.
LaPrade's—Rt. 1, Box 1488, GA 197 North at Lake Burton; 947-3312; Open April to November.
RuSharon Bed & Breakfast—177 Old Clarkesville Rd., Cleveland, GA 30528; 865-5738; Guest rooms with private baths in restored 1890s home.
Spring Hill Bed and Breakfast—New Liberty Rd.; 754-7094.

ATTRACTIONS

Babyland General Hospital—19 Underwood St., Cleveland, 30528; 865-2171; Mon. to Sat., 9:00 A.M. to 5 P.M.; Sun., 10:00 A.M. to 5:00 P.M.
Tallulah Gorge State Park—US 441 N, POB 248, Tallulah Falls, GA; 754-8257.

❧ DINING

Batesville General Store—GA 197; 947-3434.

Glen-Ella Springs Restaurant—Rt. 3, Box 3304, Bear Gap Rd.; 754-7295;
Open for dinner daily.

LaPrade's at Lake Burton—GA 197; 947-3312; April to Nov.

Mervis Sports Grill—1406 Washington Square; 754-7261.

Stoney's Family Restaurant—GA 11 and GA 197; 754-4328; Open 6:00 A.M.
to 10:00 P.M. daily.

The Last Train Restaurant—On the Square;11:30 A.M. to 3:00 P.M. Mon. to
Weds., 11:30 A.M. to 8:00 P.M. Thurs., 11:30 A.M. to 9:00 P.M. Fri. to
Sat., closed Sun.

The Trolley—1460 N. Washington; 754-5566; 11:00 A.M. to 2:30 P.M. and
5:30 to 10:00 P.M., Tues. to Sat.

❧ SHOPPING

Bill's Dish Barn—883 Historic Old 441, Hollywood, GA; 754-2048; Weds.
to Mon. 9:00 A.M. to 6 P.M.; Call first Jan. to Mar.

The Book Cellar—On the Square; 754-2717.

Burton Gallery and Emporium—Burton Dam Rd. at GA 197; 947-1351;
Mon. to Sat. 10:00 A.M. to 6 P.M., Sun. 1:00 to 6:00 P.M., closed Tues.

Co-op Craft Store—Old Train Depot, Tallulah Falls, GA; 754-6810; Mon. to
Sat. 10:00 A.M. to 5:00 P.M., Sun. 12:30 to 5:00 P.M.

Dixie Gallery Antiques—On the Square; 754-7044; Sat. to Weds. 10:00 A.M.
to 5:00 P.M.; Closed Thurs. and Fri.

Habersham Arts Council Art Gallery—S. Washington; 754-4873; Mon. to Sat.
10:00 A.M. to 5:00 P.M., Sun. 12:00 to 5:00 P.M.

Landmark Antiques and Pottery—GA 197; 947-3088; Thurs. to Mon, Spring
to Fall, 10:30 A.M. to 5:00 P.M.; Fri. to Sun., Winter.

Mark of the Potter—Rt. 3, POB 3164; 947-3440; Daily except Christmas
Day.

Once Upon a Time Antiques—808 N. Washington; 754-5789; Mon. to Fri.
10:00 A.M. to 5:30 P.M., Sat. 10:00 A.M. to 6:00 P.M., Sun. 1:00 to
4:00 P.M.

The Book Cellar—On the Square; 754-2717; Mon. to Sat. 10:00 A.M. to
5:00 P.M.

The Marketplace—Beaver Dam Rd.; 754-6226; Mon. to Sat. 9:00 A.M. to
5:00 P.M.; Habersham Plantation handcrafted furniture.

The Tin Roof—On the Square; 754-2225; Mon. to Sat. 10:00 A.M. to 5:30
P.M., closed Weds. Jan. to Mar.
The Wood Duck—Rt. 1, Box 1816; 947-3032.
Wonders Antiques—127 E. Water; 754-6883; 10:00 A.M. to 5:00 P.M. daily,
except Weds.

⅔ SPECIAL EVENTS

May—*Mountain Laurel Festival, Clarkesville*
September—*Chattahoochee Mountain Fair, Clarkesville*
December—*Christmas Night in Clarkesville*
December—*Holiday Tour of Homes*

⅔ CAMPING

Appalachian Camper Park—Rt. 2, Box 2144, Old Hwy. 441; 754-9319.
Tallulah Gorge State Park—POB 248; 754-8257; Reservations 800-864-
PARK; In Atlanta call 770-389-PARK.
Terrora Park and Campground—Tallulah Falls, GA 30573; 754-6030; Reser-
vations 800-864-PARK; In Atlanta call 770-389-PARK.

⅔ FOR MORE INFORMATION

Clarkesville Hospitality Center—Habersham Bank, POB 5; 800-822-0316 or
778-1000.
Habersham County Chamber of Commerce—POB 366, Cornelia, GA 30531;
778-4654.
Georgia State Parks and Historic Sites—404-656-3530; Park reservations 800-
864-PARK.

⅔ DIRECTIONS

From Atlanta—Take I-985/I-365 to new US 23/441.
Local—Take GA 17 out of the Sautee Nacoochee and Helen; GA 197
from Hiawassee and Lake Burton; or US 441/23 from Dillard and
Clayton.

4 Clayton, Mountain City, Rabun Gap, Dillard:

Where Spring Spends the Summer

Becky's Branch is one of many scenic waterfalls in the Chattahoochee National Forest.

From south to north along US 441, the communities of Clayton, Mountain City, Rabun Gap, and Dillard are nestled in the Little Tennessee Valley. Although within a few miles of each other, each community has its own special appeal.

Area mountains, with names like Rattlesnake, Screamer, and Wildcat, suggest you're heading into the recesses of the southern Appalachians on the way to high-country adventures. Beautiful valleys retain the feel of ancient peoples long departed.

As you enter Clayton on US 441, you'll pass the Chattahoochee Ranger District Office, where you can get maps, regulations, and directions. Generally you can camp anywhere in the Chattahoochee National Forest except within fifty feet of a trail or water. There are more than 430 miles of trails to hike, 1,000 miles of trout and warm water streams to fish, and hunting on 12 wildlife management areas. For more information, see Georgia Outdoor Recreation section.

Clayton is frequently selected by national publications as one of the top places to retire in the United States. It is still a small town with a real life Main Street. There's a hardware store that sometimes has lovely hammocks hanging in the windows, and a couple of antiques shops. The Main Street Gallery is one of three outlets of the Hambidge Center, featuring southern artists.

Not trendy or exclusive, but very clean and comfortable, is the Old Clayton Inn which has provided accommodations to visitors since the mid-1800s. It was damaged by fire and rebuilt in 1952. There are 30 rooms, all with double, queen, or king beds. Some have whirlpool tubs. The reasonable rates include cable TV and free parking, but at this writing no rooms are handicapped accessible.

The US 441 Bypass runs parallel to Main Street and is the primary travel artery for vacationers from the Deep South heading to the mountains to escape the summer heat, glimpse fall foliage, search for wildflowers along the many trails in the nearby national forests, match their skills against wild whitewaters, or ski the most southern resort in the United States. This bypass should allow Clayton to preserve what remains of its classic "downtown" area.

As you approach Clayton from the south, you'll pass Green Shutters Tea Room. There are two—the "old" one is outside Clayton on old US 441 south near the Tiger Community and the "new" one is on new US 441. Many people prefer the old one, but the new one is more conveniently located and seats more people. The menu is family style, all you can eat.

The Stockton House Restaurant overlooks Warwoman Road and Screamer Mountain. Dine buffet style or from the menu for lunch from 11:00 A.M. to 2:00 P.M. Selections include sandwiches or the lunch buffet which varies daily with choices like fried chicken livers, baked fish, fried chicken, three vegetables, and dessert. If you sleep late, you can also choose an omelet to top off your morning. Dinner is served from 5:00 to 9:00 P.M. daily. Steaks, grilled pork chops, trout, fried catfish, and pasta make it hard to save enough room for the homemade desserts. The Stockton House serves wine, and domestic and imported beer.

We were told that there's a painting of the warwoman of the Cherokee for whom Warwoman Dell is named at the library in Clayton. Vicki Rozema tells us in her book that the warwoman was an old Cherokee prophetess. According to legend, she used crystals in the dell each spring to visualize the future of the tribe.

Wildflowers like this Jack-in-the-Pulpit are abundant in Warwoman Dell.

The Warwoman Dell Recreation Area has a picnic pavilion, restrooms, and access to the Bartram Trail.

This small, secluded valley gently curves its way through the southeastern edge of the mountains to reach GA 28. On the way you'll pass by the Warwoman Dell Recreation Area, the trails to Becky's Branch Falls, Dick's Creek Falls, and the Chattooga, a National Wild and Scenic River.

The Warwoman Dell Recreation Area, about 3 miles east of Clayton, is a lovely, serene setting with picnic tables and restrooms but no camping facilities. Walk past the picnic pavilion and over the bridge to visit the confluence of three creeks and a short trail with an abundance of wildflowers.

The Willis Knob Horse Camp is off Goldmine Road about 11.6 miles down Warwoman on your right. After the right turn it's only 0.2 mile to Woodall Ridge Day Use Area and another 1.9 miles to the camp. The site has handicapped toilet facilities, drinking water, stalls, and campsites.

Warwoman Road ends at GA 28. A left turn begins a winding, scenic loop tour to Highlands, North Carolina. Follow NC 106 out of Highlands to US 441 south to Dillard, Rabun Gap, and Mountain City before returning to Clayton.

Travel US 76 East out of Clayton to visit the Chattooga River and its famous Bull Sluice rapids just after you cross into South Carolina.

This section of South Carolina is considered the foothills country. It's blessed with an abundance of outdoor recreation, lakes, and state parks.

There's a parking lot just after the US 76 bridge and a short path to some big boulders that give you a good view of the rapids. More than 50 miles of the river have been designated part of the Wild and Scenic River system. It is arguably the most scenic of the mountain streams offering commercial outfitters.

Section III takes between four and five hours to run by canoe and is a probably a little more difficult than the Nantahala, but a lot more forgiving than section IV. We think it's challenging for those of us who aren't masterful whitewater enthusiasts.

For Section IV, bring along your expert whitewater skills or a potent lucky talisman. It takes about five hours to run and is second only to the Watauga Gorge in terms of difficulty in our estimation of the Southern Highlands region. Remember Jon Voight and Burt Reynolds in those incredible river scenes in *Deliverance?* This is it folks—the filming took place here. Reynolds was so impressed with the beauty of the area that he purchased property nearby.

US 76 West out of Clayton takes you between Oakey and Timpson Mountains. The Hambidge Center's Timpson Creek Gallery is on your right about seven miles west of Clayton. US 76 soon intersects GA 197 which follows the western shore of Lake Burton. Moccasin Creek State Park and LaPrade's Restaurant are a short distance down GA 197 (for more information see the Lake District section).

For those continuing on US 76 West, the Appalachian Trail will cross the road at Dick's Creek Gap before US 76 continues 7.5 miles to Hiawassee (see Hiawassee section). Both sections of the trail from Dick's Creek are strenuous. Returning to the US 441 North route north of Clayton you'll see a couple of antiques stores, including Mountain Mama Antiques, on your way to Mountain City.

We suggest you stay at the York House Bed and Breakfast Inn as you explore this area. The main structure is a two-story clapboard log house in front of a grove of stately Hemlocks that feels like an ancient green cathedral. It is on the National Register of Historic Places and has been featured in *Historic Inns of the South* (text

The historic York House has been receiving appreciative guests since 1896.

by Hal Griesking and photos by Alan Bruie). The York House is the oldest bed and breakfast inn in Georgia.

Records tell us that in 1851 Hiram Gibson bought 1,000 acres and moved his family to Rabun County. Twenty-two years later he deeded 40 acres to his granddaughter, Mollie, and her husband, William York. Twenty-three years later Papa Bill and Little Mollie, as they came to be known, rented rooms to the surveyors and builders of the Tallulah Railroad. After the railroad was completed to Clayton in 1905, the inn had its own stop on the rail line for tourists who rode in a carriage the last ¼ mile to the inn. It had an ideal location about 60 miles northeast of Atlanta and about 45 miles southwest of Asheville.

The original structure received additions and a large dance pavilion was built in the 1920s for tourists coming to the mountains to escape the heat of the lowlands. The York House has been operated through most of its history by female descendants of Papa Bill and Little Mollie. The current owners, Ben Collins and Joey Barnes, told us the last of the Yorks to run the inn, Bea Weatherly Broadrick, lives next door and is a wonderful source of information about the inn.

Visitors will find 13 spacious nonsmoking guest rooms filled with comfortable antiques. All have private baths and entrances. We really enjoyed being pampered with breakfasts served on silver trays each morning, with pots of steaming hot coffee.

Both men have an appreciation for preservation of the historic structure and its grounds, which include pink and yellow lady's slippers, trillium, and a rare creeping cedar.

Foxfire now has a center on US 441 in Mountain City, Georgia, as well as the early collection of cabins and artifacts on the original site on the hillside overlooking the valley below. The name Foxfire comes from a lichen that glows in the woods at night in the Appalachian Mountains. Hume Cronyn and Jessica Tandy starred in the hit Broadway play *Foxfire*, named for the same lichen.

The collection of buildings, artifacts, and enterprises now collectively known as Foxfire was started in 1966 as a magazine by Rabun County High School students under the guidance of their teacher, Eliot Wigginton. In 1972, the first of the popular *Foxfire* series of books on Appalachian culture was published by Doubleday.

This book introduced a mountain woman, known as Aunt Arie, to the world. She spoke about affairs of mountain living like hog dressing and food preservation. Techniques for log cabin building were discussed and illustrated. Nine additional volumes followed, including such topics as spinning and weaving, blacksmithing, faith healing,

The Foxfire Center in Mountain City, Georgia, conducts workshops related to traditional arts and crafts each summer.

The cabins at Black Rock Mountain State Park are located high atop the Eastern Continental Divide.

Antiques and specialty shops line
US 441 in Dillard.

pottery, and chicken fighting. Foxfire also offers workshops for the
public. There were more than 40 choices in the summer of 1996.

Black Rock Mountain State Park is located on top of the Eastern Continental Divide in Mountain City. The watershed flows
toward the Atlantic on one side, while the other travels toward the
Gulf of Mexico. It also has the distinction of being the highest state
park in Georgia. Numerous vistas draw visitors to 10 cottages and
52 tent and trailer sites. Visitors will also find a 17-acre lake and hiking trails leading to Ada-Hi Falls and Tennessee Rock Overlook on
the 1,502 acres that comprise the park. Black Rock Mountain takes
its name from the presence of dark biotite-gneiss escarpments.

Proceed north on US 441 to visit Dillard and do a little antiques
or craft shopping in the shops along US 441. Mountain Sounds
Dulcimer shop is on the right as you drive north just before the turn
to the Dillard House Restaurant. The restaurant is one of the main
reasons people have been coming to Dillard for generations.

Dillard was named for the Dillard family, who came to the area
during the American Revolutionary War. Legend has it that the
wife of one of the early descendents, Mary, distracted the British
troops with a feast and managed to slip out undetected and warn
the patriots of their impending approach. Her descendents still
know how to set a great table at the Dillard House. A.J. and Carrie
Dillard started receiving paying guests in 1915. Literally millions
have had dinner or spent the night here. The Dillard House is

famous for its family-style dining, but it also offers accommodations ranging from rooms in the Old Inn to suites and cottages, a swimming pool, tennis courts, and riding stables. The gift shop offers sugar cured hams, spicy sausage, apple butter, jams, and jellies to take to all the folks back home who didn't get to come.

Treasures Old and New had a nice assortment of collectibles.

Yesterday's Treasures had lots of Roseville pottery, and Pine Cone Antiques had extensive silver, glassware, lamps and European furniture. Roseville, Watts, quilts, and collectibles abound at N and R Reflections.

Black Rock Mountain Antiques Market featured lots of antique tools, glassware, furniture, and country collectibles. Dillard Mini-Mall has 17 dealers. Mountain Keepsakes had Audubon and Wildflower prints. You'll find an assortment of colorful quilts with traditional designs at the co-op craft store. Heritage Handweavers carries a wide assortment of handwoven goods, including tablecloths, placemats, napkins, shawls, and jackets.

If you'd like to explore a bit off the beaten path while enjoying gourmet food, try Moon Lake Cafe for dinner. On the way you'll follow Betty's Creek out of Dillard through one of the most beautiful little valleys we've ever found. The turn to Moon Valley is on

Several antiques malls in Dillard entice collectors.

Moon Lake Cafe artfully combines a pastoral setting with delicious food.

your left up the hill before reaching Andy's Trout Farm. In a rustic, romantic setting overlooking a small lake, chef Robert Moon, known locally as "Buck," will prepare escargot, fresh mountain trout, rack of lamb, Veal Marsala, Chateaubriand, duck, or chicken in ways discerning palates will appreciate. Buck's sister, Laura, serves a mixed bouquet salad with delicious house dressing, and a variety of fresh breads. The fireplace in the intimate dining room is nice to chase off the chill in colder weather. And the wine list is good, so prepare to sit back, relax, and enjoy the atmosphere as well as the food.

Andy's Trout Farm on Betty's Creek is open from April to November. No license is required, no limit on fish caught and you pay $3 per pound. Cabin rentals are available. It's a great place to take small children to catch trout or to purchase trout if you prefer to eat rather than catch them.

As you drive along Betty's Creek, you'll pass the Hambidge Center on your right. Mary Crovatt Hambidge was born in Brunswick, Georgia in 1885. She later lived in New York, where she met her husband, Jay, with whom she traveled the world.

While in Greece in 1920, she began to study weaving and employed designs based on her husband's theories of "dynamic symmetry." After his death, she stayed at a friend's home in Rabun County near Mountain City and discovered the local tradition of handweaving. As she encouraged and supported Rabun County weavers, she received financial support from her friend, Eleanor Steele Rice, that enabled her to purchase 800 acres and build a large house of creek boulders along Betty's Creek.

Next came a shop called Rabun Studios on Madison Avenue in New York to market the products of the "Weavers of Rabun." Many of the weavers lived in their own houses along Betty's Creek and spun in their own homes, but several resided in the rock house on the property at various times. They produced fabric from hand-spun wool yarns. At the same time, more than 130 acres were under cultivation, employing four to six local men.

In 1944, the Jay Hambidge Art Foundation was incorporated with the belief that "agriculture and the handcrafts are the basis of

The Hambidge Center Gallery offers contemporary and folk art and hosts a large show in July.

a creative life." By the early 1960s, Mary focused on encouraging artists to build places to live and work on the property.

Eliot Wigginton met her when he was a child and corresponded with her throughout his college years. He came to Rabun County and built a cottage that he lived in for six years while teaching at Rabun County High School. He says, "Foxfire was born on her (Mary Hambidge's) kitchen table." The first *Foxfire* book is dedicated to her.

Since her death in 1974, more than 1,000 artists have lived and worked at the center which is listed on the National Register of Historic Places—a fitting legacy for a woman who believed "the world will be redeemed not through morality but through beauty."

The Hambidge Center has eight residency programs from two to eight weeks for artists in any medium, including writers, musicians, dancers, painters, and potters. Three galleries exhibit contemporary and folk art: Hambidge Center, Mainstreet Gallery, and Timpson Creek Gallery. The Hambidge Center also sponsors the Jugtown Pottery Show and the Folk Art Show.

The following are GA and area code 706 except where noted.

✍ ACCOMMODATIONS

A Small Motel—US 76, Clayton; 800-786-0624 or 782-6488.
Best Western Dillard—US 441N, Dillard; 746-5321 or 800-742-1416.
Black Rock Mountain State Park—Mountain City; 746-2141, 800-864-PARK
Days Inn—US 441, Clayton; 782-4258 or 800-DAYSINN.
The Dillard House—POB 10, US 441, Dillard, 30357; 746-5348,
    800-541-0671.
Green Shutters Inn—US 441, Clayton; 782-3342, 800-535-5971.
Lake Rabun Hotel—POB 10, Lake Raubn Rd., Lakemont, 30552; 782-4946.
Old Clayton Inn—Main St., Clayton; 782-7722.
Sky Valley Resort—Sky Valley; 746-5301 or 800-262-8259.
Shoney's Inn—US 441, Clayton; 782-2214 or 800-334-2214.
Whispering Falls Vacation Cabins—Fully equipped; accept most pets; 782-2583.
Willis Knob Horse Camp & Trail— Warwoman Rd., Clayton; 782-3320.
The York House—POB 126, Mountain City, 30562; 800-231-YORK or
    746-2068.

❧ ATTRACTIONS

Andy's Trout Farm—POB 129, Dillard, 30537; 746-2550.

Chattooga Rent-A-Raft—782-1221.

Dillard House Stables—Dillard; 746-5348.

Foxfire Museum—US 441, Mountain City; 746-5828; 9:00 A.M. to 4:30
  P.M. Mon., Weds., Thurs., and Sat.

The Hambidge Center—POB 339 Rabun Gap, 30568; 746-5718.

Southeastern Expeditions—GA 76, Clayton; 800-868-7238 or 329-0433.

❧ DINING

The Dillard House—POB 10, US 441, Dillard, 30357; 746-5348 or 800-
  541-1671.

Green Shutters—Old Hwy. 441, Clayton; 782-3342.

John and Earl Dillard's Place, Best Western—US 441, Dillard; 746-5321.

LaPrade's—GA 197 at Lake Burton; 800-262-3313 or 947-3312 for reservations.

Moon Lake Cafe—Rt. 1, Box 680, Rabun Gap, 30568; 746-2466; Reservations requested.

The Stockton House Restaurant—1 mile off US 441 in Warwoman Dell, Clayton; 782-6175.

❧ SHOPPING

Appalachian Trader Antique Mall—Warwoman Rd., Clayton, 30525; 782-2486.

Black Rock Mountain Antiques Market—US 441, POB 422, Dillard; 746-2470.

Country Antiques—Earl Circle off 441, Clayton; 782-2229.

Dillard House Gift Shop—US 441, Dillard; 746-5348 or 800-541-0671.

Dillard Mini-Mall—US 441, Dillard; 746-2127; 10:00 A.M. to 5:00 P.M.,
  except Sun, 1:00 to 5:00 P.M., closed Weds.

The Hambidge Center—Betty's Creek Rd., Dillard; 746-5718.

Heritage Handweavers—US 441, Dillard; 746-2086.

Main Street Gallery—POB 641, Clayton; 782-2440.

Mountain Mama Antiques—US 441, Clayton; 782-6232.

Pine Cone Antiques—US 441, Dillard; 10:00 A.M. to 4:00 P.M.; Closed
  Weds., Sun.

The Rocking Horse—US 441, Mountain City; 746-2004.

Timpson Creek Gallery—76 West, Clayton; 782-5164.

Treasures Old & New Antique Mall—POB 517, US 441, Dillard; 746-6566.

ᴥ SPECIAL EVENTS

July to August—*Southern Folk Expressions Art Show (Hambidge Center, 746-5718)*

ᴥ CAMPING

Black Rock Mountain State Park—Mountain City, GA; From Atlanta 770-389-
    7275 or 800-864-7275.
Copecrest—Betty's Creek Rd.; 746-2134; RVs only.
Seed Lake Campground—Primitive camping by Seed Lake; 754-6036.
Terrora Park/Tallulah Gorge—Tallulah Gorge, 12 miles south of Clayton;
    754-6036 or 800-864-7275; From Atlanta 770-389-7275.
Tugaloo Park—Primitive camping; US 23/441; 754-6036.
U.S. Forest Service—Primitive camping throughout the Chattahoochee
    National Forest; 782-3320.
Willis Knob Horse Camp and Trail—Warwoman Rd., Clayton, GA; 782-3320.

ᴥ FOR MORE INFORMATION

Rabun County Welcome Center—US 441/23, Clayton, GA; 782-5113.
Discover Upcountry Carolina Association—POB 3116, Greenville, SC 29602;
    800-849-4766 or 803-233-2690.
South Carolina State Parks—1205 Pendleton Street, Columbia, SC 29201;
    803-734-0156.
Sumter National Forest—USFS, Walhalla, SC; 803-638-9568.
Tallulah District—US Forest Service Ranger Station Office, N. Main St.,
    Clayton, GA; 782-3320.

ᴥ DIRECTIONS

I-85 from Atlanta to I-985 to US 365 to US 441 North.
I-40 or Blue Ridge Parkway from Asheville to US 23/441.

5 *Lake Rabun, Seed Lake, Lake Burton:*

Mountain Lake Country

Hall's Boat House and Marina is the site of floating church services on summer Sundays.

The Tallulah River flows southeast through Habersham County. A series of lakes created by three dams is operated by Georgia Power on the Tallulah stretch between GA 197 and US 441. The lakes created by these dams offer recreational opportunities for visitors in the resort communities that have developed along their shorelines.

The largest is Lake Burton, with 2,775 surface acres and 62 miles of shoreline. Burton's elevation is 1,866 feet above sea level. Seed Lake is the smallest, with 240 surface acres and 13 miles of shoreline at 1,752 feet elevation. Lake Rabun is the most densely populated, with modern, upscale summer homes along its 834 surface acres and 25 miles of shoreline nestled at a mere 1,690 feet above sea level. The roads are narrow as they wind between GA 197 along Burton Dam Road to Lake Rabun Road, which travels along Seed Lake and Lake Rabun to the community of Lakemont near US 441 between Tallulah Falls and Clayton.

We exited US 441 and traveled four miles to Lakemont to visit Alley's Grocery, a landmark since 1925. In fact, Mr. and Mrs. Paul Alley, who started the store, had one of the first three telephones in Lakemont. Lamar Alley runs a friendly sort of a place that is the closest source of provisions on the eastern side of Lake Rabun. Stop by and get something for a picnic at Seed Lake or Minnehaha Falls.

Almost as soon as Lake Rabun was impounded and filled in 1915, Atlanta escapees began to search for property along its shores for summer homes. Today Atlanta is less than 2 hours away and beautiful modern weekend lake houses are densely grouped among the relatively few, but equally expensive, older lake homes.

If you want to visit, you'll find three bed and breakfast inns near the lake. The most unusual is the 1922 Lake Rabun Hotel, a vision of Arts and Crafts architecture on a gentle rise across the road from the lake. It looks well-worn, just like the unparalleled collection of authentic laurel and rhododendron twig furnishings found inside. Everywhere you look there are outstanding examples of twig furniture: tables, daybeds, doorways, settees, beds, and lamps, all enhanced with the deep luster of age. Rumor has it President Jimmy Carter tried unsuccessfully to snag this collection for the White House. The hotel has 17 rooms, all of which come with ambiance and character. What they do not have are private baths with whirlpools, air conditioning, or televisions. The Lake Rabun Hotel doesn't seem particularly interested in modernization, which is, of course, a great part of its charm. Canoes are available for guests to borrow.

Across the street from the hotel is the old Rabun Cafe, now the home of Louie's on the Lake. Who else but Louie would let us

Alley's Grocery provides picnic and camping necessities.

The rustic 1922 Lake Rabun Hotel is home to an unusual collection of laurel and rhododendron twig furnishings.

Lakemont Antiques on Lake Rabun
and Burton Gallery on Lake Burton
invite shoppers to browse.

borrow his pizza pan to "carry out" our New York style pizza and
leave it on the porch for him the next day? These people have
mastered the art of relaxing. Louie's, or the Rabun Cafe as it
was known then, was the site of Saturday night square dances in
the days when only thirty or so houses lined the lake and it took
two days to travel from Atlanta. In that era people stayed for the
entire summer.

While you're in the vicinity you may want to visit Lakemont
Antiques or stop at the marina and check out some of the classic
Chriscraft models docked along the shoreline. A floating church
service is held at Hall's Boat House each Sunday morning during
the summer season.

A little less than 5 miles down Lake Rabun Road, the Rabun
Beach Recreation Area has eighty tent and trailer campsites, some
with electrical and water hook-ups, all with picnic tables, grills, and
tent pads. You'll also find hot showers and drinking water. There
are also day-use picnic tables, a roped-off swimming area on the
beach, and a boat launch. The 1.3-mile Rabun Beach Trail from
Camping Area 2 (actually the first campground you come to traveling from east to west) winds along Joe's Branch amid Catesby's Tril-

lium in late April. The easy trail takes you to two waterfalls, the 35-40 foot Panther Falls and the 50-foot Angel Falls. The area is open from mid-May to mid-November.

The Barn Inn Lodge sits on a knoll overlooking the lake. There's a nice deck with hammocks and Adirondack chairs just right for relaxing. The Lake Rabun Inn is also open to visitors. You will not find motels here, and there are limited accommodations available for visitors, so it's a good idea to arrive with reservations.

You won't find streets filled with shops but there are treasures to be found, like Minnehaha Falls on the opposite side of the lake from Lake Rabun Road. To reach the 100-foot waterfalls, turn across the bridge at the dam and follow Bear Gap Road toward the left, or east, along the lake 1.6 miles. There's a pull-off on the left and a sign pointing up the wooden steps to the easy half-mile trail to the base of the falls. A big boulder near the base of the upper falls makes a perfect seat. A fine mist fills the air, lush vegetation surrounds you, and peace prevails—interrupted only by the falling waters.

If you turn left on Bear Gap Road after crossing the bridge, you'll eventually come to Seed Lake Recreation Area down a fairly long dirt road. The reward for the drive is a pretty, shady campground with picnic sites, primitive camping, and a shallow swimming area in Seed Lake. There are bathrooms but no shower. If you're traveling with a canoe, there's a short, level carry to an easy launch.

Continuing on Lake Rabun Road, you'll pass Rabun Beach, the dam at Seed Lake, and a boat launch on your left before reaching the highest of the dams at Burton. You may continue around Lake Burton on the east side via Bridge Creek Road about eight miles to US 76 about 7.5 miles west of Clayton. Turn left on Burton Dam Road, and cross the dam toward Lil Brooks General Store before reaching Burton Gallery and Emporium near GA 197. The gallery offers gifts including folk art, wind chimes, bronze sculptures, and antique fishing tackle and decoys.

Turn right on Hwy. 197 to visit LaPrade's (rhymes with "lads") and Moccasin Creek State Park and Fish Hatchery. Burton Woods Cabins and Lodge are on the left. The new cabins have

Wildflowers like these trillium are abundant along the Rabun Beach Trail.

The lovely 100-foot Minnehaha Falls are accessed by an easy 0.5-mile trail.

Seed Lake Recreation Area offers scenic primitive campsites, picnic areas, and swimming.

central air/heat, stone fireplaces, television with VCR, telephone, fully furnished kitchens, and decks with comfortable rocking chairs.

LaPrade's is open from April 1 to the Sunday after Thanksgiving. It was founded in 1925 by John LaPrade and has been operated since 1972 by various members of the Nichols family. Most of the produce served is grown on an 80-acre farm in Clarkesville. The 20 cabins are rustic, fish-camp type and small as a rule. We liked #11, which has a fireplace; #12, which is only 12x12 but appealing; and #14 and #15, which were tucked back under the trees yet close to the lake just across the highway. There are two rental houses on the lakeside for larger groups. Two cabins are handicapped accessible. Rentals are usually weekly, three nights minimum. Guests staying in cabins can launch and keep boats in slips free of charge.

Now, let's talk food—country comfort food at its finest and most plentiful. LaPrade's can seat 150 at a time and there's a handicapped accessible ramp. Reservations are recommended. Visitors not staying in cabins can use the facilities at the marina across the road for a $3 launch fee. Boats on the lake may not have toilets, galleys, or sleeping quarters.

Burton is the site of the state record yellow perch and we feel it always helps to fish with people who know the lake and how to fish it. Such a person is Grady Sutton, who guides for all gamefish species but particularly loves going for walleye.

Guests at LaPrade's are entitled to hang their catch on the rail outside the restaurant for bragging rights. LaPrade's will ice or freeze fish for guests until their departure. Wildcat Creek, a stocked trout stream, feeds into the cove at LaPrade's. Stop by the fish hatchery just up the road for a map of fish attractors.

Moccasin Creek State Park on Lake Burton is open from 7:00 a.m. to 10:00 p.m. daily. There's an attractive campground and a handicapped accessible fishing pier on Moccasin Creek, which begins seven miles westward on the eastern continental divide. A playground, pavilion, dock, and picnic area overlook the lake. The Lake Burton Fish Hatchery is across the creek from the park. A public boat ramp is available at the hatchery. Particular campsites cannot be reserved, but types of sites may be. So if you want a premium site along the creek or the lakefront, mention type T3PR and T4PR when you call for reservations.

The following are GA and area code 706.

ACCOMMODATIONS

Burton Woods Cabins and Lodge at Lake Burton—Rt. 1, Box 1660, Clarkesville, 30523; 947-3926.
Lake Rabun Hotel—Lake Rabun Rd.; POB 10, Lakemont, 30552; 782-4946.
Lake Rabun Inn—Lake Rabun Rd., Lakemont, 30552; 782-5789, 800-762-5780.
LaPrade's—Hwy. 197 North, Lake Burton, Clarkesville; 947-3312.
The Barn Inn Lodge—Lake Rabun Rd., Lakemont, 30552; 782-5094.

ATTRACTIONS

Angel Falls—#2 Camping Area, Lake Rabun Recreation Area.
Lake Burton Guide Service—Grady and Pat Sutton; 947-3006.
Minnehaha Falls—Bear Gap Rd.
Panther Falls—#2 Camping Area, Lake Rabun Recreation Area.

DINING

Batesville General Store—Rt. 1, Box 1818, Clarkesville, 30523; 947-3434; Open daily.
LaPrade's—GA 197 North, Lake Burton, Clarkesville; 800-262-3313 or 947-3312 for meal reservations; Open Apr. to Nov.
Louie's on the Lake—Lake Rabun Rd., Lakemont; 782-3276.

SHOPPING

Barbara's Antiques—GA 197, Lake Burton; 947-1362.
Burton Gallery and Emporium—Burton Dam Rd. at GA 197, Clarkesville; 947-1351 10:00 A.M. to 6:00 P.M., Mon. to Sat., 1:00 to 6:00 P.M. Sun., closed Tues.
Lakeview Antiques—Lake Rabun Rd., Lakemont.
Landmark Antiques and Pottery—GA 197 North, Rt., Box 1, Clarkesville, 30523; 947-1278; 9:00 A.M. to 6:00 P.M., Mon. to Thurs., 9:00 A.M. to 8:00 P.M. Fri. to Sun.

Mark of the Potter—Rt. 3, Box 3164, Clarkesville, 30523; 947-3440.
One Burton Place Antiques and Reproductions—GA 197 and Laurel Lodge Rd.;
     947-1276.
The Wood Duck—Rt. 1, Box 1816, Clarkesville, 30523; 947-3032.

❧ SPECIAL EVENTS

June—*Georgia Mountain Trout Program and Contest (Moccasin Creek State Park)*
July—*Lake Burton Arts and Crafts Festival*

❧ CAMPING

Lake Rabun Recreation Area—Chattahoochee National Forest, Tallulah Ranger
     District; 782-3320.
Moccasin Creek State Park—GA 197, Rt. 1, Box 1364, Clarkesville; 947-3194
     or 800-864-PARK; From Atlanta 770-389-PARK.
Seed Lake Campground—Primitive only; GA Power, 754-6036.
Terrora Park and Visitor Center—US 441S, Tallulah Falls; 754-3276.

❧ FOR MORE INFORMATION

Lake Burton Hatchery—Rt. 1, Clarkesville, 30523.
Georgia Power Camping and Day Use Areas—754-6036.
Rabun County Chamber of Commerce/Welcome Center—US 441, POB 750, Clay-
     ton, 30525; 782-4812.
Northeast Georgia Mountain Travel Association—POB 464, Gainesville, 30503;
     535-5757.

❧ DIRECTIONS

Lake Rabun is about 5 miles from Tallulah Falls off Old US 441 via Lake
     Rabun Road. There's a very small sign pointing toward Lakemont west
     of new US 441 at the second road north of the bridge at Tallulah Falls.
From Clayton—Take old US 441 and bear to the right on Lake Rabun Road.
From Helen—Take GA 356 past Unicoi State Park and connect with GA
     197 and turn left. You're about 8 miles south of Moccasin Creek State
     Park and the fish hatchery.

6 *Hiawassee, Young Harris, Blairsville:*
Land of Enchanted Valleys

According to legend, the Cherokee and Catawba Indians were at war. Nottla, or "daring horseman," was the son of the Principal Chief of the Cherokee. He surprised and captured a Catawba village. Among the captives was Hiawassee, or "pretty fawn," the beautiful daughter of the First Chief of the Catawba. Nottla fell in love with her and demanded her hand in marriage. The Catawba Chief refused him unless he could find a place where the waters of the

The 4,784-foot summit at Brasstown Bald is the highest point in Georgia.

The Appalachian Trail stretches 2,100 miles from Springer Mountain, Georgia, to Mount Katadin, Maine.

Peggy and David Lewis provide trailside Easter breakfast for through hikers on the Appalachian Trail.

east, which were in the land of the Catawba, and the waters of the west, which were in the lands of the Cherokee, were united. The search was long for a place many did not believe could exist. He finally ventured, exhausted and discouraged, into a peaceful valley where he saw three young fawns drinking from a pool that had two streams flowing out of the valley in opposite directions. Nottla hurried back with the discovery and found his beloved near her father's wigwam. The great Catawba Chief was so enraged that he refused to honor Nottla's claim, but Nottla and Hiawassee escaped to the mountains, settling in the beautiful valley they called Hiawassee in her honor.

The Hiawassee/Towns County area was home to the Cherokee Indians until their removal in 1838. Today Hiawassee hugs the southern shores of Lake Chatuge (pronounced "sha-toog"), a 7,050-acre TVA reservoir ringed by mountains and shared with North Carolina. The lake is well known for fishing, with populations of 30 percent largemouth bass, (found in coves with structure), 50 percent spotted bass, and 20 percent smallmouth bass.

As you approach Hiawassee from the east on US 76 from Clayton, you will pass the left turn for GA 197 to visit Moccasin Creek State Park, Lake Burton, LaPrade's Restaurant and Campground, Seed Lake, and Lake Rabun (see Mountain Lake Country section). Continuing on US 76, you'll have an opportunity for a picnic with a view at Popcorn Overlook. The Appalachian Trail (AT) was constructed between 1921 and 1937. It stretches between Springer Mountain, Georgia, and Mount Katahdin in Maine, traversing 2,100 miles through 14 states. It's the longest such trail in the world.

The AT enters Towns County southeast of Brasstown Bald and skirts Rich Knob at Bly Gap, a grassy bald with scenic vistas, before exiting at the North Carolina border. The AT crosses US 76 east of Hiawassee at Dick's Creek Gap. We found Peggy and David Lewis from Greenville, South Carolina, serving breakfast on a chilly Easter morning to "through" hikers on the AT at the picnic area at Dick's Creek Gap. The Lewises are members of the South Carolina Strollers and they completed the 2,100-mile trek by a series of section hikes in 1990. They understand firsthand the importance of hospitality in the wilderness.

The section of the AT south of Dick's Creek Gap is 16.5 miles of strenuous walking with scenic views across Tray Mountain, the second highest peak along the Georgia section of the AT, to Unicoi Gap at GA 75 north of Helen. North of Dick's Creek Gap the trail is 8.7 strenuous miles through the Southern Nantahala Wilderness Area near Black Mountain at the North Carolina line. Nantahala is the Cherokee word for "noonday sun," appropriate because the deep hollows and gorges block all but the noonday sun. With more than 500,000 acres, the Nantahala is the largest of the four national forests in North Carolina.

A favorite overnight stop for hikers is the Blueberry Patch Hostel, a short distance from Dick's Creek Gap on the southern side of the highway or continue for 7.6 miles along US 76 to Hiawassee.

Hiawassee hugs the southern shores of Lake Chatuge.

Approaching Hiawassee, US 76 bears to the right as it joins GA 75 from Helen. Rather than turning toward the right at this junction, some visitors may want to follow GA 288 to Chatuge Lake Recreation Area, which has camping, boating, fishing and hiking. The recreation area can also be accessed from US 76 west of town if you prefer to drive through town first. Brasstown Bald, the highest peak in Georgia, is a short drive south of Hiawassee on GA 75 with a west (right) turn on GA 180.

On the North Carolina side of Lake Chatuge, the Jackrabbit Mountain Recreation Area is very popular. It's situated on a point studded with pines. There are 100 campsites, a swimming beach, a boat launch ramp, two picnic areas, showers, and restrooms.

To visit this unspoiled site, turn north (right) at the first traffic light onto GA 175 when entering Hiawassee from the east or south on GA 75 or GA 76. Drive about 5 miles, turn left at the sign for Jackrabbit Mountain, and go about ¾ mile to the recreation area. GA 175 continues past Jackrabbit to NC 64 between Hayesville and Franklin.

Mountain Memories Inn has rooms and suites with private baths, gas log fireplaces, Jacuzzis, and great views. A full breakfast is provided. To visit Mountain Memories Inn, turn left at the first light and go ½ mile and take a right. Turn left at the stop sign.

Mountain Memories Inn has rooms with fireplaces, Jacuzzis, and great views.

More than 200,000 visitors celebrate mountain heritage at the Georgia Mountain Fair each year.

Steve's Place Restaurant packs in the local crowd for breakfasts and Friday night seafood or rib feasts, but they offer nightly specials as well. The traditional daily menu has sandwiches, steaks, and fried chicken.

Hiawassee is also known as the home of the Georgia Mountain Fair, a twelve-day celebration of old time crafts, bluegrass music, and mountain heritage that begins the first Wednesday in August. Past fairs have featured "old ways" demonstrations of mountain arts like cider pressing, hominy making, quilting, and blacksmithing between twice-daily music shows, a replica mountain village, rides on the midway and the opportunity to hand milk a Holstein cow. There are arts and crafts for sale and pig races to watch. Georgia Mountain Fair has a campground with spots all along Lake Chatuge. The Georgia Mountain Fair attracts more than 200,000 visitors each year and has been featured in national publications. The fair, one of the most popular tourist events in the Southeast, is nonprofit and does not accept commercial exhibits.

The Georgia Mountain Fairgrounds also hosts the Spring Music Festival and the Fall Festival and Fiddlers Convention. Top country performers are also scheduled at the fairgrounds from April to November.

You'll find a no-frills fish camp at Lakeshore Cottages. On the other side of the cove is the upscale Fieldstone Inn, which overlooks the lake and has a restaurant and marina. It's on the right as you leave Hiawassee on US 76 West toward Young Harris and Blairsville.

The Fieldstone Inn has a massive, double-sided fieldstone fireplace that is the focus of a lobby and great room that overlook Lake Chatuge through a 21-foot wall of windows. There are 66 guest rooms and most have their own balconies, many with a view of the lake. There's a swimming pool and an exercise room. Inn guests have the complimentary use of a boat slip or may rent watercraft ranging from canoes to pontoon boats.

The evening buffet satisfies hearty appetites, or you can choose pastas, chicken, and steaks blackened or grilled from the menu. The soup and salad bar should satisfy lighter appetites, and the bar serves wine and beer. Habersham Winery has a tasting room open across the highway that features their Georgia vintages. Continue on US 76 to the Mountain Regional Library in Young Harris, which has an Appalachian Archives that includes books, records, and videos pertaining to the mountain way of life for those interested in learning more about the area.

Reach of Song is a drama written by Tom Detitta about the Appalachian Mountains as experienced by Byron Herbert Reece, a North Georgia writer born here in 1918. The story runs the gamut of human experience as the secluded mountain culture meets the rest of the world. Often associated with the Anderson Music Hall at Georgia Mountains Fairground, most recently *Reach of Song* has been produced at Young Harris College.

The state of Georgia owns the 503 acres on which the Brasstown Valley Crowne Plaza Resort in Young Harris was built. From the time you enter the dramatic four-story main lodge where a 72-foot fireplace dominates the Great Room, with its naturally-shed antler chandeliers and twig furniture, you realize this resort lends a new elegance to rustic and remote. One hundred and two rooms and suites are located in the lodge, which has a deep green exterior with crisp white trim and fieldstone accents that seem to blend with the lush forest surrounding it.

The Brasstown Valley Crowne Plaza Resort has one of the top-ten public golf courses in Georgia.

Choose from rooms in the main lodge, one-bedroom suites, or four-bedroom cottages with separately keyed interior and exterior entrances and a common parlor with woodburning fireplace, kitchenettes, and barbecue grills. No detail has been omitted for the pleasure and enjoyment of guests, including in-room coffee makers, hair dryers, and televisions as well as a steam sauna, whirlpool, fitness center, massage therapist, and heated indoor-outdoor pool. Children from 5 to 17 can take part in the seasonal Mountaineer Kids' Club activities like hikes, craft making, and storytelling under the supervision of trained "outdoor adventurers."

There's also a 7,000-yard, 18-hole par-72 golf course flanked by Brasstown Bald, Cherokee Indian burial grounds, and Three Sisters Mountain. The golf course was designed to be sensitive to the unique location of the property, yet it has been rated one of the top ten public courses in Georgia by *Golf Digest*. Brasstown offers equipment rental, along with golf and tennis lessons and clinics.

There are also several choices for dining, either at the Dining Room, where you'll be offered dinners ranging from trout and venison to pheasant and filet mignon, or at McDivot's, a sports pub.

On a more intimate scale, the Southern Country Inn is on US 76 after passing Young-Harris College and crossing into Union County.

To visit Brasstown Bald from Hiawassee or Young Harris heading west on US 76, turn south (left) on Track Rock Gap Road, left again on Towns Creek Road, and a final left (east) on GA 180 and follow the signs. As you travel along Track Rock Gap Road, you'll pass the Track Rock Archaeological Area on your right as you drive south. The 52-acre site contains ancient Indian petroglyphs and what the Cherokee, according to author Vicki Rozema, believed were tracks made by birds and animals while the earth was young and impressionable. No one knows for certain who made these impressions or when. Vandalism has prompted iron grates around the sites, but the petroglyphs are still clearly visible (although fading with time). The location in a low gap through the mountains may be significant. Whatever is here at Track Rock, knowledge of its origin escapes us.

Watch for the left turn onto Trackrock Church Road if you're interested in horseback riding at Trackrock Stables on more than 250 acres bordering the Chattahoochee National Forest. Many equestrians claim this stable offers the prettiest riding trails in the entire north Georgia mountain area. Best of all, they're open yearround.

The 4,784-foot summit at Brasstown Bald is topped with a small museum and theater that shows a video about the mountain, which the Cherokee knew as "itse'yi," meaning "new green place." There's a parking lot near the top that's open most of the year, even if the museum at the top is closed for the season. At the summit there's an observation tower with a 360-degree view of four states on a clear day. You can walk the steep paved 0.5-mile path that leads to the summit or you can wait for a small shuttle bus if you're here from Memorial Day through October.

Brasstown Bald is surrounded by Brasstown Wilderness Area, a part of the vast Chattahoochee National Forest, so it's particularly inspiring in spring and fall. Summer often finds the top enshrouded in cool mists and clear skies at the foot of many of the peaks of these mountain ranges. For those continuing on US 76 toward Blairsville, the southern edge of Lake Nottely touches the outskirts of town to the west on US 76 and north on US 19/129. This 4,180-acre lake has 106 miles of shoreline with somewhat limited facilities along it.

In the center of town, the old Union County Courthouse is now home to the Union County Historical Society Museum. Lodging is limited, but there are several cabins and bed and breakfasts in the area. The Butt family was one of the founding families in the area, and now Butt Antiques offers visitors some of the collectibles and antiques they have accumulated. Easterling's features collectibles and handcrafted furniture.

Turn south on US 19/129 to visit Riverside Restaurant for barbecue in Pappy's Compound, an assortment of antiques shops, ice cream parlors, and gift shops. You will also find delicious "apple trout," rainbow trout smoked over apple wood in a two-day process, and sourwood honey.

The Union County Courthouse is the home of the Union County Historical Society Museum.

The Appalachian Trail crosses US 129 near the Walasi-Yi Center at Neel's Gap.

You may also access Brasstown Bald off US 19/129 by turning east on GA 180. The Richard B. Russell Scenic Highway off GA 180 connects the area south of Blairsville with Helen. As the name implies, it is a lovely winding drive through rhododendron and laurel thickets to the Raven Cliffs Scenic Area and Dukes Creek Falls.

At the intersection of US 129 and GA 180, a west turn on GA 180 takes you past Vogel State Park and Lake Winfield Scott Recreation Area to Suches, a quiet, tiny mountain community tucked along Woody Lake on the way to Dahlonega. This is a beautiful drive as the seasons change.

If you continue south approximately 3.5 miles on US 129/19, you'll come across Neel's Gap and the Appalachian Trail. A road was cut through this area in the 1930s that opened access through the rugged area. There are several Civilian Conservation Corps (CCC) projects in the vicinity, including the Walasi-Yi Center. It took the name of the gap the Cherokee knew as "Frog Place" because legend says a Cherokee brave saw a giant frog here while hunting. The stone structure was originally built as an inn by the CCC.

The AT crosses here about 2 miles from the Blood Mountain Archaeological Area. Theories about the origin of the name "Blood

Mountain" include battles between the Cherokee and the Creek, and battles between the Cherokee and the South Carolina militia during the Revolutionary War. Whatever happened, it was a site reputed to hold lots of arrowheads, or "points," as they're often called, before hikers searched the area. It's also one of those extraordinary "ancient" places scattered throughout the mountains of the Cherokee.

A little farther south US 19 bears to the right toward Dahlonega. Look for a pile of stones at the "T," where US 129 intersects US 19 north of Dahlonega and a historic marker at Trahlyta's Grave. Legend tells us she was a beautiful Cherokee maiden who was kidnapped by a suitor and taken to a distant land. Her beauty was preserved with the aid of a magical spring from which she drank. Deprived of these waters, she soon began to age and was returned to her home, dying. It is considered good luck for passersby to add a stone to the pile. There are other stonepiles found throughout Cherokee country. They frequently, as in the case of Trahlyta's grave, marked trails at the intersection of routes, but are reported to mark Indian graves in stories told by elder members of the community. At this point, a right (north) turn takes you toward Dockery Lake and Suches. A left (south) turn takes you to Dahlonega.

It is considered good luck for travelers to add a stone to Trahlyta's Grave.

The following are Hiawassee, GA 30546 and area code 706 except where noted.

❧ ACCOMMODATIONS

Blood Mountain Cabins—US 19/129, Blairsville; 800-284-6866.
Brasstown Valley Resort—US 76, Young Harris, 30582; 800-201-3205 or 379-9900.
Fieldstone Inn—3499 US 76 West; 896-2262 or 800-545-3408.
Lake Nottely Vacation Rentals—2942 Nottely Dam Rd., Blairsville 30512; 745-4119.
Lake Winfield Scott Recreation Area—GA 180, Blairsville, 30512; 745-6928.
Misty Mountain Inn and Cottages—4376 Misty Mountain Ln., Blairsville, 30512; 800-346-045 5 or 745-4786.
Mountain Memories Inn—385 Chauncey Dr.; 896-8439 or 800-335-VIEW.
Souther Country Inn—2592 Collins Ln., Blairsville, 30512; 800-297-1603.
Vogel State Park—7485 Vogel State Park Rd. off GA 180, Blairsville, 30512; 745-2628 or 800-864-PARK; Metro Atlanta 770-389-PARK.

❧ ATTRACTIONS

Brasstown Bald—896-2556; Memorial Day to Oct., and weekends in early
    spring.
DeSoto Falls Scenic Area—US 129 & 19 North; 745-6928.
Duke's Creek Falls—Richard B. Russell Scenic Hwy.
Fred Hamilton Rhododendron Gardens—US 76 West, Georgia Mtn. Fairgrounds;
    896-4966.
Georgia Mountain Fair—POB 444, US 76 West, 896-4191.
Lake Nottely—US 19/129 North, Blairsville, 30512.
Mountain South Outfitters—Hwy. 76 W; 379-2096.
Raven Cliffs Scenic Area—Richard B. Russell Scenic Hwy.
The Reach of Song—Young Harris College, Clegg Fine Arts Bldg.; 896-3388.
Track Rock Gap Archaeological Area—Trackrock Gap Rd.; 745-6928.
Trackrock Stables—4890 Trackrock Campground Rd., Blairsville, 30512;
    745-5252.
Union County Historical Society Museum—Old Union County Courthouse,
    Blairsville, 30512; 745-5493; Weds. to Sat., June through Nov.

❧ DINING

Brasstown Valley Resort—Young Harris; 379-9900.
Cherdan's Seafood Company—715 N. Main St.; 896-3815; Dinner 4:00 to
    10:00 P.M., closed Mon.
Riverside Restaurant at Pappy's—US 19/129, 5 miles south of Blairsville;
    745-9885.
Steve's Place—US 76; 896-3668; Breakfast, lunch, dinner.
The Fieldstone Inn—US 76, POB 60, 30546; 896-2262 or 800-545-3408.

❧ SHOPPING

Easterling's Collectibles—US 76; 800-448-4271.
Habersham Winery Tasting Room—3370 US 76; 11:00 A.M. to 7:00 P.M. Mon.
    to Sat.
The Mountain Homestead—US 76 West, POB 332; 896-2568.

❧ SPECIAL EVENTS

May—*Georgia Mountain Fair Spring Music Festival*
August—*Georgia Mountain Fair*

October—*Fall Festival and Georgia State Fiddlers' Convention (896-4191)*
December—*Mountain Country Christmas*

⌘ CAMPING

Bald Mountain Campground and Resort—Fodder Creek Rd.; 896-2274.
Jackrabbit Mountain Recreation Area—North Carolina; 704-524-6441.
Lake Chatuge Recreation Area, Chattahoochee Nat. Forest—US 76; 896-4191,
   896-2600.
Track Rock Campground & Cabins—Off US 129; 745-2400.

⌘ FOR MORE INFORMATION

Blairsville/Union County Chamber of Commerce—POB 727, Blairsville, GA
   30512; 745-5789.
Towns County Chamber of Commerce—Hwy. 76 West; 896-4966 or
   800-984-1543.
USDA Forest Service—Brasstown Ranger District; 745-6928.
USDA Forest Service—Wayah Ranger District, 90 Sloan Rd. (off US 64 west
   of Franklin), Franklin, NC 28734; 704-524-6441.

⌘ DIRECTIONS

From Atlanta—Take I-985 to US 129 at Gainesville and follow the signs
   from 129 to GA 75.
From I-40 at Asheville, NC—Take US 23/441 to Clayton, GA, then US 76
   West.
From I-85—Exit scenic US 441 north to Clayton and turn west on US 76,
   a beautiful drive with many scenic overlooks as you cross the Blue
   Ridge Mountains.

7   *Georgia Outdoor Recreation*

The northeast Georgia highlands have been the getaway region for more than a century for people living from Atlanta south into Florida. Those who could afford to do so left the hot climate and disease-bearing mosquitos during the summer for the cool cabins and resorts in the mountains.

Improved road systems and a better standard of living have put these cooler climes within reach of most people today. The communities recognizing this have put their best efforts forward in developing attractions, lodging, and dining for the millions of tourists who come here each year—often regardless of season.

Some tourists come to lounge and relax in quiet surroundings of a bed and breakfast, while many come for the outdoor activities

Whitewater kayaking, canoeing, and rafting draw visitors to north Georgia.

that abound here. The following is a sample of what you may find to burn calories, concentrate on a game or quiescent sport, or travel on foot or horse to remote areas. Northeast Georgia has something for everyone.

The following are GA and area code 706 except where noted.

❧ STATE PARKS

State parks were originally lands set aside to be preserved or to be developed within specific guidelines. The parks with camping, cabins, and lodges were operated, and still are, to be economical to the general public. Their popularity grew to the point that some parks are booked a year in advance. To stay at a popular park requires advanced planning. The following northeast Georgia parks are very popular and there are phone numbers at the end of the list for you to call for reservations.

Amicalola Falls Park and Lodge—Star Rt. Box 215, Dawsonville, 30534; 265-8888; Lake fishing, swimming pool, hiking, nature trails, pedal boats, launching ramp, picnic sites, and 25 sites for tents/RVs.
Black Mountain Park—PO Drawer A, Mountain City, 30562; 746-2141; Lake fishing, swimming pool, hiking, nature trails, picnic sites, 10 cottages, and 52 sites for tents/RVs.
Moccasin Creek Park—Rt. 1, Box 1634, Clarkesville, 30523; 947-3194; Lake and stream fishing, hiking, nature trails, pedal boats, launching ramp, water skiing, dock, picnic sites, and 54 sites for tents/RVs.
Tallulah Gorge Park—POB 248, Tallulah Gorge, 30573; 754-8257; Hiking and nature trails.
Terrora Park & Campground—POB 248, Tallulah Gorge, 30573; 754-6036; Lake and stream fishing, swimming beach, tennis, picnic sites, and 50 sites for tents/RVs.
Unicoi Park & Lodge—POB 849, Helen, 30545; 878-2201; Stream fishing, hiking, nature trails, tennis, picnic sites, 100 rooms in the lodge, and 120 sites for tents/RVs.
Vogel Park—7484 Vogel State Park Rd., Blairsville, 30512; 745-2628; Swimming beach, pedal boats, lake and stream fishing, hiking and nature trails, 36 cottages, and 110 camping sites.

For reservations in any of these parks, call 770-389-PARK in Metro Atlanta or call 800-864-PARK outside Atlanta. For more information and

Visitors to Vogel State Park enjoy swimming, fishing, hiking, and miniature golf.

brochures, call 404-656-3560 or write Georgia State Parks, 1352 Floyd Tower E., 205 Butler St., SE., Atlanta, 30334.

✺ BIKING

Northeast Georgia biking is an up-and-down love affair. There are some fairly level rides along valley floors if you like touring. Contact Tourism Division, POB 1776, Atlanta, 30301; 404-656-3590 and ask for *Georgia Bicycle Touring Guide.* It contains 10 routes for touring, but only one ride takes you 120 miles though the mountains, from Lookout Mountain in Chattanooga to Black Rock Mountain State Park in Rabun County.

Mountain biking is the "real thing." Its popularity has exploded, but unfortunately that popularity has not been developed in northeast Georgia. There are trails in the Chattahoochee National Forest. Contact Toccoa Ranger District, Suite 5, Owenby Bldg., E. Main St., Blue Ridge, 30513; 632-3031.

✺ CAMPING

Camping was once a fairly rugged adventure, but today's campgrounds are plush. Your RV can hook up to receptacles and you immediately have a new front yard. Tent camping is still popular, but it too has been enhanced. Rain doesn't come through the roof like it once did because of new fabrics. So if you haven't been camping in a while, try it—you'll probably stay with it. You'll find campgrounds near most lakes, streams or flat spots on mountains. The following will give you an idea of what is convenient in northeast Georgia. Check the other Georgia sections for other commercial camping areas.

Camping areas in Chattahoochee National Forest:

Andrews Cove—10 campsites with hiking and fishing; Take GA 75 north of Cleveland 14 miles.

Cooper Creek—17 campsites with hiking and fishing; Take GA 60 North from Dahlonega for 26 miles, turn right on F.S. 4 for 6 miles.

Deep Hole—8 campsites with hiking and fishing; Take GA 60 North from Dahlonega for 27 miles.

DeSoto Falls—24 campsites with hiking and fishing; Take US 19 North from Dahlonega for 18 miles.

Dockery Lake—11 campsites with fishing and hiking; Take GA 60 North from Dahlonega for 12 miles, turn east on F.S. 654 for 1 mile.

Dockery Lake offers 11 primitive campsites for trout fishermen.

Frank Gross—11 campsites with fishing; Take GA 60 North from
    Dahlonega for 27 miles, turn south on F.S. 69 for 5 miles.

Lake Chatuge—30 campsites with boating, fishing, and hiking; Take US 76
    northwest from Hiawassee for 2 miles, turn south on GA 288 for 1 mile.

Lake Winfield Scott—36 campsites with fishing, hiking, and electric powered
    boats; Take US 19/129 south from Blairsville 10 miles, turn west on
    GA 180 for 7 miles.

Medicine Bow—Rt. 8, Box 1780, Dahlonega, GA 30533; 864-5928. This is
    an outdoor school for all ages that offers camps for canoeing, archery,
    flute making, art with natural dyes, Indian sign language, hide tanning,
    and Native American ceremonies.

Mulky—10 campsites with fishing and hiking; Take GA 60 north from
    Dahlonega for 26 miles, turn right on F.S. 4 for 5 miles.

Rabun Beach—80 campsites with hiking, boating, fishing, swimming, and
    dump station; From Clayton go south on US 123/441 for 7 miles,
    turn west on unnumbered county road for .1 mile, turn south on GA
    15 for 2 miles, turn right on County Rd. 10 for 5 miles.

Tallulah River—17 campsites with fishing and hiking; From Clayton go 8
    miles west on US 76, turn north on unnumbered county road for 4
    miles, turn northwest on F.S. Rd. 70 for 1 mile.

Tate Branch—19 campsites with fishing and hiking; From Clayton go 8
    miles west on US 76, turn north on unnumbered county road for 4
    miles, turn northwest on F.S. Rd. 70 for 4 miles.

Waters Creek—8 campsites with hiking and fishing; Take US 19 north from
    Dahlonega for 12 miles, turn northwest on F.S. 34 for 1 mile.

Willis Knob—8 campsites with fishing, hiking, and horse trails; From Clayton
    go east on Warwoman Rd. for 11.6 miles, turn right on Goldmine Rd.
    (gravel), look for signs to Woodall Ridge Day-Use Parking area on left.

Contact US Forest Service, 508 Oak ST. NW , Gainesville, GA 30501;
    404-536-0541. Ask for *Recreation Opportunity Guide* and camping guides.

Scenic waterfalls and primitive campgrounds are found throughout the
Chattahoochee National Forest.

CANOEING/RAFTING

Canoeing flat water is available on the lakes along the Tallulah River and
others (see the fishing section), but what many outdoor enthusiasts want is
whitewater, and the Chattooga is the ultimate ride.

Rafting looks fun and easy. One of those is true. Easy, it ain't! You get a
workout paddling and there is some risk. At the very least, you'll get soak-
ing wet, so dress appropriately.

Here are some outfitters who will take you on streams of varying difficulty. Be sure to ask what skill level is required of you.

Appalachian Outfitters—POB 793, Dahlonega, 30533; 864-7117; Chestatee and Etowah Rivers.

Canoe-the-Hooch Outpost—Rt. 4, Box 4548, Cleveland, 30528; 865-5751; Upper Chattahoochee has Class II, Lower Chattahoochee has Class III rapids (this run is for intermediate and advanced canoeists); Rafts available.

Chattooga Rent-A-Raft—Rabun County; 782-1221.

Medicine Bow—Rt. 8, Box 1780, Dahlonega, 30533; 864-5928; Canoeing instructions.

Nantahala Outdoor Center—POB 1390, Clayton, 30525; 800-232-7238.

Southeastern Expeditions—On US 76 southeast of Clayton; 800-868-7238 or 782-4331; Chattooga and Ocoee Rivers; Overnight and other packages available.

Wildewood Outpost—POB 999, Helen, 30545; 800-553-2715 or 865-4451; Rent rafts or canoes for self-guided or guided trips down the Chattahoochee River; Reservations suggested.

We recommend *North Georgia Canoeing*, by Bob Sehlinger and Don Otey, for detailed information.

⅔ FISHING

The Tallulah River flows south out of North Carolina with six dams forming Lakes Burton, Seed, Rabun, Tallulah, Tugaloo, and Yonah.

Lake Burton, the largest in the chain, is serviced by LaPrade's Marina, Rt. 1, Clarkesville, GA 30523; 947-3003. You can hire a guide to fish for your favorite game fish. The lake has trout, walleye, bream, catfish, smallmouth bass, and largemouth bass. The state record yellow perch (2 pounds, 8 ounces) was caught here in 1980. Boat rentals and bait available.

Lake Seed is a small, shallow reservoir suitable for small boats and canoes. Bass, bream, catfish, perch, and trout abound.

Lake Rabun is suitable for motor boats. Flipping and pitching techniques come in handy for fishing the numerous boat houses and docks. Clay points and coves will also hold fish. In 1982, the state record northern pike was landed, weighing in at 18 pounds, 2 ounces. Bass, bream, catfish, perch, and trout are the primary species here.

Tallulah Lake is a riverine, only 63 acres, of bass, bream, catfish, perch, and trout.

Tugaloo Lake has limited access. Bank and wade fishing are options. A lake with as little fishing pressure as this one receives should make the action come faster. You'll find bass, bream, catfish, perch, and trout here. A 3-pound, 3-ounce, redeye bass caught from the Tugaloo River made the state record book in 1990.

Yonah Lake has bass, bream, catfish, perch, and trout within its 325 acres.

Chattooga River in Rabun County (GA/SC border) offers anglers rainbows and browns, but only after a hike through rugged country.

Dockery Lake, north of Dahlonega on GA 60, is stocked with trout during trout season. Fishing is restricted to the trout season.

Trout anglers will find *Trout Fishing in North Georgia* and *Trout Streams of Southern Appalachia* by Jimmy Jacobs indispensable.

Lake Chatuge at Hiawasse (GA/NC border) provided the state record smallmouth bass (7 pounds, 2 ounces) and hybrid bass (25 pounds, 8 ounces). There is excellent spotted bass and largemouth bass angling also.

For fishing regulations contact Wildlife Resources Division, 2150, Dawsonville, 30501.

North Georgia rivers and lakes provide rewarding opportunities for anglers.

❧ GOLF

Brasstown Valley Crowne Plaza Resort—Young Harris; 800-201-3205; Eighteen
    holes.
Heritage Golf Course—Ramsey Rd., Clarkesville; 754-8313; Nine holes.
Coach Cave Memorial Golf Course—Demorest; 778-3000; Nine holes.
Innsbruck Resort—Helen; 800-642-2700; Eighteen holes.
Mountain Harbour and Resort—389-8111.
Rabun County Gold Club—Old US 441, Clayton; 782-5500; Nine holes.
Ski Valley Resort—Rabun County; 746-5303; Eighteen holes and driving range.

❧ HORSEBACK

Georgia's horse trails take you through many scenic areas and offer easy to difficult rides. Check with the stables in the area you plan to be for details. Compare this section with the Virginia Outdoor Recreation horseback section.

Chattahoochee Horse Hotel—Rt. 2, Box 2357, Clayton, 30535; 782-4385.

Dillard House Stables—Old Dillard Rd., Dillard, 30537; 746-2038 or 746-5348; Reservations requested; Beginners to advanced riders; Open year-round.

Gold City Corral—Rt. 3, Box 510, Dahlonega, 30533; 864-6456; Lodging, dining, and much more.

Horse Outfitters—Dahlonega; 30533; 864-9333; Guided trail rides, overnight camping, and summer horse camps.

Rabun County Recreation Park—Clayton, 30525; 782-4600.

Smokey Mountain Stables—POB 149, Wiley, 30581; 782-5836; Between Clayton and Tallulah Falls; Wooded trail, moonlight and group rides.

Sunburst Stables—Rt. 1, Sautee, 30571; 878-2095.

Trackrock Riding Academy—4890 Trackrock Campground Rd., Blairsville, 30512; 746-5252.

Twin Oak Stables—Rt. 1, Box 1264, Blairsville, 30512; 745-5349.

Willis Knob Horse Trail—Take Warwoman Dell east from Clayton; 782-3320; Two moderate-to-difficult trails—Rocky Gap is 12.5 miles long and Willis Knob is 15 miles long; Contact Forest Service for maps and brochures of other horse trails (508 Oak St. NW, Gainesville, GA 30501; 404-536-0541); Contact Tallulah Ranger District, POB 438, Tallulah, GA 30525; 782-3320 for reservations at Willis Knob Horse Camp.

HIKING/NATURE TRAILS

Hiking is serious walking, nature trails are for looking. The Appalachian, Bartram, Benton MacKaye, and Duncan Trails are serious. Let's start with those.

The AT's southern terminus is Springer Mountain. It's a 79-mile hike to Bly Gap on the North Carolina border and is all within the Chattahoochee National Forest. The trail marker is a 2x6-inch vertical, white paint blaze. Access to the AT can be made at Amicalola Falls State Park (access trail takes you up Springer Mountain), Logan Turnpike Trail, Blood Mountain Spur Trail, Woody Gap, Neels Gap, Dick's Creek Gap, Hogen Gap, and Unicoi Gap. Contact Georgia AT Club, POB 654, Atlanta, GA 30301 for more information.

William Bartram hiked through north Georgia in the mid-1770s. His entire trek was 900 miles. You have 37 miles in Georgia running from the west fork of the Chattooga River, across Rabun Bald to the GA/NC border. If you choose to begin at the river, take Warwoman Road east from

Thirty-seven miles of the Bartram Trail traverse some of the most beautiful country in north Georgia.

Clayton 8 miles to intersection with GA 28. To begin at Rabun Bald, take US 441 north from Clayton, turn east on GA 246, go about 7 miles (the road changes to NC 106 at the border), turn south at Scaly, NC, onto Hale Rd. for 2.1 miles, take F.S. Rd. 7 for 1.1 miles. The hike to the bald is 2 miles with an elevation of 1,150 feet. Contact Tallulah Ranger District, POB 438, Clayton, GA 30525; 782-3320 for maps and more information.

Hiking areas in Chattahoochee National Forest include:

Anna Ruby Falls—In Unicoi State Park, two trails; A .4-mile trail parallels Smith Creek and ends at the base of the falls. The Lion's Eye Trail near the Visitor's Center is an interpretive walk for persons with visual and physical disabilities. Take GA 75 northeast from Helen for 1 mile to Robertson, turn northeast on GA 356 for 1.5 miles, go left on the entrance road at sign, and follow signs for 3.5 miles to parking area.

Brasstown Bald—Highest mountain in Georgia (4,784 feet) is open from late May through October; Take US 19/129 south from Blairsville for 8 miles, turn east on GA 180 for 9 miles, then north on GA 180 spur for 3 miles.

Dukes Creek—Dukes Creek Falls drops 300 feet into a scenic gorge; A one-mile walk.

Lake Burton Wildlife Management Area—There are 10 trails ranging from 1.1 to 6.6 miles in the Lake Burton WMA. Moccasin Creek Trail is 6.1 miles long. The others are Falls Mountain, Bramlet Ridge, Pigpen Ridge, North Fork, Deep Gap, Parks Gap, Deer Gap, Addis Gap to Dick's Gap (AT), and Addis Gap to Tray Gap (AT). Contact Game & Fish Division, 205 Butler St. SE, Room 1362, Atlanta, 30334; 404-656-3524. Ask for Lake Burton WMA trails map.

Warwoman Dell—Dense forest on Warwoman Creek; 3 miles east of Clayton on Warwoman Rd.

Look in the Camping section above for sites with hiking. Also contact US Forest Service (address in this section) and ask for *Recreation Opportunity Guide* and hiking guides.

〜 SKIING

There is only one ski slope in Georgia. Ski Valley Resort, Rabun County: 746-5302 or 746-5015; Five slopes open from mid-November to late February, weather permitting.

Wade Stephens of Kennesaw, Georgia, "Casper" to his Appalachian Trail buddies, heads to Baltimore to visit his lady love via the scenic route.

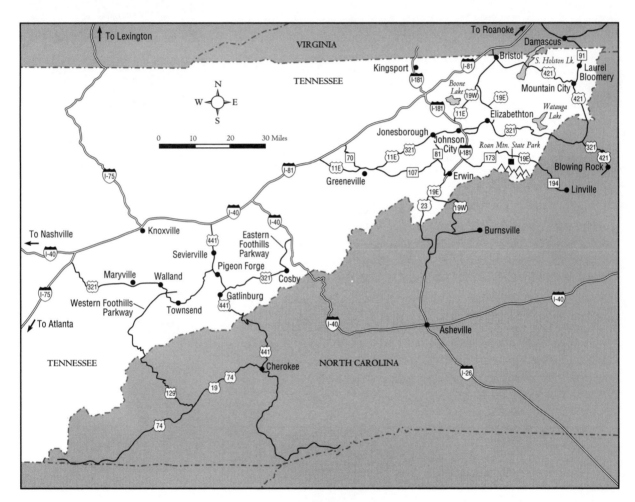

TENNESSEE

Tennessee

Tennessee

East Tennessee is best known for the outdoor recreation offered by thousands of acres of national forest and the Great Smoky Mountains National Park (GSMNP). Unlike the mountain communities in north Georgia and western North Carolina, east Tennessee was not easily accessed by coastal residents seeking respite from summer heat, but the Tennessee Valley became a major route for settlers heading West.

The great Tennessee Valley runs southwest to northeast in an undulating series of ridges from Knoxville to Bristol along I-40 and I-81. This pattern is intersected by the rising mass of mountain ranges to the southeast near the North Carolina border.

Knoxville served as the first capital when Tennessee became the sixteenth state admitted to the Union in 1796. Frontiersmen like Daniel Boone and Davy Crockett lived here when settlers traveled through the Great Valley of east Tennessee along the former Great Warrior's Path of the Cherokee on their way to the western frontier. Many historic sites associated with this era of our nation's history are open to the public. On an athletic note, fall football weekends at the University of Tennessee are enthusiastically attended.

Visitors from the west should begin near Knoxville along I-40 and travel south into the GSMNP via Townsend to Cades Cove or through Sevierville, Pigeon Forge, and Gatlinburg to Newfound Gap in the heart of the park.

As you travel east in the Great Valley, you encounter the home of President Andrew Johnson and Davy Crockett's birthplace in Greeneville; and Jonesboro, the oldest town in Tennessee, with its historic bed and breakfast inns, specialty and antiques shops, National Storytelling Festival, and appetizing eateries. Race fans come from all over the United States to the NASCAR track at Bristol. The tour continues to the Tri-Cities of Kingsport, Bristol, and Johnson City and heads deeper into the mountains and highland lakes of the Cherokee National Forest near Erwin, Elizabethton, and Mountain City before returning to I-81 near Abingdon, Virginia, or heading for the Blue Ridge Mountains in nearby North Carolina.

Our favorite trip in this area is the Wilderness Week in Pigeon Forge each January for a week of intensive information about the GSMNP and environs ranging from discussions about black bear habitats to wintertime hikes of two to seven hours' duration. The mountains are wonderful in winter and scheduled guided hikes are an excellent introduction. Stay in Gatlinburg, voted number-one mountain getaway, or Pigeon Forge, voted number-one shopping spot in the South, by readers of Southern Living magazine and you've got a vacation spot with something for everyone.

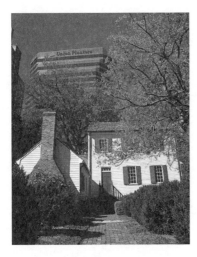

The 1792 Blount Mansion was the home of the first governor of the Southwest Territory.

✢ DIRECTIONS

I-40, I-75, and I-81 intersect in East Tennessee.

8 *Knoxville:*
Big Orange Country

Knoxville is the largest city in East Tennessee and the third largest in Tennessee, with a population of nearly 170,000. It hosted 10 million visitors during the 1982 World's Fair, and sometimes it seems there are nearly that many University of Tennessee, or "Big Orange," fans here during football season. With more than 26,000 students, the university is a vital part of the city.

Knoxville is strategically located where the confluence of the Holston and French Broad Rivers forms the Tennessee. Although the Great Smoky Mountains are visible to the south, Knoxville is actually situated in the Great Valley of East Tennessee.

According to Edward Luther in *Our Restless Earth*, this valley is about 45 miles wide with its eastern edge buried by the Great Smoky Mountains. The valley floor consists of a series of undulating ridges that resulted from the compression from the Southeast (see Great Smoky Mountains section).

Knoxville began as a settlement in 1785 on a land grant given to Revolutionary War veteran James White of North Carolina. The White homestead was a frequent stopping point for settlers traveling west, so he added structures to house his guests and a stockade for protection. At this time the settlement was known as White's Fort. Today the James White Fort is open for tours of the original "great house," kitchen, guest house, smoke house, a small museum, and blacksmith shop. The fort is a combination of modern reconstruction and original structures.

The settlement that would become Knoxville began at White's Fort in 1785.

The original "great house" at White's Fort is open to visitors.

The Sunsphere has dominated the Knoxville skyline since the 1982 World's Fair.

In the fall of 1791, the city was officially founded and named for Gen. Henry Knox, President Washington's Secretary of War.

The governor of the "Territory South of the River Ohio," William Blount, moved his capital from Rocky Mount between present-day Bristol and Johnson City to White's Fort in 1792. When Tennessee was admitted to the Union in 1796, Knoxville became the first capital of the state and remained so until 1812.

Knoxville is bisected by I-40 into northern and southern portions and into eastern and western divisions by Gay Street and Henley Street, which becomes the Chapman Highway (US 441) over the Tennessee River to the south on the way to Sevierville. There are many places to visit, including the site of the World's Fair, Cumberland Avenue/University of Tennessee/Neyland Drive, Market Square, and Old City District.

The World's Fair Park includes the Sunsphere, a landmark from the 1982 World's Fair, which dominates the Knoxville skyline. Found on Henley Street, it houses a Visitor's Center that is filled with smiling faces and information about the area. The walkway behind the center leads to the Candy Factory, a collection of shops and galleries, and the Knoxville Museum of Art. You can visit the gallery, great hall, museum shop, and cafe daily except Monday. We were lucky enough to catch a traveling Rodin exhibit of more than 70 works the summer we visited Knoxville.

Several galleries, studios, and antiques and specialty shops are in the 1920s Victorian houses along 11th and Laurel across from the Candy Factory and the Museum of Art. The same area is the home of Fort Kid, a popular playground built by volunteers along the steep hillside at the western edge of the park.

The Middleton House Bed and Breakfast Inn has 15 guest rooms with private baths, king or two double beds, phones, and cable TV. A full breakfast and an evening reception are included in the tariff. It is centrally located on Hill Avenue off Henley.

The Knoxville Museum of Art is just behind the Sunsphere.

Begin your tour with the Cumberland Avenue/UT/Neyland Drive area. Cumberland Avenue becomes Kingston Pike as it runs alongside the campus of the University of Tennessee. Sites along Kingston Pike include the Armstrong-Lockett House (Crescent Bend) and Confederate Memorial Hall, headquarters to Confederate Gen. James Longstreet during the Civil War siege of Knoxville. Crescent Bend was built in 1834 near the bend of the same name in the Tennessee River. It is now home to the Toms Collection of eighteenth-century English and American furniture and an English silver collection dating from 1670 to 1820.

Confederate Memorial Hall was known as Bleak House by its builder, Robert Houston Armstrong. Some historians refer to it as the Armstrong House. During the siege of Knoxville by Confederate forces from November 17 to December 2, 1863, Confederate Gen. James Longstreet and his staff occupied the Armstrong House. Longstreet placed sharpshooters in the tower windows and cannons on the lawn. In this same tower, three portraits etched on the wall are labeled "Men who were shot up here." Windows were broken and bullet marks riddled the walls but the house survived. A series of landscaped terraces lead to Fort Loudoun Lake/ Tennessee River.

Sam and Andy's across from UT has juicy burgers. The Orangery on Kingston Pike offers selections like escargot in puff pastry and lobster flamed in cognac and a good wine list. Naples

The University of Tennessee is a vital part of Knoxville's cultural resources.

Italian Restaurant is also a popular Kingston Pike destination because of its romantic atmosphere and delicious food.

The Maple Grove Inn is a lovely Georgian-style home west of downtown off Kingston Pike. It is situated on 15 acres, complete with pool and tennis court. The attractive bedrooms and suites offer amenities like fireplaces, whirlpool tubs, saunas, and private porches.

The McClung Museum on UT campus may be accessed by Kingston Pike or Neyland Drive. The museum has collections in archaeology, art, geology, and local history and is open daily. Neyland Drive skirts the university to the south of the football stadium parallel to the Tennessee River.

For scenic dining, try Calhoun's Restaurant, which overlooks the river, or the Tennessee Riverboat Company, which offers a variety of cruises aboard the Star of Knoxville ranging from sightseeing to buffet dinner cruises. Board at Neyland Drive, east of Gay Street.

The Blount Mansion was the home of William Blount, the first governor of the Southwest Territory. Legend has it that Blount's wife refused to move to the Tennessee wilderness until he built her a proper home along the banks of the Tennessee River.

Development in downtown Knoxville along the Tennessee River includes parks, restaurants, and riverboat cruises.

Construction of the mansion began around 1792. The mansion was the finest of its kind and possibly the first frame house built west of the Appalachian Mountains. Visitors will find an extensive collection of late eighteenth-century furnishings.

Lest you envision the Market Square Mall as the usual suburban indoor mall, let us explain that it's actually an outdoor mall with inviting shops and restaurants like Tomato Head for great pizza, creative salads, and tasty sandwiches, and the Soup Kitchen for excellent soups and fresh breads. If you haven't worked up an appetite, check out Krutch Park on your way to the East Tennessee Historical Center at the corner of Market Street and Clinch Avenue. This area is the focus of many of the activities associated with the Dogwood Arts Festival held each spring. It's a lovely spot during any season.

Turn east on Main Street and north on South Central to visit the Old City District. This area of Knoxville was the bustling warehouse district of the nineteenth century and now houses restaurants, nightclubs, microbreweries, antiques malls, art galleries, and specialty shops.

While touring the Old City, we enjoyed the blue-plate specials at Patrick Sullivan's. The 1888 building once stood at the center of trade in an area known as the Bowery. Commerce ruled during the daytime, but its night life was full of dance-hall girls providing entertainment for the farmers, salesmen, and buyers who flocked to the thriving commercial center. Today this revitalized area offers a pleasant afternoon's diversion.

Knoxville has a long tradition of excellent dining at Regas, which in addition to numerous other awards, was voted one of the top restaurants in the South by *Southern Living* magazine readers in 1996. That came as no surprise to the Regas family, as they've been serving award-winning food since 1919.

We were pleased with the quietly elegant setting, non-smoking areas, and aged beef. Early evening dinner specials from 5:00 to 6:30 P.M. Monday through Saturday include shrimp, sole, scrod, prime rib, chicken, and pasta. All entrees include salad, starch or fresh vegetable, and an assortment of freshly

Krutch Park is a cool, green oasis at the southern end of Market Square Mall.

The East Tennessee Historical Center is one of the most popular museums in Knoxville.

The revitalized Old City District is one of Knoxville's most popular attractions.

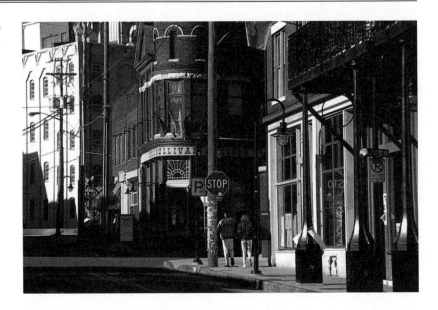

baked breads. Try to save room for their special cheesecake with fresh raspberries.

Other restaurants of note in the area include the JFG Coffee House on Jackson and Harold's Deli on Gay Street for hefty kosher sandwiches. The restored 1909 Bijou Theatre now hosts the East Tennessee Hall of Fame for the Performing Arts, and serves as the arena for all sorts of entertainment. The Tennessee Theatre, also on Gay Street, started showing films in 1928. Today this movie palace shows movies to the accompaniment of old-fashioned popcorn and a "mighty Wurlitzer" organ.

Of interest to young and old alike is the Ijams Nature Center, an 80-acre bird sanctuary on the Tennessee River. The Discovery Trail takes you on a tour of the woodlands, pond, and gardens. One trail is paved and handicapped accessible, and there's a boardwalk around the pond. The museum is in a 1910 house that has been refitted with nature displays.

Sharp's Ridge Memorial Park is located at the highest elevation in Knoxville. It is a favorite bird-watching site during spring and fall migrations. More than 133 species have been sighted in the park. Several picnic tables and shelters are available, and the park is reached via Fairfax Street off Broadway.

The Tennessee Theatre is a fine example of the movie palaces of the 1920s.

If you're really serious about antiques, you'll want to make sure you're here on the third weekend of the month for the Knoxville Flea Market, one of the area's biggest and best.

The wide range of activities available in Knoxville makes it a good weekend getaway or stopover on your way to the Great Smoky Mountains National Park.

The following are Knoxville, TN and area code 423 except where noted. Unless otherwise indicated, admission is charged.

ACCOMMODATIONS

Days Inn—Several locations, including I-40/75 west on Lovell Rd., 966-5801; or east at I-40 Exit 394 (5423 Asheville Hwy.); 637-3511, 800-DAYSINN.

Hampton Inn—Two locations, I-40 at exit 395, 525-3511; and west at 9128 Executive Park Dr.; 693-1101, 800-HAMPTON.

Holiday Inn World's Fair—525 Henley St., 37902; 522-2800, 465-4329, 800-854-8315.

Hyatt Regency—500 Hill Ave., SE, 37915; 637-1234, 800-233-1234.

Maple Grove Inn—8800 Westland Dr.; 690-9565, 800-645-0713.

Middleton House Bed and Breakfast Inn—800 W. Hill Ave. at the Henley St. Bridge; 800-583-8100, 524-8100.

The Middleton House Bed and Breakfast Inn is located near the Sunsphere Park.

ATTRACTIONS

Armstrong-Lockett House—2728 Kingston Pike, 37919; 637-3163; Tues. to Sat., 10:00 A.M. to 4:00 P.M., Sun. 1:00 to 4:00 P.M.

Bijou Theatre—803 Gay St., 37902; 522-0832.

Beck Cultural Exchange Center—1927 Dandridge Ave., 37915; 524-8461; African-American history; Free; Tues. to Sat., 10:00 A.M. to 6:00 P.M.

Blount Mansion—200 W. Hill Ave., 37901; 525-2375. Closed Mon.

Confederate Memorial Hall—3148 Kingston Pike, 37919; 522-2371; Tues. to Fri., 1:00 to 4:00 P.M.

Ijams Nature Center—2915 Island Home Ave., 37920; 577-4717; Free.

James White Fort—205 East Hill Ave., 37915; 525-6514; Mon. to Sat., 9:30 A.M. to 4:30 P.M., Mar. 1 to Dec. 15.

Knoxville Museum of Art—1050 World's Fair Park Dr., 37916; 525-6101; Closed Mon.

McClung Museum of the University of Tennessee—1327 Circle Park Dr., 37996-
    3200; 974-2144. Free; Daily except holidays.
John Sevier Home—1220 W. Governor John Sevier Hwy., 37920; 573-5508;
    Daily except Mon. and major holidays.
Sharp's Ridge Memorial Park—521-2090; Free.
Tennessee Riverboat Company—300 Neyland Dr., 37902; 800-509-BOAT,
    423-525-STAR.
Tennessee Theatre—604 Gay St., 37902; 525-1840.

✍ DINING

Bennett's Pit Barbeque—8413 Kingston Pike, World's Fair Park; 690-4030.
Butcher Shop—801 W. Jackson Ave.; 637-0204.
Calhouns—400 Neyland Dr.; 673-3355.
Copper Cellar—1807 Cumberland Ave., 673-3411; or 7316 Kingston Pike,
    673-3422.
Harold's Deli—131 Gay St.; Breakfast, lunch, daily except Sun.
Manhattan's—101 S. Central; 522-4463; Lunch, dinner.
Naples Italian Restaurant—5500 Kingston Pike; 584-5033; Lunch, dinner daily.
Old College Inn—2204 Cumberland Ave.; 523-4597; Lunch, dinner daily.
The Orangery—5412 Kingston Pike; 588-2964.
Patrick Sullivan's—100 N. Central in the Old City; 522-4511.
Regas Restaurant—318 N. Gay; 637-9805.
Sam and Andy's Deli—1800 Cumberland Ave., 524-9527.
Soup Kitchen—1 Market Square Mall, 546-4212; and 9246 Park West Blvd.,
    539-6500; Lunch, early dinner, daily (lunch only on Sun.).
Spaghetti Warehouse—200 East Jackson in the Old City; 637-9706.
Tomato Head—12 Market Square Mall; 637-4067; Lunch daily, dinner Fri,
    to Sat.
Ye Old Steak House—6838 Chapman Hwy.; 577-9328.

✍ EVENTS

April—*Dogwood Arts Festival begins the second Friday and lasts 17 days; Held at Market
    Square Mall; 687-4561.*
Esau's Antiques and Collectibles—*Third weekend every month; 588-1233; I-40
    East, Rutledge Pike Exit.*
Tennessee Valley Fair—*Chilhowee Park, begins Friday after Labor Day and lasts nine
    days; 637-5840.*

SHOPPING

Candy Factory—408 Tenth St., 37916; 546-5707.
Farmers' Market—I-640 Exit 8 near East Town Mall; 524-FARM.
Jackson Antique Marketplace—E. Jackson St. in the Old City; 521-6704.
Key Antiques—South Central in the Old City; 546-2739.
The Museum Shops of Knoxville—At the Candy Factory.
Old City District—Jackson and Central.

FOR MORE INFORMATION

Knoxville Convention and Visitor's Bureau—POB 15012, 37901; 423-523-7263, 800-727-8045.

DIRECTIONS

Knoxville is within one-half day's drive of much of the eastern United States via I-75, I-40, or I-81.
I-40 East—Take Exit 388 to the Visitor's Center on Henley Street.
I-40 West—Exit 388A to James White Parkway, exit on Cumberland Avenue, and continue to Henley Street.

9 *Sevierville:*
Home of Dolly Parton—and More

Hometown gal Dolly Parton is a favorite of country music fans around the world.

The community now known as Sevierville was settled about 1783 as "Forks of Little Pigeon." In 1785, the Treaty of Dumplin Creek between John Sevier, acting as the governor of the State of Franklin (see Greeneville, Tri-Cities, and Elizabethton sections) and chiefs of the Cherokee Nation opened territory south of the French Broad River to settlement. The town was renamed to honor John Sevier.

There are several stops along US 66/441 off I-40, including the antiques malls and the Sevierville Welcome Center on the approach to Sevierville, the home of country music star Dolly Parton.

We diligently avoid this route in mid-October. During peak foliage season, traffic literally creeps through the Great Smoky Mountains National Park (GSMNP) and is backed up coming and going at Exit 407 off I-40, the Sevierville exit.

Despite the proliferation of fast-food restaurants, shopping malls, and motels along US 441 as it skirts the western edge of town, Sevierville manages to retain its small-town flavor, providing tourists with a breath of fresh air.

The beautiful domed courthouse built in 1896 dominates downtown Sevierville, and many of the shops and restaurants we like to visit are in its shadow along Court Avenue and Bruce Street. The large four-faced clock in the dome is the original Seth Thomas and it chimes the time on the half-hour in measured tones that, like the town, have remained consistent for the past 80 years.

For the last several years, we have stopped in Sevierville for lunch at Josev's at 130 West Bruce because the food is always good, the decor is soothing, and the service is excellent. Turn east off US 441 South onto Bruce Street. If you're traveling south on US 441 this will be a left turn after the first traffic light in Sevierville.

Josev's second-story restaurant on the right across from the courthouse is open for soups, salads, and sandwiches for lunch with specials that vary from salads and blackened salmon with penne pasta and basil sauce to chicken parmigiana. Alcoholic beverages are not served, but you may bring your own wine to savor with dinner entrees like crab, stuffed rainbow trout, blackened chicken pasta, or aged filet mignon.

Several antiques malls invite collectors to stop and browse.

Just down Bruce Street you'll spot 131 Antiques on the right as you head east. They had a large selection of collectibles and antiques the last time we stopped.

Annie's Antique Mall is also on Bruce Street, as is the Sevier County Heritage Museum. You can rejoin US 441 by turning right onto Parkway and continuing to Forks of the River Parkway, which unites with US 441.

Golfers may want to make their way back to the US 411/441 intersection (which is also Main Street in Sevierville and becomes the Chapman Highway to Knoxville), turn west on US 411, and continue to the intersection with the Old Knoxville Highway. Take a right to try your luck on the links at Eagle's Landing Golf Club, an 18-hole par 72 facility.

Spelunkers may be more interested in turning to the east on US 411 to visit the Forbidden Caverns. These caverns have a long history of human inhabitants, ranging from Eastern Woodland Indians to moonshiners during the 1920s. The caverns were opened to the public in 1967. In addition to unusual formations, the caverns contain the largest wall of cave onyx found in the world.

If you continue down US 441 toward GSMNP, you'll soon feel the pace quicken as you begin to notice the beginnings of the tourist mecca Pigeon Forge has become.

How about a cold beer and barbecue? You'll definitely need to stop by Damon's on US 441 between Pigeon Forge and Sevierville because it's one of only two restaurants in the area that serves beer.

Another of our traditional stopping points along US 441, especially during the fall apple season, is the Apple Barn and Restaurant.

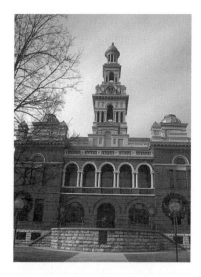

The 1896 domed courthouse dominates Sevierville's downtown.

The peaceful small-town streets invite visitors for a leisurely stroll around the courthouse square.

It has greatly changed since its humble beginnings in 1910 as a dairy barn along the banks of the Little Pigeon River between Sevierville and Pigeon Forge. Today, neatly tended apple trees cling to the hillside and produce some of the finest apples we've ever tasted. We usually take home several bags of Mutsu to family and friends.

The Apple Barn also serves up tasty concoctions featuring apples—fried pies, fritters, dumplings, and muffins—along with fresh and frozen apple cider, apple butter, and apple syrup. Breakfast, lunch, and dinner are served in a casual setting at the restaurant next door and there's even a winery. But it's those wonderful apples that keep us coming back.

Sevierville and Pigeon Forge are so close in proximity that several of the motels and bed and breakfasts in the Pigeon Forge area have Sevierville mailing addresses, even though they are best accessed on the way to Pigeon Forge. These include Oak Tree Lodge, Comfort Inn Apple Valley, Blue Mountain Mist B&B, Von Bryan Inn, and the Wonderland Hotel (see Pigeon Forge section).

Oak Tree Lodge offers 160 acres and a riding stable with horses for hire in addition to TVs, balconies, fireplaces, waterbeds, and handicapped accessible facilities. Comfort Inn Apple Valley has

The Apple Barn offers bushels and bushels of fresh apples in season and apple concoctions ranging from cider to fritters.

69 rooms with TVs, private balconies, heated pool, hot tubs, fireplaces, and refrigerators.

For a quiet evening meal in an elegant setting, look for Five
Oaks, a two-story white house just across from the turnoff to
Applewood and adjacent to the first of many outlet malls to come
as you approach Pigeon Forge. The restaurant is housed in a structure that was once the center of a horse breeding farm. The Five
Oaks Factory Stores next door are just the beginning of the outlet
mall shopping experience in the Sevierville-Pigeon Forge area.

The following are Sevierville, TN 37862 and area code 423 except where noted.

✑ ACCOMMODATIONS

Blue Mountain Mist B&B—1811 Pullen Rd.; 428-2335, 800-497-2335.
Comfort Inn Apple Valley—1850 Parkway, Pigeon Forge, TN 37868;
     428-1069, 800-233-3443.
Comfort Inn Mountain View Suites—860 Winfield Dunn Pkwy.; 428-5519,
     800-228-5150 in TN; 800-441-0311 out of state.
Hampton Inn—681 Winfield Dunn Pkwy.; 429-2005, 800-HAMPTON.
Oak Tree Lodge—1620 Parkway; 428-7500, 800-637-7002.
Von Bryan Inn—2402 Hatcher Mtn. Rd.; 453-9832, 800-633-1459.
The Wonderland Hotel—3889 Wonderland Way; 428-0779,
     800-428-0779.

✑ ATTRACTIONS

Eagle's Landing Golf Club—1556 Old Knoxville Hwy.; 429-4223.
Forbidden Caverns—455 Blowing Cave Rd.; 453-5972; Apr. 1 to Dec. 1.
Lee Greenwood Theater—870 Winfield Dunn Pkwy.; 453-0777,
     800-769-1125.
River Islands Golf Course—9610 Kodak Rd.; 933-0100.
Walden's Creek Horseback Riding—Walden's Creek Rd., 429-0411.

✑ CAMPING

East Knoxville Dumplin Valley KOA—933-6393.

✑ DINING

Damon's—US 441 Pkwy.; 428-6200

Five Oaks Inn Restaurant—1625 US 441 Pkwy.; 453-5994.

Josev's Restaurant—130 W. Bruce St.; 428-0737; Tues. to Sat., 11:00 A.M. to 3:00 P.M., Brunch Sun. 11:00 A.M. to 2:00 P.M., dinner 4:00 to 9:30 P.M. Tues. to Sat.

SHOPPING

Annie's Antique Mall—137 Bruce St.

Antique Mall—131 Bruce St.; 428-0001, Mon. to Sat. 10:00 A.M. to 6 P.M,. Sun., 12:00 to 6:00 P.M.

Apple Barn Cider Mill and General Store—230 Apple Valley Road; 453-9319; Daily.

Five Oaks Factory Stores—US 441 Pkwy.; Daily.

Ogle and Webb General Store—128 Court Ave.; 453-5751.

Ole Smoky Antique Mall—TN 66; 429-0100; Daily.

Rocky Top Trail Shop—912 Wears Valley Rd.; 429-2242.

Smoky Mtn. Knife Works—TN 66; 453-5871; Daily.

FOR MORE INFORMATION

Sevierville Chamber of Commerce—866 Winfield Dunn Pkwy.; POB 4280; 453-6411, 800-255-6411.

You'll find concrete figures from angels to mermaids at Teague's on TN 66 north of Sevierville.

DIRECTIONS

From I-75—Take I-40 east to Exit 407 about 10 miles east of Knoxville.

From I-81—Take I-40 west to Exit 407.

From I-85—Take US 441 north for the scenic route through the north Georgia mountains and the southern entrance to the GSMNP via Cherokee, North Carolina.

10 *Pigeon Forge:*
From Mountains to Malls

In the eighteenth century, huge flocks of now extinct passenger pigeons migrating through the valley inspired the naming of the river that flows through Pigeon Forge. The community along the Pigeon was originally called Fanshiers after one of the early settlers in the area, Richard Fanshiers. It was later renamed "Pigeon" from the river and "Forge" from the iron works on the river. Only the Old Mill hints of the community that once thrived here along the tumbling Pigeon River in the shadow of the high peaks of the Smoky Mountains.

Southern Living magazine's Readers' Choice Awards in 1996 proclaimed Pigeon Forge to be the number-one shopping spot in the South. It is also a gateway to diverse outdoor recreational opportu-

The Old Mill along the Pigeon River is one of the rare National Register of Historic Sites properties in Pigeon Forge.

nities within the 800 square miles of the Great Smoky Mountains National Park (GSMNP) and thousands of acres in nearby National forests.

Pigeon Forge is action packed, fast paced, and especially appropriate for the young and the young at heart who enjoy shopping malls, arcades, bumper cars, helicopter rides, miniature golf, or bungee jumping. Youthful entertainment abounds at the Carousel Fun Center, Ogle's Water Park, and Parkway Speedway. And there are many other such offerings along US 441, also known as "the Parkway."

Although Pigeon Forge is home to only 3,248 yearround residents, there are accommodations for 35,000, so unless you're planning a trip during peak foliage season, you shouldn't have any problems finding food and lodging to suit almost any budget, from tent camping to bed and breakfasts with outstanding views and menus.

The Department of Tourism, local businesses, and area individuals host Wilderness Week each January, one of the finest opportunities you'll ever find to learn more about the flora, fauna, history, and topography of the Smokies.

During the winter season, we recommend the Heartlander Country Resort, "home" of Wilderness Week. The rooms are comfortable and it has both indoor and outdoor pools, but no restaurant as of this writing. Along the US 441 strip you'll also find the Capri Motel, which has a large pool and reasonable rates, and the River Place Inn, River Lodge and Willow Brook Lodge, all offering in-room Jacuzzi, fireplace suites, and heated pool.

Campers will appreciate the 150 shady sites (tent and full hook-ups) on the Little Pigeon River offered by Creekstone Outdoor Resort. It also offers a pool, tennis and basketball courts, cable TV, river tubing, and fishing.

Day Dreams Country Inn Bed and Breakfast is within walking distance of the bustle of Pigeon Forge, and is situated on three surprisingly peaceful acres. Owners Bob and Joyce Guerrea invite you to enjoy the appealing sound of the rushing water of Mill Creek as it passes in front of the two-story western cedar and hemlock log home. They stayed here after reading about it in *Country Magazine*, fell in love with it, and have owned it since 1994.

The Day Dreams Country Inn Bed and Breakfast is a peaceful retreat in the heart of Pigeon Forge.

Six large antiques-filled bedrooms with private baths and Jacuzzis or clawfoot tubs, along with country breakfasts of bacon, eggs, link sausage, waffles, or turnovers are designed to please.

We especially liked the Rose Room, with its handsome antique walnut bed and clawfoot tub. If you raise the windows you can drift off to sleep to the sounds of the creek below.

One bedroom has been constructed with handicapped access. Accommodations for children are available by special arrangement. Sorry, no pets. Televisions are available on request. It's best to book well in advance, especially during fall (the same goes for all area bed and breakfasts).

Hilton's Bluff Bed and Breakfast invites visitors to enjoy amenities including king-sized beds, Jacuzzis, in-room television, private balconies, rocking chairs along the long western exposure porch, and a southern gourmet breakfast in this hilltop hideaway. Hosts Norma and Jack Hilton have been greeting visitors since 1990. There are no rooms with formal handicapped access at this time. Limited accommodations for children are by special arrangement. Sorry, no pets.

Although it has a Sevierville mailing address, Blue Mountain Mist Bed and Breakfast is reached by turning east at red light No. 7

The Blue Mountain Mist Bed and Breakfast has 12 rooms in the main house and separate couples-only cottages.

in Pigeon Forge. This newly reconstructed Victorian was designed to function as a bed and breakfast by Sarah and Norman Ball. Twelve rooms with private baths in the main house and couples-only cottages have kept loyal patrons coming back since 1987. Our favorite room in the big house is Sugarlands, with its double bed and double-wide whirlpool tub, complete with mountain view. The cottages have large Jacuzzis, gas fireplaces, televisions with VCR, charcoal grills, and picnic tables.

Blue Mountain Mist is located on 60 acres that were part of Sarah's family's farm. Her dad, Estel Owenby, grew up inside the park in the Greenbriar community. To this day, he continues to perform traditional sacred harp singing in the area. If you are interested in music and you've never heard the plaintive mountain melodies of shaped note, or sacred harp singing, try to make it to a performance for a unique evening's entertainment. Meetings of shaped note singers are held locally each month if you'd like to learn more.

Norman's grandad, Houston Ball, was a lumberman at Elkmont, as were so many of the local men. His grandmother was the cook at the old Wonderland Hotel, which was also at Elkmont. In addition to their renowned mountain hospitality, Sarah and Norman represent a wealth of information about the history of the area as well.

Outlet shopping malls along US 441 in Pigeon Forge, with more than 200 shops open yearround, offer everything from cookware and Danskin tights to stereo equipment and hiking boots. Shoppers disappear for hours in those malls during pre-Christmas shopping blitzes only to emerge exhausted, delighted, and laden with packages.

Dollywood opens in late April and Dolly Parton greets visitors on opening weekend. Ms. Parton was a graduate of Sevier County High School in nearby Sevierville, and she lends her support to the theme park named in her honor in various ways. The 29 rides and attractions and 40 live shows daily, pack in the crowds at the height of the season, so a springtime weekend visit may be the right choice for you if you want to avoid summer lines waiting to ride the Thunder Express, Log Flume, and the Smoky Mountain Rampage. You'll also find an assortment of rides suitable for small children, and mountain craft demonstrations ranging from blacksmiths and potters to weavers and glassblowers.

Due to popular demand, Dollywood also hosts a series of weekend Winter Crafts Workshops during January, February, and March. Crafts being taught vary, but range from blacksmithing to dulcimer making. Dollywood also supports a raptor rehabilitation program. Raptors are such birds of prey as eagles, hawks, and owls. Some of Dollywood's raptors are unable to be released due to the injuries they have sustained (sometimes, we are sorry to say, at the hands of man).

This owl is one of the residents at the raptor rehabilitation program supported by Dollywood.

The Old Mill was built in 1830 by William Love after he dammed the river to create the mill pond. It has been operating continuously for more than 150 years and still grinds grain into flour and meal every day except Sunday. The mill, of hand-hewn construction, is on the National Register of Historic Sites. Guides are available from April to November.

More than 70 area restaurants serve visitors to Pigeon Forge. Have you ever eaten chicken, herb-basted potato, BBQ ribs, corn on the cob, and dessert while watching a "South vs. North" rodeo? If you have, you've been at the Dixie Stampede Dinner Attraction.

For a quick lunch or dinner, J&S Cafeteria features tasty home-style cooking for tastebuds yearning for fresh vegetables, roast beef, meatloaf, fried chicken, breads, and pies.

Speaking of tastebuds, if lamb, pasta, and veal appeal to yours, be sure to visit our favorite Pigeon Forge restaurant, Chef Jacques' tiny Tastebuds, just down Wears Valley Road between Pigeon Forge and Townsend. We can highly recommend the lamb, scallops, sun-dried tomato pasta, or red snapper diablo. The food is wonderful and the presentations appealing from start to finish. Don't be fooled by its unassuming appearance. Reservations are recommended regardless of the season, for Chef Jacques has an appreciative local following. Bring along your own bottle of wine and relax, for Jacques prepares everything as it is ordered—well worth the wait!

Most Pigeon Forge restaurants do not serve alcohol, but many allow you to bring your own wine.

The Von Bryan Inn has an outstanding mountaintop view.

Seven miles down Wears Valley Road toward Townsend, visitors will see the sign on the right at Hatcher Mountain Road for Von Bryan Inn. Innkeepers JoAnn and D.J. Vaughn have been here since 1988. In addition to a 360-degree mountaintop view, which is outstanding during any season, the Von Bryan offers six rooms with private baths and a chalet for groups of four to six. Children over 10 are welcome in the house and the chalet is appropriate for youthful travelers of any age. There's a big swimming pool and a 12-person hot tub with a 70-mile view up the Tennessee Valley to the Cumberland Mountain Range.

Their son, David, led us to the especially attractive wood-and-glass enclosed Garden Room, which has great views and a reading loft. The White Oak suite has a sitting area and a corner Jacuzzi.

Continuing down Wears Valley Road, signs to your left direct you to the "new" Wonderland Hotel, built by the most recent proprietors of the "old" Wonderland Hotel at Elkmont when their lease with GSMNP expired. Although newly built, it attempts to retain vestiges of rusticity with front porch rockers and swings, ceiling fans, and wood paneling. Cabin rentals are also offered. Their country restaurant serves three meals daily.

The Wonderland also operates a stable with horses for hire or facilities for your personal use if you're traveling with your equine friends. The hotel is 9 miles from Pigeon Forge and 6 miles from Townsend off US 321 (Wears Valley Road). It can also be reached via scenic Highway 73, also known as Little River Road.

Continue on US 321 to Townsend or cut through to Little River Road, and turn east toward Gatlinburg and Sugarlands Visitor's Center before returning to Pigeon Forge. Little River Road is lovely, but you'll need to check for road closures during winter.

Pigeon Forge itself is easily accessed by major highways. It's a good headquarters for families exploring the Smokies because there's something here for everyone.

The following are Pigeon Forge, TN 37863 and area code 423 except where noted.

❧ ACCOMMODATIONS

Blue Mountain Mist B&B—1811 Pullen Rd., Sevierville, TN 37862; 428-2335, 800-497-2335.

Capri Motel—4061 Parkway; 453-7147, 800-528-4555.

Day Dreams Country Inn B&B—2720 Colonial Dr.; 428-0370,
    800-377-1469.

Days Inn—1841 Parkway; 428-3353, 800-DAYSINN.

Hampton Inn—2760 N. Parkway; 428-5500, 800-HAMPTON.

Heartlander Country Resort—2385 Parkway; 453-4106, 800-843-6686.

Hidden Mtn. Log Cabins and Chalets—Rt. 5, Box 338A, Sevierville, 37862;
    453-9850.

Hilton's Bluff Inn B&B—2654 Valley Heights Dr.; 428-9765,
    800-441-4188.

Holiday Inn Resort—3230 Parkway; 428-2700, 800-HOLIDAY.

River Lodge—1351 Parkway; 453-0783, 800-233-7581.

River Place Inn,—3223 Parkway; 453-0801, 800-428-5590.

Von Bryan Inn—2402 Hatcher Mtn. Rd., Sevierville, 37862; 453-9832,
    800-633-1459.

Willowbrook Lodge—3035 Parkway; 453-5334, 800-765-1380.

Wonderland Hotel—3889 Wonderland Way, Sevierville, 37862; 428-0779,
    800-428-0779.

ATTRACTIONS

Carousel Fun Center—2879 Parkway; 428-1988.

Dixie Stampede Dinner Attraction—3849 Parkway; 453-4400, 800-356-1676;
    Mid-March to Dec.

Dollywood—1020 Dollywood Lane; 428-9488, 800-DOLLYWOOD;
    Daily, Memorial Day to Labor Day.

Five Oaks Stables—1650 Parkway; 428-9764.

Ogle's Water Park—2530 Parkway; 453-8741; Daily, June to Aug.

The Old Mill—453-4628, Mon. to Sat. yearround, guided tours Apr. to Nov.

Parkway Speedway—3632 Parkway; 428-0555. March to Dec.

Smoky Mountain Jubilee—2115 N. Parkway; 453-0165; Mon. to Sat. May to
    Nov., weekends Jan. to Apr.

Smoky Mountain Tours—436-3471, 428-3014.

DINING

Bennett's Pit Barbeque—Parkway; 429-2200.

Damon's at Five Oaks—1640 Parkway; 428-6200; 11:00 A.M. to 3:00 P.M.,
    3:00 P.M. to closing.

Eddie's Heart and Soul Cafe—2251 Parkway; 453-0833.

J&S Cafeteria—2255 Parkway; 429-8070; Menu 429-3070.
Tastebuds Cafe—Wears Valley Rd. (US 321); 428-9781.

✌ SHOPPING

Belz Factory Outlet World—2655 Teaster Ln. (stop light #3); 453-3503;
    Daily.
Pigeon Forge Factory Outlet Mall—2850 Parkway; 428-2828; Daily.
Tanger Factory Outlet Center—175 Davis Rd,; 428-7001 or
    800-4-TANGER; Daily.

✌ SPECIAL EVENTS

Contact Bob Easton at 423-429-7350 for information regarding the following.
January—Wilderness Wildlife Week of Nature
February—Storytelling Festival
November through February—Winterfest

✌ CAMPING

Creekstone Outdoor Resort—304 Day Springs Rd.; 453-8181, 800-848-8181.
Pigeon Forge KOA—3514 Cedar Top Ln.; 423-453-7903, 800-KOA-7903
    (reservations only).

✌ FOR MORE INFORMATION

Pigeon Forge Department of Tourism—POB 1390-G; 800-251-9100.
Great Smoky Mountains National Park—107 Park Headquarters Rd.,
    Gatlinburg, 37738; 436-1200.

✌ DIRECTIONS

From Atlanta—I-75 to US 321 to Townsend and Pigeon Forge.
From I-40 about 10 miles east of Knoxville, TN—Exit 407 to Sevierville and
    Pigeon Forge.
From Blue Ridge Parkway—Exit at Cherokee and continue north on US 441
    to GSMNP, Gatlinburg, and Pigeon Forge.

11 *Gatlinburg*
Gateway to the Smokies

Known as White Oak Flats in the early 1800s, Gatlinburg was voted the number-one mountain getaway in *Southern Living* magazine's Readers Choice Awards for 1996. Like most of the communities bordering the Great Smoky Mountains National Park, it is a town of dichotomies. You can view it with eyes that see only the glitz, or you can look beyond the superficial "tourist traps" and find people and places very much in touch with the beauty and culture of the mountains.

This unofficial honeymoon capital of the South frequently suffers from weekend traffic congestion during the summer, but most

Gatlinburg, nestled among towering peaks, is the northern entrance to the Great Smoky Mountains National Park.

profoundly in October, so consider yourself warned. We love its quiet beauty in winter and are never disappointed with the lovely Appalachian spring season.

Gatlinburg rests at the northern edge of the GSMNP and the only central entrance, US 441. The city is ringed by mountains and streams.

Parking can be a challenge, but you'll find trolleys to drop you off at more than 100 locations. The route is color coded to make it easier to catch the right trolley. For example, the yellow route runs to the Great Smoky Arts and Crafts Community. One dollar buys you unlimited access to the trolleys as you travel along the loop visiting craftsmen and artists in their galleries. There are four other trolley routes, including the red route to Dollywood and Gatlinburg Golf Course and the green route to Ski Mountain Road. The trolleys provide environmentally and user friendly transportation between Gatlinburg and Pigeon Forge, allowing you to concentrate on Gatlinburg itself instead of the traffic.

Prepare yourself for mountain-to-mountain shopping. The tiny hamlet of Gatlinburg offers more than 400 specialty shops ranging from Irish linens and Belgian lace to stuffed black bears and tee shirts. The shops have enough stone and dark brown alpine trim to retain the appeal of a mountain hamlet amid the proliferation of shops carrying items you don't need but just can't do without, and probably won't find elsewhere.

You'll find an excellent selection of very reasonably priced crafts at the Arrowcraft Shop, one of Gatlinburg's oldest and finest shops. It's located on the US 441 Parkway near the heart of downtown Gatlinburg, next to Arrowmont School. We found notecards, earrings, shawls, baskets, woodcrafts, and pottery that made perfect presents for lucky recipients back home.

You can arrange to stay in the dormitory at the Arrowmont School of Crafts while you take an intensive week-long series of classes in woodturning (they're well known throughout the country for the quality of work represented by their program), pottery, basketry, jewelry making, etc.

The Smoky Mountain Arts and Crafts Community is also a

The Arrowcraft Shop has one of the area's finest selections of crafts.

must. It's located 3 miles east of downtown Gatlinburg off US 321
North. More than 80 local artists and craftsmen open their galleries to the public daily along an 8-mile auto loop. For a special
outing, consider the Wild Plum Tearoom for lunch. It's on the
Smoky Mountains Arts and Community tour and sits amid a cool
plum grove in a rustic setting. Reservations are accepted.

The Wild Plum Tearoom is on the
Smoky Mountain Arts and Crafts
Community loop tour.

　　　Hikers will want to visit Tom Brosch's shop, the Happy Hiker,
near the Sugarlands entrance to the GSMNP in Burning Bush
Plaza. He has a good supply of warm, lightweight hiking clothes,
topo maps, and trail guides. He volunteers his capable leadership
for day hikes, as do most of his staff, during Wilderness Week in
Pigeon Forge.

　　　Past hiking trips they've led include Cucumber Gap near Elkmont, Hen Wallow Falls near Cosby; and the Old Settlers Trail.
Even the most inexperienced did quite well with him in the lead,
but it does help if you've been walking regularly. Most importantly,
Tom loves to hike. He'll share his extensive knowledge of the area
as you decide where to go for the day or the weekend.

　　　Gatlinburg's skiing at Ober Gatlinburg keeps downtown
bustling during winter, and the midtown tramway operates yearround for a view of the resort town below. In the winter, the tram
ride is free if you have an area ski lift ticket. There are eight ski
trails, an indoor ice skating rink, and several eateries.

　　　For those of you interested in an award-winning photographer's perspective of the Smokies, a visit to Ken Jenkins' shop,
Beneath the Smoke in Gatlinburg, is a worthwhile stop. The shop
offers his photography, slide shows, gifts, photography workshops,
and a large selection of books and calendars about the area.

　　　Old Smoky Outfitters is nearby at 511 Parkway and offers full
and half-day guided trips for fly-fishing and bass fishing. They'll also
arrange seasonal small- and big-game hunts, southern Appalachian
history tours, and nature hikes. Trout fishing peaks in the Smokies
in the springtime. Trout anglers have more than a dozen streams to
fish. Little River is probably the most popular destination.

　　　We found some interesting accommodations in Gatlinburg. The
Gatlinburg Inn is one of the older structures downtown and has

The 1930s Buckhorn Inn is a gracious mountain retreat.

Each room at Hippensteel's Inn opens onto a veranda with a lovely view of the mountains.

hosted many honeymooners and vacationers since its construction in 1937. It no longer operates a dining room, but maintains 67 rooms and 7 suites and is still owned and operated by the family of the original builder, Rel Maples. It is open from April to November.

Contrast the Gatlinburg Inn, in the heart of downtown Gatlinburg, with the Buckhorn Inn, which was built in 1938 and features six guest rooms and four cottages on 40 secluded acres past the craftman's loop east of Gatlinburg on Tudor Mountain Road. Tastefully decorated with Oriental rugs and antiques, the Buckhorn retains the flavor of a 1930s mountain resort. Full breakfast is served. A gourmet dinner is available in the dining room by special arrangement.

The spectacular view from the porch of the inn is of Mount Le Conte. A foot trail invites visitors to explore the acreage. The inn is an all-season property, as are most of the bed and breakfasts in the area around Gatlinburg.

To reach Hippensteel's Inn, a modern construction with a decidedly nouveau Victorian style, turn east at traffic light No. 3 onto US 321. After 3 miles, turn onto Glades Road beside Battles Supermarket and follow the signs. Vern Hippensteel is a well-known local artist whose prints decorate the walls of the modern inn, which boasts a spectacular mountain view from each of the generously proportioned rooms.

Without a doubt, the most unusual lodging to be found in the vicinity is Le Conte Lodge, 6,593 feet atop Le Conte Mountain overlooking Gatlinburg. The retreat was started in 1926 by Jack Huff and the Huff family ran the lodge until 1960. In order to stay at Le Conte, you'll need reservations. And to get there, you'll need to undertake a 5- to 8-mile hike, depending on which route you choose. Alum Cave Trail is the shortest and steepest, and Boulevard the longest. Rainbow Falls, Trillium Gap, and Bullhead have varying mileages and topographies but will take the average hiker about five hours.

We journeyed up Alum Cave Bluff Trail to Le Conte Lodge one May afternoon several years ago and were rewarded with an extraordinary sunset view of the Smokies at Cliff Tops. As for our dinner of canned meats and vegetables, well, we figured it was a matter of priorities. At least we didn't have to carry the canned beef up the mountain ourselves. Llamas carry supplies to the lodge via Trillium Gap Trail, usually on Mondays, Wednesdays, and Fridays.

There's no electricity in the cabins, so light and heat are provided by kerosene. In addition, there's no opportunity for bathing until you traipse back down the mountain (the Boulevard is much better downhill than up) to Gatlinburg. The trip to the outhouse can get a little chilly, so be sure to pack a flannel shirt and some toasty socks, even if you don't think you'll need them.

You'll want to get up early to experience Myrtle Point, although few of the fifty guests the lodge can accomodate make it to the spectacular sunrises. Le Conte is open from late March to mid-November.

Less adventuresome but very comfortable choices include the Oak Square Motel, the Travelodge, and Rocky Waters Motor Inn.

Many Gatlinburg restaurants serve alcoholic beverages, and several open for evening hours only are worth special mention, including the Peddler at 820 River Road, where meat lovers can choose their steaks from "the peddler." They also offer chicken and seafood, and, for no extra charge, a nice view of the river. Reservations are not accepted, so you may find yourself waiting at the bar on a busy Friday night.

The Park Grill at 1110 Parkway is a newer establishment and features steaks, chicken, prime rib, mountain trout, pasta, and salads in an attractive setting of native stone and wood. Don't be surprised to hear the sounds of birds singing—the sweet sounds are piped in. Try to be seated near the waterfall at the back of the restaurant.

Maxwell's offers a traditional setting for fresh seafood, prime rib, lamb, and a good wine list at 1103 Parkway. Don't miss the Caesar salad.

Bennett's Pit Barbeque is open for breakfast, lunch, and dinner, and is reliable for casual dining. For "home cooking," head for Ogle's Buffet for breakfast, lunch, and dinner. They've been serving Gatlinburg for more than 50 years.

Although Ruby Tuesday originated in Knoxville, it's now owned by Morrisons. It remains a good choice for casual dining at 449

Le Conte Lodge offers rustic accommodations in a wilderness setting high atop Mount Le Conte. *(Photo by Douglas H. Brown)*

Parkway. The Pancake Pantry on the Parkway serves breakfast all day for late risers and lunch until 3:00 or 4:00 P.M., depending on the season.

If you happen to be in town during breakfast hours, treat yourself to brunch at the Burning Bush Restaurant at the southern edge of town just before you enter the GSMNP near the Sugarlands Visitor's Center. You may prefer to sip a sunrise daiquiri or a bloody mary rather than coffee for an eye opener as you sample generous portions of bacon, sausage, fried pork chops, country fried chicken breasts, country ham with red-eye gravy, or Smoky Mountain Rainbow Trout along with eggs, stewed apples, grits, sliced tomato, home fried potatoes, hot biscuits, and sausage gravy. Ask if seating is available in the atrium, which overlooks the GSMNP. You can also choose a nonalcoholic fruit beverage while you twirl a lazy Susan loaded with muffins and fresh fruit. They offer an excellent lunch and dinner menu as well.

If you're ready to walk off breakfast or brunch, look for the beginnings of the 2-mile Gatlinburg Trail just beyond the Burning Bush Restaurant parking lot. This trail roughly parallels US 441 to the Sugarlands Center, which is your best source of information about the GSMNP. (For more information, see GSMNP section.)

For a spectacular view of mountain life and spring wildflowers, check out the Roaring Fork Motor Nature Trail just off Airport Road in downtown Gatlinburg. The winding 5.5-mile Roaring Fork Motor Nature Trail travels through a pleasant hardwood forest setting, across tumbling streams, and past the remnants of family farms. A self-guided booklet is available at the start of the trail. Although the trail is one taken by car, you will have the opportunity to hike a little if you'd like to visit the pioneer homesteads of Alfred Reagan and Ephriam Bales up close.

Smoky Mountain Tours has pick-ups in both Pigeon Forge and Gatlinburg, and offers a variety of tours ranging from 2 to 7½ hours.

Be sure to see for yourself what makes Gatlinburg a favorite mountain getaway for generations of visitors before you head through the GSMNP on your way to Cherokee via US 441.

The following are Gatlinburg, TN 37738 and area code 423 except where noted.

✂ ACCOMMODATIONS

Best Western Crossroads Motor Lodge—440 Parkway; 436-5661, 800-225-2295.
Buckhorn Inn—2140 Tudor Mountain Rd.; 436-4668.
The Colonel's Lady—1120 Tanrac Trail; 436-5432; Four suites and four
   rooms, private baths, some with spas, fireplaces, and cable TV.
Gatlinburg Inn—755 Parkway; 436-5133.
Gazebo Inn—417 Airport Rd.; 436-2222.
Hippensteel's Mountain View Inn—POB 707; 436-5761, 800-527-8110.
Holiday Inn—520 Airport Rd.; 436-9201, 436-4878, 800-HOLIDAY.
Le Conte Lodge—250 Apple Valley Rd., Sevierville, TN 37862; 429-5704.
Mountain Laurel Chalets—440 Ski Mountain Rd.; 436-5277, 800-626-3431.
Oak Square at Gatlinburg—River Rd; 436-7582, 800-423-5182.
Ramada Inn—756 Parkway; 436-5191; 800-933-8678.
River Terrace Resort—240 River Rd.; 436-5161, 800-251-2040.
Rocky Waters Motor Inn—333 Parkway; 436-7861, 800-824-1111.
7th Heaven Log Inn—3944 Castle Rd.; 430-5000, 800-248-2923; Over-
   looks the 7th green, all rooms with private baths.

✂ ATTRACTIONS

Arrowmont School of Crafts—556 Parkway; 436-5860.
Gatlinburg Municipal Golf Course—453-3912; Eighteen holes; Yearround.
Gatlinburg Sky Lift—765 Parkway; 436-4307.
Great Smoky Arts and Craft Community—POB 807; Hwy. 321 N; 671-3600.
Great Smoky Mountain Tours—POB 278, 436-3471, 428-3014,
   800-962-0488.
Ober Gatlinburg—1001 Parkway; 436-5423.
Old Smoky Outfitters—511 Parkway; 430-1936.
Roaring Fork Motor Nature Trail—Turn onto Airport Road at traffic light No.
   8 on the Parkway in downtown Gatlinburg.
Smoky Mountain Angler—376 East Parkway; 436-8746.

✂ DINING

Bennett's Pit Barbeque—714 River Rd.; 436-2400.
The Burning Bush—Parkway at GSMNP; 436-4168. Breakfast, lunch, dinner.
Maxwell's Beef and Seafood—1103 Parkway; 436-3738; Dinner daily.

Ogle's Buffet Restaurant—Parkway; 436-4157; Breakfast, lunch, dinner.
The Pancake Pantry—Parkway; 436-4724.
The Park Grill—1110 Parkway; 436-2300; Dinner daily.
The Peddler—820 River Rd.; 436-5794.
Ruby Tuesday—449 Parkway; 436-9251; Daily.

SHOPPING

Arrowcraft—576 Parkway; 436-4604; Daily.
Beneath the Smoke—Parkway, 436-3460.
The Happy Hiker—Burning Bush Plaza; 436-6000, 800-HIKER01.

SPECIAL EVENTS

April—*Spring Arts Fest*
April—*Annual Easter Craft Show; Easter weekend*
April—*Wildflower Pilgrimage*
November—*Annual Christmas Craft Show; Thanksgiving weekend*
December—*Annual Twelve Days of Christmas Craft Show*

CAMPING

Smokemont Campground—GSMNP; 800-365-2267, 436-1293.

FOR MORE INFORMATION

Gatlinburg Chamber of Commerce—423-430-4148, 800-568-4748.
Gatlinburg Welcome Center—US 441 South; 436-0519; Daily.
Great Smoky Mountains National Park—107 Park Headquarters Rd.;
    436-1200.
GSMNP Sugarlands Visitor's Center—436-1293.

DIRECTIONS

From Atlanta—Via I-75 to US 321 to Townsend and Gatlinburg.
From I-40 about 10 miles east of Knoxville, TN—Exit 407 to Sevierville, Pigeon
    Forge, and Gatlinburg.
From Blue Ridge Parkway—Exit at Cherokee and continue north on US 441
    to GSMNP and Gatlinburg.

12 Walland, Townsend, Cades Cove:
Quiet Side of the Smokies

Cades Cove is billed as "the most popular site in the most visited national park in the United States." A premier fall foliage viewing area, Cades Cove is south of Townsend in the Great Smoky Mountain National Park (GSMNP).

Townsend was founded around 1902 to meet the transportation and housing needs of the lumber industry in the area. It was named for Col. W. B. Townsend, president of the Little River

The Shay engine at the Little River Railroad Museum sits on its own section of railroad track.

Lumber Company and the Little River Railroad. Years later, the Little River Lumber Company sold much of its land to become what is now part of the GSMNP. The Little River Railroad and Lumber Company Museum does an excellent job of telling the story of the railroad and lumber company operations with a timeline from early settlers to W. B. Townsend and the building of the railroad.

We visited with museum volunteer Don Headrick, who explained that the engine proudly sitting out front on its own section of track is old No. 2147, a Shay engine once used to haul men and logs down the steep mountain grades. There are several innovations on the old engine that will be a treat for railroad aficionados.

You won't find immense outlet shopping malls or go-cart tracks in this peaceful community located in the Tuckaleechee Valley. You will find quiet mountain roads and spectacular bed and breakfasts like the Inn at Blackberry Farm at Walland about 5½ miles north of the Townsend Visitor's Center on West Miller's Cove Road off Highway 321 South. Watch carefully for Miller's Cove Road because when we visited there was not a sign announcing the inn at Blackberry Farm at the turnoff. The 3½ mile drive along the nar-

The four-star Inn at Blackberry Farm sits amid 1,100 acres.

row two-laned country road does not hint at what lies ahead until
you see the gleaming white fences and the inn gracefully nestled
along the crest of a small ridge that overlooks a lake and provides a
sweeping mountain vista.

In the 1930s, as Florida and Dave Lasier explored the site that
was to be their mountain estate, Florida snagged her silk stockings
on a blackberry bush and the site was named Blackberry Farm. The
initial nine-bedroom house was completed in 1940 and was built
of native mountain stone, shingles, and slate.

Fifty years later, Kreis and Sandy Beall transformed the 1,100-
acre estate into an inn open to the public. The attention given to
details in all areas has earned the inn coveted membership in the
Relais and Chateaux Hotels Association, usually associated with
European castles and chateaux. Additionally, it has been named one
of the top 10 country house hotels in the United States and is a
Four Star resort.

All 29 rooms are tastefully decorated with lovely antiques,
feather mattresses, and chintz, which create the feel of an English
country inn. Particularly pleasing are Solomon's Seal, with its king-
size bed and great view in the guest house; Teaberry, which has a
sitting area and a fireplace; and the Cardinal Suite, which has three
bedrooms with private baths off a private living room area common only to these rooms (great for couples traveling together).
TVs and phones are available on request. Ramps are provided for
handicapped access in the Indian Paint room.

The package price includes three meals prepared daily by Executive Chef John Fleer, whose award-winning "foothills cuisine,"
described as a creative merger of haute cuisine and the best of traditional country cooking, is receiving national attention.

Guests are invited to explore the vast acreage surrounding the
inn by bicycle (Schwinn 10-speed mountain bikes are available for
guests), golf cart, or while walking a 3-mile paved nature trail.
GSMNP forms one border of Blackberry Farm and the Trunk
Branch Hiking Trail accesses the GSMNP trail system.

You'll also find a heated swimming pool, complete with mountain view, and four tennis courts. Wet a line in Walland Pond,

The design of the Richmont Inn was inspired by the traditional cantilevered barns of the area.

which is stocked with bass and bream; Singing Brook Trout Pond or Hesse Creek with your choice of spinning and fly rods. Lessons, if you want them, are available. Guests are provided with everything from snacks and picnic lunches to robes and binoculars. Generally, children under 10 are not suitable guests at Blackberry Farm.

The Richmont Inn outside Townsend is another beautiful bed and breakfast, this one of more recent construction. The cantilevered barns native to the area were the inspiration for its unique design. Inside you'll find floor-to-ceiling glass to enjoy the views from the great room and 10 large rooms with private baths and appealing amenities.

Innkeepers Susan and Jim Hind are corporate escapees who delight their guests with special touches like award-winning desserts served with freshly ground coffee by candlelight each evening. There are individual room controls for piped in music, wood-burning fireplaces or gas logs, whirlpool tubs, bathrobes, coffee makers, and hair dryers.

The rooms are named for early Appalachian settlers. Our favorite was the Chief Attakullakulla, which had skylights over a king-size bed as well as the double-size spa tub—talk about star-

Richmont Inn's dining room's floor-to-ceiling glass showcases the view.

gazing in style. There's also a private third-story balcony and a wood-burning fireplace. There is one handicapped accessible room on the first floor.

Susan is a graduate of the Culinary Institute of New York and prepares daily breakfast specials along with a breakfast bar offering cereal, juice, and fresh fruits. Rates include full breakfast and evening desserts for two. Golf privileges are extended to guests at the 18-hole Laurel Valley Country Club.

Although Cades Cove itself is crowded on crisp fall days, Townsend generally maintains an air of calm. This may be due in part to the relatively few motels here (as compared to Pigeon Forge and Gatlinburg). You'll really be disappointed if you arrive on a summer weekend without reservations only to find there are no rooms available, so we strongly suggest you call ahead.

Several establishments offer cabin rentals. Hideaway Cottages (just off US 321) allows well-behaved children and pets. One of their more secluded cabins, the Crow's Nest, makes a great honeymoon or anniversary hideout.

In addition to the campground at Cades Cove, Tremont Hills Campground on the Little River has RV and tent sites, pool, laundry, and bathhouses. Lazy Daze Campground is also on the Little River and has 75 sites, pool, and playground. Tuckaleechee Campground and Horse Camp offers RV hook-ups, horse campsites with a 28-stall covered horse shelter, and tent camping.

If you're a horse lover but don't actually own one, you have an excellent opportunity for some time in the saddle at Cades Cove Riding Stable or Davy Crockett Riding Stable off TN 73 near the GSMNP boundary.

There are definitely fewer restaurants on this side of the mountains. You'll see the Kinzel House as you enter Townsend from the north at the intersection of US 321 and Old Tuckaleechee Road.

They serve breakfast, lunch, and dinner. The country ham breakfast with homemade biscuits is a big favorite. Luncheon fare includes sandwiches, vegetable plates, and salads. The dinner menu features sandwiches, salads, steaks, chicken (charbroiled and fried), and specialty items like trout dijon topped with scallions, herbs,

The Kinzel House is a Townsend dining tradition.

and spices and baked in butter, and steak au poivreau, a 10-oz. New York strip, coated with coarsely ground pepper, sautéed with green onions in butter, deglazed with brandy and sherry, and served with chutney over a brown sauce. Reservations are recommended, especially for the busy Friday night all-you-can-eat seafood buffet. The Sunday buffet is almost as popular. The Kinzel House staff will proudly tell you they serve only "real" mashed potatoes, "homegrown" green beans, and desserts and breads made from scratch.

The Mill House Restaurant is 15 minutes north of Townsend in a historic house overlooking the Little River. Turn east off US 321 on Melrose Station Road near the Walland Post Office, cross the bridge, and make an immediate left. The Mill House is open only on Fridays and Saturdays and specializes in fine dining including selections like Delmonico steaks, chicken breasts sautéed in herbs and white wine, and catfish served in a white wine herb sauce.

The Donut Shoppe has more than 50 varieties of breakfast pastries including bagels, muffins, and fritters. Owner Melody Willard whipped us up a "country breakfast" including coffee, eggs, biscuits, and bacon that was greatly appreciated one cool January morning.

Several restaurants are located at the southern end of Townsend on the way to Cades Cove. The Timber's Restaurant is in a log building near the intersection of US 321 and Wears Valley Road. The menu ranges from Belgian waffles and country ham breakfasts to burgers, prime rib, and seafood for dinner.

There are some unusual shopping opportunities in the area. Wild Flowers by Native Gardens on US 321 is open April through June and offers about 100 varieties of plants. If you can keep the roots moist, you have a good chance of returning home with a legal reminder of the beautiful flowers you see blooming along trails in the GSMNP. Remember: It is illegal to harvest flowers along the trails. Some species have such a limited gene pool that to remove specimens could place the plant on the endangered list, so deal only with a licensed commercial grower or retailer like Native Gardens.

The Dogwood Mall sells traditional handcrafted dulcimers by Robert Mize, a craftsman whose techniques are described in detail in *Foxfire III,* one of the popular series of books produced in the late 1970s and early 1980s by the students in Rabun Gap, Georgia, to chronicle Appalachian arts and crafts (see Clayton-Rabun Gap, Georgia, section).

Other area craftsmen are represented at the Nawger Nob Craft Settlement on US 321. Furniture, baskets, woodcarving (tools and supplies also offered), pottery, dulcimers by Mike Clemmer of Wooden Strings, jellies, and jams are offered for sale. Our favorite items were lovely handpainted parchment lamp shades by Marcia Hardwick. Yoder's Deck and Lawn Furniture had an impressive inventory of pressure-treated pine Amish loveseats and chairs. The River View Antique Mall has an assortment of collectibles and antiques, everything from furniture to glass.

If you're visiting Townsend between March 15 and November 15, consider seeing Tuckaleechee Caverns, also off US 321. Located on Dry Valley Road, Tuckaleechee Caverns exist because the stream that left Cades Cove went underground when it entered the appropriately named Dry Valley and carved out the caverns. The underground creek surfaces eventually as Short Creek and flows past Terry's Trout Farm on its way to the Little River. Cherokee Indians probably discovered the cavern but the modern story begins with two young explorers living out their own version of a Mark Twain novel.

Bill Vanada and Harry Myers made this secret place their own private world as children, exploring almost a mile into the depths of the cavern with their homemade lights. As adults, they ventured to Alaska to work and save money for four years in order to open the caverns to the public. Tons of gravel, cement, and sand, and endless days of back breaking work later, they'd carried enough supplies into the cavern to build the walkways that visitors have followed through the cavern since 1953. Vanada eventually bought out his partner and his family continues to operate the cavern today with more than 50,000 annual visitors.

Townsend also has an in-town horsedrawn carriage service, the Hayburner Express, which offers a variety of rides, from 15 minutes to half-day cookouts.

A jogging/bicycle trail through
Townsend is visitor friendly.

If you prefer getting around town on your own steam, there's a jogging/bicycle trail through the center of Townsend.

Townsend's efforts to prevent the kind of explosive growth that occurred in Pigeon Forge have been successful so far, but the nearness of Cades Cove draws increasing numbers of tourists and spawns the businesses that serve them.

The following are Townsend, TN 37882 and area code 423 except where noted.

✎ ACCOMMODATIONS

Best Western Valley View Lodge—US 321, POB 148; 448-2238.
Days Inn—US 321; 800-DAYSINN.
Family Inn of America—7239 E. Lamar Alexander Pkwy.; 448-9100.
Hampton Inn—7824 E. Lamar Alexander Pkwy.; 448-9000,
    800-HAMPTON.
Hideaway Cottages—984-1700.
Highland Manor Motel—7766 E. Lamar Alexander Pkwy.; 448-2211.
The Inn at Blackberry Farm—1471 West Millers Cove Rd., Walland, 37886;
    984-9850.
Richmont Inn—220 Winterberry Ln.; 448-6751.
Talley Ho Inn—8314 TN 73; 448-2465, 800-448-2465

✎ ATTRACTIONS

Cades Cove Riding Stable—4035 E. Lamar Alexander Pkwy, Walland; 448-
    6286.
Davy Crockett Riding Stable—232 Stables Dr.; 448-6411; Daily.
Little River Railroad & Lumber Company Museum—US 321; 448-2211; Year-
    round.
The Hayburner Express—448-0325.
Tuckaleechee Caverns—825 Caverns Rd.; 448-2274; Mar. 15 to Nov 15.

✎ DINING

Kinzel House—US 321; 448-9075.
The Donut Shoppe—US 321; 448-0606; Open 6:00 A.M.
The Mill House—Rt. 1, Box 1597, Melrose Station Rd., Walland, TN
    37886; 982-5726; Weekends.
The Timbers Restaurant—Year round; 7:00 A.M. to 10:00 P.M.; 448-6838.

The Hayburner Express—448-0325.
Tuckaleechee Caverns—825 Caverns Rd.; 448-2274; Mar. 15 to Nov 15.

DINING

Kinzel House—US 321; 448-9075.
The Donut Shoppe—US 321; 448-0606; Open 6:00 A.M.
The Mill House—Rt. 1, Box 1597, Melrose Station Rd., Walland, TN
    37886; 982-5726; Weekends.
The Timbers Restaurant—Year round; 7:00 A.M. to 10:00 P.M.; 448-6838.

SHOPPING

Antiques and Uniques—US 321; 448-1033; Daily; 10:00 A.M. to 7:00 P.M.
Backcountry Outdoor Supply Center—448-6628.
Nawger Nob Craft Settlement—US 321; 448-2259.

SPECIAL EVENTS

September—*Old Timers Day*

CAMPING

Cades Cove Campground—GSMNP.
Lazy Daze Campground and Motel—8429 TN 73, POB 214; 448-6061.
Little River Village Campground—8533 TN 73; 448-2241.
Tremont Hills Campground—TN 73; 448-6363.
Tuckaleechee Campground and Horse Camp—448-9608.

FOR MORE INFORMATION

Townsend Visitors Center—Lamar Alexander Parkway; 448-6134.

DIRECTIONS

From the West—Exit I-40 about 15 miles west of Knoxville at Exit 364 onto
    US 321 to Maryville, Walland, and Townsend.
From the North and East—Exit I-40 in Knoxville at US 129 to join US 321 at
    Maryville.
From the South and West on I-75—Take Exit 18 onto US 321.

13 The Great Smoky Mountains:
Place of the Blue Smoke

Glacier action formed streams filled with huge boulders throughout the Smoky Mountains.

According to Karen Wade, the thirteenth superintendent of the 520,197-acre Great Smoky Mountains National Park (GSMNP), the Park is "open space used for the restoration of the spirit and nourishment for the soul." Eight-and-a-half million of us journey to Shaconage, "place of the blue smoke" as the Cherokee called these mountains, every year. The GSMNP draws higher numbers of annual visitors than any other park in the United States.

The Smoky Mountains are the oldest existing mountains in the world. There may have been older ones but, if they existed, they have been worn away.

About 250 million years ago, the African and North American tectonic plates met. When this mountain building collision ended, the two continents separated, forming the Atlantic Ocean. Some of the original African plate is now part of our southeastern coast.

According to Edward T. Luther in *Our Restless Earth, The Geologic Regions of Tennessee,* the area has an intensely active geologic history. The forces that generated this activity are believed to originate far eastward from the widening of the bottom of the distant Atlantic Ocean.

Since their formation, the Smoky Mountains have moved about 100 kilometers (61 miles). Much of the land in the Southern Highlands is crowded with tremendous thrust faults. Movement has occurred along them in a northwestward fashion that is measured in miles at various points. Imagine a giant shoving force from

the southeast folding layers of sedimentary rocks on top of crys-
talline bedrock like an accordion. You'll be glad to know that none
of these faults has been active for millions of years.

Except along fault lines, you won't find many fossils in the
rocks here because they're too old, but the range of biodiversity
present in the Park challenges the imagination. Abrahms Creek in
Cades Cove is the lowest point in the Park at 840 feet above sea
level. Clingman's Dome towers above the other peaks at 6,643 feet.
In between live more than 1,300 species of flowering plants, 2,000
species of mushrooms, 125 species of trees, 200 species of birds,
about 50 species of fish, and 60 species of mammals.

In fact, the GSMNP has been designated an International Bios-
phere Reserve, an honor bestowed by the United Nations in recognition of the international significance of the natural resources
found here. It is part of one of the largest unbroken wilderness
areas in the eastern United States. Glacier action at the edge of the
Smokies formed streams filled with huge boulders that you see as
you travel through the region.

US 441 passes through the towering
peaks of the Great Smoky Mountains
National Park at Newfound Gap.

The idea for the Park originated with Horace Kephart when he
visited the Smokies in 1904. During the 1920s, the desire to preserve the remaining virgin forest in the heavily logged region gained
momentum and the Great Smoky Mountains Conservation Association was born.

The GSMNP was established on June 15, 1935, with donations from private citizens, including public school children; financial backing from Tennessee and North Carolina; and a five-
million-dollar donation from John D. Rockefeller Jr. In additional
to its unique biodiversity, the Park is unique in that it is the only
one given to the government by the "people."

More than 1,008 improved campsites, 100 primitive sites, and
800 miles of hiking and horseback trails, including the famous
Appalachian Trail, affectionately known as the AT, crisscross the
Park. Other outdoor activities include fishing, biking, cross-country
skiing, campfire programs, annual festivals, pioneer life exhibits,
and ranger walks.

The trees at higher elevations are particularly sensitive to air-

Not only airborne pollutants but wooly aphids are attacking many of the Frasier firs.

born pollutants because they remain fairly constantly shrouded in a fine mist that includes suspended particulates, effectively bathing them in pollutants. It remains the mission of the National Park Service to protect these half-million acres placed in trust with the Federal government. For this reason, there are no entrance fees for the Park, although during the recent years of Congressional budget cutting, the GSMNP has felt the pinch of cutbacks in all areas.

Today there are several active citizens groups attempting to help meet the gaps. Friends of the Park has the primary goal of finding funding for continuation of projects like the 1995 restoration of the firetower atop Mt. Cammerer, which was built by the Civilian Conservation Corps (CCC) in the 1930s. The Great Smoky Mountain Natural History Association is a nonprofit publication arm of the Park whose revenues return directly to support the Park's interpretive programs (their publications are excellent). Other groups study air pollution, reintroduction of red wolves, black bear population and habitat, as well as help maintain trails.

One such group, the Appalachian Black Bear Rehabilitation and Release Center, is involved in planning and fundraising efforts to provide a facility for rehabilitation and release of orphaned and injured black bears. During years with a low mast crop production, bears move greater distances to forage and find themselves in areas outside the Park.

In addition to the problems that inevitably arise when bears and humans intermingle, obstacles like Interstate 40 take a tremendous toll on the mother/cub groups. Without the protection of their mothers these orphaned cubs become malnourished and weakened. Sometimes, in misguided attempts to render assistance and offer food to foraging bears, tourists may seal the bears' fate by creating what are called nuisance bears, so it's best to leave these concerns to the professionals.

As the formerly remote Appalachian region becomes more populated, the Park and the surrounding National Forests and communities of East Tennessee, western North Carolina, and northern Georgia come under increasing pressure to maintain the aesthetic qualities that have drawn visitors from across the United States and Europe to the area since the 1830s.

The timber industry entered the picture in the early 1900s. Many of the beautiful green slopes you presently see were virtually denuded by clear cutting.

Railroads eventually were needed to haul lumber and some vestiges of these old railroad beds remain. In fact, the Little River Road (Scenic TN 73) between Townsend and Sugarlands Visitor Center is built on the bed of the tracks of Little River Lumber Company's Little River Railroad. The last day of lumber cutting was in 1938.

The Sugarlands Visitor Center is just inside the park entrance at Gatlinburg.

Several stands of virgin forest remain deep within the Smokies, protected through the years by their inaccessibility. Most of the land you now see has been reclaimed by nature under the watchful eye of the GSMNP.

A good place to start your tour of the GSMNP is the Sugarlands Visitor Center just inside the Park entrance at Gatlinburg. As you might expect, it was named for the sugar maple trees in the vicinity. It's one of three visitors centers in the GSMNP and it's a good source of information about park activities including naturalist-led hikes, wildflower pilgrimages, and road closings. The bookstore has a wide variety of publications for sale. This is also the place to secure back-country camping permits. Pets are allowed in the Park on leashes, but are prohibited on trails or cross-country hikes.

As you leave the Sugarlands parking lot, turn right onto Little River Road and begin the scenic drive to Laurel Falls and the Cove

Mountain Fire Tower, one of only five firetowers left in the GSMNP. Most have been abandoned due to the availability of aerial surveillance.

The drive to Fighting Creek Gap offers a great view of LeConte. A trailhead at the top of Fighting Creek Gap leads 1.3 miles to Laurel Falls and has been paved due to its heavy use. Although it can be somewhat treacherous when ice-covered, this is usually a gentle trail. Steep cliffs line the trail at several points before Laurel Branch forms double cascades at the falls. Older children and adults may want to continue the unpaved portion of the trail 2.7 miles to Cove Mountain through a section of virgin hemlock and poplar.

Elkmont Campground is about 5 miles from Sugarlands. It has 220 sites and is open yearround, with greatly reduced numbers of sites available during the winter months. In season the rates are $11 per night with a seven-day stay limit. There are no camper hook-ups but you'll find water, picnic tables, and restrooms in shady sites, some of them along the river.

The Little River Trail follows an old railroad bed of the Little River Railroad Company. Wildflowers are abundant along this trail. About one mile from the trailhead, a pretty little cascade is formed by Huskey Branch, named for Sam Huskey, who owned the store in the middle of Elkmont.

Historian Bill Hooks helped us to imagine the activity that took place in this area when Elkmont was a thriving lumber community. The remnants of the Wonderland Hotel in the ghostly resort community at Elkmont hint at the lively dances held here on summer Saturday nights during the roaring twenties. Since the 1920s, several cabins in the area were leased to members of the Wonderland Club, but the Park Service declined to renew any leases after 1992. This decision generated controversy, not only from the previous leaseholders but also from visitors who feel it is a mistake for GSMNP to continue to abandon the Elkmont area.

Meigs Falls can be seen along Little River Road where Meigs Creek empties into Little River. A deep sinkhole on the side of the road, known as the Sinks, was caused by loggers using dynamite to break up a log jam around the turn of the century.

The old Wonderland Hotel saw its last visitor in 1992.

The "Y" at Little River is a popular swimming hole.

As the road goes under an overhanging rock known as Indian Head you may see the resemblance that earned the rock its name.

Just before you reach the turnoff to Cades Cove, you'll see the confluence of the Middle and West Prongs of the Little River with the East Prong, which is a popular swimming hole. The "Y," as it's called, has an assortment of rocks perfect for sunbathing. The Chestnut Top Trail opposite the river offers a good opportunity for spotting wildflowers.

The campground at Cades Cove has 161 campsites with 35 trailer spaces, water, and picnic tables but no showers or hookups for trailers.

Bicycle rentals are available at the Cades Cove Bike Shop. Horses may be rented by the hour at Cades Cove Riding Stable or you can arrange an evening hayride.

An 11-mile paved loop around the cove is a popular bicyclist destination, especially on Wednesday and Saturday mornings when it is closed to motorized traffic until 10:00 A.M. from June through Labor Day.

Pioneer cabins and farmsteads dot the cove, reminding us of the history of the former inhabitants. The eastern end of the cove was settled first because it was higher and drier than the western end.

By 1936 all of the homesteads in Cades Cove had become the property of the National Park Service.

Orchards and crops were planted on the flat land while cabins were usually placed on the less productive slopes. The census of the cove reached a peak in 1850 with more than 130 households in the valley, but by 1860 only about 40 families remained.

The Civil War was particularly difficult for the small community as it was part of a state that was decidedly Confederate, but local sympathies lay largely with the Union. Of the young men who went to war from the cove, about ten joined the Union forces while three allied themselves with the Confederates.

During the Depression, the most profound influence on the cove in more than 100 years came in the form of surveyors and land agents seeking the land for a national park. When the government took over the land for the park in the 1920s, some restrictions were placed on the inhabitants who wished to remain on their land. No electricity would be provided, but several families elected to live under these conditions rather than leave their homes.

By 1936, all of Cades Cove was transferred to the National Park Service. But the memory of the community is celebrated twice a year by those who were born and raised here. As Cades Cove people gather to celebrate their beloved homeplaces, mountain music echoes through some of the most beautiful scenery in the world.

If you've managed to find yourself in Cades Cove on a crisp fall day and you're spending most of your time inching along behind a string of automobiles, consider taking Rich Mountain Road out of the cove. Watch carefully for the turnoff on a gravel road to the north just after you pass the Methodist Church. The narrow road climbs over the ridge, offering a nice perspective of Cades Cove before dropping into Townsend.

Continuing on the Cades Cove loop, you'll come to the trail to Abrahms Falls, a popular hike. It's 2.5 miles from the trailhead between signposts #10 and #11 on the Cades Cove Loop Trail to the 25-foot waterfall. A small swimming pool is formed at the base of the falls, so be prepared to splash about a bit.

This is a moderate hike covering a 400-foot ascension along its length. Several creeks with foot logs for crossing can be found along the way, but it is suitable for school-age children and adults.

Wildlife viewing is a favorite pastime in Cades Cove.

The trail is lined with mountain laurel, rhododendron, and wildflowers. The Cades Cove Nature Trail is an easy half-mile walk highlighting the use of native plants by pioneers.

The Gregg-Cable house was home to Aunt Becky Cable until her death in 1940. It has been moved from its original site to the Cable Mill area at the western end of the cove. The mill, mill race, and dam are all in their original locations. The Cades Cove Visitors Center is open daily from mid-April through October and offers information on Park activities in the area.

If you are interested in environmental educational opportunities, contact the folks nearby at the Great Smoky Mountains Institute at Tremont located off the Cades Cove Road.

Tremont in Walker Valley was a former Job Corps camp, before being established as an environmental center. It is presently operated by the Great Smoky Mountains Natural History Association. Yearround programs are offered for individuals or school groups interested in learning more about the geology, wildlife, and flora of the Smoky Mountains. Lodging and family-style meals are provided on site for a reasonable cost. Recent programs included Cherokee Earth Skills, Photography Workshops, Naturalist Weekends, Elderhostel, and Wilderness Adventure Camps (ages 13 to 17). Fees vary.

Returning to our US 441 Smoky Mountain tour, a turn to the left out of the parking lot at Sugarlands Visitor Center leads you back onto US 441, also known as the Newfound Gap Road, south toward Cherokee, North Carolina.

The present route for this road was established in the 1920s. If you're on US 441 during weekends in July, August, or October, you may feel like you're in a parking lot. In winter, snow may temporarily close it. The reason millions of people travel this road anyway is that there are some really spectacular sights as you follow the rushing cascades of the Little Pigeon River and catch glimpses of landmarks along the way.

Besides natural features, you'll see engineering marvels like "the loop," a 360-degree switchback that loops back on itself as the road makes its way up a narrow, steep portion of the route. The

US 441 follows the rushing waters of
the Little Pigeon River through the
Great Smoky Mountains National Park.

presence of both natural and engineering wonders, added to the
sheer numbers of people traveling this road, explains the traffic
problems encountered during peak times.

Five miles from Sugarlands the road passes the Chimneys Picnic
area, where you'll find picnic tables and restrooms. Two miles from
this point you'll see the parking area for the trailhead for Chimney
Tops, 4,755 foot rocky twin spires that reminded the white settlers
of stone chimneys. As you might expect, the four-mile round trip
trail is strenuous and steep (climbs over 1,300 feet), but it rewards
intrepid hikers with an eagle's view of Sugarlands (northwest), Mt.
LeConte (northeast), and Mt. Mingus (southeast). There are hand-
and foot-holds to allow experienced pre-teens and older hikers to
scale the formidable formation waiting at the top of the trail.

The next must-see along US 441 is Clingman's Dome, the
highest peak in the GSMNP. The dome is reached by a 7-mile spur,
Clingman's Dome Road, off US 441 to the right, which takes you
nearly to the top of the 6,641-foot summit before leaving the last
0.5 mile to a paved trail that steeply rises 330 feet along its length.
This means that if you're willing to take your time, you can experience this incredible view even if you're wheelchair bound.

You'll notice many of the Frasier firs are being killed by wooly aphids. Although strategies for halting their destruction are being evaluated, this tree may soon become endangered at the current rate of devastation.

A tower at the summit of Clingman's Dome has a 360-degree view on clear days. Hikers on the Appalachian Trail reach their highest point along its length at Clingman's Dome so it's all down-hill, in a manner of speaking, from here.

While you're at Clingman's Dome, consider a visit to the most accessible of the balds in the park, Andrew's Bald. Grassy balds in the Smokies may have been caused by lightning fires or prolonged drought and kept cleared by cattle grazed upon them by early set-tlers like Andrew Thompson, for whom this bald was named. The Park Service has established special management practices to pre-serve Andrew's Bald, which has an outstanding rhododendron dis-play in June.

The summit at Clingman's Dome is 6,643 feet above sea level.

The 4.2-mile round-trip hike begins to the left of the paved Clingman's Dome Trail. It climbs a little over 600 feet, so even seven- and eight-year-olds can master it successfully and play in the thick grass of the bald. It's a great spot to savor a picnic lunch as you gaze at the peaks in the distance. Clingman's Dome Road is closed in winter and is used for cross-country skiing and sledding if US 441 remains open.

As you continue along US 441, you'll reach Newfound Gap on the Tennessee-North Carolina Line at 5,000 feet. According to *Mountain Roads and Quiet Places,* Indian Gap was thought to be the lowest point in the area, so when this point was found to be lower it was called the "new-found gap." Up to 69 inches of snow fall here each year.

As you approach Cherokee, you'll reach the Oconaluftee Visi-tor's Center and the Mountain Farm Museum. An easy 1.5-mile trail along the river to Cherokee originates near the entrance to the Mountain Farm Museum.

Nearby Smokemont Campground has 140 campsites. Cosby and Deep Creek Campgrounds have 175 and 108 sites, respec-tively. There are several smaller campgrounds including Abrahms

The easy hike to Hen Wallow Falls is one of our favorites.

The Old Settler's Trail passes along old settlements and through hardwood forests.

Creek, Balsam Mountain, Big Creek, and Look Rock. A long, winding dusty dirt road takes you to Cataloochee Valley, where you'll find historic structures, some beautiful countryside, and a 27-site campground.

When considering the seasons of the Smokies, know that wildflowers peak in the mountains in late April and early May but are found as early as March. Favorites like Spring Beauties, Hepatica, Trillium, Trout Lilies, and Lady's Slippers are joined by a host of silent sentinels witnessing the spring dramas that unfold each year. A park-wide annual Wildflower Pilgrimage is held in late April.

We especially liked the easy-to-moderate hike to Jakes Creek and Cucumber Gap just off the historic Elkmont Loop. You may see Galax blooming along another of our favorite easy trails, which leads to Hen Wallow Falls 2.0 miles from the Cosby Campground parking lot on TN 32 on the northeastern end of the GSMNP. Porter's Creek Trail, which requires a more moderate energy expenditure, is also excellent for wildflower viewing.

Heat and humidity will be punctuated with afternoon showers from June through August so dress in cool cottons and invest in insect repellent, especially if you'll be hiking along streams. The autumn colors tend to peak around mid-October but can vary with the local weather patterns up to two weeks either way. This is prime Smoky Mountain time for many visitors. To save you from the traffic on US 441 and in Cades Cove, we suggest you tour the Western Foothills Parkway from Walland, the Eastern Foothills Parkway into Cosby, or the Cataloochee Valley on the southeastern side of the Park.

Winter weather can vary from sunny skies with highs in the 60s to lows in the 20s. In some years, enough of a January thaw takes place to make you remember spring. Its a good idea to dress in layers if you intend to visit the high country. Although there's not a lot of snow at the lower elevations, storms can blow up quickly dropping the temperature below zero and leaving a foot of snow. Winter snowfall transforms the landscape into a wonderland, but makes for treacherous travels. However you reach the Smokies, we hope you'll allow yourself many opportunities to experience their unparalleled beauty.

❧ FOR MORE INFORMATION *(Area Code 423)*

You can get information and make reservations for the 161 sites at the GSMNP, Cades Cove, Elkmont, and Smokemont Campgrounds by phoning 1-800-365-CAMP (Visa and Mastercard accepted). Camping fees are $11 per night with a 7-day maximum stay during peak season (May 1 to October 31). Budget constraints have caused closure of the campground during winter months.

Friends of GSMNP—134 Court Ave., Sevierville, TN 37862; 453-6231.

Great Smoky Mountains National Park Headquarters—436-1200.

Great Smoky Mountains Natural History Association—115 Park Headquarters Rd.; 436-0120.

Appalachian Black Bear Rehabilitation and Release Center, Inc.—POB 53446, Knoxville, TN 37950; 531-0914.

Great Smoky Mountains Institute at Tremont—9275 Tremont Rd.; 448-6709.

❧ DIRECTIONS

Located within 550 miles of half the population of the United States, the GSMNP is the most visited national park in the National Park system. There are several approaches:

• I-40 east of Knoxville to US 66 (exit 407) to Sevierville, Pigeon Forge, and Gatlinburg.

• Exit 386B from I-40 west of Knoxville onto US 321 to Maryville, Townsend, and Cades Cove.

• Exit I-40 north of Asheville, NC, to Cosby via the eastern Foothills Parkway.

• From Asheville, NC, via the Blue Ridge Parkway to Cherokee, NC, the home of the Eastern Band of the Cherokee Indians and the southern entrance to the GSMNP on US 441.

14 Greeneville:
The Great Tennessee Valley

Greene County was the birthplace of legendary frontiersman Davy Crockett.

Greeneville is the second oldest town in Tennessee. It was founded and named for Revolutionary War hero Gen. Nathanael Greene in 1783 by the authority of the State of North Carolina. It began with a 300-acre tract of land owned by Robert Kerr centered on the Big Spring behind the present site of the library on Main Street. In 1784, North Carolina ceded its western lands to the central government created by the Articles of Confederation.

By December 1784, a group of citizens of the Washington District in what is now east Tennessee, decided that since they were now without the protection of North Carolina, their interests were best served by the creation of a new state, named for Benjamin Franklin. John Sevier (see Johnson City and Elizabethton sections) was elected governor of the State of Franklin and established its first capital at Jonesboro. By the next year, the capital of the State of Franklin had been moved to Greeneville.

In the meantime, North Carolina thought better of its decision to cede these lands and rescinded the action. The North Carolina government wanted to reestablish its authority over the area. To further complicate the situation, there were factions that had remained loyal to the government of North Carolina (see Johnson City section).

Several attempts to admit Franklin as the fourteenth state in the Union failed. The Franklin legislature elected Evan Shelby to succeed John Sevier when his term expired in the fall of 1787, but he refused to serve. Without leadership, the movement toward statehood failed and the State of Franklin quietly ceased to exist.

In 1789, North Carolina again ceded its western frontier and the area was given the title "Territory of the United States of America South of the River Ohio," commonly known as the Southwest Territory. William Blount was appointed governor and began to direct the territory toward statehood (see the Bristol section). On June 1, 1796, George Washington signed legislation making Tennessee the sixteenth state in the Union.

The original Greeneville courthouse, a log structure, was dismantled and sent to Nashville for the 1896 sesquicentennial. Because the original structure was never returned, Greeneville erected a replica in 1966.

Greeneville has a large number of historic buildings downtown. The Welcome Center has an assortment of brochures, including a self-guided tour of the buildings in the Historic District. The 1821 Dickson-Williams Mansion on Church Street is open for tours. Such notables as Presidents James K. Polk and Andrew Jackson, Henry Clay, and the Marquis de Lafayette were entertained here. The house was used as both Union and Confederate headquarters at various times during the Civil War.

In 1864, Confederate Gen. John Hunt Morgan, an overnight guest, was killed here in a surprise attack by Union troops. Like most of east Tennessee, Greeneville had a strong, predominantly Unionist sentiment.

You'll also find the Nathanael Greene Museum and several antiques malls downtown. The museum offers information about Greeneville's early history and men like John Sevier, Davy Crockett, and President Andrew Johnson.

Greeneville was the home of Andrew Johnson, the seventeenth president of the United States. A true example of the "American dream," this man, who was an indentured servant in his early years, rose to hold the highest office in the land during our nation's darkest hours.

In 1861, Tennessee was clearly divided over the issue of slavery with east Tennessee being strongly pro-Union. A state convention called in February 1861 yielded results clearly favoring the Union. When the events at Fort Sumter prompted Lincoln to call for two Tennessee regiments to help put down the rebellion, another con-

Andrew Johnson, the seventeenth president of the United States, was born in Greeneville.

vention was called before the requested troops could be sent or refused. This time the vote was strongly pro-separationist. Tennessee seceded from the Union and ratified the Confederate Constitution in August 1861. Much of upper east Tennessee area remained sympathetic to the Union cause.

According to *Tennessee Historical Markers*, former Governor Johnson was appointed military governor of Tennessee by President Lincoln after the occupation of Nashville by Union forces in 1862. Johnson tried to force citizens to swear an oath of allegiance to the Federal government, going so far as to imprison Confederate supporters who refused and seize their properties within the state. He was selected by President Lincoln for the vice-presidency in 1864 and he assumed the presidency after Lincoln's assassination.

Two of his homes, his tailor shop, and a visitor's center await your exploration in downtown Greeneville. Tours are conducted hourly most days. The official Andrew Johnson Presidential Library is at Tusculum College, a few miles east of town on TN 107. The library is open to the public if you're interested in visiting the picturesque campus and learning more about Andrew Johnson.

There are several bed and breakfasts in Greeneville. The Big Spring Inn on Main Street is within walking distance of downtown. The Greek Revival home has six guest rooms, a swimming pool for summer evenings, and a cozy fireplace that's perfect when there's a nip in the air. The two acres of shady, pleasantly landscaped grounds are enticing.

We visited Oak Hill Farm Bed and Breakfast on a sunny April afternoon. Only 3 miles north of town, the road to the yellow farmhouse on top of the hill seemed to carry us much farther. The bird's-eye view from the hill top is of the Appalachians and the Cumberland chain.

The modern house (built in 1981) has lots of old-fashioned touches like the wide front porch, just right for rocking or visiting with one of the friendly Brittany Spaniels languishing in the sun. Modern amenities include a swimming pool and a master suite with king-size bed, fireplace, Jacuzzi, and sitting area.

Full breakfasts including eggs cooked to order, biscuits and gravy, and country ham are included. Dinner can be arranged with advance reservations. One of the owners, Bill Guinn, is an artist and a past chairman of the Tennessee Council of Trout Unlimited, so he can help you if you're interested in slipping away to wet a line while you're here.

The newly restored General Morgan Inn is conveniently located downtown.

Contrary to the popular ballad of the 1950s, Davy Crockett was not "born on a mountaintop in Tennessee." As you travel down US 11E between Greeneville and Jonesboro, you'll see signs directing you 3.3 miles to Davy Crockett's Birthplace State Park along the banks of the Nolichucky River.

A tour of the Visitor's Center and Museum will reacquaint you with this colorful hero. It's like stepping back into the 1950s for those of us who grew up watching Davy's adventures on television, wearing coonskin caps at every opportunity, carrying Davy Crockett lunchboxes to school, and remembering the Alamo.

Davy was born on August 17, 1786, to John and Rebecca Hawkins Crockett. Ten years later his parents opened a tavern along the road from Knoxville, Tennessee, to Abingdon, Virginia.

The Big Springs Inn welcomes visitors to historic Greeneville.

The newly refurbished General Morgan Inn is a downtown landmark.

Although there's considerable doubt that he "killed a bar when he was only three," he was unsurpassed as a hunter. In a single winter he was credited with killing 105 bears.

He was a fiddler of a gregarious nature, so he was naturally drawn to large gatherings and festive events. The appeal of "politickin'" for him was not surprising. He was sent to Congress and records of several of his speeches remain. No stranger to hyperbole, picture the five-foot, nine-inch Crockett addressing his fellow congressmen: "I can outlook a panther and out stare a flash of lightning, tote a steamboat on my back and play rough and tumble with a lion."

Crockett was initially aligned politically with Andrew Jackson, but a disagreement brought the full force of the Jackson political machine in middle Tennessee against him and he lost his seat in Congress.

Shortly after that he left for Texas—and the Alamo. Legend has it that Crockett played his fiddle for his friends while passing the time before the fateful battle. He was captured and executed on March 6, 1836, after Santa Anna's army seized the Alamo. Crockett almanacs were published for twenty years after his death, continuing his legacy of tall tales and homespun comedy.

The park has picnic tables with grills, camping, playgrounds, and an outdoor pool.

The Snapp Inn Bed and Breakfast is on your left before you reach the park. The lovely 1815 Federal-style home is a bed and breakfast with two bedrooms with antiques and private bath. The reasonable rates include a full breakfast.

Kinser Park has 108 campsites overlooking the Nolichucky River, a nine-hole golf course, swimming pool, tennis courts, bath houses, picnic tables, and a boat ramp.

The Nolichucky District of the Cherokee National Forest begins about 6 miles south of town and is part of the largest wildlife management area in Tennessee. The trail system is excellent throughout the Cherokee National Forest. Some trails are shared with mountain bikers, while others are designated for foot traffic only. The forest also encompasses designated wilderness areas like Sampson Mountain, southeast of Greeneville. The Andrew Johnson Unit has a black bear reserve.

Davy Crockett's legacy of hyperbolic homespun humor lives on.

There are five camping sites in the Nolichucky District including the Horse Creek Recreation Area off TN 107 east of Greeneville. TN 107 is a scenic drive through largely undeveloped farm land along the historic Nolichucky River valley to Jonesboro, your next stop.

The following are Greeneville, TN 37743 and area code 423 except where noted.

☙ ACCOMMODATIONS

Big Spring Inn—315 N. Main; 638-2917.
Days Inn—935 E. Andrew Johnson Hwy. (11E Bypass), 37745; 639-2156.
General Morgan Inn and Conference Center—111 N. Main; 787-1000,
    800-203-5555.
Hilltop House B&B—6 Sanford Circle off US 70; 639-8202.
Holiday Inn—1790 East Andrew Johnson Hwy.; 639-4185,
    800-HOLIDAY.
Nolichucky Bluffs—301 Kinser Park Lane; 787-7947, 800-842-4690; Two
    bedroom cabins.
Oak Hill Farm—3035 Lonesome Pine Trail off US 70; 639-2331,
    639-5253.
Snapp Inn—1990 Davy Crockett Park Rd., Limestone, TN 37681;
    257-2482.

☙ ATTRACTIONS

Andrew Johnson National Historic Site—College and Depot St.; 638-3551;
    Daily except New Year's Day, Thanksgiving, and Christmas.
Dickson-Williams Mansion—114 W. Church; 638-8144; Mon. to Sat., 10:00
    A.M. to 2:00 P.M.
Doak-Johnson Heritage Museum—Tusculum College; 636-8554; Mon. to Fri.,
    9:00 A.M to 5:00 P.M.; Free.
Historic Greeneville District—638-4111; Guided walking tours.
Nathanael Greene Museum—101 W. McKee; 636-1558; Feb. to Dec., Tues. to
    Sat., 10:00 A.M. to 4:00 P.M.; Free.
President Andrew Johnson Museum and Library—Tusculum College; Mon. to Fri.,
    9:00 A.M. to 5:00 P.M.; Free.

DINING

Augustino's—US 11E, 3465 E. Andrew Johnson Hwy.; 639-1231.
Brumley's at the General Morgan Inn—Main St.; 787-1100.
The Butcher's Block—125 Serral Dr.; 638-4485.
The Tannery—117 E. Depot; 638-2772.

SHOPPING

Greeneville Antique Market—117 W. Depot St.; 638-2773.
Ye Old Tourist Trap—204 E. Depot St.; 639-1567.

SPECIAL EVENTS

May—Greenespring

CAMPING

Davy Crockett Birthplace State Park—Rt. 3, Box 103A, Limestone, TN 37681;
    257-2061.
Horse Creek Recreation Area—TN 107, Cherokee National Forest; 638-4109.
Kinser Park Golf Course/Campground—650 Kinser Park Ln.; 639-5912.

FOR MORE INFORMATION

Greene County/Greeneville Chamber of Commerce Partnership—115 Academy St.;
    638-4111.
Nolichucky Ranger District—Office of the Cherokee National Forest, 120
    Austin Ave.; 638-4109.

DIRECTIONS

From the West—Take I-40 to I-81 and exit on US 11E.
From the East—TI-81 to US 11E.
From East Tennessee—Take US 11E/321, TN 107, or I-81 to TN 172.

15 Jonesboro:
Oldest Town in Tennessee

Jonesboro was established in 1779 by the General Assembly of the State of North Carolina because North Carolina had authority over what is now called east Tennessee. The settlers in the area did not recognize the authority of North Carolina and founded the State of Franklin. They elected John Sevier their governor and selected Jonesboro as the state's first capital.

Jonesboro was simultaneously a seat of civilization and the edge of the wild west of the 1780s. Andrew Jackson lived at the Christopher Taylor house on Main Street, and practiced law here as a public

Jonesboro is a small town with quiet streets and friendly shopkeepers.

The National Storytelling Festival is held in October.

prosecutor from 1788 to 1789. Taylor was a veteran of the French and Indian War and served as a major in the American Revolution.

Three Tennessee presidents, Jackson, Polk, and Johnson, stayed at the Chester Inn on Main Street. One of the historic markers along West Main Street describes the publication from 1819 to 1820 of the first periodicals in the United States devoted to the abolition of human slavery, *The Manumission Intelligencer* and *The Emancipator.*

Jonesboro is probably best known for the National Storytelling Festival sponsored by the National Association for the Preservation and Perpetuation of Storytelling (NAPPS). All kinds of stories and storytellers are featured here: Jack tales, nature tales, animal fables from American Indians, African folk tales and fables, cowboy stories, fairy tales, and tales of frightful apparitions. Many of us grew up close to the storytelling tradition, listening at our mamas' knees to tales of Davy Crockett, "haints," mountain panthers, and the Underground Railroad.

The annual festival is a delightful experience even though it places lots of people in close proximity in a town of only 3,400. Somehow Jonesboro seems to accommodate them all. Well, maybe not literally, as the only accommodations in Jonesboro are bed and breakfast inns. So on storytelling weekends, people often arrange to stay in motels or bed and breakfasts in nearby Johnson City, Greeneville, Kingsport, or Erwin. Everybody agrees it's a minor inconvenience when it's weighed against the kind of feeling the town maintains.

In 1969, Jonesboro became the first Tennessee town, yes that's the whole town, to be placed on the National Register of Historic Places. Not the least among its many attractions is the fact that Jonesboro is still a small town with quiet streets in the evening, good neighbors, and courtesies for strangers. The ambience can make you feel like you've stepped back in time. The town's multi-million-dollar restoration program has helped create an appealing, old-fashioned environment with brick sidewalks, underground wiring, and attractive lighting.

There's also a "new" visitor's center, built in 1982. It makes no pretense at architectural conformity but it isn't obtrusive and it certainly is helpful and interesting.

The Jonesboro-Washington County History Museum inside the Visitor's Center displays changing exhibits addressing themes of unsung heroines of northeast Tennessee, exhibiting 200 years of Tennessee quilts, and covering the history of Jonesboro and its citizenry. A walking-tour brochure that describes the history and architecture of many of Jonesboro's oldest structures is available.

The Jonesboro Antique Mart has been one of our regular stops for years. The 22 dealers inside offer a good variety of glassware and some outstanding furniture finds. The Pig and Slipper also has antiques and collectibles. Nifong's Crafts and Woods Products is a do-it-yourself woodworker's dream with unfinished wooden table tops, legs, bed posts, spindles, knobs, shelves, and brackets.

There are several good lunch destinations. In town try the Old Sweet Shop for sandwiches, salads, and a variety of ice cream treats including a classic banana split and milk shakes. The Main Street Cafe across from the Chester Inn has soups, sandwiches, and creative salads.

The Parson's Table has luncheon selections that include a beef stroganoff using filet mignon over rice pilaf, fettucine with a medley of shrimp, crab, and whitefish in a sherried lobster sauce, or lasagna with three cheeses, spinach, onions, and carrots and a red sauce.

You may prefer to drive out to the popular Harmony Grocery off TN 81N, especially if it's a pretty afternoon. Selections include crawfish pie, fried alligator tail, sausage and seafood gumbo, red beans and rice, and a variety of steaks, chops, and chicken dishes, including pan-fried veal with Creole sauce and broiled chicken with sweet brown sauce and mushrooms. Appreciative diners also select fried, blackened, or broiled shrimp, scallops oysters, or catfish. You may want to brown bag at dinner, because no alcohol is served here. Ditto for the Parson's Table.

There are several bed and breakfasts in Jonesboro. The Hawley House is across the railroad track on Woodrow Avenue. The 1793 log-and-stone dwelling is believed to be the oldest building in Tennessee's oldest town. It has a comfortable wraparound porch, queen-size poster beds, private baths, and air conditioning.

Down the street is Jonesboro Bed and Breakfast in the 1848 Shipley-Bledsoe House. The house on the hill across from the Parson's Table

The Parson's Table offers lunch and dinner seating.

The 1848 Jonesboro Bed and Breakfast is filled with antiques but has such modern amenities as central heat and air, TVs, and telephones.

The 1850 Aiken-Brow House Bed and Breakfast is located in the Jonesboro Historic District.

has a formal living room with antiques and a grand piano. Visitors may choose from three large bedrooms with poster beds and one with double canopy beds. All have central heat and air, and some have TVs and phones. Bathrooms may be private or shared. A full breakfast is served.

The Cunningham House is across from the Christopher Taylor Log House and down an alley on the left beside Main Street Cafe as you travel west along Main Street. Tours, as well as bed and breakfast accommodations, are available in the 1840 two-story home filled with period antiques.

The Aiken-Brow House is an 1850s Greek Revival structure that is a little tricky to find on Third Avenue South, unless you realize that the left turn onto Third Avenue does not immediately follow Second on your right as you drive west on Main Street. The three guest rooms have private baths. The Crockett Room has a nice poster bed and the Sevier Room has a big brass bed.

The Wetlands Water Park has a giant water slide, lap pool, concessions, and a picnic area for family fun from May to September.

Regardless of the season, Jonesboro's charming, historic environment, coupled with its small-town hospitality, makes it one of our favorite towns in the Southeast.

The following are Jonesboro, TN 37659 and area code 423 except where noted.

ACCOMMODATIONS

Aiken-Brow House—104 Third Ave. S; 753-9440.

Bugaboo B&B—211 Semore Dr.; 753-9345.

Cunningham House—119 W. Main; 753-9292.

Hawley House B&B—114 E. Woodrow Ave.; 753-8869.

Jonesboro B&B—100 Woodrow Ave, POB 722; 753-9223.

The Old Yellow Vic Bed and Breakfast—411 W. Main St.; 753-9558; Two rooms, private bath, shared bath, air conditioning, no smoking.

The Tea Room—130 W. Main; 753-0660.

ATTRACTIONS

Discover Jonesboro's Times and Tales Tour—117 Boone St.; 753-1010; Story-telling inside historic homes and buildings.

Jonesboro/Washington County History Museum—117 Boone St.; Daily; Admission; 753-5961.

Wetlands Water Park—Jonesboro Parks and Recreation; 753-1553.

DINING

The Harmony Grocery—1121 Painter Rd.; 348-6183; Exit 45 off I-81, call for hours and directions; Closed Mon.

Main Street Cafe—117 W. Main; 753-2460; Mon. to Fri., 11:00 A.M. to 6:00 P.M.; Sat., 11:00 A.M. to 4:00 P.M., closed Sun.

Old Sweet Shop—129 E. Main; 753-8851.

The Parson's Table—Woodrow Ave.; 753-8002; Lunch, dinner; closed Mon.

SHOPPING

Jonesboro Antique Mart—115 E. Main; 753-8301.

Nifong's Crafts and Wood Products—122 E. Main; 753-4551.

Old Town Hall—144 E. Main; 753-2095.

Pig and Slipper—117 E. Main; 753-2141.

The Salt House—127 Fox St; 753-5113.

✣ SPECIAL EVENTS

July—Historic Jonesboro Days
October—National Storytelling Festival
December—Christmas in Old Jonesboro (progressive dinner; contact the
    Jonesboro Civic Trust; 753-5281)

✣ CAMPING

Davy Crockett Birthplace State Park—Off US 11E, 1245 Davy Crockett Rd.,
    Limestone 37681; 257-2167.
Home Federal Park Campground—1.7 miles from historic district; 753-2036.

✣ FOR MORE INFORMATION

Historic Jonesboro Visitor's Center—117 Boone St.; 753-1012; 800-400-4221;
    Daily.
National Association for the Preservation and Perpetuation of Storytelling—POB 309;
    753-2171.

✣ DIRECTIONS

From Knoxville—Take I-40 to I-81 and exit I-181 toward Johnson City. Take
    Exit 38 off I-181 to TN 354 (Boones Creek Road) to Jonesboro. This
    is a pretty drive through rolling green hills. As you drive down TN 354
    you will pass Semore Drive on your left 5.6 miles from the exit at I-
    181. This is the location of Bugaboo B&B. Continue 0.5 mile to cross
    US 11E/321. The road is now called Boone Street and the Visitor's
    Center is in the modern brick building to your right. Main Street is
    straight ahead.
You can also travel to Jonesboro via US 11E from Johnson City, TN 107
    from Greeneville, or TN 81 from Erwin.

16 Bristol, Kingsport, Johnson City:
The Tri-Cities

BRISTOL—A TALE OF TWO CITIES

The land that now is part of Bristol, Tennessee-Virginia was once part of a Cherokee settlement known as "Big Meet Camp." Legend has it that the name arose from the deer and buffalo that were drawn to the canebrakes to feed after visiting nearby salt and sulfur deposits.

The Cherokee abandoned Big Meet Camp and ceased their prolific production of arrowheads and spearheads after they sold fifty thousand acres of land, including the site of modern Bristol, to the Loyal Land Company of England in 1756.

A few years later a stockade and trading post established on the site of Bristol was host to John Sevier during the planning for the Battle of Kings Mountain that led to a strategic defeat of the British by the Overmountain Men in 1780 (see Elizabethton section).

Other names for the future twin cities followed, including Kings Meadow and Goodson, named for two colonels who figured prominently in the development of the area by the predominantly Scotch-Irish settlers coming to the new frontier. The survey establishing the dividing line between the states of Virginia and Tennessee was disputed until 1802.

The Bristol International Motor Speedway is the home of the Volunteer 500.

By 1856, the Virginia side of the town was incorporated as Goodson and the Tennessee side as Bristol, named after Bristol, England.

During the Civil War, the railroad line connecting Bristol and Chattanooga was the supply line between Virginia and the "Deep South" beyond Chattanooga. Several encounters took place between Union and Confederate forces in and around Bristol and portions of the town were burned twice.

In 1881, the governments of both sides of the town established the middle of Main Street as the dividing line and renamed it State Street. Tennessee formally ceded the northern half of the street to Virginia in 1901, officially ending the dispute that started more than 100 years earlier.

In 1910, a luminous sign was erected over State Street to symbolize the unity that had finally come to Bristol, Tennessee-Virginia.

Today Bristol stretches alongside Interstate 81. As the speeding motorists travel the interstate, thousands will make their way to the Bristol International Motor Speedway off US 11E, home of the world's fastest half-mile NASCAR track. If it's a race weekend, you'll know by the crowded driving conditions along Route 11E from Johnson City (also known as the Volunteer Parkway) and TN 394 (the Bristol Beltway) as well as the scarcity of accommodations throughout the surrounding area including Abingdon, Virginia; Boone, North Carolina; and Johnson City, Kingsport, Jonesboro, Greeneville, and Mountain City, Tennessee. It goes without saying that if you're the type of traveler who usually prefers serendipity, you would be well-advised to make sure your journey to this area on a race weekend includes advance reservations.

Bristol also claims the honor of being the "birthplace of Country Music." Ralph Peer of the Victor Talking Machine Company recorded titles that launched the careers of Jimmie Rodgers, the Stonemans, and the Carter family in a recording studio established in Bristol in 1927. Radio Station WOPI featured the Carter Family and other performers while WCYB aired "Farm and Fun Time," a showcase for musicians playing what would come to be known as bluegrass.

The late Bill Monroe, credited with being the father of bluegrass, formed his band in 1939. Many believe that the addition of Lester Flatt and his banjo playing partner, Earl Scruggs, was a critical factor in the development of what came to be known as the bluegrass style. Flatt and Scruggs were based in Bristol for a time and have said that being on WCYB was their first "big" break.

A mural on the wall outside Lark Amusement Company at 824 State Street depicts this part of Bristol's history. If you enjoy seeing beautiful old Wurlitzer juke boxes be sure and walk around front to check out the collection inside the building.

Record collectors will want to scout the area for 78s of the Carter Family on the Conqueror label. You might even consider making the trek to the Carter Family Fold and Museum in nearby Hiltons, Virginia, at Moses Springs. In addition to the museum in the A. P. Carter Store, many locals visit the Fold that is still the scene of weekly country music performances Carter family style. One of the members of this legendary family, June Carter Cash, is the only person with the distinction of having a mother, uncle, aunt, and husband in the Country Music Hall of Fame in Nashville.

The mural at Lark Amusement Company portrays Bristol's part in the evolution of country music.

Avid country music fans may want to visit the birthplace and early childhood home of country music legend Tennessee Ernie Ford in a little frame house at 1223 Anderson Street that also serves as the headquarters of the Bristol Historical Association.

If you're really lucky (or you planned well) you don't even have to leave town to hear live country music because the Paramount Theatre Center for the Arts, a renovated 1931 movie palace on State Street, offers Pickin' at the Paramount, an acoustic bluegrass and country music heritage performance one evening each month. The Paramount also hosts regular theatrical productions by Theatre Bristol throughout the year.

While you're downtown visit some of the antiques malls and shops on State Street including Heritage Antiques and Collectibles, Mary Ann Stone Antiques and Interiors, and Antiques Unlimited, or turn north on Commonwealth Avenue to visit A Abe's or the Bristol Antique Mall.

Several interesting spots are 5- to 15-mile trips from Bristol. Bristol Caverns off scenic US 421 is 5 miles southeast of town and 200 million years old. Local legend claims the caverns and the underground river through them were used as an Indian attack and escape route by allowing the Indians to appear to vanish before the settlers' eyes. The 78-acre cave is filled with fascinating geological formations.

Rocky Mount is a two-story log structure that was built in 1770–72 by William Cobb. At this time, the area that we now know as east Tennessee was part of North Carolina's western holdings. North Carolina later ceded this area to the central government formed under the United States Constitution. It then was known as the Territory of the United States South of the Ohio River or the Southwest Territory.

William Blount was appointed Governor and Superintendent of Indian Affairs of the Southwest Territory by George Washington in 1790. He came to live with the Cobb family, which made Rocky Mount the site of the first territorial seat of government of the Southwest Territory. In 1792 the capital was moved to Knoxville as westward growth continued. (See Knoxville section.)

Rocky Mount is now the property of the State of Tennessee. The house, grounds, outbuildings, and the Massengill Museum of Overmountain History are open for viewing daily except weekends in January and February, Thanksgiving, and December 21 to January 5.

Rocky Mount was the capital of the Southwest Territory from 1790 to 1792.

✌ ACCOMMODATIONS

Comfort Inn—2368 Lee Hwy., I-81 Exit 5, Bristol, VA; 540-466-3881, 800-221-2222.

Days Inn—536 Volunteer Pkwy, Hwy 11E South, Bristol, TN; 423-968-2171.

Glencarin Manor—224 Old Abingdon Hwy, Bristol, VA 24201; 540-466-0224; Built in 1842, this lovely old home has four rooms with private baths; Full breakfast; Children over six by arrangement; Smoking restricted; No pets.

Hampton Inn—3299 West State St., Bristol, TN 37620; 423-764-3600, 1-800-HAMPTON.

HoJo Inn—975 Volunteer Pkwy., Hwy. 11E South, Bristol, TN; 423-968-9474, 1-800-446-4656.

New Hope Bed and Breakfast—822 Georgia Ave., Bristol, TN 37620; 423-989-3343; Four rooms with private baths, seasonal rates.

✌ ATTRACTIONS

Bristol Caverns—Box 851, Bristol, TN 37621; 5 miles southeast of Bristol; 423-878-2011.

Carter Family Museum—A. P. Carter Hwy., Hiltons, VA; 540-386-6054.

Paramount Theatre Center for the Arts—518 State St., Bristol, TN 37620; Box Office 423-968-7456.

Rocky Mount Museum—200 Hyder Hill Rd., Piney Flats, TN 37686; 423-538-7396.

✌ DINING

Athens Steakhouse—Corner of Volunteer Parkway and 8th; 423-652-2202; 105 Goodson, 466-8271; Open 4:00 P.M. until closing except Sunday.

Sandy's—2871 W. State St., Bristol, TN; 423-968-9278; 11:00 A.M. to 9:00 P.M. daily.

The Troutdale Dining Room—412 6th Street, Bristol, TN; 423- 968-9099; 5:00 p.m. to closing, daily except Sunday.

℅ SHOPPING

A Abe's Antiques—411 Commonwealth Ave., Bristol; 466-6895.
Antiques Unlimited—620 State St., Bristol; 764-4211.
Bristol Antique Mall—403 Commonwealth Ave., Bristol; 466-4064.
Heritage Antiques—625 State St., Bristol; 669-0774.
Mary Ann Stone Antiques and Interiors—610 State St., Bristol; 968-5181.

℅ SPECIAL EVENTS

September—*Autumn Chase Festival, Bristol Chamber of Commerce (20 Volunteer Pkwy., Bristol, TN 37620, 423-989-4850)*
Throughout the year—*Bristol International Motor Speedway (POB 3966, Bristol, TN 37625; 423-764-1161)*

℅ CAMPING

Bristol/Kingsport KOA—Exit 63 from I-81, 1.5 miles to KOA, 423-323-7790, 1-800-KOA-7640.

℅ FOR MORE INFORMATION

Bristol/Tennessee Virginia Chamber of Commerce—POB 519, Bristol, VA 24203; 423-989-4850; 20 Volunteer Parkway, Bristol, TN

℅ DIRECTIONS

Bristol straddles the TN-VA state line on I-81. You can't miss it.
Locally US 11E parallels I-81 through Greeneville, Jonesboro, and Johnson City before entering Bristol.
US 421 enters Bristol from Boone, NC, via Mountain City, TN.

KINGSPORT—Along the Great Warrior's Path

Kingsport was once known as Long Island by the Cherokee who hunted and traded here along the Holston River. The site of

Long Island was strategically situated along the Warrior's Path, or the Great Indian War Trail, which traveled through the Great Valley and reached to neighboring settlements with a series of connecting trails. The Cherokee allowed traders to join the island encampment as early as the mid-1700s.

A peace treaty in 1761 promoted the passage of travelers going west through the area. So many settlers came to Long Island with the intention of continuing their journey by water that an area known as the Boat Yard developed as a gateway to the west on the opposite shore of the Holston River. The Boat Yard was a point of departure and center of commerce from 1768 to 1850.

The Cherokee eventually rose up against the invasion of their homelands by hoards of settlers and attacked the settlements along the Holston, Watauga, and Nolichucky but were driven back by the militias of Tennessee and Virginia at Long Island. In 1781 a peace treaty was negotiated and in 1806 the Cherokee ceded Long Island and additional extensive holdings in Tennessee and Alabama.

In 1976, a part of this island was returned to the Cherokee by the city of Kingsport. This was in accordance with instructions of the Mead Company, which owned Long Island at the time and donated a portion of it to the city.

To visit this site travel west on US 11W to the Netherland Inn Road. You will travel along the North Fork of the Holston River and enter the Boat Yard District, now a city park. Park and walk down the path to the swinging bridge to reach Long Island.

The Netherland Inn was built in 1802 to help develop the Boat Yard. After receiving a stage contract, the inn and tavern became a coach stop in 1818 along the Old Great Stage Road from Washington City (which became Washington, D.C.) to Nashboro (Nashville). The three-story inn hosted Tennessee Presidents Jackson, Johnson, and Polk and is now a museum open on weekends in the Boat Yard complex overlooking the Holston. It has been restored and contains many of the original furnishings.

The second historic structure of interest in Kingsport is the Exchange Place, also known as the Gaines Preston Farm at 4812 Orebank Road. This was a relay station where teams of horses were

The swinging bridge at the Boat Yard District Park leads to Long Island, the historic meeting grounds of the Cherokee.

The Netherland Inn is now a museum filled with period antiques and exhibits.

Swimming, boating, and fishing are popular at Warrior's Path State Park.

exchanged for the stagecoach. The name comes from the opportunity passengers had to exchange their Tennessee and Virginia currencies at the store here. A spring Festival and Herb Sale held here is considered one of the top 25 events in the Southeast.

The 870-acre Warrior's Path State Park is 3 miles southeast of Kingsport on the shores of TVA's Patrick Henry Reservoir. More than 130 campsites have tables and grills. Of these, 94 have water and electrical hook-ups. Picnic tables and grills dot the water's edge.

Paddle boats and small fishing boats are available for rent at the marina. There is no park fee for fishing but you must have a valid Tennessee fishing license if you're over 13. Visitors will also find an 18-hole par 72 golf course, an olympic-size pool, and a water slide. Horseback riding is available through the park stables.

Bays Mountain Park and Planetarium is a 3,000-acre nature preserve with 22 miles of hiking trails around a 44-acre lake and the ridges surrounding it. The river otter's pool is a favorite stop among the animal and habitat exhibits but deer, wolves, and bobcats viewed in their woodland habitats are popular as well.

Bays Mountain also features an active weekend schedule of star watches, barge rides along the lake, and special programs about topics ranging from wildflowers to wolves. The barge rides are quite popular, so make arrangements as soon as you arrive.

Kingsport has a half-dozen or more excellent antiques malls along Broad Street offering nearly 100,000 combined square feet of browsing.

You might want to search out the Mezzanine Tea Room at Home Sweet Home if you're in the vicinity between 11:00 A.M. and 3:00 P.M. Wednesday to Saturday and treat yourself to an inspired dessert while you contemplate your purchases.

The following are Kingsport, TN 37660 and area code 423 except where noted.

ACCOMMODATIONS

Comfort Inn—I-81 at Fairlane Dr., 60 rms., pool; 239-7447, 800-228-5150.

Comfort Inn—Kingsport, 100 Indian Center Ct.; 122 rms.; pool; 378-4418, 800-221-2222.

Days Inn Downtown—805 Lynn Garden Dr.; 247-7126, 800-DAYS-INN.

Fox Manor Bed and Breakfast—1612 Watauga St.; 378-3844; Four bedrooms with antiques and high ceilings; Two rooms have shared baths, two have private baths, three have fireplaces; Breakfast and high tea served; Smoking restrictions.

Holiday Inn Express—4234 Fort Henry Dr.; 49 rooms; 239-3400, 800-HOLIDAY.

Shadowilde Manor—252 Ollis Bowers Rd.; 323-3939; Three bedrooms with private baths; Pool; Gazebo on 60 acres; Full breakfast; Smoking restrictions; Children over 14; Dog kennel.

Ramada Inn—2005 La Masa Dr.; 195 rms; pool; 245-0271, 800-228-2828.

ATTRACTIONS

Bays Mountain Park and Planetarium—853 Bays Mountain Park Rd.; 229-9447; Daily except New Year's, Thanksgiving, Christmas Eve, and Christmas; Admission.

Boat Yard—Riverfront Park, Netherland Inn Rd.; 229-9457.

Exchange Place—Gaines Preston Farm, 4812 Orebank Rd; 288-6071; Open May to Oct., Thurs. to Fri., 10:00 A.M. to 2 P.M., Sat. to Sun., 2:00 to 4:30 P.M.; Admission.

Netherland Inn Historic House Museum—2144 Netherland Inn Rd.; 246-6262; Open weekends; Admission.

DINING

Amato's—121 Jack White Dr.; 245-4043; Mon. to Thurs., 11:00 A.M. to 10:00 P.M.; Fri. to Sat., 11:00 A.M. to 11:00 P.M., Sun., 11:00 A.M. to 9:00 P.M.

Giuseppe's Lounge—2538 East Stone Dr.; 288-5265; Mon. to Fri., 11:00 A.M. to 11:00 P.M., Sat., 4:00 P.M. to 11:00 P.M., Sun., 12:00 to 9:30 P.M.

Harmony Grocery Co.—I-181 at Eastern Star Rd., 1121 Painter Rd; 348-6183; Closed Mon.

Olde West Dinner Theater—3520 Hwy. 75; 323-1468.

Skoby's—1001 Konnarock Rd.; 245-2761; Mon. to Thurs., 4:30 to 10:00 P.M., Fri. to Sat., 4:30 to 11:00 P.M., closed Sun.

Wright's Country Cuisine—109 Jack White Dr.; 245-2565.

SHOPPING

Adams Company and Friends, LTD.—231 Broad St.; 247-9775; 10:00 A.M. to 5:30 P.M., Mon. to Sat., 1:00 to 5:00 P.M. Sun.

Anchor Antiques—137 Broad St.; 378-3188, 11:00 A.M. to 5:00 P.m., Mon.
    to Sat.
Colonial Antique Mall—245 Broad St.; 246-5559; 10:00 A.M. to 5:30 P.M.,
    Mon. to Sat., 1:00 to 5:30 P.M. Sun.
Haggle Shop Antique Mall #1—146 Broad St.; 246-8002; 10:00 A.M. to 5:30
    P.M., Mon. to Sat., 1:00 to 5:30 P.M. Sun.
Haggle Shop Antique Mall #2—147 Broad St.; 246-6588; same hours as #1
Home Sweet Home—Mezzanine Tearoom, 122 Broad St.; 246-1331; 10:00
    A.M. to 5:30 P.M., Tues. to Sat., dining 11:00 A.M. to 3:00 P.M. Wed.
    to Sat.

✎ SPECIAL EVENTS

April—*Exchange Place Spring Festival and Herb Sale*
May—*Netherland Inn's Season Opening Celebration*
July—*Funfest*
September—*Exchange Place Fall Festival*
December—*Christmas at Allandale Mansion*

✎ CAMPING

Bristol-Kingsport KOA Campground—425 Rocky Branch Rd., Blountville, TN
    37617; 423-323-7790, 800-KOA-7640; 73 sites; Pool; Yearround.
Warrior's Path State Park—POB 5026, Kingsport, TN 37663; 423-239-
    8531; or TN Dept of Conservation, 800-421-6683.

✎ FOR MORE INFORMATION

Kingsport Convention and Visitors Bureau—POB 1403, Kingsport, TN 37662;
    423-392-8820, 800-743-5282.

✎ DIRECTIONS

From the West—I-81 to I-181 and take Exit 57B to Bays Mountain or
    Exit 55 on East Stone Drive
From the East—Take I-81 to Exit 59 on TN 35, also known as Fort Henry
    Drive To visit Warriors Path State Park go north to the turn at Hem-
    lock Rd. or continue on Fort Henry Drive to downtown Kingsport.
Many of the downtown streets radiate like spokes from a wheel hub at his-
    toric Church Circle.

JOHNSON CITY: HOME OF EAST TENNESSEE STATE UNIVERSITY

Johnson City was once known as the village of Green Meadows. It was renamed three times before it became Johnson City in 1869. Former titles include Blue Plum, Johnson's Depot, and Haynesville in honor of Landon Carter Haynes whose estate, the Tipton-Haynes Historic Site, is now owned by the Tennessee Historical Commission.

The site of the original town has been greatly transformed since those days, most recently by the urban renewal projects of the 1970s, the presence of 12,100 students at East Tennessee State University (ETSU), and a 1996 population of about 50,000 residents.

In addition to motels along US 11E, the Hart House Bed and Breakfast has three comfortable second-floor guest rooms with private baths. Queen-size beds, color cable TVs, full breakfasts, and an exercise room round out the amenities in this 1910 Dutch Colonial home located within a few blocks of I-181.

The Antique Village, Memory Lane Antique Mall, and the Hands On Regional Museum on Main Street are interjecting new life into the downtown area. The Hands On Museum offers more than 50 exhibits and interactive displays designed to play on each of the senses for a memorable learning experience. One of the downtown antiques malls fills a three-story building with an interesting assortment of antiques and collectibles. Another has an

Young Hunter Steadman thoroughly enjoys the life-size cockpit of one of the exhibits at the Hands On Museum.

The Tipton-Haynes Farm was the site of the Battle of the State of Franklin in 1788.

especially large selection of antique living room and dining room furniture. Every time we visit, it seems a new shop has appeared to entice us to Main Street.

The Tipton-Haynes Historic Site is south of town on S. Roan. The site is along an old buffalo trail that was visited by Woodland Indians and later by the Cherokee. The trail became the Stage Road and the home was built along it in the 1780s by Col. John Tipton. The dispute that took place here between Tipton, a North Carolina magistrate and John Sevier, the governor of the State of Franklin became known as the Battle of the State of Franklin.

According to *Tennessee Historical Markers,* a publication of the Tennessee Historical Commission, the area had been under the jurisdiction of the state of North Carolina, which for various reasons first ceded the area to the newly established central government and then reversed its position.

During this time, the State of Franklin was created in December 1784 by east Tennessee pioneers who already had experience in self-government about 15 years earlier in the self-governing Watauga Association (see Elizabethton section). The Franklinites, as they came to be called, elected John Sevier to be their first governor.

When news was received in the area that North Carolina had rescinded its land cession, the Franklinites refused North Carolina's demands that the state be dissolved. For a while there were parallel governments. One represented North Carolina and the factions in the area loyal to it. The other represented the proposed State of Franklin and those loyal to it. The Franklin faction sent repeated envoys to Washington requesting recognition of the proposed new state but their efforts failed. Of course, the Franklinites refused to acknowledge North Carolina's right to collect taxes from the citizens of what they considered another state.

The North Carolina sheriff confiscated persons and property of John Sevier for taxes in the winter of 1788 and took them to the home of another North Carolina loyalist, Magistrate John Tipton. When Sevier returned to his home and discovered what he considered the theft of his property, he marched with a group of men to John Tipton's home and demanded the return of his property. A contingent of Tipton allies resisted, a fight ensued, and in the melee Sheriff Pugh was killed and two of Sevier's sons were captured. The dispute threatened to escalate but intermediaries of both men were able to intervene. North Carolina Governor Caswell took a moderate stance, and the losses on both sides were kept to a minimum.

East Tennessee State houses the B. Carroll Reece Museum and the Ambrose Manning Collection in the Sherrod Library that is part of the Center for Appalachian Studies and Services. The museum has a collection of frontier artifacts and antique musical items. The Ambrose Manning Collection is part of the Appalachian Archives, an extensive collection of music of the Appalachians including many recordings available for research purposes.

The following are Johnson City, TN 37601 and area code 423.

✌ ACCOMMODATIONS

Broadway Motel—2608 N. Roan; 282-4011.
Comfort Inn—1900 S. Roan; 928-9600.
Days Inn—2312 Brown's Mill Road; 282-2211.
Hampton Inn—508 N. State of Franklin Rd.; 929-8000.
Hart House B&B—207 E. Holston Ave.; 926-3147.
Holiday Inn—101 W. Springbrook Dr.; 282-4611, 800-HOLIDAY.

❧ ATTRACTIONS

Carroll Reece Museum—East Tennessee State University Campus; 929-4392; Daily.

Center for Appalachian Studies and Services—East Tennessee State University; 929-5348.

Hands On Regional Museum—315 E. Main St.; 928-6508, 928-6509.

Tipton-Haynes Historic Site—2620 S. Roan St. or Exit 31 off I-181; 926-3631; Daily Apr. 1 to Oct. 31, Mon. to Fri. Nov. 1 to Mar. 31.

❧ DINING

The Apex—604 W. Market; Burgers and beer; 926-9931.

The Cottage—705 W. Market; Burgers and beer; 928-9753.

The Firehouse Restaurant—627 W. Walnut; 929-7377.

Galloways Restaurant—807 N. Roan; 926-1166.

Olde West Dinner Theater—3520 Hwy. 75; 283-4974.

Peerless Steak House—2531 N. Roan; 282-2351.

Picadilly Cafeteria at the Mall—282-4327.

Poor Richard's Deli—825 W. Walnut; 926-8611.

Red Pig Barbeque—2201 Ferguson Rd.; 282-6585.

Sunny's Cafeteria—1000 S. Roan; 926-7441.

❧ SHOPPING

Antique Village—228-230 E. Main St.; 926-6996.

Memory Lane Antique Mall—324 E. Main St.; 929-3998.

❧ FOR MORE INFORMATION

Johnson City Convention and Visitors Bureau—603 E. Market, POB 180, Johnson City, TN 37605; 461-8000.

❧ DIRECTIONS

I-81 and exit I-181 to Johnson City.

US 11E from Greeneville or Jonesboro.

US 19/23 from Asheville, NC.

17 *Erwin:*
The Beauty Spot

As you drive toward Erwin from Johnson City, the mountains begin to rise around you. You have entered the high country of the Cherokee National Forest of Unicoi County.

Unicoi, we were told, means "place of the white man." The first white people to enter this area were Long Hunters from North Carolina. Settlers first located in the cove between Unicoi and the Nolichucky River around 1772. Andrew Jackson came up with a group of his friends from Jonesboro in 1788 to race his horse along the half-mile track. Jackson rode the horse himself because his jockey was ill. He lost the race by inches.

The Buffalo Valley Resort and Golf Course nestles among the peaks of the Cherokee National Forest.

Unicoi County was formed in 1876. The county seat was first called Longmire, then Vanderbilt, and then Ervin. The Post Office made a mistake and changed the "V" to "W" and that's what it's been called ever since.

The area is relatively undeveloped for tourism, which means much of its natural beauty is yet undisturbed. However, US 19/23 is being upgraded to four lanes across the mountains from Asheville to join I-181 from Johnson City, so development will begin to increase rapidly in the near future. There are at least four good reasons to visit Unicoi County: railroading, Blue Ridge Pottery, Beauty Spot, and the Nolichucky River.

Erwin was the home of Southern Potteries, Inc., the makers of the highly collectible Blue Ridge pattern. Southern Pottery was started by the CC&O Railroad in 1920 and employed 1,200 during peak production, most of them young women from the mountains. An excellent display of Blue Ridge Pottery is open from May to October at the Unicoi County Heritage Museum at the National Fish Hatchery property. Southern Pottery went out of business in 1957 and the colorful flower designs have only grown in popularity since.

Erwin Pottery is owned and operated by Negatha Peterson, a former Southern Pottery employee. She makes original designs and reproductions of Blue Ridge. She bought at least one original mold for each Blue Ridge piece when the pottery closed and is frequently called upon to replace missing parts for special pieces like teapots, sugar bowls, etc. There's a Blue Ridge Pottery Club Show and Sale at the Apple Festival each fall.

Much of Erwin's growth resulted from its part in the railroad industry in the area. The need for a north-south rail line was talked about for years before anyone braved the rugged terrain to actually build it. It took nearly thirteen years and several changes within the corporate structure of the railroad itself for the reality to be achieved in 1899.

Initially Erwin was the home of the repair shops for the Carolina, Clinchfield, and Ohio (CC&O) railroad. In 1909, the Superintendent, Car Service, and Master Agent arrived. The general offices relocated to Erwin in fall of 1926 and remained until 1983 when the railroad merged with CSX Seaboard System. Trains still run through the area and many of the antiques shops have railroad memorabilia for sale.

Several miles past the Tipton-Haynes Historic site on the way to Erwin you'll see the Buffalo Valley Resort and Golf Course and the Farmhouse Gallery and Gardens. The Farmhouse Gallery owners share their vast knowledge of gardening, wildflowers, and wildlife habitat with visitors. One of the owners is a wildlife artist with a studio in an old log cabin on the 70-acre property. The other half of this talented duo grows and sells wildflowers and herbal teas.

As you approach Erwin you will pass through the tiny community of Unicoi. Crackerbee's Antiques was filled with collectibles, including a Watts bean pot that now rests comfortably on our kitchen shelf. A surprising number of items are stacked from the floor to the ceiling and inside every nook and cranny.

Nearly half of Unicoi County's 118,400 acres lie within the Cherokee National Forest. Thirty miles of the Appalachian Trail pass through the rugged county. A turn east on TN 107 takes you to the Beauty Spot, a relatively accessible site with a breathtaking mountain-top view that is reached entirely by gravel road after the turnoff of TN 107. A map is available from the Unaka Ranger District office in Erwin to help you locate the turnoff. The Unaka Mountain Auto Tour map routes you to TN 395 and returns you to Erwin.

The view is always impressive on a clear day, but you'll rarely find a crowd even during autumn.

The panoramic view from the Beauty Spot can be enjoyed in all seasons.

Continuing toward Erwin, you'll find the Erwin National Fish Hatchery. It grew out of legislation in 1894 providing $12,000 for the establishment of a fish hatching station. The hatchery initially provided rainbow trout fingerlings. Presently the hatchery ships 15 million rainbow trout eggs all over the United States and supplies brood fish to other hatcheries.

The former superintendent's residence, built in 1903, is now the Unicoi County Heritage Museum. Everything in it was either donated or loaned by families in the community. The Blue Ridge

Pottery Room is in the dining room. Upstairs there's a recreation of Erwin's Main Street complete with boardwalk, an apothecary shop, doctor's office, and combined dentist office/barber shop. Visitors are invited to use the picnic pavilion and walk the self-guided nature trail on the 30-acre property. A picnic lunch would be a perfect accompaniment on a crisp fall day.

If you travel west on TN 107 toward Greeneville, you'll be traveling along the historic Nolichucky Valley, a pleasant alternative to US 11E or I-81 for those traveling toward the Great Smoky Mountain National Park. As you follow along the river, you'll understand why the Indians named it "rushing waters."

Rapids are classified using an international scale with Class I rapids being the easiest to get through and Class VI probably being survivable. Class III/IV means they're challenging. The upper Nolichucky has nearly a dozen of these rapids. The lower section is broader and much gentler with occasional Class II/III rapids and enough ripples to keep you interested. There are several outfitters in the area. The headwaters of the Nolichucky River are at Mount Mitchell, and the put-ins for the upper section are in North Carolina as well.

Cherokee Adventures is located 1 mile out of Erwin on TN 81/107 toward Jonesboro. They specialize in water sports along the Nolichucky, including the wild and scenic trips on the upper section and the gentler float trips through the lower section.

The following are Erwin, TN 37650 area code 423.

❧ ACCOMMODATIONS

Tumbling Creek Mountain Inn B&B—Rt. 2, Box 380 A, 37650, 743-5308.
Buffalo Valley Resort/Family Inns of America—Rt. 2, Hwy. 19/23, Unicoi, TN 37692; 743-6438.

❧ ATTRACTIONS

Cherokee Adventures—Looking Glass Mtn.; 743-7733.
Nantahala Outdoor Center—4 Jones Branch Rd.; 743-7400.
Erwin National Fish Hatchery—1715 Johnson City Hwy., 743-4712.

Farmhouse Gallery and Gardens—Old Erwin-Johnson City Hwy., Unicoi,
   743-8799, 800-952-6043.
Unicoi County Heritage Museum—1715 Old Johnson City Hwy., 743-9449.

✍ DINING

Elms Restaurant—202 S. Elm St.; 643-6181.

✍ EVENTS

April—*April Garden Party at the Farmhouse Gallery and Gardens*
May—*Ramp Festival at Flag Pond*
October—*Apple Festival*
October—*Autumn Jubilee and Open House at the Farmhouse Gallery and Gardens*

✍ SHOPPING

Farmhouse Gallery and Gardens—Rt. 2, Box 112, Unicoi, TN 37692;
   743-8799, 800-952-6043.
The Hanging Elephant Antique Mall—219 S. Main; 743-9661; Daily.
Main Street Antique Mall—105 S. Main St.; 743-7810 .

✍ CAMPING

Rock Creek Recreation Area—USDA Forest Service; 743-4452.
Limestone Cove Recreation Area—USDA Forest Service; 743-4452.

✍ FOR MORE INFORMATION

Erwin/Unicoi Chamber of Commerce—POB 713, Bank of TN Bldg., 37650;
   743-3000.
Unaka Ranger District—USDA Forest Service, 1205 N. Main St., 743-4452.

✍ DIRECTIONS

From I-81—Exit I-181 to Johnson City and continue to Erwin via 19/23.
From Asheville—Take US 19/23.
From Jonesboro—Take TN 81 to TN 107.

18 Elizabethton, Roan Mountain, Watauga Lake:
Land of the Overmountain Men

Elizabethton was founded on the site of a Cherokee village known as "Old Fields" near the shoals in the Watauga River now known as Sycamore Shoals. The Watauga settlement was believed to be on land claimed by Virginia, but the boundary line placed it in North Carolina's jurisdiction.

The first settler in the area was William Bean in 1768. He was soon followed by James Robertson, who would later lead an expedition to found the middle Tennessee settlement that would become

Roan Mountain State Park is known for its grassy balds and natural rhododendron gardens.

Nashville. Robertson, according to Donald Davidson in his book, *The Tennessee*, got lost in the mountains on his way back to North Carolina but managed to survive and bring a group of settlers back. North Carolina, however, paid them little attention and the settlers decided to establish their own government known as the Watauga Association to represent their interests.

The Watauga Association sent emissaries to the Cherokee at Chota and negotiated a ten-year lease of the lands they were occupying thereby skirting the issue of buying the land from the Cherokee or fighting them for possession.

In the spring of 1775, negotiations here with the Cherokee led to the purchase of lands along the Watauga, Holston, and New (then known as the Great Canaway) Rivers that they had earlier leased.

This was the site of the gathering of the "overmountain men" as they went to meet British forces at King's Mountain, South Carolina on Sept. 25, 1780. According to *Tennessee Historical Markers*, a publication of the Tennessee Historical Commission, British Maj. Patrick Ferguson threatened to burn the homes of the Wataugans if they continued to aid the revolutionists. Their reply was a gathering of men from the Watauga, Holston, and Great Canaway, along with members of the North Carolina militia.

Davidson tells us that Major Ferguson brought 1,100 British and Tories to the encounter at King's Mountain, South Carolina, as a part of Lord Cornwallis' campaign through the Carolinas that started after Charleston fell in May 1780. In one fateful day, the Overmountain Men killed Ferguson and either killed or captured his entire command. It was a resounding defeat with fewer than 30 Overmountain Men lost. Many historians feel the defeat was the turning point of the Revolutionary War in the South.

The self-reliant settlers eventually declared themselves the State of Franklin and chose frontiersman and hero of the Battle of King's Mountain John Sevier as their first governor. Sevier, also known as Nolichuckey Jack according to Davidson, was Tennessee's first frontier hero. His military genius and ability to lead successfully in battle against the British and the Cherokee was the source of his fame. He is believed to have fought 35 battles and won them all. The war whoop his men used when engaging the enemy in battle may have traversed the years as the Rebel Yell of Confederate soldiers.

So popular was Sevier that he was the governor of the "lost" State of Franklin and also the first governor of Tennessee when it was eventually admitted to the Union, although he had been arrested for treason as the governor of Franklin. He held the office five additional terms before retiring from public office (see Johnson City section).

More about the colorful history of our fledgling nation's first wild west settlement can be discovered at Sycamore Shoals State Park. The site includes a reconstruction of Fort Watauga, a museum and interpretative programs, as well as July performances of the outdoor drama *The Wataugans.*

Other historic sites include the Doe River Covered Bridge, which was handbuilt by craftsmen in 1882. It is believed to be the oldest covered bridge in use in Tennessee today and is on the National Register of Historic sites. A week-long covered bridge celebration is held each June.

Elizabethton is situated in Carter County in the midst of 84,500 acres of the Cherokee National Forest at the intersection of the Watauga and Doe Rivers.

The babbling waters of the Doe are well-known for stream fishing. The 72-acre trout-filled Little Wilbur Lake below Watauga

The Doe River Covered Bridge is an Elizabethton landmark.

Dam is also very popular. Primitive campsites are available near the Little Wilbur with picnic tables, grills, and a bathhouse.

Watauga is an inviting TVA lake, nestled among the surrounding mountain peaks like a jewel in a crown. With 6,430 surface acres and 106 miles of meandering shoreline with very little development, it offers outdoor enthusiasts ample opportunities for fishing, boating, swimming, and water skiing with plenty of elbow room. There are several popular picnic sites along the lake, including Shook Branch and Watauga Point, which both have swimming areas. Camping is available at the Carden's Bluff Campground.

Watauga Lakeshore Resort and Marina has a motel, cottages, fishing, ski boat and pontoon boat rentals, a swimming pool, and the Captain's Table Restaurant.

About 60 miles of the Appalachian Trail are in Carter County, including a portion that runs along the shoreline of Watauga Lake and a portion that traverses the Roan High Knob at Roan Mountain State Park.

Roan Mountain State Park is named for the 6,285-foot peak that towers above it and is one of the most popular parks in the upper east Tennessee Region. It has 20 cabins, two campgrounds with bathhouses, playgrounds, picnic tables, hiking, three cross-country ski and snow shoe trails, and a swimming pool. The longest stretch of grassy balds in the southern Appalachians stretches from Carvers Gap to Big Hump Mountain and vies for the distinction of being the prettiest portion of the Appalachian Trail system.

This former mountain homestead is now a museum at Roan Mountain State Park.

One of the largest natural rhododendron gardens in the world is at the top of the Roan. The bloom tends to be in the last half of June and it is an impressive array of red, pink, and purple Catawba rhododendron flaming along the mountain peaks.

Spring is also a wonderful time to visit. Wildflowers and wild alpine strawberries have lured us to the Roan since childhood. Fall foliage puts on a showy display. The brilliance of new-fallen snow and stillness broken only by the swish of skis meeting snow is enticing, if somewhat difficult to predict.

The weather changes quickly here and often without warning. We've been nearly blown off the top in a sudden late spring storm. We've set out in a snowstorm that turned to drizzle and we've climbed through early morning fog to discover a brilliant expanse of blue sky broken only by puffy white clouds drifting overhead, but we've never been disappointed. It's a beauty in all seasons.

The following are Elizabethton, TN 37643 and area code 423 except where noted.

❧ ACCOMMODATIONS

Days Inn—505 W. Elk Ave., 543-3344, 800-DAYS-INN.
Head Fer the Hills Log Cabin Resort—631 Cowan Town Rd., Butler, 37640; 768-3346, 800-705-7724; Log cabins with modern amenities; gas-log fireplaces; open-air hot tub; Near Watauga Lake.
Hunter Cottage Bed and Breakfast—213 S. Riverside Dr.; 542-9268, 800-876-3604; Victorian home with two rooms, private baths, and antiques; Overlooking Doe River Covered Bridge.
Old Main Manor—708 N. Main; 543-6945; Four rooms with feather downs, Private or shared bath; Children welcome; Landscaping; Jacuzzi.
Roan Mountain State Park—Rt. 1, Box 236, Roan Mtn.; 772-3303.
Watauga Lakeshore Resort—Rt. 2, Box 379, Hampton, 37658; 725-2201.

❧ ATTRACTIONS

Sycamore Shoals State Historic Area—1651 W. Elk Ave; 543-5808; Daily.

❧ DINING

Captains Table at Lakeshore Resort—Hwy. 321, Hampton; 725-2201.
Classic Malt Shop—630 Broad St.; 543-7141.
Dino's—420 E. Elk Ave; 542-5541.
O'Dellys—two locations; US19E/321, 543-3354; Roan Mtn. State Park 772-4700; May to Oct.
Ridgewood Restaurant—Bluff City Hwy., Hwy 19E; 538-7543; Closed Mon.
Southern Restaurant—408 East Elk Ave; 542-5132.

❧ SHOPPING

Antiques on Elk—509 E. Elk Ave.; 542-3355; Mon. to Fri., 10:00 A.M. to 6:00 P.M., Sat., 10:00 A.M. to 4:00 P.M.
Duck Crossing Antique Mall—515 E. Elk Ave.; 542-3055; Mon. to Sat., 10:00 A.M. to 5:00 P.M.

❧ SPECIAL EVENTS

May—*Annual Roan Mountain Wildflower Tours and Birdwalks; Roan Mountain State Park; (772-3303)*

June—*Slagle's Bluegrass Festival, Slagle's Pasture (Old Hwy. 19E; 542-8615)*

June—*Covered Bridge Celebration (547-3850)*

June—*Rhododendron Festival (772-3303)*

July—*Outdoor Drama The Wataugans (543-5808)*

September—*Overmountain Victory Trail events (543-5808)*

October—*Mountain Harvest Festival (524-3131)*

October—*Autumn Leaf Specials (train rides, 753-5797)*

❧ CAMPING

Carden's Bluff—US 321, Watauga Lake, USDA Forest Service; 542-2942.

Dennis Cove—Dennis Cove Rd. off US 321 in Hampton, USDA Forest Service; 542-2942.

Pioneer Landing—Rt. 1, Box 2735, Butler, 37640; 768-3164; 100 sites; Electric hook-up; Yearround.

Roan Mountain State Park—Rt. 1, Box 236, Roan Mountain; 772-3303, 772-4178.

TVA Watauga Dam—Little Wilbur, off Siam Rd.

❧ FOR MORE INFORMATION

Elizabethton/Carter County Chamber of Commerce Tourism Council—500 19E Bypass, POB 190; 547-3852, 800-347-0208.

Watauga Ranger District—Cherokee National Forest, Rt. 9, Box 2235; 542-2942.

❧ DIRECTIONS

From I-81—Exit to I-181 to Johnson City and take US 321 to Elizabethton.

From Bristol—Take US 11E toward Johnson City and turn left on four-laned US 19E to Elizabethton.

From Boone, NC—Take scenic US 321 to Watauga Lake and Hampton and turn right on US 19E to Elizabethton or turn left on US 19E to Roan Mountain.

19 Laurel Bloomery, Mountain City:
Land Between Two States

The gift shop at the former location for Iron Mountain Stoneware offers crafts from throughout the South.

IN 91 from Damascus, Virginia, takes you along the Daniel Boone Heritage Trail through Laurel Bloomery, a tiny community in a pretty valley southwest of Bristol and northwest of Mountain City in a remote section of the Cherokee National Forest.

In addition to its scenic attractions, Laurel Bloomery is known for Iron Mountain Stoneware. Although the stoneware is not in production at this writing, a gift shop at the site of the factory store offers attractive, tasteful, and functional stoneware bowls, plates, platters and accessories from craftsmen throughout the South.

As you continue along US 91 you will notice Donnelly House Antiques on your left. The lovely old farmhouse is chock-full-to-overflowing with antiques and collectibles.

The beautiful grounds and impressive appearance of the Butler House Bed and Breakfast catch your eye as you enter Mountain City on US 91, but no sign announces that the 1870 structure situated on 15 manicured acres is a bed and breakfast.

Owners Joan and Bill Trathen showed us the very unusual winding stairway in the entry hall that splits half-way to the second floor. The ceilings rise to 14 feet, comfortable antiques fill the four guest rooms, and the library is well stocked. Three of the rooms have double beds, one has twins, and all have private baths. Our favorite was the Wagner Room, with its big brass bed.

A full breakfast is served and ranges from casseroles to waffles. The Butler House is on the National Register of Historic Places. The day we stopped by, the inn was filled with guests attending the NASCAR race in Bristol.

Within 30 miles of this peaceful retreat you can visit historic Abingdon, Virginia, Backbone Rock State Park or Boone, North Carolina. The Appalachian Trail, Watauga Lake, and the Virginia Creeper Trail are within 15 miles, so Mountain City is an excellent choice if you prefer to spend your vacation in the great outdoors.

The Butler House Bed and Breakfast is a National Register of Historic Places property.

The Welcome Center is in a new log cabin on US 421. Inside you'll find information and a museum. Behind the Welcome Center facility is a campground with picnic area and full hook-ups that is open yearround.

Roan Valley Golf Estates and the Golf Course Restaurant are on your right as you continue on US 421 to Boone. You will pass through the former trading ground of the Indians and the Long Hunters in the little community of Trade just before you cross into North Carolina.

Shortly after entering North Carolina, US 421 merges with US 321 from Watauga Lake at the Clayhouse Restaurant.

At this point, you can proceed south on US 421 to Boone and Blowing Rock, which is near the Blue Ridge Parkway.

The following are Mountain City, TN 37683 and area code 423.

☙ ACCOMMODATIONS

The Butler House Bed and Breakfast—309 N. Church St. (Hwy 91); 727-4119
Creek Side Guest House—Rt. 4, Box 350; 727-6853; One unit on creek, private, golf course nearby.
Days Inn—Hwy. 421; 727-7311, 800-329-7466.
Roan Valley Golf Estates—Hwy 421S; 727-5756, 800-444-6615; 7 cabins.

☙ ATTRACTIONS

Johnson County Welcome Center and Museum—Hwy. 421 south of Mountain City; 727-5800; Yearround; Free.

❧ DINING

Roan Valley Golf Course Restaurant—Hwy. 421S; 727-5756, 800-444-6615.

❧ SHOPPING

Donnelly House and Antique Shop—TN 91; 777-9005.
Iron Mountain Stoneware—Rt. 1, Box 1, Laurel Bloomery, TN; 727-8888.

❧ CAMPING

Johnson County Welcome Center Campground—Hwy. 421, Mountain City, TN 37683; 423-727-5800.

❧ FOR MORE INFORMATION

Welcome Center and Museum—POB 1, Hwy. 421, Mountain City, TN 37683; 423-727-5800; Daily.
Appalachian Trail—POB 807, Harper's Ferry, WV 25425; 304-535-6331.
Cherokee National Forest—USDA Forest Service, Elizabethton, TN 37643; 542-2942.
TVA Dams—Watauga Lake; 542-2951.

❧ DIRECTIONS

Scenic TN 91 from Damascus, VA.
US 321 from Watauga Lake.
US 421S from Bristol, TN-VA.
US 421 North from Boone, NC, and the Blue Ridge Parkway at the Boone/ Blowing Rock Exit.

20 *Tennessee Outdoor Recreation*

Each of the states we write about seems to have one or two outstanding forms of recreation. Virginia has mountain trails for hiking, biking, and horses. Georgia has hiking and wilderness camping. North Carolina has more waterfalls, whitewater, and golf courses. Tennessee has countless campgrounds and outstanding fishing. Tennessee has more and larger rivers, one of the factors that kept the Blue Ridge Parkway from being routed through the state. The Tennessee River alone has more fish species than any other freshwater river in the world.

Just in case you would rather golf, camp, or hike, here are some relaxing and stimulating outdoor opportunities from which to choose.

The following are TN and area code 423 except where noted.

STATE PARKS

Davy Crockett Birthplace—1245 Davy Crockett Park Rd., Limestone, 37681; 257-2167; 66-acre historic park, swimming pool, Nolichucky River fishing, picnic, museum with videos and items, birthplace cabin, and 65 campsites.

Roan Mountain State Park—Rt. 1 Box 236, Roan Mountain, 37687; 800-421-6683, 772-3303; Cabins, camping, hiking, fishing, pool, tennis, playgrounds, visitor's center, museum, restaurant, picnic areas, and gift shops.

Fishing is great for trophy striper on Boone Lake in East Tennessee.

The Appalachian Trail passes through 3 East Tennessee counties on its 2,200-mile trek from Georgia to Maine.

Sycamore Shoals State Historic Park—1651 W. Elk Ave., Elizabethton, 37643; 543-5808; Museum, reconstruction of Fort Watauga, visitor's center, gift shop, picnic areas, canoes access, boat launching ramp, fishing, and hiking trail.

Warrior Path State Park—POB 5026, Kingsport, 37663; 239-8531; Snack bar, camp store, gift shop, picnic areas, canoe access, fishing, boat launching ramp, water skiing, boat rental marina, swimming, gold course, bike trails and rentals, tennis, playgrounds, nine miles of hiking trails, stables (rental), disc golf, and recreation center on shores of Ft. Patrick Henry Lake.

For more information contact Tennessee State Parks, 401 Church St., Nashville, 37243-0446; 800-421-6683.

✍ BIKING

Although biking is very popular, there are not many companies set up for guided touring or backwoods pedaling.

Cherokee Adventures—Rt. 1 Box 605, Erwin, 37650; 800-445-7238, 800-838-7238; (tri-cities area); Bike tours.

✍ CAMPING

There is no lack of camping sites in east Tennessee, especially around the GSMNP. This is by no means an exhaustive list but a good place to start. If you call a campground that is full, ask for names and phone numbers of nearby campgrounds that meet your requirements.

GSMNP has several campgrounds but some are closed due to lack of funding. To learn which campgrounds are open and secure maps, call 800-365-CAMP. Also look in the GSMNP section of this book.

Big Meadow Campground—8215 Cedar Creek Rd., Townsend, 37882; 448-0625; Ninety-six sites, hook-ups, dumping station, toilets, showers, fishing, swimming, and more.

Cherokee Adventures—Rt. 1 Box 605, Erwin, 37650; 800-445-7238, 800-838-7238; (tri-cities area); 20 sites, showers, toilets, fishing, and more.

Crazy Horse Campground & RV Resort—4609 E. Foothills Pkwy., Gatlinburg, 37738; 800-528-9003; Cabins, 207 sites, swimming pool, water slide, trout pond, laundry, store, recreation center, and more.

Fort Wear Campground—2630 Sequoia Rd., Pigeon Forge, 37863; 800-452-9835; 175 sites, hook-ups, dumping station, toilets, showers, laundry, store, fishing, and more.

Great Smoky Jellystone Resort—POB 282, Gatlinburg, 37738; 800-210-2119, 487-5534; 105 sites, laundry, store, hook-ups, dumping station, toilets, showers, pool, and more.

Lazy Daze Campground—8429 Hwy. 73, Townsend, 37882; 448-6061; 75 sites, hook-ups, dumping station, toilets, showers, fishing, game room, swimming pool, and more.

Little River Village Campground—8533 Hwy. 73, Townsend, 37782; 448-2241; 145 sites, hook-ups, dumping station, toilets, showers, fishing, swimming, store, and more.

Mill Creek Resort—449 Mill Creek Rd., Pigeon Forge, 37863; 428-3498; 74 sites, hook-ups, dumping station, toilets, showers, laundry, store, pool, and more.

Nolichucky Gorge Campground—Jones Branch Rd., Erwin, 37650; 743-8876.

Peaks of Rich Mountain Campground—736 Dry Valley, Townsend, 37782; 448-9567; 12 sites, hook-ups, dumping station, toilets, showers, and more.

Persimmon Ridge Campground—1521 Persimmon Ridge Rd., Jonesboro, 37659; 753-1555; 48 sites, hook-ups, dumping station, toilets, showers, swimming pool, and more.

Ripplin' Waters Campground—930 Winfield Dunn Pkwy., Sevierville, 37876, 453-4169; 155 sites, hook-ups, dumping station, toilets, showers, swimming pool, fishing, and more.

Riverbend Campground—2479 Riverbend Rd., Pigeon Forge, 37863; 800-477-1205, 453-1224; 100 sites, hook-ups, dumping station, toilets, showers, fishing, and more.

Riverside Campground & Resort—4280 Boyds Creek Hwy., Sevierville, 37876; 800-341-7534, 453-7299; 150 sites, hook-ups, dumping station, toilets, showers, fishing, store, pool, and more.

Riverview Campground—213 Webb Rd., Townsend, 37782; 448-6800; 71 sites, hook-ups, dumping station, toilets, showers, fishing, swimming, and more.

Roan Mountain State Park—Rt. 1 Box 236, Roan Mountain, 37687; 800-421-6683, 772-3303; 107 sites, hook-ups, dumping station, toilets, showers, fishing game area, restaurant, and more.

Rocky Top Campground—469 Pearl Ln., Blountville, 37617; 800-452-6456; 42 sites, full hook-ups, store, antiques, laundry cabins with TV, and full baths.

Shady Oaks Campground—210 Conner Hgts. Rd., Pigeon Forge, 37863; 453-3276; 100 sites, hook-ups, dumping station, toilets, showers, swimming pool, fishing, and more.

Tremont Hill Campground—POB 5, Townsend, 37882; 448-6363; 145 sites, hook-ups, dumping station, toilets, showers, fishing, store, swimming, and more.

Tuckaleechee Campground & Horse Camp—7259 Alexander Pkwy., 37782; 448-9608; 65 RV sites, 50 tent sites, hook-ups, dumping station, toilets, showers, fishing, swimming, and more.

Twin Creek RV Resort—114 Low Gap Rd., Gatlinburg, 37783; 800-252-8077, 436-7081; 75 sites, hook-ups, dumping station, toilets, showers, fishing, store, swimming pool, and more.

USDA Forest Service—Rock Creek Park, Rock Creek Rd., Erwin, 37650; 743-4452; 37 sites, full hook-ups, dumping station, toilets, showers, fishing, swimming pool, and more.

"Z" Buda's Smokies Campground—4020 Parkway, Pigeon Forge, 37863; 453-4129; 300 sites, full hook-ups, dumping station, toilets, showers, swimming pool and more.

✍ CANOEING/RAFTING

Let's get on some of east Tennessee's bumpy water. In mid-March we were driving down I-40 on the east side of the Smoky Mountains headed toward the North Carolina border. Interstate 40 runs parallel to the Big Pigeon River and you can look into the gorge to see it flowing.

From the elevation of the highway the white caps look gentle and the river serene. In fact, all the scenery is gorgeous. Our destination was Smoky Mountain Outdoors Unlimited in Hartford where we planned to cruise down the Big Pigeon with Daniel Jennette. Jennette began his whitewater rafting company in 1993 after spending nine years working with other rafting companies.

Let us set the rafting scene for you. Late winter dumped lots of snow and cold weather on east Tennessee. The Pigeon River walls were dripping with icicles and patches of snow. The water temperature was a chilly 45 degrees. Standing at the launch site, we saw the current was swifter and much stronger than it appeared from the highway about 500 feet above.

Bedecked in wet suits that felt like garbage compactors compressing our lungs, we were ready to launch. The discomfort of the wet suits disappeared the instant we hit the water. We had something far more important to worry about than breathing.

It's hard to imagine an adult with a sane mind getting into frigid water on purpose, yet there we went. All of us committed to ride 6½ miles downstream back to headquarters.

Remember the gentle white-capped rapids? At least the white was right. Those waves went up and down like a washboard of tidal waves six feet tall—not small, not gentle. We bucked and bounced for well over an hour.

Here is what you can expect when rafting over those 6 miles; 43 Class I and II rapids, 14 Class IIIs, and 4 Class IVs. The Class IV rapids are named Powerhouse, Lost Guide (but they teased us by calling it Lost Guest), Double Reaction, and Accelerator.

Jennette said when the water was 15 feet higher than normal, he made the 6½-mile trip in 17 minutes. During normal operation for guests, the trip takes more than two hours, allowing time for swimming and surfing.

Until you experience a raft ride, you don't appreciate the skill it takes to maneuver one. All of Jennette's guides are required to make 40 training trips. It is important to your safety that your guide learns the river and how to get through the torrents successfully.

There are bad places to turn over and there are good ones. Jennette's guides stop to let guests swim and surf in the safe areas. Surfing involves getting the raft on top of a standing wave. You stay still while the water rushes under you.

If you're looking for a place to have fun away from the crowds of Gatlinburg, try Smoky Mountain Outdoors Unlimited, only 30 minutes from Gatlinburg. They also offer lower Pigeon River trips for a less rambunctious float and a full-day trip (lunch included) down the French Broad River on Sundays for a more leisurely pace.

In addition to rafting, Smoky Mountain Outdoors Unlimited offers guided fly- and spin-fishing for trout, and hiking (day trips and overnight trips), rope courses, horseback riding, canoeing, kayaking, and team building. Camping is available at headquarters. Smoky Mountain Outdoors Unlimited, 3299 Hartford Rd., Hartford, TN 37753; 800-771-7238. Call for reservations, directions, and brochure.

B-Cliff Whitewater Rafting—Rt. 1, Box 2335, Elizabethton, 37643; 423-542-2262. Watauga River.
Big Pigeon Rafting—POB 49, Hartford, 37753; 800-GET-WWET; Raft 5 miles of the Big Pigeon.

Whitewater rafting offers thrills on the Big Pigeon River at Hartford.

Cherokee Adventures—Rt I Box 605, Erwin, 37650; 800-445-7238, 800-838-7238; (tri-cities area); Watauga, Nolichucky, Pigeon, and French Broad Rivers.

Rip Roaring Adventures—800-449-RAFT; Rafting in the Smokies, canoeing, and camping.

Rapid Descent River Co.—POB 89, Hartford, 37752; 800-455-8808; Pigeon River rafting.

Smoky Mountain Outdoors Unlimited—3299 Hartford Rd., Hartford, 37753; 800-771-7238; Rafting the Big Pigeon and French Broad Rivers.

Smoky Mountain River Co.—Hartford Rd., Hartford, 37753; 800-238-6925, 423-487-3971.

Wahoos Adventures—800-444-RAFT. Rafting Ocoee, Pigeon, and Nolichucky Rivers; Canoeing, cabins, and camping.

The Whitewater Company—3485 Hartford Rd., Hartford, 37753; 800-RAFT-H20; Trips on the upper and lower Pigeon River.

➢ FISHING

Boone, Ft. Patrick Henry, South Holston, and Watauga Lakes are in the most northeastern corner of the state. These have smallmouth bass, largemouth bass, crappie, trout, catfish, white bass, walleye, and bream.

Fishing in the lakes for most species is best from February into June, then from October into December. Trout and walleye fishing are best from November until April in the tailwaters.

Boone and Ft. Patrick Henry have striped bass (also called stripers or rockfish) and the hybrid (striper X white bass). These fish grow to 60 and 20 pounds, respectively. Fishing in the headwaters and tailwaters is best from June through August for these fish. Guide Tom Richards has caught 13 freshwater stripers over 50 pounds from Boone and Ft. Patrick Henry. Tom Richards, 1512 Lawrence St., Kingsport, 37660; 246-7628. Tom guides for stripers, hybrids, trout, largemouth bass, and smallmouth bass.

Nolichucky River is one of the best smallmouth streams in Tennessee. The area near Greeneville has floatable and wadeable waters. A small jig (1/16- or 1/8-ounce) with a plastic curlytail grub works well when cast upstream of shoals and retrieved just fast enough to keep the jig from hanging in the rocks.

Other streams popular with anglers are Big Pigeon, French Broad, Hiwassee, Holston (see VA Outdoors section), and Ocoee Rivers.

Boone Lake is home of the Tennessee state record hybrid, about 3 times the size of this 7-pounder.

Douglas Lake, northeast of Sevierville, is best known for crappie. It also has largemouth bass, catfish, and bream. You may find some sauger and white bass in the headwaters during the cold months. Ted Kramer guides on Douglas for crappie, 587-4931.

The following companies guide for trout.

Old Smoky Outfitters—511 Pkwy., Gatlinburg; 423-430-1936.
Smoky Mountain Outdoors Unlimited—3299 Hartford Rd., Hartford, 37753; 800-771-RAFT (7238); Fly- and spin-fishing for trout in the Smokies, Tennessee, and North Carolina.

For more information contact:

Tennessee Angler Magazine—5550 Boy Scout Rd. Franklin, TN 37064; 615-790-0487.
TroutSouth—POB 344, Andersonville, TN 37705; 494-6235.

✍ GOLF

Andrew Johnson Golf Course—615 Lick Hollow, Greeneville, 37743; 800-421-2149, 636-1476; 18 holes
Bent Creek Golf Resort—3919 E. Parkway, Gatlinburg, 37738; 436-3947; 18 holes.
Buffalo Valley Golf Club—90 Country Club Rd., Erwin, 37650; 800-882-0096, 928-1022; 18 holes.
Eagle's Landing Golf Course—1556 Old Knoxville Hwy., Sevierville, 37876; 429-4223; 18 holes
Elizabethton Municipal Golf Course—Golf Club Rd., Elizabethton, 37744; 542-8051.
Gatlinburg Country Club—520 Dollywood Ln., Gatlinburg, 37738; 453-3712; 18 holes.
Graysburg Hills Golf Course—910 Graysburg Hills Rd., Greeneville, 37743; 234-8061; 27 holes.
Holston Valley Golf Course—300 Golf Course Rd., Bristol, 37620; 878-2120; 18 holes.
Kinser Park Golf Course—780 Kinser Park Ln., Greeneville, 37743; 639-6406; 9 holes.
Lambert Acres Golf Club—3402 Tuckaleechee Pk., Maryville, 37801; 982-9838; 27 holes.

Nolichucky Golf Course—5297 Asheville Hwy., Greeneville, 37743; 639-1622; 9 holes.

River Islands Golf Club—9610 Kodak Rd., Sevierville, 37862; 800-34RIVER, 933-0100; 18 holes.

Roan Valley Golf Estates—POB 138, Mountain City, 37683; 800-444-6615, 727-7931; 18-hole championship course.

Steele Creek—20 Little Ln.., Bristol, 37620; 764-6411; 9 holes.

Tri-Cities Golf Club—2354 State St., Bristol, 37620; 323-4178.

Warrior's Path State Park—POB 5026, Kingsport, 37663; 423-239-8531, 800-421-6683; 18 holes.

✴ HORSEBACK

All commercial stables and guided horse rides are around the GSMNP. They range from a few hours on the trail to several days and nights out. If you haven't ridden a horse in a while, be kind to yourself. Start out with just a couple of hours in the saddle. Riding a horse for too long can put a pain where you don't want it.

Cades Cove Riding Stables—4035 Alexander Pkwy., Walland, 37886; 448-6286; Guided horseback and carriage rides through foothills; Hayrides in Cades Cove.

Cedar Ridge Riding Stables—Hwy. 441, Sevierville, 37862; 428-5802; Guided trail rides.

Davy Crockett Riding Stables—820 Caverns Rd., Townsend, 37882; 448-6411; Guided trails in Smokies; Horse boarding.

Double M Ranch—4033 Miser Station Rd., Townsend, 37882; 995-9421, 995-2972; Horse riding in Smoky foothills; Hiking, biking, and fishing.

Douglas Lake View Riding Stables—1650 Providence Rd., Sevierville, 37862; 428-3587; Guided rides, horseback swim ride, moonlight rides, and overnight camping.

Gannon's French Broad Outpost Ranch—Del Rio, 37821; 800-995-POST; Gannon offers a Riverside Ride (scenic, easy, 1½ hour ride), Ridge Ride (more difficult, better views on this 2½ hour ride), and an Overnight Package (two days and two nights).

McCarter's Riding Stables—Hwy. 441 S., Gatlinburg, 37738; 436-5354; Guided mountain rides in the park.

Twin Valley B&B Horse Ranch—2848 Chilhowee Rd., Walland, 37886; 800-872-2235, 984-0980; Mountain rides (your horse or theirs).

Tuckaleechee Campground & Horse Camp—7259 Alexander Pkwy., Townsend,
37782; 448-9608; 65 RV sites, 50 tent sites, hook-ups, dumping station, toilets, showers, fishing, swimming, and more.

Walden's Creek Horseback Riding Stables—2709 Walden Creek Rd., Sevierville,
37862; 429-0411; 500 acres of riding in valleys, mountains, and streams.

Willowbridge Farm—2920 Jones Coor Rd., Sevierville, 37862; 453-2257;
Unguided and guided horse trails in Smokies foothills.

〰 HIKING/NATURE TRAILS

If you are an inexperienced hiker, it's appropriate to learn from someone who can teach the things you need to know. Do you know why and how to apply mole skin? Are your hiking boots broken in? Do you know how to read a map? Do you know what to do if confronted by a bear? These are a few of the simple things. We learned the hard way that there are many facets to a safe hike.

Chances are if you are hiking a popular trail in the Smokies and need help, someone will come along within 24 to 48 hours. Each year we hear about people lost in the mountains with varying outcomes. The point is be prepared, have a plan, and leave your itinerary with someone.

The following are experienced hiking guides and are worth the investment for future hikes. While you are with them, ask lots of questions.

The Happy Hiker—Burning Bush Plz., Gatlinburg; 436-6000, 800-HIKER01.

High Country Adventures—Rt. 1, Box 412, Ocoee, 37361; 800-233-8594;
Hiking, cabins, camping, and more.

Old Smoky Outfitters—511 Pkwy., Gatlinburg; 423-430-1936.

Smoky Mountain Outdoors Unlimited—3299 Hartford Rd., Hartford, 37753;
800-771-RAFT (7238); Day or overnight trips into the Smokies, Pisgah National Forest, or Cherokee National Forest.

You will find other outdoor information in many of the Tennessee sections.

Hiking the Appalachian Trail offers many spectacular views, but few can rival this vista from Max Patch, near Hartford, Tennessee.

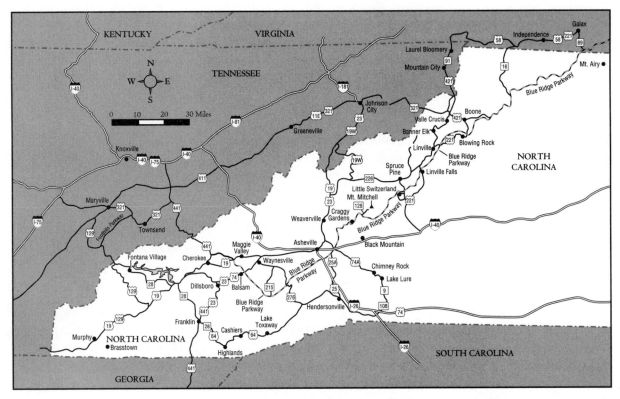

NORTH CAROLINA

North Carolina

North Carolina

North Carolina contains the largest area of the Southern Highlands. We like to arrange the sections so you complete a loop, but that isn't conveniently done where there is so much area to cover and so many mountains to climb. So we've divided North Carolina into one loop tour and one somewhat linear trek. The "somewhat linear" tour zigzags along the Blue Ridge Parkway from Cherokee to the North Carolina-Virginia border.

The Highlands of North Carolina are in the western portion of the state. Our loop tour begins in the northwest at Fontana Dam and Lake. Next we go southwest to Franklin and Highlands, then northeast to Cashiers, east to Hendersonville, northwest to Waynesville and Maggie Valley, then southwest to Dillsboro. From Dillsboro you are less than a leisurely two-hour drive back to Fontana.

You may have noticed that we did not include Asheville in the loop tour, which we should have, but we saved it because it is on the edge of the Parkway. If you are only exploring the loop tour, we suggest you flip to the Asheville section after you've visited Hendersonville, in order to include it.

Our Blue Ridge tour starts at the southern terminus in Cherokee. First there is a section about the Parkway's history and some of the highlights along it. From Cherokee we go to Balsam, then Asheville. We take a side trip north to Weaverville, then a scenic back road up a mountain to the Parkway. Then it's on to the higher Highlands; Little Switzerland, Spruce Pine, Linville, Banner Elk, and Valle Crucis. Our last two Highlands destinations are Boone and the "Crown Jewel of the Blue Ridge Mountains," Blowing Rock.

As part of our serendipity in researching this book, we discovered Mt. Airy, which did not appear on our original list of places to visit. It's our last stop just off the Parkway near the Virginia Border. Mt. Airy is downhill from the Highlands and Fancy Gap, Virginia, on US 52. Antiques shops and fruit stands led us astray from the mountains into the home of Andy Griffith.

The final North Carolina section gives you a taste of the outdoor activities available. North Carolina is waterfall country. Some are along the roadside and many require a hike. Hiking seems to be the favorite pastime in western North Carolina.

We've included many sources for maps and detailed information about certain areas such as the national forests, hiking trails, horse trails, and much more. There is a lot to do here, and we hope you enjoy your exploration of North Carolina's Highlands.

We regret we had to omit so many interesting and extraordinary towns, attractions, and, especially, foods. We hope you will explore some of these omissions yourself. After all, your serendipitous discoveries will be all the more exciting.

This bronze statue of a young girl drinking water is just one of many items around Pack Square reflecting Asheville's historical and cultural elements.

21 *Fontana:*

Best Kept Secret in the Smokies

As noted at the end of this section, there are many ways to reach Fontana Dam, North Carolina. We came from Middle Tennessee via I-40, turned onto US 321 at exit 364 about 15 miles west of Knoxville, crossed Fort Loudoun Dam, and went through Maryville to Walland, where we got on the Western Foothills Parkway.

The scenic Foothills Parkway parallels the northwestern boundary of the Great Smoky Mountains National Park (GSMNP). It remains incomplete at this writing, but 23.1 miles of the proposed 72 miles have been completed since construction began on February 9, 1960. The section we traveled extends 16.6 miles from Highway 321 at Walland, Tennessee, to Highway 129 at Chilhowie Lake.

Scenic vistas greet you along the top of Chilhowie Mountain. The best known is the Look Rock, which purports to have a vista reaching to the Cumberland Mountains in Middle Tennessee on a clear day. There is a tower a short walk from the Look Rock Campground. Part of the GSMNP, this rustic camp has 92 tent and RV sites with picnic tables, flush toilets, and cold running water. This campground almost always has spaces available—the busiest times are the Fourth of July and fall foliage weekends.

Turning east on Highway 129, we passed Calderwood Lake and, before we reached the junction of NC 28, we took 316 curves in 11 miles on what is believed to be the curviest road in the world. (I know *we* believe it.)

You're looking from the top of Fontana Dam, the highest in the eastern United States, at the Little Tennessee River as it exits the turbines 480 feet below.

Making our way along this zigzagging stretch, known as "the Dragon," our supply of adrenaline was depleted—not from the curves, but from the motorcyclists who were buzzing by us like jet-powered mosquitoes.

We were passed on curves and hills like we were motionless, and by comparison we were. Cyclists dressed in expensive looking racing garb on high-performance cycles were testing their machines—and themselves—on the hills and curves. We saw a cyclist standing at the apex of a sharp curve videotaping other cyclists zooming down the hill, then around a tight turn. We later learned that "the Dragon" claims about six lives a year. At those speeds the chance of a simple maiming doesn't seem likely. To be fair, some cyclists, albeit few, cruised at safe speeds.

Aside from the aggravation from speeding cyclists, the drive is stunning. There are pull-offs for viewing, picnicking, and fishing.

At the junction where US 129 meets NC 28 is a campground for motorcyclists only. We turned east on NC 28 and enjoyed a peaceful, scenic drive to Fontana Lake and Dam.

Fontana Dam is the highest dam in the eastern United States, 480 feet high, and the eighth highest in the world. On January 1, 1942, construction began on the dam less than a month after the bombing of Pearl Harbor to provide critically needed hydroelectric power.

Virtually overnight, Fontana became a village with a school, hospital, and churches. Twenty-four hours a day, seven days a week, workmen excavated, drilled, formed, and poured 2.8 million cubic yards of concrete until 1944, when the first water was released to fill the lake. The first electricity was wired to a secret location in the community of Oak Ridge. Slowly at first, the lake began to attract vacationers, anglers, and boaters. The village became the nucleus of cottages and service centers that today is Fontana Village Resort.

The resort is now a major attraction in the southern Highlands. Its close proximity to many other attractions, including Joyce Kilmer Memorial Forest, excursions on the Great Smoky Railway, whitewater rafting, guided tours of the dam, and to nearby cities of Bryson City, Cherokee, Dillsboro, Franklin, Maggie Valley, Waynesville, and Gatlinburg, make it an ideal vacation spot. Fontana is

Fontana Dam's observation building extends from the eighth tallest dam in the world.

This pool surrounded by rooms is just a small part of the large Fontana Village Resort.

within a few hours of Knoxville, Atlanta, Charlotte, Birmingham, Chattanooga, and Nashville.

Fontana Village Resort is a one-stop destination. You have a choice of places to stay, including the resort's inn, cottages, houseboats, or campgrounds.

A variety of foods is available from the cafeteria, including pizza and snacks, and fine dining is served in the inn. You can prepare your own meals in your cottage.

The village is in a "dry" county. Bring your own or drive 35 miles to Bryson City for alcohol. The general stores will supply your basic grocery needs.

Geri Mendillo, with Fontana Village Resort, took us on tour of the inn, restaurants, and cottages. Some of the cottages are original to the village of dam workers, and most have been renovated.

All cottages offer kitchenettes with stoves and refrigerators. The cottages range from moderately furnished, featuring 1950s furnishings and atmosphere, to luxury cabins with central heat and air, two baths, TV/VCR, modern appliances, fireplace, and Jacuzzi.

There are swimming pools, craft classes, trout pond, mountain bike trail, horseback riding, tennis, hiking, museum, fitness center with classes, along with many other facilities and recreation opportunities. It would take weeks for you do every thing Fontana Village has to offer.

The Appalachian Trail crosses over Fontana Dam. You may prefer to walk some of the other trails off NC 28 or off the dam road. There is an incline tram you can take from the Visitor's Center on the dam down to the powerhouse.

Hollywood has also discovered Fontana. Part of the movie *Nell* was filmed on Fontana Lake. Nell's cabin can be seen by taking the Nell Tour. You will hear about how the site was selected and learn about moviemaking at this remote location.

Fontana Village Resort—Hwy. 28, Box 68, Fontana Dam, NC 28733; 800-849-2258, 704-498-2211.

✎ DIRECTIONS

Atlanta—North on US 19, turn northwest (left) on NC 28 to the resort.

Knoxville—South on US 129 to Maryville, southwest on US 411, south on US 129, northeast on NC 28 to the resort.

Chattanooga—Northeast on I-75 to Sweetwater, turn east on TN 68, turn northeast on US 411, turn south on US 129, northeast on NC State Route 28 to the resort.

Charlotte—West on I-85, northwest on US 74 to Blue Ridge Parkway near Asheville, BRP to Cherokee, NC, southwest on US 19, turn northwest (right) on NC 28 to the resort.

Columbia—North on US 26 to BRP near Asheville, BRP to Cherokee, NC, southwest on US 19, turn northwest (right) on NC 28 to the resort.

Winston-Salem—West on I-40 to BRP near Asheville, BRP to Cherokee, NC, southwest on US 19, turn northwest (right) on NC 28 to the resort.

22 *Franklin:*
Where the Beauty Never Ends

Franklin lies among the gorgeous foothills of the Smokies between Atlanta and Asheville. It is a special place for you do to some sightseeing and gem mining.

Our favorite route for reaching Franklin from Fontana involves traveling east on NC 28 past the Tsali Campground, turning left on US 74, and continuing to Needmore Road. The road sign is small, but if you look for an auction building on your right you should be able to find the turn without much trouble. It's well worth the effort. Needmore is paved most of the way, but there is a 3-mile section that is still gravel. Its chief attraction is that it runs along side the Little Tennessee River with frequent pull-offs used for camping, fishing, and picnicking. We have seen families camping in the wide area between the road and the river. These unmanaged primitive sites for tents looked like a great place to enjoy the woods and river. There are several swinging bridges spanning the Little Tennessee where you can see anglers fly-fishing and swimmers frolicking in the shallows.

This road is a charmer, and we fervently hope it remains unchanged for the enjoyment of future travelers and nature enthusiasts. We heard there were plans to widen the road. "Improving" the road would damage its appeal. The road isn't one on which you can make up time, but one where you can delight in your time spent traveling.

Turn left at Tellico Road and left across the bridge on Carnes. Your final turn will be a right onto Bryson City Road (NC 28) to Franklin.

Author Cathy Summerlin ventures across a swinging bridge that spans the Little Tennessee River on Needmore Road between Franklin and Fontana.

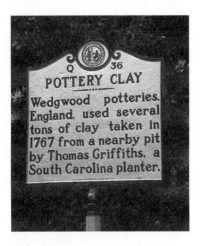

This marker across the road from Cowee Creek Pottery also lets you know you are close to Snow Hill Inn.

Cowee Creek Pottery, north of Franklin, specializes in artistic and functional pottery. The shop is a pleasant place to browse.

Needmore Road joins NC 28 north of Franklin. If you are coming in from that direction, when you see the historic marker "Pottery Clay," that reads "Wedgwood potteries, England, used several tons of clay taken in 1767 from a nearby pit by Thomas Griffiths, a South Carolina planter," you are near two places you should visit.

From Franklin, go north 8 miles on NC 28 to reach the same historic marker across the road from Cowee Creek Pottery, your first stop. Jonathan Deeks and Jennifer Phillips have had their shop in the historic old West Mill Store since 1986. You will find a wide variety of pottery in the studio, and three black cats that take their siestas on the drying racks. There are functional pieces, like lovely and serviceable berry bowls, and unusual and imaginative decorative pieces—something for most needs and tastes.

Cowee Creek runs next to the pottery studio, parallel to West Mills Road. Take this short road to the junction and turn left on Snow Hill Road. Up this road on the right is one of our favorite bed and breakfasts.

Sitting on the apex of a hill is the spacious Snow Hill Inn, owned by George and Rita Sivess. The two-story home doesn't look like a former schoolhouse, but it was built as one in 1914.

An old photo downstairs reveals a much more academic structure prior to the addition of the porch by the WPA in the 1930s. One of the desks from the school sits by the front door, and the carved initials of students of long ago are visible on the walls of one of the upstairs rooms.

This graceful old building has taken on new life under the watchful eyes of its owners. George and Rita were living in Knoxville where George was the operations manager for Kimberly Clark. Who can blame them for deciding to stay in the southern Highlands area rather than moving every two to three years as George's job required? It seems quite fitting that they came home to Snow Hill after traveling the United States, because Rita's grandfather helped build the school and her father learned the three R's within its walls.

Innkeeping seems to suit them quite well, as they'll happily share their love of the area and their appreciation for the inn and its history with their guests. They provide lots of attention to details that insure the comfort of visitors not the least of which are snacks at your bedside, beverages in the hallway refrigerator, and nightly desserts served at nine. Indulge yourself in the likes of decadent fudge pie or delicious butterscotch cake.

Breakfast is served from 8:30 to 10:00 A.M., generally. Rita bakes and George whips up the omelets while guests enjoy the early morning mists kissing the North Carolina mountains outside the glass-enclosed dining room.

George and Rita Sivess are innkeepers at Snow Hill Inn. Rita's grandfather built a schoolhouse in 1914 that now, after remodeling, offers travelers excellent accommodations and dining.

The two large downstairs rooms have 12-foot ceilings. All rooms have private baths and large windows looking over the rolling hills. Upstairs are four more rooms, including one suite that runs the entire length of the house on one side for special occasions. The old school's kitchen still serves as the kitchen today, with all modern amenities added for Chef George's convenience.

Guests are invited to enjoy their collection of regional books. Be sure to ask George about his collection of Indian points from the Franklin area, as well the location of the ancient fish trap nearby.

When you get back on NC 28 heading south toward Franklin, you'll see Mason Mountain Mine on your left. The mineral-rich Cowee Valley area has been exploited by companies like Tiffany's. Franklin has 13 gem mines where you can buy dirt to try sifting for rubies, sapphires, garnets, rhodolites, moonstones, and many other gems. Some of the mines guarantee you'll find a ruby. You can pan and sift for your own gems from native soil, or from native plus "imported" soils intended to enrich your find.

Most of the gem mines are north of Franklin; there are five on Cowee Creek Road alone. Gem hunting should be viewed as entertainment. Some people visit "their" mine several times a year as a hobby. There is one company that lets you pay to dig your own mine. You never know when you might get lucky, but the consensus is the best the area had to offer was taken years ago. However, there continue to be a few valuable finds.

In 1963 a rare translucent ruby was found, which weighed 163 carats uncut. A 1½-pound blue sapphire was found at the Mason

Mary Carriker examines a gem that she discovered on her annual birthday trip to Mason Mine from her home in Georgia. This trip to "her" mine was on her ninety-fourth birthday.

Mine. It brought the "miner" $30,000. Richard Peek at Mason Mountain Mine said he and his staff take dirt from up the mountain on the property for their operation. They don't do any commercial mining until they find a rich spot.

While we visited with Richard Peek, Wendell and Quentin Carriker arrived to get mining gear and some dirt for their mother. Mary Carriker was there to celebrate her ninety-fourth birthday. She looked at least 20 years younger to us. She was a delight to talk with, bragging about her five sons, two of whom brought her to "work" in the mine each year from her home in Cairo, Georgia. She started coming here when she was 90.

If you want to become a miner, here are a few tips: Go prepared to get dirty, and take along a towel, something padded to sit on, insect repellent, and sunscreen. Prices vary from 50 cents a bucket to $50 ($5 to $10 average range) and some mines charge an admission fee.

You can see an ancient fish trap in the Little Tennessee River across the road from the entrance to Mason Mountain Mine. Look for a "V" made of rocks. Indians chased the fish into the head of the V while others held baskets at the narrow end to collect the fish.

As you approach Franklin on Highway 28 you'll see the Blaine House Bed and Breakfast on your left. The Sunset Restaurant on your right is a good choice for country-style cooking. Stay on Highway 28 through town to visit the Visitor's Center on Porter Street.

In addition to an appealing assortment of shops and public gardens, Main Street is home to the Macon County Historical Museum in the 1904 J.R. Pendergrass Building. Here you will see examples of vintage clothing, tools, books including a Bible written in Cherokee, weavings, and quilts. Visitors will also learn that tourism began in the area in the late 1820s when wealthy South Carolina planters traveled north to escape the heat. Gifts are available for purchase as well, ranging from jewelry to books and tee shirts.

The Tartan Museum gives visitors a chance to learn about their heritage should they be descendants of one of the many Scots who settled the southern Highlands. Docent Charlie Rhodarmer explained the evolution of the Tartan plaids.

Franklin's Tartan Museum offers Scottish descendants an opportunity to research their family tartans.

As early as the 1690s it was written that you "could tell from whence a man came by the colors he wore." This was most likely due to the variations in color achieved with plants that were available for natural dyes in any given locality. Within a locality, a weaver who devised a particularly popular Tartan plaid color scheme might find the design subtly changed by another weaver.

Some families trace their Tartan to an ancestral portrait with a particular Tartan depicted that may in fact have been only a favorite color scheme of the wearer or a special gift. In short, there is no way to canonize the Tartans, but many of us enjoy trying to find this link with our ancestors. This museum is the only one of its kind in the United States and it is a good place to begin your search for your family Tartan.

The Old Jail Museum is open on weekends and is filled with gems and information about mining in North Carolina. It is behind Memorial Park, which honors the county's service men and women.

The gazebo is the site of Picking on the Square each Saturday night during summer.

The Frog and Owl is a great spot for lunch or dinner. We had Caesar salad with salmon and a slice of pecan tart with caramel whipped cream and vanilla sauce that was so tasty Vern had to sit on his hands to keep from licking the plate.

This old loom shows how tartan patterns were woven.

The Rev. Henry Burton took time out from busily greeting guests to explain to us that owner Geri Royal was a broad jumper in high school and her pals called her "Frog." Her first restaurant had a family of owls in the tree outside so the name evolved and stuck! By any name, the food is delicious.

Lucio's Italian Restaurant has appetizers like escargot and stuffed artichoke hearts, pastas including spaghetti, linguine, fettucine, manicotti, penne, and tortellini along with chicken, veal, and seafood.

As you're leaving Franklin, you can see many natural wonders. You will find details in the North Carolina Outdoor Recreation section and at the beginning of the section on Highlands, North Carolina, which is next on our list while traveling the southern Highlands along US 64.

The following are Franklin, NC 28734 and area code 704.

✐ ACCOMMODATIONS

Blaine House B&B—611 Harrison Ave.; 349-4230; 3 rooms and breakfast.
Buttonwood Inn—50 Admiral Dr.; 369-8985; 4 rooms and breakfast; March to December.
The Franklin Terrace—67 Harrison Ave.; 800-633-2431, 524-9707; 1 cottage, 9 rooms, Breakfast; April to November.
Heritage Inn B&B—101 Heritage Hollow; 524-4150; 6 bedrooms, private baths and entrance; Queen beds; Full breakfast; Evening desserts.
Snow Hill Inn—45 Snow Hill Rd.; 369-2100; 8 rooms, Private baths; Breakfast.
The Summit Inn—125 E, Rogers St.; 524-2006; 13 rooms; Breakfast.

✐ ATTRACTIONS

Franklin Gem & Mineral Museum—In the old jail on the square; 369-7831; Open weekends; Free admission.
Macon Country Historical Museum—36 W. Main St.; 524-9758; Closed January; Free admission.
Mason Mountain Mine—895 Bryson City Rd; 524-4570.

Perry's Water Gardens—Off Cowee Creek Rd. beyond Snow Hill Rd.; 524-3264; 13 acres of sunken gardens of lotus plants (large enough to support a child), largest aquatic nursery in United States, exotic fish, and much more; Free admission.

Scottish Tartans Museum—33 E. Main St.; 524-7472; History of kilt and weaving of the Tartan, as well as influence of the Scots on Appalachian and Cherokee culture and North Carolina.

Wayah Bald—Drive east from Franklin on US 64 W. for about 5 miles to Mount Hope Baptist Church, then turn right onto Loafer's Glory, then left on SR 1310 (Wayah Road). At Wayah Gap take the side road to the right; it leads to the top of Wayah Bald and the lookout tower.

✒ DINING

Courthouse Plaza—15 Courthouse Plaza; 524-5885; Breakfast and lunch.

Hickory Ranch Restaurant—126 Palmer St.; 369-9909; Lunch and dinner.

Mountain Vittles—103 Highlands Rd.; 524-9980; Breakfast, lunch, and dinner.

Summit Inn—125 E. Rogers St.; 524-2006; Dinner.

Sunset Restaurant—214 Harrison Ave.; 524-4842; Breakfast, lunch, and dinner.

✒ SHOPPING

Bachelor's End—1646 Bryson City Rd.; 524-4883.

Books Unlimited—372 Westgate; 369-7942.

Cowee Creek Pottery—20 W. Mills Rd; 524-3324.

Franklin Flea and Craft Market—199 Highlands Rd.; 524-6658.

Friendly Village Antique Mall—85 Palmer St. 524-8200.

Pieces From the Past—30 E. Main St.; 524-0814.

Quinlan Estate Antiques—161 Highlands Rd.; 524-0096.

Spirit Interiors Antique Shop—2794 Georgia Rd.; 524-0418.

✒ SPECIAL EVENTS

May—*Mountain Artisans May Fair and Craft Show; 524-3405*

June through October—*Picking on the Square (music on the downtown square every Saturday night)*

June—*Blue Ridge Gospel Weekend; 524-7799*

July—*Annual Macon County Gemboree; 524-3161*
August—*Franklin's Foot Stompin' Festival; 524-3161*
August—*Scottish Heritage Week; 524-7472*
October—*Annual Leaf Lookers Gemboree; 524-3161*

﹏ CAMPING

The following are Franklin, NC 28734 and area code 704.

Cullasaja River Campgrounds—6269 Highlands Rd.; 800-843-2795, 524-2559; 64 trailer sites with hookups, 30 tent sites, showers, toilets, camp store.
Downtown RV Park—160 Palmer St.; 369-2125; 11 trailer sites with hookups, showers, toilets; April to October.
Kountry Kampground—2887 Georgia Hwy.; 524-4339; 77 trailer sites with hookups, 10 tent sites, showers, toilets; April to October.
Mi Mtn. Campground—29 Kirkland Rd.; 524-6155; 32 trailer sites with hookups, 15 tent sites, showers, toilets, camp store.
Morrison Campground—29 Bates Branch Rd.; 524-4783; 15 trailer sites with hookups, 4 tent sites, showers, toilets.
Rainbow Spring Campground—7984 Old Murphy Rd.; 800-524-8293, 524-6376; 35 trailer sites with hookups, 11 tent sites, showers, toilets, camp store.
Rose Creek Mine & Campground—115 Terrace Ridge Dr.; 524-3225; 28 trailer sites with hookups, 4 tent sites, showers, toilets, camp store.

﹏ FOR MORE INFORMATION

Franklin Area Chamber of Commerce—425 Porter St., Franklin, NC 28734; 800-336-7829, 704-524-3161; Be sure to get the *Walking Tours* brochure.
Smoky Mountain Host of North Carolina—4437 Georgia Hwy., Franklin, NC 28734; 800-432 HOST.

﹏ DIRECTIONS

Franklin is at the junction of US 64 and US 23/441 in Macon County.

23 *Highlands:*
High Altitude and Attitude

"We discourage bus tours—it's too dangerous," is what we were told by the Highlands Chamber of Commerce. The community rests on a large, flat mountain top at 4,118 feet above sea level. The Cherokee called the Highlands plateau "Hills of the Sky." Today you have to drive the ever-climbing meanders of asphalt to get there regardless of your starting point. Despite the adventuresome mountainous roads, Highlands was voted as one of the top-three mountain getaways by readers of *Southern Living* magazine.

As we drove from Franklin up US 64, there were many scenes we would have liked to photograph, but the narrow roads and traffic prevented this. On a few occasions we would turn around, go back to the spot, and try to catch a break in traffic to snap a picture. This technique failed more often than not.

The magnificent Lower Cullasaja Falls plunges 250 feet into the gorge, but there is only room for about six vehicles to park along the highway, and the lack of space causes traffic jams. We "circled" the parking area until we were able to get in and take photos. The drivers seemed very tolerant of "gawkers," probably because they were, like us, waiting their turn.

The next falls upstream has a large parking lot, which is usually full during the summer. The stream of visitors walking up and down the trail to the 75-foot falls is often as large as the Cullasaja River itself.

Cullasaja Falls was its original name, but the Civilian Conservation Corps (CCC) dubbed it "Dry Falls" while constructing the

Between Franklin and Highlands on US 64 you will see many waterfalls and cascades. This is one of numerous cascades on the Cullasaja River.

path and observation points. The new name stemmed from the wide, washed-out area behind the falls that lets you walk to the other side without getting drenched. You will get "moist" from the blowing droplets if you stay behind the plunging water for more than a minute, but the experience is worth it. The terrain is untamed and beautifully rugged except for the easy walk to Dry Falls.

Vanhook Glade Campground is the only National Forest Service campground in the area. The entrance is a short distance from Cliffside. It has 21 campsites, 13 with hook-ups for small RVs. Cold showers are available at Cliffside Lake at no charge. Camping fee is $8 per night.

Closer to Highlands is a waterfall you can drive under. Bridal Veil Falls is 120 feet high. The best photography is from across the highway from the falls.

You'll know you are almost to Highlands when you see the Sequayah Lake and Dam on your right. Wright Square at the corner of Main and First Streets houses the National Forest Service information office and shops.

Summer vacationers began coming in the late 1800s. Today many professional people own homes here, and the community

You will know you are entering Highlands when you see Sequayah Lake spilling over a dam.

Highlands has long been a mountain retreat from the summer heat of the lowlands. Highlands Inn (pictured) and Old Edwards Inn await you downtown; both are listed on the National Register of Historic Places.

caters to this influx that swells the winter population from fewer than 2,000 to more than 20,000 during summer.

Main Street is wide enough for parking on both sides and down the middle. Shops abound. Downtown are two inns on the National Register of Historic Places, Old Edwards Inn and Highlands Inn. Central House Restaurant is well over 100 years old. The Highlands Inn, built in 1880, accommodates children and guests in wheelchairs, whereas the Old Edwards cannot. Comfortable areas are provided for smokers at both inns.

Leaving Highlands and heading for Cashiers on US 64, there is another sight you won't want to miss halfway between the two towns, Whiteside Mountain. Unfortunately, when we were there the light was low and the white did not stand out, but the high cliffs did. The north and south cliff faces range from 400 to 750 feet high. The granite cliffs look down 2,100 feet to the Chattooga River Valley.

Whiteside Mountain, part of the eastern continental divide, is described as one of the oldest mountains on this planet. The summit is 4,930 feet above sea level; to get there you must hike along a 2-mile loop trail from the parking lot at the end of Whiteside Mountain Road (NC 1690) off US 64. You can enjoy the view

Tourists are the main business of the many shops you'll find in Highlands.

from an overlook where you'll see the headwaters of the Chattooga River and, if you relish more hiking, a spur trail takes you to Devil's Courthouse to the north, at an elevation of 4,485 feet.

If you visit Whiteside in spring or summer, look for Peregrine falcons. They make their home on the mountain faces during this time. Once their native habitat, they were eradicated and later reintroduced in 1985. Rappelling and climbing are restricted during their nesting season.

When leaving the mountain, turn right on US 64 to go to Cashiers.

The following are Highlands, NC 28741 and area code 704 except where noted.

Age-old inns such as this one, Old Edwards Inn, are still very popular today, but there are many newer ones if you are looking for a modern touch.

❧ ACCOMMODATIONS

The Chandler Inn—POB 2156; 526-5992; I efficiency, 14 rooms, 6 fireplaces, breakfast, golf.

Colonial Pines Inn—Rt. 1, Box 22-B; 526-2060; I cottage, 5 rooms, private baths, full breakfast.

Dogwood B&B—Hwy. 64E; 526-3152.

Edgewater—Cullasaja Dr.; 526-4733; 2 suites with kitchen and bath, canoeing.

The Guest House—Rt. 2, Box 649N; 526-4536; 4 rooms with full baths, breakfast, TV.

The Highlands Inn—POB 1030; 526-5036; 30 rooms, breakfast, golf, tennis; April to November.

Lakeside B&B—1921 Franklin Rd; 526-4498; Restored 1930s hunting lodge overlooking lake, bedrooms with private bath, gourmet breakfast, canoeing.

The Laurels: Freda's B&B—Rt. 2, Box 102; 526-2091; 4 rooms with private baths, 2 fireplaces, English breakfast, afternoon tea, fishing, boats; May to November.

Long House B&B—POB 2078; 800-833-0020, 526-4394; 4 rooms with private baths, hearty breakfast.

Mirror Lake Lodge—23 Cullasaja Dr.; 526-5947; 3 rooms, breakfast, fishing, canoes/boats/rafts.

Morning Star B&B—480 Flat Mountain Rd.; 526-1009; Bedrooms with private bath, a suite with whirlpool, gourmet breakfast.

The Old Edwards Inn—POB 1030; 526-5036; 19 rooms, Continental breakfast, golf, tennis; April to November.

Ye Olde Stone House B&B—1337 S. 4th St.; 526-5911; 1 chalet, log cabin, 4 rooms, full breakfast.

4½ St. Inn—22-A 4½ St.; 526-4464; 10 rooms with private baths, gourmet breakfast, hot tub; May to November.

ATTRACTIONS

Highlands Chamber Music Festival—526-9060; Performances Sunday afternoons and Tuesday evenings July to August.

Highlands Nature Center & Biological Station—526-2623; Summer activities for all ages.

Highlands Playhouse—POB 896; 526-2695; Plays and dates vary; Tickets $7 to $20.

DINING

Central House—In the Old Edwards Inn; 526-5036; Fresh seafood, beef chicken, pastas, seasonal specialties.

Highlands Seafood & Smokehouse—Hwy. 64 .; 526-4799; Barbecue, smoked trout.

Lakeside Restaurant—Smallwood Ave.; 526-9419; Casual; Serious cuisine.

Michael's Cafe—Behind Wright Square; 526-4188; Fine dining.

Paoletti's Restaurant—E. Main St.; 526-4906; Italian dining, good wine list.

On the Verandah—Hwy. 64 W.; 526-2338; Contemporary American, wine bar, Sunday brunch.

Wolfgang Green's—E. Main St.; 526-3807; American, authentic German cuisine, wine and espresso bar, outdoor dining.

SHOPPING

C.K. Swan Antiques—4th at Pine; 526-2083; Fine art, antiques, eccentricities.

Custom House—Carolina Way; 526-2665; Handmade American crafts, Southern Piedmont antiques.

Country Inn Antiques—Main St.; 526-9380; American country antiques.

The Elephant's Foot Antique—Hwy. 64 E.; 526-5452; Antiques, decorative furniture.

Farmers Market—Main at Hwy. 106S; 526-4382; General store.

Fletcher & Lee—Mountain Brook Ctr.; 526-5400; English and French antiques.

Hanover House Antiques—Rt. 2, Box 659; 526-4425; English pine and oak chests, dressers, tables, cabinets.

I'm Precious Too!—Main St.; 526-2754; Unique items.

Lick Log Mill—Hwy. 106S; 526-3934; American basketry.

Main Street Cottage—Main St.; 526-8126; Art, gifts, gourmet sauces.

Mountain Makings Art & Crafts Shows—Sassafras Campground on Hwy. 28S; 526-3181; Fine arts and crafts, 100 exhibitors with live Celtic music.

Needlepoint of Highlands—Picket Fence; 526-3901; Handpainted needlepoint canvasses, wools, special fibers for stitching.

Spring Street Gallery & Gardens—271 Spring St.; 526-5464; Original art, pottery, handcrafted jewelry, patio and lawn furnishing, twig furniture.

CAMPING

Vanhook Glade Campground—Highlands Ranger District, POB 1299, Highlands, NC 28741; 526-3765; 4 miles west of Highlands on Hwy. 64; 21 sites for tents and small trailers, restrooms, showers at Cliffside Lake adjacent to campgrounds.

Highlands RV Park—1104 Chestnut St.; 526-5985; 5 trailer sites with hookups, laundry; May to November.

Sassafras Gap Campground—Hwy. 28S; 526-9909

FOR MORE INFORMATION

Highlands Chamber of Commerce—396 Oak St.; 526-2112.

DIRECTIONS

From Asheville—Take I-40 to Waynesville, then NC 23, which becomes US 23/441, in Franklin take US 64 for 11 curved, scenic miles. About 65 miles.

From Atlanta area—Take I-85 to Gainesville, GA, then US 441 to Dillard, GA, then GA 246 that becomes NC 106, which takes you into Highlands. About 125 miles.

From Greenville, SC—Take US 123 to Senca, Hwy. 28 to Highlands. About 85 miles.

24 *Cashiers and Lake Toxaway*

CASHIERS: Ancient Beauty and Contemporary Solitude

At an elevation of 3,487 feet is the quiet village of Cashiers. Casual Cashiers has one traffic light regulating its 1,200 inhabitants at the crossroads of US 64 and NC 107. If you are looking for a secluded getaway, you've found it. Cashiers is pronounced "Cash-ers," not (as we've heard for years) like the people who ring up your groceries.

You may enjoy AAA Four-Diamond accommodations at Innisfree Inn or remove yourself to the isolated Honeymoon-Anniversary Cabin at High Hampton Inn and Country Club.

If golfing is high on your list, then High Hampton Inn and Country Club offers you all you want among gorgeous vistas. (© 1994 by Lavidge & Assoc.)

Innisfree Inn, 6 miles north of Cashiers, has made a name for itself as a romantic inn. It has elegant rooms and an extravagant suite with a bathing chamber overlooking the mountains from a whirlpool built for two. As you can imagine, this suite is in demand by newlyweds and couples celebrating anniversaries. Candlelit breakfast in the tower is one more romantic touch. Innisfree Inn tenders quiet cottages among the beautiful surroundings.

For a one-stop destination, you couldn't ask for a better place than High Hampton Inn and Country Club. Golf is a main attraction, but there are many activities to mention, so here goes: wildflower workshops, conservation retreat, literary conference, bird watching, tennis (7 courts), picnic, children's programs for all ages, hiking on 8 trails, mountain biking, exercise room, gift shops, guided walks, canoeing, paddle boating, row boating, sail boating, fishing, fly-fishing lessons, archery, croquet, bridge games and tournaments, swimming, sunbathing on the beach, rocking on the porch, fine dining, tavern (one of only a few in the county), and even a kennel for your best friend.

The Hampton Inn, once a private summer home, is the heart of a 1,400-acre estate with a 35-acre lake and 18-hole golf course designed by George W. Cobb. The 120 rooms with private baths and suites are available on the American plan (three meals daily). Tipping is discouraged. Coat and tie are required for the evening meal. All of this is offered from April through October.

Remember the Honeymoon-Anniversary Cottage? It's secluded in a back area on the lake with a roof-high water wheel, deck, and fireplace. You get there by walking down a path or paddling a canoe. Meals are taken in the dining room.

About a quarter-mile from Cashiers on NC 107N is Oakmont Lodge. Guest Quarters is located amid an outdoor museum of yesteryear's farm implements, and across the pond from White Goose Cafe, where we enjoyed our pond-side dinner on the porch, which was comfortably cool during August. There were a few ducks and one white goose lounging along the bank, where two sunken boats seem to have been forgotten a decade ago.

Dining pond-side to a chorus of ducks and one goose creates an unusual and pleasant experience at the White Goose Cafe.

Guest Quarters has combination sitting room-bedrooms, private baths, desks, coffee makers, and cable TV. Two cabins and one large cottage have fireplaces and equipped kitchens. There is also a 100-year old chestnut log cabin on its own acre for honeymooners. A claw-foot tub polishes off the atmosphere of yesteryear.

The essence of Cashiers is hushed and half-hidden among the natural beauty of the lower Blue Ridge Mountains. You'll find few distractions here. Getting away from it all was never more fun.

LAKE TOXAWAY

The Greystone Inn earned AAA's Four-Diamond Award. Listed on the National Register of Historic Places, it was built in 1915 by Lucy Armstrong Moltz as her home on the lake—a six-level Swiss mansion. In addition to the mansion, today's Greystone Inn offers you the choice of staying in Hillmont with 12 rooms or in the 2 luxurious Lakeside Suites.

This is the place to be pampered! The spa at Greystone Inn offers sauna, massage, facial, French manicure, ultimate foot treatment, salt glow/loofah and more. You can continue your relaxation on a champagne cruise. This is a full-service resort of exceptional quality.

Here is luxury with history, beauty with pampering. As grand as the outdoor vistas are in North Carolina, at Greystone Inn you can experience grand vistas and accommodations that satisfy your desire for indulgences. (© 1995 by T. L. Schermerhorn)

Lake Toxaway has 640 acres where you can fish, ski, swim, or sail. A picnic lunch can be ready for you to take along on an electric boat ride to a distant shore or, if you prefer, you can hike among the 3,000 acres of wilderness, taking in waterfalls and mountain-top vistas. There's also a par 72, 18-hole golf course, swimming pool, and croquet.

From a delightful breakfast to a gourmet dinner, you will be pleased with the extraordinary dining experience at Greystone Inn.

Continue on US 64 to Brevard, then into Hendersonville.

The following are Cashiers, NC 28717 and area code 704 except where noted.

➣ ACCOMMODATIONS

The Greystone Inn—Greystone Lane, Lake Toxaway, 28747; 800-824-5766, (NC only) 966-4700.

High Hampton Inn & Country Golf Club—POB 338; 800-334-2551 ext. 151, 643-2411; 130 rooms, breakfast.

Innisfree Victorian Inn—POB 2464, Glenville, NC 28736; 743-2946; 8 cottages, 9 rooms, breakfast.

Laurelwood Mountain Inn Motel—POB 188; 743-3034; 18 rooms, cable TV, phones, refrigerators; Suites and cottages available.

Millstone Inn—POB 949; 743-2737; 4 suites, 7 rooms, gourmet breakfast, fishing, good view of Devil's Courthouse and Whiteside Mountain.

Oakmont Lodge—Rt. 3, Box 71; 743-2298.

➣ ATTRACTIONS

Cashiers Chamber of Commerce has free brochures and audiotapes for rent for driving tours among the mountains, lakes, and valleys.

Cashiers Sliding Rock—Nature's water slide on the Chattooga River; Perfect for small children; Take 107 S. 1.5 miles, turn west on Whiteside Cove Rd. to bridge, park on right and follow short trail.

Silver Run Falls—A 40-foot cascade, is 3 miles south of Cashiers on Hwy. 107; Park in gravel area and follow the trail to the falls and picnic area; There's a good swimming hole for those who like cold water.

Whitewater, Drift, Rainbow, Turtle, and Bust-Your-Butt Falls—Whitewater Falls, the highest in the eastern United States, is about 13 miles from Cashiers; Follow 107 S. about 8 miles across NC/SC border, go 1 mile, turn left on first paved road (Wiggington/SC 37-413), which

Swimming and other water sports, including sailing and fishing, attract people to the High Hampton Inn. (© 1994 by Lavidge & Assoc.)

ends in 2 miles, turn left on SC 130, which becomes NC 128, and follow the signs; Park in marked area; Hiking is not necessary to view the fall; Trails take you to top and bottom of falls, but hiking to the top is not recommended as several fatalities occur each year.

Other laudable falls are downstream but you must maneuver some seriously steep terrain. Go south on Whitewater Road about a mile, turn left on gravel road, go 4 miles, park past the bridge, and follow the trail on the right. Drift, Rainbow, Turtle, and Bust-Your-Butt Falls are 6 miles beyond Whitewater Falls on the Horsepasture River. From a paved pull-off in the right, over the guard rail are fairly steep trails leading down to the river, where the trails level at the river.

There are more hiking/nature trails in the area.

Return by going north on NC 281, turn left (west) on US 64 back to Cashiers.

⅍ DINING

Liquor cannot be sold by the drink, but "brown bagging" is acceptable in most restaurants.

Carolina Smokehouse—Hwy. 64 W; 743-3200; Barbecue.
Cornucopia Restaurant—Hwy. 107 S; 743-3750; Continental cuisine, deli sandwiches.
High Hampton Inn—Hwy. 107; 743-4211; American foods, full buffet.
Horacio's Restaurante—Hwy. 64E; 743-2792; International cuisine, seafood.
Market Basket—Hwy. 107; Hot rock cooking, varied menu.
Martine's—Hwy. 107S; 743-3838; Continental cuisine, soups and sandwiches.
The New Mica's—US 64E; 743-5740; Fine dining; Reservations preferred.
White Goose Cafe—Hwy. 107S; 743-5410; Sandwiches, casual fare.

⅍ SHOPPING

Balderdash Antiques—Hwy. 107N; 743-5499.
Basketworks—Hwy. 107S; 743-5052.
Books & Specialty Shop—Hwy. 107S; 743-9930; New, used, and rare books.
Lyn Holloway Antiques—Crossroads of Hwys. 64 & 107; 743-2524; English, Continental, and American antiques.
Main Street Workshop & Store—743-2437; Shaker Furniture, antiques, baskets.
Suzanne's—Hwy. 64 E; 743-2009; Lizzie High Dolls, Dept. 56, gifts.
Wormy Chestnut Antiques—Hwy. 64 W; 743-3014.

Comfort is the first rule of hospitality, and the tasteful decor of this sunroom at Greystone Inn made us feel snug and cozy. (© 1996 by T. L. Schermerhorn)

❧ CAMPING

The following are area code 704.

Arrowmont Stable & Cabins—Rt. 66, Box 135-B, Cullowhee, NC 28723;
743-2762; 12 tent sites, 3 cabins, showers, toilets, fishing, horseback
riding; May to September.
Ralph J. Andrews Park—School Creek; 743-3923; 47 lakefront sites with full
hook-ups, laundry, showers, dump station; April to October.
Singing Water Camping Resort—860 Trout Creek Rd., Tuckasegee, NC 28783;
293-5872; 58 trailer sites with hook-ups, 68 tent sites, showers, toilets,
camp store; May to October.

❧ FOR MORE INFORMATION

Cashier Area Chamber of Commerce—POB 238; 743-5941
Jackson County Travel & Tourism Authority—116 Central St., Sylva, NC 28779;
800-962-1911.

❧ DIRECTIONS

From Atlanta area—Take I-85 to Gainesville, GA, then US 441 to Dillard,
GA, then GA 246, which becomes NC 106; in Highlands take US 64.
About 150 miles.
From Asheville—Take NC 191 and NC 280 to Brevard, then US 64 west to
Cashiers. About 65 miles.
From Greenville, SC—Take US 123 to Senca, follow SC 28 to junction of
107, which takes you into Cashiers. About 70 miles.
Lake Toxaway is 10 miles east of Cashiers on US 64.

25 *Hendersonville, Flat Rock, and Lake Lure*

HENDERSONVILLE: THE APPLE OF NORTH CAROLINA'S EYE

Hendersonville rests on a mountain plateau 2,200 feet above sea level between the Blue Ridge and Great Smoky Mountains. This region, known for its apples, is also known as "Land of the Sky."

Hendersonville is a popular retirement area, in part because it offers four seasons (something Florida lacks!); blooming flowers in the spring, cooler summers, the color of fall foliage and snow in winter (although it melts quickly).

Hendersonville, known for its apples, has also developed an outstanding reputation among antiques hunters.

Today, Hendersonville, a favorite summer resort for more than a century, offers tourists antiques shopping, variety of dining experiences, recreation in the mountains (see North Carolina Recreation section), bed and breakfasts, specialty shops, and a rich history.

We were especially taken with the layout of Main Street. Less than 30 minutes south of Asheville, downtown Hendersonville was entered on the National Register of Historic Places in 1988. The once four-lane Main Street has been transformed into a two-lane winding way with large planters of flowers at the intersections, trees, and piped in music along the sidewalks. The term "user friendly" certainly applies here.

Our stay at the Waverly Inn was one of the most comfortable of our travels. Innkeepers John and Diane Sheiry and Darla Olmstead create an "easy" atmosphere from their social hour on the front porch between 5:00 and 6:00 P.M. to the spacious accommodations. There are large sitting rooms on each floor. We especially enjoyed watching night fall while rocking on the second-floor balcony.

The Waverly Inn has 13 rooms, 1 suite, private baths, and is open yearround. Our bedroom suite had a four-poster canopy bed and the sitting room had a desk, TV, couch, and plenty of room for guests to entertain visitors.

Fresh coffee is ready around 7:30 A.M. and breakfast is served between 8:00 and 9:00 A.M. Newspapers await you in the dining room. Picnic lunches are available on request.

The Waverly Inn, the oldest surviving inn in the city, is listed on the National Register of Historic Places and selected for *Innkeepers' Register*. It has received positive reviews from *The New York Times, Southern Living, The Discerning Traveler*, and the Summerlins.

The site was purchased on January 15, 1898, by Mrs. Maggie Anderson. She and her sister Bessie Egerton ran the inn until they defaulted on their bank note after a hurricane that hit Miami in September 1926 devastated the tourism business they depended on.

The inn became a boarding house for teachers in the area before it became an inn known for its homecooked meals that kept folks lined up on the porch.

There is always a friendly atmosphere on the front porch of the Waverly Inn during the social hour when guests get better acquainted.

Next door to the Waverly Inn is Claddagh Inn, built at the beginning of the 1900s.

May 13, 1988, John and Diane Sheiry and Diane's sister, Darla Olmstead, purchased the inn. The Waverly Inn is on the left at the corner of Eighth Avenue and North Main Street.

Next door to the Waverly Inn is Claddagh Inn. Built between 1888 and 1906 as the Smith-Green House, the structure evolved into the inn it is today in the 1980s. The Claddagh (pronounced "claw-da") is a Gaelic symbol of two hands, a heart, and a crown representing love and friendship.

Park Deli Cafe makes large, luscious sandwiches and soups. We recommend that you split your sandwich with someone to save room for their fabulous desserts (caramel apple granny, espresso cheesecake, mocha hazelnut torte, fruit pies). You also have your choice from a menu of fifteen pasta dinners, barbecue ribs, prime rib, and salads.

Expressions, also on Main Street, combines upscale dining with casual attire. They offer saffron seafood stew and smoked salmon tartar with sundried mashed potatoes, sautéed escargot appetizers, salads, trout, swordfish, chicken breast stuffed with portobello mushrooms, feta cheese and roma tomatoes, rack of lamb with Dijon rosemary crust and garlic flan, and filet of beef with béarnaise sauce. It's no wonder they've received a Mobile three-star rating.

Hendersonville's Main Street winds its way among flowers, benches, music, and creatively decorated store fronts.

Sinbad, another fine dining restaurant for the casually dressed, offers tastes of Lebanon, Greece, and India, with appetizers like lamb sautéed with garlic, lemon, wine and coriander, grape leaves stuffed with currents, rice, pine nuts, onion, and dill, or tabouleh salad. Entrées include grape leaves stuffed with ground lamb, rice, and pine nuts, and sautéed shrimp in curry sauce. Dinners come with salad, rice, and fresh vegetables.

For the musical enthusiast, the Hendersonville Symphony presents a combination of professional quality with hometown spirit. The sixty-piece orchestra's caliber ranks with those in much larger metropolitan areas.

From Hendersonville you have easy access to the Carl Sandburg National Site, the Flat Rock Playhouse, Chimney Rock, Lake Lure, the Folk Art Center, Pisgah National Forest, Brevard Music Center, Cradle of Forestry Interpretive Center, and the Biltmore Estate in Asheville.

It's 24 miles to Asheville, 169 miles to Atlanta, 112 to Charlotte, 146 to Columbia, South Carolina, and 131 to Knoxville.

FLAT ROCK

Three miles south from Hendersonville via US 25 is Flat Rock. This was home to Carl Sandburg the last 22 years of his life. Now it's a National Historic Site that provides us with an insight of how he and his family lived on this 240-acre farm. The home, "Connemara," was built in 1838 by Christopher Memminger of Charleston. Today, it's much as it was when Sandburg was alive. In addition to viewing his collection of 10,000 books, you may tour the grounds and hike through the rolling hills.

Considered one of the ten best summer stock theaters in the country, the Flat Rock Playhouse bills itself as "Broadway in the mountains." It presents *The World of Carl Sandburg, Rootabaga Stories,* among other plays, and you can listen to dramatic readings and the musical renditions of Sandburg's *The American Songbook,* as well as comedies and dramas.

Just down the road from Sandburg's home is Old Teneriffe Inn. An inn for more than 100 years, you can walk trails through acres of old trees, play tennis, or enjoy listening to the birds from the stone verandahs.

Highland Lake Inn is a bed & breakfast lodge with cabins, kitchen-equipped cottages for 90 guests, and conference facilities for 500 people. You can play tennis, swim in an Olympic-sized pool, bike, hike in their 180 acres, and play golf.

The Wrinkled Egg, as unusual as its name, claims to have "funky" American art, imported garden tools and statuary, fresh baked bread from a wood-fired oven, and summer camp surprise packages.

LAKE LURE

Approximately 15 miles east of Hendersonville via Highway 64 is Chimney Rock Park and the 1,500-acre Lake Lure. Chimney Rock is probably one of the best known attractions in the area. This monolith offers sightseers a grand vista. You will take an elevator through solid rock for 26 stories. Also in Chimney Rock Park is the 404-foot Hickory Nut Falls. You may recognize it from the movie *The Last of the Mohicans,* which was partially filmed here.

The New York Times called Lake Lure Inn the "little Waldorf of the South" in 1928. It has a long tradition of quality service that was enjoyed by F. Scott Fitzgerald, Emily Post, and President Franklin Roosevelt.

A member of Historic Hotels of America, the inn has also earned AAA's Three-Diamond Award. Fifty rooms echo a bygone era with the comforts of a modern vacation. You can swim, hike, play tennis, go boating, and enjoy other water sports in Lake Lure, or go horseback riding. You may prefer fishing in the lake for trout, bass, and catfish. *National Geographic* magazine called Lake Lure one of the most beautiful manmade lakes in the world.

You may want to take advantage of Lake Lure Tours. You can choose a covered tour boat for an hour ride on the lake, or a sunset romantic dinner tour for two (cozy blankets are provided for the boat ride back after dark). The tours are offered from March to November, seven days a week.

At this point, we direct you to Waynesville via US 74A north to I-40 west to the junction of US 19/23/74 to begin closing the loop tour. Although Asheville seems the next logical destination, we saved that city for the linear tour using the Blue Ridge Parkway as the backbone.

Chimney Rock is instantly recognizable. Thousands of visitors come here yearly to be awed by the view. *(Courtesy of Chimney Rock Park)*

Lake Lure, "one of the most beautiful man-made lakes in the world" according to *National Geographic,* offers romantic boat rides and fishing. Lake Lure Inn will share its historic past and three-diamond accommodations with you. *(© Tim Barnwell)*

On US 19/23/74, you'll pass near the towns of Candler, Canton, and Clyde. This is a more scenic route than the interstate, and you have the opportunity to visit a couple of interesting antiques stores.

In Candler, Copper Kettle Antique Mall is on the south side of the road. They had a completely restored 1929 Ford pick-up, one room filled with tools, spinning and flax wheels, gas stoves, corn shellers, crocks, and a wooden cart when we visited. Antiquers will want to take advantages of the reasonable prices and varied collections.

In Clyde, look for the Trading Post. It has pre-1950s furniture, glassware and estate items.

The following are Hendersonville, NC 28792 and area code 704 except where noted.

✺ ACCOMMODATIONS

Apple Inn—1005 White Pine Dr., 28739; 800-615-6611, 693-0107.
Echo Mountain Inn—2849 Laurel Park Hwy., 28739; 693-9626.
The Claddagh Inn—755 N. Main St.; 800-225-4700, 697-7778.
Etowah Valley B&B—Country Club and Gold Course, POB 2150, 28793; 800-451-8174, 891-7022.
The Greystone Inn—Greystone Lane, Lake Toxaway, 28747; 800-824-5766, (NC only) 966-4700.
Highland Lake Inn—POB 1026, Flat Rock, 28731; 800-762-1376, 693-3868.
Lake Lure Inn—POB 10, Lake Lure, 28746; 800-277-5873, 625-2525.
Mill House Lodge—POB 309, Flat Rock, 28731; 800-736-6073, 693-6077.
Old Teneriffe Inn—POB 1378, Flat Rock, 28731; 800-617-6427, 698-8178.
Rubin's Osceola Lake Inn—POB 2258, 28793; 800-468-3540, 692-2544.
The Waverly Inn—783 N. Main St.; 800-537-8195, 693-9193; E-mail jsheiry@aol.com.
Westhaven B&B—1235 5th Ave.; 693-8791.
Woodfield Inn—POB 98, Flat Rock, 28731; 800-533-6016, 693-6016.

✺ ATTRACTIONS

Carl Sandburg Home—1928 Little River Rd., Flat Rock, 28731; 693-4178.
Flat Rock Playhouse—POB 310, Flat Rock, 28731; 693-0731.
Hendersonville Depot—Corner of Maple and 7th Ave.; 697-9614, 692-3135.

Within walking distance of downtown Hendersonville, the Waverly Inn provides guests with quiet rooms and extra-special amenities.

Jackson Park Nature Trail—Off Four Seasons Blvd. east of Hendersonville;
   1.5-mile self guided tour with 17 stops; A brochure describes each stop
   along the trail; A portion of the trail is paved and wheelchair accessible.
Skyland Cinema—538 N. Main St.; 697-CINE; Small cabaret theatre in the
   Arts Center serving light foods, beer, and wine; Features Hollywood,
   foreign, and independent films for patrons 21 and older.

✒ DINING

Days Gone By—303 N. Main St.; 693-9056; Soda fountain, sandwiches.
China Grill—211 Asheville Hwy.; 696-0031.
Expressions—114 N. Main St.; 693-8516.
Hannah Flanagan's Pub—300 N. Main St.; 696-1665; Fine dining.
Highland Lake Inn—Highland Lake Rd. off Hwy. 25, Flat Rock, 28731;
   800-762-1376, 693-3868.
Hubert's—Hwy. 64W; 693-0856.
McGuffey's—1800 Four Seasons Blvd.; 697-0556.
Park Deli Cafe—437 N. Main St.; 696-3663.
Quarter House—1508 Asheville Hwy.; 692-1529.
Sinbad—133 4th Ave. E; 696-2039.

✒ SHOPPING

Antiques, Etc.—147 W. 4th Ave.; 696-8255; European and American
   antiques, silver matching service, decorative items.
The Brass Latch—117 S. Main St.; 693-7505; Vintage textiles, antique furniture, linen, laces, jewelry.
Brightwater Art Glass—502 N. Main St.; 697-6842; Custom stained glass,
   windows.
Calico Galley—317 N. Main St.; 697-2551; Local artists, crafts, antique
   glass.
Days Gone By—303 N. Main St.; 693-9056; Soda fountain, drugstore collectibles.
Main Street Antique Mall—429 Main St.; 696-8202; 2 floors, 30 dealers,
   antiques, collectibles, estate jewelry.
Mast General Store—527 N. Main St.; 696-1883; Restored 1905 emporium,
   old-time mercantile items, outdoor gear.
South Main Street Antiques—119 S. Main St.; 693-3212; Antiques, collectibles, primitives, art.

Village Green Antique Mall—424 S. Main St.; 692-9057; Antiques, collectibles in 12,000-square-foot mall.

Wagon Wheel Antiques—423 N. Main St.; 692-0992; Southern period pieces.

The Wrinkled Egg—2710 US Hwy. 25, Flat Rock, 28731; 696-3998.

❧ SPECIAL EVENTS

Apple Festival—201 S. Main St.; 697-4557; Annual four-day festival on Main Street; Entertainment, sporting events, arts, crafts, apple products, children's activities, King Apple Parade.

Farm City Day—First Saturday in October; Jackson Park; Taste of rural life from making shingles to milking cows.

❧ CAMPING

Call for details.

Alpine Woods RV Park—800-445-4355, 692-6011.

Big Willow Campground—693-0187.

Creekside Mountain Camping Resort—800-248-8118, 625-4257.

Lake Lure Campground—625-9160.

Lakewood RV Resort—800-767-2330, 697-9523.

Mills River Recreation Area and Campground—877-3265.

Red Gates RV Park—685-7707.

❧ FOR MORE INFORMATION

Chamber of Commerce—330 N. King St. Hendersonville, NC 28793; 692-1413.

Henderson County Travel and Tourism Visitors Center—201 S. Main St., Hendersonville, NC 28793; 800-828-4244, 693-9708.

❧ DIRECTIONS

From Asheville—Go south on I-26 or US 74.

From Atlanta area—Take I-85 to Gainesville, GA, then US 441 to Dillard, GA, then GA 246 that becomes NC 106; in Highlands take US 64 into Hendersonville.

Flat Rock is 3 miles south of Hendersonville on US 25.

Lake Lure is 15 miles east of Hendersonville via US 64.

26 *Waynesville:*
Fashionably Old-Fashioned

Haywood County was a tough place to live in the first half of the 1800s. Any white person could come in, claim the land he wanted, make improvements, and register a deed to make it legal. Settlers could own slaves, kill Indians, and hunt buffalo. A jail was built two years before a courthouse. Being placed in public stocks and having one's hands branded were punishments for stealing and killing white people.

Travel was limited to foot, ox-drawn wagons, and horseback until 1828, when a stagecoach ran through Waynesville from Greeneville, Tennessee, to Greenville, South Carolina. It took more than 50 years before the first railroad came to town in 1880. In 1850, Haywood County recorded 5,931 whites, 710 Indians, 418 slaves, and 15 free Negroes.

The railroad and the Civil War changed Haywood County in the last half of the 1800s. Nearly a thousand men left to fight after North Carolina seceded from the Union in 1861. No major battles were fought in the county until April 1865, when one skirmish took place a month after the war was over.

Waynesville was first advertised as a tourist destination when Col. and Mrs. W.W. Stringfield built and opened Haywood White Sulfur Springs Hotel in 1878.

Seven years later, Bowling Hall built Hallcrest on top of Hall Mountain. His home was originally in his apple orchard a little north of Waynesville. Today that home is Hallcrest Inn.

Russell and Margaret Burson bought the land in 1979, estab-

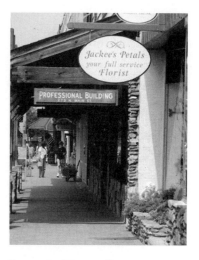

Downtown Waynesville seems redesigned for tourists, from the Mast General Store to Curbside Market, which carries many out-of-state newspapers.

Hallcrest's specially crafted dining tables with large Lazy Susans create a home-style setting for breakfast guests preparing to indulge in award-winning cathead biscuits.

lishing an inn. Martin and Tesa, their son and daughter-in-law, are the innkeepers today.

Breakfast is as good as it gets with Martin's award-winning cathead biscuits heading up a country breakfast of scrambled eggs, grits, country ham with red-eye gravy, bacon or sausage, apples, jam, and jellies. All meals are served on special tables that are giant Lazy Susans. (In case you've not had a cathead biscuit, it's a biscuit as big as a cat's head.)

Dinner, served Monday through Saturday at 6:00 P.M., consists of fried chicken, country-style steak, ribs, pork loin, barbecue meatballs, chicken pie, apple/cheese casserole, broccoli casserole, squash casserole, tomatoes, pickled cucumber, and fresh farm produce in season.

Sunday lunch, at 1:00 P.M. is always honey-glazed ham and some type of chicken or roast beef and a medley of vegetables.

There are 7 rooms with private baths in the main house. None are wheelchair accessible. Four additional rooms are off the side porch. There are rocking chairs on the porch so you can admire the valley while you relax after a delectable, generous meal.

When you arrive, you'll notice the big cast-iron bell in the side yard. Martin rings the bell to wish each departing guest a safe journey.

Up on Main Street in Waynesville, you'll find many shops of interest. As you walk, notice that Main is the highest point in town—all side streets run downhill. You can sit along the street on benches to rest or read the newspaper. Curbside Market carries many out-of-state newspapers and a wide variety of magazines (even *Opera Quarterly*). They also sell produce and essentials.

Waynesville is geared to tourists looking for variety. You'll notice boutiques, galleries, sandwich shops, even a place whose business is making micro-brewery beers. You'll need several hours to comb the town.

Mast General Store on Main Street is one of five such stores in the state. It offers outdoor clothing, hats, shoes, hiking boots, household products, and camping gear. If you want to see early 1900 department store architecture, you'll want to look around the old Mast General. It was restored but not tampered with.

Picnic Pleasantries Cafe is a convenient place to pick up a pic-

The typical late 1800s architecture of the Museum of North Carolina Handicrafts sets the mood for the treasures you'll see inside.

nic lunch. Located in the back of Smith's Drugs, you can also get breakfast and lunch specials.

Other choices include Duvalls on Walnut Street for meat-and-three dining, Whitman's Bakery, Charlie's Corner, and O'Malley's Pub. And don't forget Bosu's for buying wine and delicacies.

The Museum of North Carolina Handicrafts is in the old two-story white frame Shelton House beneath shady hemlock and maple trees. Built between 1875 and 1880, the home remained in the family until 1977 when Charles E. Ray, a direct descendant, conveyed the property to the Museum of North Carolina.

It houses unique collections of traditional handicrafts by some of the state's most renowned artisans. Handcrafted dulcimers, carved wooden bowls, pottery pitchers, bowls, vases and urns, an early Edison phonograph, and a Navajo collection that Shelton brought back with him after serving as superintendent of the Navajo Indian School in Shiprock, New Mexico, are a sampling of the many items on display.

The late Edd Presnell's exhibit is hands-on. He carved many small bowls from different woods to show what each wood looked like. He asked that the display be open so that visitors could feel

The quilt craze of today had its origin many years ago. This hanging quilt is one of many examples found in the Museum of North Carolina Handicrafts.

the wooden bowls for texture and heft. Museum hours change seasonally, so call to confirm tours.

In late July, an 11-day festival kicks off with a parade downtown. Called Folk Moot USA, it is a gathering of more than 300 international performers of dance and musical instruments who travel to surrounding cities, including Maggie Valley and Asheville. If you are in the area, you will enjoy seeing the colorful native costumes, hearing native instruments, and feeling the excitement of mountain cloggers and Italian, Russian, Chinese, Irish, and other dancers perform their traditional folk dances. This festival was chosen on of the top 20 events held in the southeast by the Southeastern Tourism Society.

Next stop on the loop tour is Maggie Valley. Take US 276 north from town and follow the signs to US 19 and Maggie Valley.

The following are Waynesville, NC 28786 and area code 704 except where noted.

⤞ ACCOMMODATIONS

Belle Meade Inn—POB 1319; 456-3234; 4 rooms with private baths, breakfast, bicycles, fishing, tennis.

Boyd Mountain Log Cabins—Rt. 2, Box 176; 926-1575; 4 cabins (some sleep up to 8), fishing, biking, hiking, horse facilities.

Grandview Lodge—809 Valley View Cir. Rd.; 800-255-7826; 2 apartments, 9 rooms, breakfast, restaurant, golf.

Hallcrest Inn—299 Halltop Cir.; 800-334-6457, 456-6457; See text above.

Haywood St. House B&B—409 S. Haywood St.; 456-9831; 4 rooms, breakfast.

Herren House—200 East St.; 800-284-1932, 452-7837; Victorian inn, 6 rooms, private baths, full country breakfast.

Mountain Mist Vegetarian Health Retreat—420 Country Club Dr.; 452-1550; 5 rooms, breakfast, tennis, golf.

Old Stone Inn—900 Dolan Rd.; 800-432-8499, 456-3333; 4 suites, 18 rooms, breakfast, golf, restaurant, special packages.

The Snuggery—602 N. Main St.; 456-3660; 4 rooms, breakfast, golf.

The Swag Country Inn—Rt. 2 Box 280-A; 926-0430; 3 cabins, 12 rooms, breakfast, fishing, golf, jogging/nature trail; May to October.

Ten Oaks—803½ Love Lane; 800-563-2925, 452-4373; 4 rooms, breakfast, golf.

Waynesville Country Club Inn—POB 390; 800-627-6250, 456-3551; 3 condos, four cottages, 90 rooms, breakfast, pool, golf, tennis.

Yellow House—610 Plott Creek Rd.; 800-563-1236; 6 rooms, private baths, fireplace, wet bar or refrigerator in room, breakfast, appetizers, picnic baskets, lily pond.

ATTRACTIONS

Museum of North Carolina Historic Handicrafts—307 Shelton St.; 452-1551.

DINING

Duvall's Restaurant—1104 N. Main St.; 452-9464; Three meals daily.

Full Circle Cafe—166 Main St. (downstairs); 456-3050; Sandwiches, vegetarian foods, coffees, munchies.

Hallcrest Inn—299 Halltop Cir.; 800-334-6457, 456-6457.

The Old Stone Inn—900 Dolan Rd.; 456-3333; Mountain bistro; Dinner from 6:00 to 8:00 P.M.

Maggie's Galley and Seafood Restaurant—456-8945.

O'Malley's Pub & Grill—295 N. Main St.; 452-4228; Lunch, dinner, a touch o' the Irish.

Picnic Pleasantries Cafe—Downtown; 452-0027; Breakfast, sandwiches; Free delivery.

SHOPPING

The Antique Place—460 Hazelwood Ave.; 456-5610; Antiques, collectibles, refinishing.

Antiques Today & Tomorrow—241 N. Main St.; 456-8832; Antiques, collectibles; 3,000-square-foot store.

Barber's Orchard Antique Mall—727 Balsam Rd.; 456-7229; Antiques, collectibles; 7,000-square-foot store, 15 dealers.

Cabin Fever—2221 Dellwood Rd. W; 926-9066; Antiques, rustic pine furniture, pottery, wrought iron.

Craft Collection—305 Miller St.; 456-5441; "Yearround craft show"; Sales, classes, supplies.

Country Antiques—611 Walker Rd.; 456-5250; Primitives, general antiques.

The Glass Giraffe—110 Depot St.; 456-6665; Wide and varied glass products, glass working studio, supplies, classes.

Magnolia Antiques Mall—322 Branner Ave.; 456-5054; Antiques, art, collectibles, solid wood furniture of Western NC in 14,000-square-foot store; Refinishing, restoration.

Mast General Store—148 N. Main St.; 452-2101; General merchandise from earrings and hats to tents and hammocks in 10,000-square-foot restored 100 year-old store.

Thad Wood's Antique Mall & Auction—Waynesville Plaza, Russ Ave.; 456-3298; Antiques, collectibles in 25,000-square-foot store; Auctions Friday & Saturday at 7:00 P.M.

Trunks & Treasures—607 Dellwood Rd.; 456-8998; Trunks, jewelry, antiques.

SPECIAL EVENTS

Folk Moot USA—POB 658; 452-2997; Annual festival of international dancers and musicians; Haywood County Visitors Information, POB 125 Waynesville, NC 28786.

Trout Festival—POB 308; 456-3575; Crafts, conservation educational programs, children's programs, music, trout races (money prizes), adopt-a-trout, seminars, soft ball; Late May.

CAMPING

Winngray Family Campgrounds—625 Jonathan Creek Rd.; 926-3170; 125 trailer sites with hookups, 35 tent sites, showers, toilets, camp store, fishing.

FOR MORE INFORMATION

Haywood County Visitors Information—POB 125 Waynesville, NC 28786; 926-5426, 704-456-3021.

Tourism Development Authority—POB 1079, Maggie Valley, NC 28751; 926-5426.

DIRECTIONS

From Knoxville or Asheville—Take Exit 27 from I-40 and follow US 23/74, take Waynesville exit.

From Atlanta—Take I-85 to Gainesville, GA, then US 441 to Dillsboro and then take US 74 to Waynesville.

27 Maggie Valley:
The Playground

Jack Setzer thought his community needed a post office. Jack lived in a valley surrounded by mountains up to 6,000 feet high and it was a 5-mile ride to pick up mail for the valley residents. That was in December 1890.

Jack went through the channels to establish a post office in his home. After jumping through the bureaucratic hoops, it got down to naming the office. He was asked to submit three names: he chose Cora, Mettie, and Maggie Mae, the names of his three daughters. He also added Jonathan's Creek because they lived on the stream named for Jonathan McPeters, one of the area's earliest settlers (1788).

Perspectives above Maggie Valley are incredible—you couldn't ask for more inspiring views.

By return mail Jack learned that his settlement would have a post office and the community would be officially known as Maggie, North Carolina.

There was a movement to change the name in 1950 by the "newcomers" to the valley, but Jack and the other oldtimers fought to keep it. As you know, they won—and capitalized on it. They named "Maggie" patron saint of the valley.

Today, businesses are spread out over the 3-mile-long main street, Soco Road/US 19. A description of Maggie Valley would sound like one of a strip mall because it is not unlike a long strip mall—just about every thing of interest is along the straight drive from one end of town to the other. Finding any place is fairly simple; just look left and right.

Entering Maggie Valley past the junction of US 276 and US 19 you'll see Yesterday's Crafts, which has antiques and collectibles, on the left, Mini-Apolis Grand Prix Park on your right, Pressley's Campground on the right, Back Door Grill and J. Authur's Restaurant on the left, Stompin' Ground on the right, Comfort Inn, Cabbage Rose, Joey's' Pancake House, Arf's, and so on until you reach Ghost Town in the Sky on the right.

Turn right at Ghost Town, then make a quick left on Fie Top Mountain Road to get to one of the coziest Smoky Mountain bed and breakfasts. As you climb the steep road that leads to Smokey Shadows Lodge, you'll see signs of encouragement painted by Ginger and Bud Shinn along the way. We encourage you to follow their advice and "keep coming," because the steep 1.5-mile drive from Maggie Valley will eventually lead you to a peaceful, isolated inn. There is a 100-foot long back porch that makes you seem like you're a million miles from the hustle and bustle below.

In addition to the majestic mountain vista, you'll be treated to birds singing, wind whispering through the trees, crickets chirping and baby squirrels dancing up and down the porch railing as the smells of Ginger's cooking drifts out to the porch. Ah . . . Ginger's cooking.

She somehow manages to put on a spread that's inventive but meets our definition of "comfort food" at its finest. Lots of folks drive from nearby communities just for dinner, so be sure to give her

Smokey Shadows Lodge offers simple but very comfortable bedrooms in the stone and log inn.

a call for reservations. This is a "Mom and Pop" (and daughters, Tracy and Amie Jo) operation, and they cook for you, serve it to you, and sit down and keep you company while you eat it family-style. (You can ask for a secluded table for a romantic candlelit meal, if you prefer.) In fact, staying at Smokey Shadows makes one mindful of a nice visit to a favorite aunt and uncle who just happen to live in a beautiful, rustic log and stone home in the Smoky Mountains.

Smokey Shadows Lodge is made of stone and logs that came from an old grist mill in the Cataloochee Valley. There are 12 simply furnished rooms with private baths in the main lodge and 1 cabin with 3 beds upstairs and 1 double bed downstairs. There are lots of thoughtful touches in the rooms, like feather mattresses (also known as ticks) on the beds and little bouquets of fresh flowers. The atmosphere is relaxed and easygoing whether you're sitting on the porch in a rocker or pulling the latch string on your door as you prepare to drift off to sleep to the sounds of crickets chirping along Jonathan Creek as it tumbles down the hillside.

When leaving Smokey Shadows, turn right on Fie Top Mountain Road to reach Cataloochee Ranch. The ranch was started as a horseback riding livery by Tom Alexander in 1934 in the Cataloochee Valley. Great Smoky Mountain National Park (GSMNP) maintained an annual lease agreement with him until 1938 when he purchased the present 1,000 acres and set up the ranch.

Fifty to 75 percent of visitors to the ranch participate in horseback riding. There are lessons for beginners and limited facilities to board horses for nonguests. April to November is their regular season, with some limited wintertime accommodations for skiers at the nearby Cataloochee Ski Area.

Marked hiking trails offer pedestrians access to the trail system of the GSMNP about 1.5 miles from the lodge. Other activities are fishing in the stocked trout pond, tennis, outdoor hot tub, swimming (heated indoor pool), volleyball, badminton, croquet and, of course, horse shoes—this is a horse ranch after all.

There are 10 rooms in the main lodge, 3 suites, 7 cabins, and 4 romance cabins with whirlpool tubs, private decks, views, and fireplaces. Some of the cabins have quiet, unobstructed views of the Smokies.

The den at Smokey Shadows Lodge has TV, books, and games to occupy you, but the view out the back door is far more impressive. The photograph on the cover of this book was taken from the backyard.

The ride up to Ghost Town is the first exciting step toward a day of rides, amusements, and shopping on top of the mountain.

Gun fights in the street are daily fare in Ghost Town; to heighten your excitement take a ride on the roller coaster.

Ghost Town was an idea R.B. Coburn had in 1960 when he was vacationing at Smokey Shadows Lodge. Coburn left Smokey Shadows to fly his family to Disneyland. Along the way they stayed in a motel next to an old Wild West attraction. Inspired, Coburn returned to Maggie Valley and bought Buck Mountain for his western theme park.

He had to lower the mountain by 70 feet to make room for the town and amusement park. Building the Incline Railway was a hazardous and difficult feat. A bulldozer had to be attached to safety cables, then pulled up and down the mountain side, a 30 to 77 percent grade. The chair lift was added two years later. We enjoyed the trek uphill in the incline car and the trip back down in the chair lift. It was especially delightful to see parents in the chairs with excited children. At the top you will be driven by bus to the Ghost Town and ride areas. Gun fights occur on Main Street among the many shops offering various foods and gifts, "saloons," and other activities. One admission price includes unlimited rides. One of us loved the roller coaster, Black Widow, but the other one had to have both feet firmly on the ground.

The annual Folk Moot USA performs opening night at the Stompin' Ground each year. Headquartered in nearby Waynesville, this ensemble of international dancers and musicians plays in other areas during their 11-day festival (see Waynesville section for more

The Stompin' Ground in downtown Maggie Valley supplies the square dance and country music and the dance floor, you supply the stompin'.

information). Other folk music can be heard here most nights. Blue-grass and mountain music keep the cloggers clogging and the square dancers do-si-do-ing. Stop in and join the fun.

Dillsboro is the last stop in our loop tour. You have the option of taking the more scenic route via US 19 west from Maggie Valley, turning south (left) onto the Blue Ridge Parkway, then going west (right) on US 23/74 to Sylva, then Dillsboro. You can take the short-cut by going back toward Waynesville where you get on US 23/74.

The following are Maggie Valley, NC 28751 and area code 704.

✎ ACCOMMODATIONS

Cataloochee Ranch—Rt. 1 Box 500; 800-868-1401, 926-1401; 11 cabins, 15 rooms, breakfast, restaurant, golf, fishing, horseback riding, snow skiing.
Ketner Inn & Farm—POB 1628; 926-1511; 5 rooms, breakfast.
Maggie Valley Resort & Country Club—340 Country Club Rd.; 926-1616; 11 villas, 64 rooms, breakfast, restaurant, pool, golf, tennis.
Smokey Shadows Lodge—POB 444; 926-0001; 12 rooms with private baths, 2 cottages, breakfast, restaurant, pool, jogging/nature trail, majestic view (featured in this book's cover photograph).

Ketner Inn offers farm-life accommodations just outside Maggie Valley.

✎ ATTRACTIONS

Cataloochee Ski Area— December to March. 800-768-0285.
Ghost Town in the Sky—POB 369 (US 19 at Fie Top Mountain Rd.); 800-446-7886, 926-1140.
Lindsey Miniature Village—250 Soco Rd.; 926-6277; Seasonal displays of villages, railroad, flower gardens in miniature, doll exhibits.
Maggie Valley Opry House—US 19; Bluegrass & mountain music, nightly at 8; May to October.
Mini-Apolis Grand Prix—US 19; 926-1685; Go-carts, amusements, shops, gem mine.
Soco Gardens Zoo—904 Soco Rd.; 926-1746; Guided tours, snake shows, covered walkways, animals.
Stompin' Ground—9 Soco Rd.; 926-1288; Nightly music and dancing for the family; No alcohol.
The Valley Art Gallery—POB 1238; 926-1200; Art works, materials, painting demonstrations.

❧ DINING

Arf's—1316 Soco Rd; 926-1566; American menu.

The Back Door Grill & Bar—611 Soco Rd.; 926-2229; Salads, sandwiches, and full meals; bar and karaoke on Sunday and Thursday nights.

Cataloochee Ranch—Fie Top Mountain Rd; 800-868-1401, 926-1401; Southern Appalachian cuisine; Reservations requested.

Country Vittles Restaurant—907 Soco Rd.; 926-1820; All-you-can-eat and full menu.

J. Authur's Restaurant—801 Soco Rd.; 926-1817; Prime rib, seafood , gorgonzola cheese salad, full bar.

Joey's Pancake House—1315 Soco Rd.; 926-0212; Breakfast from 7:00 to 11:00 A.M.

Saratoga's Cafe—735 Soco Rd.; 926-1448; Steaks, fish, chicken, sandwiches, homemade soup; Jazz on Wednesday nights; Entertainment Friday and Saturday nights; No cover charge.

Smokey Shadows Lodge—POB 444 (Fie Top Rd.); 926-0001; Candlelight dinner, honeymoons, weddings, reunions; Reservations only.

❧ SHOPPING

Cabbage Rose—Olde Town Plaza; 926-3079; Dept. 56, Snowbabies, year-round Christmas shop.

Fugate's Flea Market—US 19; 926-0865; Antiques, collectibles, 70 booths.

Geisha Gardens—Rt. 1, Box 512, Fie Top Mountain Rd; 926-1182; Authentic Oriental gift shop.

Lavender & Lace—901 US 19; 926-0877; Lace, linen, antiques, teas, candies.

Maggie Mountaineer Crafts—606 Soco Rd.; 926-3129; Local artisans produce pottery silk flowers, baskets, crafts.

Soco Crafts and Tower—US 19; 926-1626; "Most photographed view in the Smokies"; 9-story observation tower.

Soco Gardens Zoo and Gift Shop—904 Soco Rd.; 926-1746; Animal collectibles, wind chimes, crafts.

Sweet N Sassy—822 Soco Rd.; 926-3585; Homemade candy, quilts, crafts.

❧ SPECIAL EVENTS

May—*Rally in the Valley Hot Air Balloon Festival*

June to July—*Mountaineer Antique Auto Show (US 271)*

July—*Maggie Valley Arts & Crafts Fair*

July—*Folk Moot USA*
July—*Maggie Valley Gem, Mineral, Art, & Jewelry Show*
August—*Larry's Jazz Reunion*
October—*High Country Quilt Show*
October—*America's Clogging Hall of Fame Competitions*

CAMPING

Happy Valley RV Park—813 Soco Rd.; 926-0327; 24 trailer sites with hookups, showers, toilets; April to November.
Meadow Brook Resort— Indian Creek Rd.; 926-1821; 31 trailer sites with hookups, showers, toilets, fishing.
Pressley's Campground and RV Park—US 19; 926-1904; Creek side, RV hook-ups, tent sites, pool, games, TV, trout pond.
Smoky View Travel Trailer Park Resort—846 Soco Rd.; 926-1245; 10 trailer sites with hookups, 10 tent sites, showers, toilets, fishing, camp store.
Soco Gap Campground—Rt. 1, Box 538; 926-3635; 15 trailer sites with hookups, 25 tent sites, showers, toilets, camp store; May to November.
Village Campground—POB 535; 926-1083; 50 acres on Jonathan Creek for RVs, hook-ups, showers, dump station, grills, tables.
Winngray Family Campground—625 Jonathan Creek Rd., Waynesville, NC 28786; 926-3170; Closer to Maggie Valley, there are 100 full hook-ups, showers, phone hook-ups, camp store, game room, restrooms, fish pond, bottled gas, laundry.

FOR MORE INFORMATION

Maggie Valley Convention and Visitors Bureau—621 Soco Rd., Maggie Valley, NC 28751; 800-MAGGIE1, 926-1686.

DIRECTIONS

Take Exit 20 off I-40 on to US 276, then turn west on US 19 to Maggie Valley.
From Waynesville—Go east on US 74, then turn west on US 19.

28 Dillsboro:
A New Spirit Springs from the Past

We arrived in Dillsboro about sunset. Coming in from the direction of Sylva, we were on Haywood Street. The Jarrett House, on the National Register of Historic Places, was the last building on the right before the junction with US 441.

When we walked in to register for our room, people were walking out groaning. We learned these were people who tried to eat everything set before them. The Jarrett House earned its reputation for a good and generous meal a century ago. The tradition continues. Now we understood why the parking lot was full, as full as the people who were getting up from the tables.

Constructed in 1884 by William Dills, the Mount Beulah Hotel attracted passengers off the new railroad. Dills named the

Dillsboro's century-old Jarrett House provides the same family style dining that our great-grandparents would have enjoyed here. After eating all-you-can-eat, you may want to sleep it off in one of the hotel's newly renovated rooms.

inn and the mountain facing it Beulah, for his daughter. By 1886, people were coming to "summer" in Dillsboro. Frank Jarrett bought the hotel in 1894 from Dills, changed its name to Jarrett Springs Hotel, taking advantage of the sulphur spring behind the inn.

Springs became popular "healing places" throughout the South (see the Shatley Springs story in the Troutdale, VA, section). Jarrett promoted the spring with much hyperbole and built a summer house over it with encircling seats so guests could invigorate themselves by sitting in the water as well as drinking it.

"DILLIEBIRD"

The rare bird that some people say Dillsboro is really named after. It returns to this very spot every spring after wintering on the roof of a condo in Boca Raton.

Dilliebird welcomes tourists to one of the many shops that have made Dillsboro a shopper's paradise.

Although the spring was popular, Jarrett's wife, "Miss Sallie" earned the real kudos. She created a menu backed by good cooking that established the Jarrett House as *the* place to eat. It's true Frank Jarrett developed a new way to cure hams, but it was Miss Sallie's cooking that became the main attraction. Items on Miss Sallie's menu were "fried ham on great platters with red-eye gravy, hot buttermilk biscuits, sourwood honey, homemade butter, and fresh vegetables." At every meal, the platters of country ham and bowls of red-eye gravy keep coming to the tables causing strong men to weep—"because they couldn't eat as much as they wanted!"

Jim and Jean Hartbarger bought the hotel in 1975. They and their two sons, Buzz and Scott, lived in two rooms behind the front desk. After getting the "feel" of operating a successful restaurant, adding trout and fried chicken to the menu (that still keeps 'em moaning), the Hartbargers took on the formidable task of reconditioning the rooms.

"Formidable" is an understatement. Previous owners had tried to "modernize" the rooms by cutting off the legs of old beds and nailing the headboards to the walls. Old furniture had been painted pink, yellow, and blue. After years of work the hotel now has comfortable rooms for guests, but the renovation continues.

Our room was tastefully done with a gorgeous antique bedroom suite of walnut. It rendered the feeling of being in the hotel in its heyday, 113 years ago. We spent part of the evening rocking on the second-story balcony—delightful.

Buzz and Scott, having grown up in the inn, brought their wives, Mary and Sharon, into the business. Sharon showed us around and shared "inn stories" with us. One we found particularly appealing: Jim Hartbarger was sent a key by John Vaught Jr. in 1995. John had bought a house and, while moving in, found the key in the basement. The key had Jarrett Springs Hotel on it. The couple who sold John the house kept the key from the time they spent their honeymoon at the hotel in 1935 or 1936. It took 60 years for the key to return home.

William Dills founded New Webster in 1884 to become the terminus for the Western North Carolina Railroad until the tunnels were completed through Cowee Mountain. New Webster was named "Dillsboro" in 1899.

The young community had several inns similar to the Jarrett House, and soon it attracted travelers by rail to the cool mountain air. After the construction of good highways through North Carolina, visitors merely passed by on their way to more distant places. In short, Dillsboro's light faded.

Ironically, as traffic continued to increase along these very roads, eventually more people began to stop. Dillsboro's light began to shine again because it made itself attractive to travelers. Dillsboro is a town of fewer than 200 souls known as Jackson County's growing craft village.

The former home of C.J. Harris, a pioneer miner, was converted into Riverwood Shops. Once you visit these shops you will understand one of the reasons the community has grown in popularity. Within the limited space of a hilltop overlooking two streams are many shops with local artists who spin and weave, carve wood, hammer pewter, and much more.

Rustic Dillsboro Inn has gardens and decks on the trout-stocked Tuckasegee River. The waterfall next to the inn creates a relaxing atmosphere. Also here to help you relax are fireplaces, a wood-fired cedar hot tub, massage, yoga classes, gourmet coffee, teas, and full breakfasts. All rooms have private baths and are smoke-free.

Historic Olde Towne Inn's large front porch overlooks shops and the railroad tracks. Built in 1878, this restored home has 3 guest rooms with private baths. You'll enjoy a full country breakfast, which you'll need for energy to visit all the nearby shops.

Olde Towne Inn is one of several inns welcoming tourists to Dillsboro. You will want to spend at least 2 days taking in all the sights and shops in this unusual village.

Riding in old-fashioned train cars of the Great Smoky Mountain Railway is one of the highlights of visiting Dillsboro.

Just 25 minutes south of the Great Smokies Park, Dillsboro is the main departure depot of the Great Smoky Mountains Railway. Hop on board for Whittier, Bryson City (depot), Almond, Wesser, Nantahala, Topton, Andrews (depot), Marble, and Murphy.

All these towns along the railroad were founded in the 1800s and retain their charm and character today. Tracks laid between 1852 and 1882 for Western North Carolina Railroad linked Asheville to Waynesville; two years later they reached the old city of Charleston, now Bryson City. The tracks stretched to Murphy by 1891.

Now you can ride the 67 miles from Dillsboro to Murphy in comfortable, reconditioned coaches. You may choose to sit in a coach, club car, dining car, crown coach, or the open car for better viewing. The caboose is available for private parties only.

The railway operates four diesel-electric locomotives and one Baldwin steam engine, No. 1702, which is a movie star (*This Property Is Condemned*, starring Robert Redford, Natalie Wood, and Charles Bronson). Today many excursionists want to see the Tuckasegee River site made famous by the train wreck scene for *The Fugitive*, starring Tommy Lee Jones and Harrison Ford. The GSM Railway operates from June to October and carries 175,000 passengers annually.

Floyd McEachern (right) began his Historical Train Museum, and was later joined by Bill Randall, to fulfill his dream—a huge model of trains, tracks, and landscape that may reach completion by the year 2000.

Adjacent to the GSM Railway train station is the Floyd McEachern Historical Train Museum. Floyd and Bill Randall have created a treasury of trains. Railroad devotees will love this place! From numerous turn-of-the-century models (string-pull, wind-up, and electric) to memorabilia from the original iron horses going back 140 years, make up more than 3,000 items on display. If you had a model as a child, we bet you'll find one like it here.

An extensive scale model railroad and environs, including mountains with 1,200 trees, switching yard, and more, is being added to yearly. Only one-third of the landscaping for the elaborate model was complete when we visited in the summer of 1996. It will take about three more years of work before it performs as Floyd and Bill envision it.

There aren't many old fashioned soda shops left in this world, but there is one on Front Street in Bradley's General Store. Yummy!

Across the railroad tracks, over a small stream, and up the hill are the Riverwood Shops. One of the highlights here is Riverwood Pewter. Dee Shook has been handcarving pewter for 49 years.

Time Capsule Bookstore is the place to look for rare, old, out-of-print, and *new* books on Appalachian history, Civil War, Native

Bradley's General Store includes an old-timey soda fountain that still whips up great shakes, malteds, sodas, and pies.

America, the South, railroads, nature, and many other topics of regional interest.

Dillsboro's appearance hasn't changed much since 1889. And the best thing is that its heart is still warm and friendly, welcoming you to stay awhile.

To get back to Fontana, go west on US 74 then take NC 28 west. This concludes our loop tour. Next we'll take a linear tour along the Blue Ridge Parkway, beginning in Cherokee and ending in Mount Airy.

The following are Dillsboro, NC 28725 and area code 704 except where noted.

Dee Shook planned to retire the year after this photo was taken, following a half century of handcarving pewter.

ACCOMMODATIONS

Applegate Inn—163 Hemlock St.; 586-2397; 4 rooms, breakfast.
Dillsboro Inn—POB 270; 586-3898; 2 apartments, 4 rooms with private baths, breakfast, fishing.
Jarrett House—POB 219; 800-972-5623, 586-0265; 21 rooms, breakfast, restaurant; Open April 15 through October, weekends in November, and first two weekends in December.
Olde Towne Inn—POB 485; 586-3461; 3 rooms, breakfast.
Squire Watkins Inn—POB 430; 586-5244; 3 rooms, 2 suites, private baths, breakfast.

ATTRACTIONS

Great Smoky Mountain Railway—POB 397; 800-872-4681, 704-568-8811.
Floyd McEachern Historical Train Museum—586-4085.

The handsome Squire Watkins Inn is just up the road from where the train wreck in the movie *Fugitive* took place.

DINING

Dillsboro Smokehouse—267 Haywood St.; 586-9556; One block from the depot; barbecue baby back ribs, chicken, beef, and pork, smoked turkey, Lunch and dinner; Carry out.
Jarrett House—POB 219; 800-972-5623, 586-0265; See details in text.
Well House—Riverwood Shops; 586-8588; Open yearround for lunch, serving deli sandwiches, homemade soups, daily specials, desserts; Dine in or take out .

⤳ SHOPPING

Several shops make up Riverwood at the corner of River Road and US 441. Some are listed below.

Apron Shop—586-9391; Offers locally made aprons, quilts, pillows, baskets, crafts.

Bateman's Jelly Shop—Front St.; 586-9650; Features locally made jellies, jams, preserves, relishes, syrups, cider, honey.

Bradley's General Store—On Front St.; great old time soda fountain sundries; Country gifts, home furnishings.

The Cheddar Box—On Haywood St.; 586-4442; Fine cheeses, teas, coffee beans, homemade candies, cookbooks .

Dogwood Crafters—Webster St., between Jarrett House and Riverwood Shops; 586-2248; Over 100 crafters offer items for sale.

Duck Decoys—POB 717; 586-9000, 586-2940.

The Golden Carp—Webster St.; Home accessories, baskets, antiques, collectibles, gifts.

The Imagination Station—Set back off Haywood St.; 586-3353; Locally handcrafted folk art, wood carvings, bird houses and feeders; March to December.

Mountain Pottery—586-9183; Makes pottery while you watch; Offers handmade porcelain, stoneware, and Raku from over 50 artists.

Oaks Gallery—A Riverwood Shop; 586-6542; A showcase for over 90 local artists; Weaving, glass, wood, pottery.

Old School Antique Mall—5 miles south of Dillsboro on Hwy. 441; 586-8097.

Nancy Tut's Christmas Shop—POB 130; 800-742-7155, 586-5391; On Haywood St. beside the Jarrett House; Everything for Christmas including Dept. 56, Thomas Clark, and collectibles; April to December.

Puzzle Emporium—Church St.; 586-1114; Puzzles from around the world for all ages.

Riverwood Pewter Shop—586-6996; Wide variety of pewter items, some made in the shop.

The Silver Hammer—Set back off Haywood St.; 586-3180; Offers handcrafted sterling silver jewelry, gifts.

Time Capsule—586-1026; Used, rare, and out-of-print books with several specialties; New regional books; At the Riverwood Shops.

Venture Out—POB 638; 586-1464, 800-586-1464; Full line of camping, backpacking, and hiking clothes, gear, and supplies.

Yes Dear—271 Haywood St.; 586-2826; Gifts, antiques.

✒ SPECIAL EVENTS

April—Dillsboro Easter Bonnet Parade; Easter Sunday at 1:00 P.M., Show off your bonnet to be judged (outrageous hats are encouraged); Contact Susan Leveiller at 704-586-6542.

June—Dillsboro Heritage Festival; Foods, crafts, antiques, mountain music; Contact Susan Leveiller at 704-586-5477.

December—Dillsboro Luminaries; First two Fridays and Saturdays in December; All of Dillsboro is aglow with light from thousands of candles; At 5:00 P.M., local merchants serve refreshments as brass ensembles and choral groups play and sing carols; Call 704-586-2155 or 800-962-1911.

Seasonal—Wildflower Work Shops; Spring, summer, fall; Contact George Ellison at 704-488-8782.

✒ CAMPING

Fort Tatham Campsites—Rt. 2 Box 206, Sylva, NC 28779; 586-6662.

Laurel Bush Campground—15 Tunnel Mountain Rd., Sylva, NC 28779; 704-586-8346; 20 trailer sites with hookups, 10 tent sites, shower, toilets, boat/raft rental, fishing; May to November.

✒ FOR MORE INFORMATION

Jackson County Travel & Tourism Authority—116 Central St., Sylva, NC 28779; 800-962-1911.

✒ DIRECTIONS

From East or West—Take Exit 27 off I-40, then US 23/74 to Exit 81.

From Atlanta area—Take I-85 north to US 441; Dillsboro is on US 23/441.

29   *Blue Ridge Parkway:*
The Best of Then Is Now

A drive along the Blue Ridge Parkway not only arouses your sense of reverence for the countryside, but also makes you wonder how early Americans could make a living farming among these mountains.

The Blue Ridge Parkway runs uninterrupted for 469 miles allowing motorists, hikers, and bicyclists views of blue-misted mountains, waterfalls, rolling pastures, wildflowers, forests, and gorges. It is the world's first parkway designed exclusively for leisurely travel and recreational use.

The Blue Ridge Parkway is free from commercial development and congestion. Trees and plants border the parkway, pull-offs for viewing the scenery are fairly frequent, as are campgrounds, picnic areas, and wayside exhibits. Mileposts along the Parkway let you know where you are and help you locate attractions.

It wasn't until 1987 that the ground broken at Cumberland Knob, North Carolina, became the completed Parkway. In 1967, only 7.5 miles remained incomplete, but what a 7.5 miles!

Grandfather Mountain remained "un-parkwayed" due to environmental considerations. The question was, "How do we build a road at 4,100 feet elevation without damaging one of the world's oldest mountains?"

After much thinking and consulting, National Park engineers decided a bridge was needed. Construction began on a bridge, or viaduct, to curve around the mountain and over Linn Cove in 1979. The completed viaduct is 1,243 feet long, containing 153 segments weighing 50 tons each. Construction was difficult. Engineers had to create ways of working from the viaduct they were building in front of them.

Ribbon-cutting ceremonies at the completion of the Blue Ridge Parkway occurred on Sept. 11, 1987, exactly 52 years after the first spade of dirt was turned. Linn Cove Viaduct, at milepost 304.6, was the last link in a long road that connects the Great Smokies with the Shenandoah Valley. Traversing the Blue Ridge Mountains, the road has 26 tunnels, and passes through 29 counties in two states encompassing 85,000 acres as it crosses 181 miles of US forests and 11 miles of Qualla Boundary Cherokee Indian Reservation.

Between April 1939, when the Blue Ridge Parkway (BRP) opened, until January 1990, it was determined that 500 million people had visited the scenic road. Someone took those numbers a step further to calculate that it cost about 26 cents per visitor to build the road. (Try to figure the total cost. We'll fess up later.) The original concept to build a road for relaxation and recreation, and to preserve the natural beauty around it, did not change from conception to implementation. The means and methods did.

It is not likely in today's political environment of Congress threatening to sell national parks to private enterprise this project would have ever had a hope of completion. That the Blue Ridge Parkway exists today is the result of a combination of fortuitous circumstances.

The concept of a road traversing the Southern Appalachians has surfaced off and on since the early years of the automobile. The idea for the BRP drew its first breath during the Great Depression as a child of the National Industrial Recovery Act of 1933 that ordered the Public Works Administration (PWA) to prepare a comprehensive program that would include construction, maintenance, and improvement of public highways and parkways.

During 1933, President Franklin Roosevelt visited the Skyline Drive that was being built by the Civilian Conservation Corps (CCC) in Virginia's Shenandoah National Park. When it was suggested that a similar road be built through the mountains to connect the Shenandoah with the Great Smoky Mountains National Park in North Carolina and Tennessee, Roosevelt approved. Late that year, $16.6 million was allocated for a scenic roadway linking the two national parks.

The road was to be a joint project of the Commonwealth of Virginia, the state of North Carolina, and the Federal government. Procedures called for the states to acquire rights-of-way and donate them to the United States. Federal entities then would provide funding for design, construction, and supervision. Surveyors were in the field in 1934 and the first construction on a 12-mile section just south of the Virginia-North Carolina border began in late summer 1935.

In 1936, Congress put the Parkway under the jurisdiction of National Park Service of the US Department of Interior. This meant the BRP would be considered a resource of national merit "to conserve the scenery and the natural and historic objects and the wildlife . . . and to provide for the enjoyment of the same in such manner and by such means as will leave them unimpaired for the enjoyment of future generations."

Even with this boost in esteem for the project, there was turmoil. Tennessee was not unlike a child seeing others get a bag of candy—she wanted some too. Squabbling, or put more diplomatically, negotiations began. Tennessee proposed a different route that would leave North Carolina out. The squabble finally got down to the number of bridges that would have to be built to bring the road in on the north side of the GSMNP compared to the route through North Carolina to the south side. Tennessee had too many major rivers to span, therefore too many more dollars would have had to be spent. North Carolina won her original position: a two-state road connecting the national parks.

Politics aside, out in the mountains the magnitude of the project soon became apparent. The route of the 469-mile parkway had to be established through rugged country that had few roads. There were no maps for some sections of the mountains and other areas had only been sketched by the Appalachian Trail Club.

Landscape architects and surveyors began wandering through the woods talking with local people about where the best scenic views were, working from one side of the ridge to the other, discussing the advantages, scenic or monetary, of locating the corridor here or there.

The red-orange Mountain Ash berries are as pretty in the fall as rhododendron are in the spring. Flora along the Parkway were an attraction long before the road was completed in 1987.

Next, landscape architects worked with engineers to determine where to build bridges and where to blast tunnels. Every foot of the BRP was planned carefully.

With the path of the road chosen, the states had to begin securing the rights-of-way from private landowners. The Blue Ridge Mountains have had inhabitants for more than 200 years and obtaining rights-of-way meant talking with the mountain people one at a time, on a case-by-case basis. The inhabitants needed to hear what the project was about, be convinced the road would be good for them, and know they would get a fair price for their land.

Most of the mountain people were in favor of the road. But most of them, as well as most county and state officials, thought it was just another road to get their wares to market. Hence began the ongoing campaign to define a national parkway.

There was no precedent in 1933, certainly not in magnitude, for a 469-mile road that had recreational pleasure travel as one of its primary purposes. New policies had to be created and decisions based on those policies had to be made. Very early on, the "scenic highway" concept evolved into an elongated park containing a road designed to please motoring viewers by revealing the beauty, charm, and interest of a portion of the indigenous American countryside.

This meant not only protecting the narrow corridor but also establishing some sort of protection for views from the road. Policies calling for leases and scenic easements were initiated. Over the years, this approach has required public relations with sensitivity and constraint in order to convince those who owned the property the BRP passes through that this road was indeed a national resource, a creation in which they could all take pride. It is to the enduring credit of the BRP personnel over the years that their high standards were not relaxed, and to the credit of the mountain residents that they joined in the effort.

As the Parkway grew in miles and in reputation, there were significant donations of private lands. These included the Moses H. Cone estate (1948), the Julian Price Memorial Park (1949), and the Linville Falls Recreation Area, purchased and donated by John D. Rockefeller Jr. (1952).

Construction on the Parkway did not have to wait for all the lands to be acquired by the two states and donated to the Federal government. The need during the Great Depression was to put people to work. The BRP was built one section here, one section there, until all were joined.

A stipulation in early contracts required contractors to hire labor from rolls of the unemployed in the county where the work would take place. About 90 percent of the labor force came from local "creeks and coves." Only specialized labor was imported. On any given job, those laborers might have joined road engineers, bridge engineers, architects, landscape architects, foresters, heavy equipment operators, mechanics, and masons to carry out some often unique requirements.

For example, specialists were brought in to build the splendid stone bridges and retaining walls that have become the Parkway's trademark. These gifted stonemasons were Spaniards and Italians who developed a friendly rivalry to see who could build the finest bridges and walls in the shortest time at the lowest cost.

Tunnels presented other problems. An entire mountainside could not be blasted away allowing the debris to fall where it may. The idea was to reveal, but at the same time protect the beauty of the mountain terrain. Blasting crews had to learn how much dynamite was "just enough."

Imagine the scope of landscaping the parkway. No National Park Service had attempted such an enormous undertaking. What you see is the result, not what they had to work with. Farms, land that had been burned over, and eroded and timber harvested land had to be reclaimed.

In the process, mountain people learned about soil conservation, fire control, erosion prevention, and crop rotation, whereas the National Park Service learned about blending the motor road with its environs. All involved were moving the vision from an abstraction to a reality.

Work slowed considerably during World War II, but afterward construction resumed in earnest. The next-to-last section, around the city of Asheville, was finished in 1967. The final section,

Great care was taken when constructing tunnels and the road bed so that rock blasted loose would not scar the mountainsides or leave debris.

around Grandfather Mountain, was opened to traffic 52 years to the day from the beginning, September 11, 1987.

Oh, yes, the total cost of building the parkway was $130 million.

HIGHLIGHTS ALONG THE SOUTHERN HALF OF THE BRP

We'll begin at Oconaluftee Visitor's Center in Cherokee, North Carolina (milepost 469), working our way 250-something miles northeast to the Virginia border pointing out some highlights. There are numerous panoramic views; many have self-guiding trails, exhibits, waterfalls, and other places of interest.

MILEPOST 469 ▪ Southern terminus of BRP at Cherokee, NC, at junction with US 441.

MILEPOST 431 ▪ Richland Balsam's self-guiding trail (moderate 1.47 miles) takes you through a remnant spruce-fit forest. Highest point on the parkway, 6,047 feet elevation.

MILEPOST 422.4 ▪ Devil's Courthouse is a rugged exposed mountaintop rich in Cherokee legends. A moderate to strenuous .42-mile walk to the bare rock summit earns you a spectacular view of Pisgah National Forest.

MILEPOST: 408.6 ▪ Mount Pisgah was part of the Biltmore Estate. The estate became home of the first US forestry school and the nucleus of the Pisgah National Forest. There are self-guiding trails, ranger talks, books and craft sales, camping, and camp store. Frying Pan Mountain Trail is a moderate-to-strenuous 1.06 miles.

MILEPOST 382 ▪ Folk Art Center offers sales and exhibits of traditional and contemporary crafts and books of the Appalachian Region. Interpretive programs, gallery and library. A section of the Mountain-to-Sea Trail runs 7.5 miles from Folk Art Center to milepost 365, moderate.

Craggy Gardens is true to its name with the added allure of views to stimulate your sense of wonder.

MILEPOST 363.4-369.6 ▪ Craggy Gardens seem covered with purple rhododendron in mid-June. Craggy Pinnacle Trail (moderate .73 miles), other trails and road to picnic area and trails (367.6). Book and craft sales in the Visitor's Center.

MILEPOST 355.4 ▪ Mount Mitchell State Park reached via NC 128 has a picnic area, lookout tower, exhibit, restaurant and is the highest point east of the Mississippi River at an elevation of 6,684 feet. Snow has been recorded here during every month of the year. Often overcast and windy. For a day-hike, follow the orange blaze from the parking lot along Black Mountain Crest Trail. A rugged mile-long trail to Mt. Craig (6,645 feet). Ask for more information at the concession stand.

MILEPOST 339 ▪ Crabtree Meadows. Walk to Crabtree Falls via a strenuous two-mile loop trail. You will find a campground, camp store, books and crafts, ranger talks, and hiking.

MILEPOST 331 ▪ Museum of North Carolina Minerals interprets the state's mineral wealth. There are more than 300 different kinds of rocks and minerals. You can prospect for gems and minerals in the area. The Visitor's Center has books and crafts for sale and demonstrations.

MILEPOST 316.3 ▪ Linville Falls roars through a dramatically rugged gorge. The Visitor's Center has books and crafts for sale, ranger talks, camping, trails to overlooks and fishing. This 7,600-acre tract has been preserved to provide a primitive natural environment. The steep walls of the gorge enclose Linville River that descends 2,000 feet in only 12 miles. Access to Linville Gorge Wilderness Area is by foot trails via a Forest Service Road off US 221 at the Linville Falls community exit.

MILEPOST 308.3 ▪ Flat Rock is worth the easy walk (.63 mile) for the superb view of Grandfather Mountain and Linn Valley. Grandfather Mountain is the site of the annual Highland Games and Gathering of Scottish Clans.

MILEPOST 305.5 ■ Beacon Heights Parking Area is trailhead for Tanawha Trail.

MILEPOST 304.4 ■ Linn Cove Viaduct. The Visitor's Center has books and crafts for sale. Linn Cove Trail, wheelchair accessible, is an easy .16 mile long to the base of the viaduct.

The Linn Cove Viaduct is a modern engineering marvel. *(Courtesy of Blue Ridge Parkway)*

MILEPOST 299.9 ■ Boone Fork parking area. You can connect with Tanawha Trail (13.5 miles, easy-to-moderate), Daniel Boone Scout Trail and Nuwati Trail. The Boone Trail connects with Grandfather Trail that takes you to Linville Peak, 5,280 feet high.

MILEPOST 295.1-298 ■ Julian Price Memorial Park, the former retreat of an insurance executive, offers a variety of short trails and a lake. Here is a lovely place to picnic, camp, fish, rent a canoe/ boat, hike and wade in a stream. From Price Park you can hike the Tanawha Trail from milepost 297.1 to 305.5 at Beacon Lights parking area. Price Trails are Price Lake Trail (moderate, 2.3 miles), Green Knob Trail (moderate/strenuous 2.3 miles), and Boone Fork Trail (moderate/strenuous 4.9 miles) that connects with Tanawha Trail then the Daniel Boone Scout Trail.

MILEPOST 292-295 ■ Moses H. Cone Memorial Park has 25 miles of carriage roads, ideal for hiking and horseback riding within its 3,600-acre environs. Flat Top Manor houses the Parkway Craft Center where books and crafts are for sale and demonstrations. Fishing is available as are canoe/boat rentals. At Moses Cone you can hike on 11 trails, including the Rich Mountain Road, Ducan Road, Deer Park Road, Flat Top Road, Watkin Road, Black Mountain Road, and the Maze. Here is a good place to cross-country ski when there is snow.

MILEPOST 285.1 ■ Boone's Trace that Daniel Boone blazed to the west, crosses near here.

MILEPOST 272 ■ E.B. Jeffress Park has a self-guiding trail (easy half-mile loop) to the Cascades and another trail goes to the old cabin and church. The view of the falls is better from the bottom.

MILEPOST 264.5 ▪ Tom Dula Overlook offers a magnificent view and a good place to picnic. Maybe pull out your guitar and sing a chorus of "Hang down your head Tom Dooley."

MILEPOST 258.6 ▪ Northwest Trading Post is sponsored by the Northwest Development Association to keep alive the old crafts within North Carolina's 11 northwestern counties. Demonstrations, and books and more than 250 different crafts for sale.

MILEPOST 238.5-244.7 ▪ Doughton Park was named for Congressman Robert L. Doughton, a staunch supporter and neighbor of the parkway. One of the best locations to see deer. Camping, ranger talks, camp store, restaurant, hiking and fishing are available. Books and crafts for sale. The largest recreation area on the BRP. Bluff Mountain Trail parallels BRP to milepost 244.7 and is a moderate 7.5-mile hike. Cedar Ridge Trail is another moderate hike of 4.2 miles.

MILEPOST 238.5 ▪ Brinegar Cabin was built by Martin Brinegar about 1880 and was lived in until his death in the 1930s when the homestead was purchased by the Parkway from his widow. The original cabin stands here today. Demonstrations and hiking available.

MILEPOST 217.5 ▪ Cumberland Knob, at 2,885 feet, is a delightful spot to walk (easy half-mile) through fields and woodlands. The Visitor's Center has books and crafts for sale. You can picnic and hike here also. This is the site of the first spade full of dirt turned to begin construction on the BRP.

MILEPOST 216.9 ▪ The BRP crosses the North Carolina/Virginia border. The 1749 party that surveyed the boundary included Peter Jefferson, father of Thomas Jefferson.

There are 216 miles of the upper parkway we didn't cover in this book. We strongly recommend you get one of the free Blue Ridge Parkway Maps available at all Visitor's Centers. If you are interested in hiking, ask for a map of trails in that district. You can usually only get maps of trails at the closest Visitor's Center to the trails.

You can use the Blue Ridge Parkway as the backbone of your vacation, seeing the sights along the way or getting off to visit the cities, communities, and countryside attractions we write about.

The mountains sometimes make it difficult to reach another destination without going around the long way, when in reality, it is the shortcut. More than a few times we heard, "You can't get there from here." Of course that isn't true, it just takes a good map and some time to make your way over, around, and through the mountains, but that should be part of your enjoyment.

If you prefer a flatland vacation, we recommend you read our book *Traveling the Trace* (Rutledge Hill Press, 1995), which takes you on another parkway from Nashville, Tennessee, to Natchez, Mississippi. The scenic Natchez Trace Parkway was built under the same guidelines as the Blue Ridge Rarkway.

We hope you are inspired by this book and find its contents helpful in discovering the Southern Highlands. Its abundant history, breathtaking views, and modern roads offer you a chance to experience the past, revel in nature, and sample southern hospitality in some of the South's best locales. We wish you a gratifying journey!

Turn the page to begin at the southern terminus of the Parkway in Cherokee, North Carolina.

30 Cherokee:
Home of the Eastern Band of the Cherokee

Historically, one of the most meaningful dances of the Cherokee people was the Eagle Dance. Visitors to the summertime outdoor drama *Unto These Hills* can see this dance performed. *(Courtesy of Cherokee Tribal Promotions)*

The town of Cherokee is located within the 56,000 acres of scattered tracts of land known as the Qualla Boundary, the home of the Eastern Band of the Cherokee. According to Horace Kephart in *The Cherokee of the Smoky Mountains*, this is but a fragment of their ancient holdings, which included land in eight states and totaled more than 135,000 square miles.

The Cherokee language evolved from the same root as Iroquoian languages, but no one is certain of the tribe's origins. The Cherokee lived in villages with log huts and cultivated crops long before they encountered white men.

The center of government was the council house, which was generally at the center of the stockaded Cherokee towns. Women and "ordinary" members of the village did not attend council meetings, but each of the seven traditional clans was represented: ani-awi (Paint Clan); ani-gategewi (Raccoon or Wild Potato Clan); ani-sahoni (Panther or Wild Cat Clan); ani-gilohi (Long Hair or Wind Clan); ani-tsiskwa (Bird Clan); ani-wahiya (Wolf Clan); and ani-awi (Deer Clan). The ancient Cherokee code found only two crimes punishable by death: marrying within the clan and murder.

The principal chief of the Cherokee Nation was the head of all civil and religious affairs. Separation of powers was achieved by having a chief warrior who was the chief official of military affairs. He was aided by the counsel of the War Woman, an aged and honorable woman of the tribe, often the widow of a former principal chief.

The earliest treaty was made with the Cherokee by whites in 1684. Over 150 years and 30 broken treaties later, an agreement between a small faction that did not include the principal chief or his representative, and the United States government forced the Cherokee to abandon their traditional homeland at gunpoint.

The story of the Cherokee removal begins with the arrival of British colonists before the American Revolution. The French and the British were competing for territory and most of the native tribes allied with the French. The Cherokee sided with the British against both their neighboring Indian adversaries and the colonists who were infringing on Cherokee lands along the river valleys in North Carolina, Tennessee, and Georgia.

PAINT CLAN

Paint Clan is one of the seven clans of the Cherokee shown at the base of the hand-carved statue of Sequoyah.

This alliance proved costly for the Cherokee, who were attacked by an overwhelming force of armed colonists from what is now eastern Tennessee, western North Carolina, and northern Georgia during the summer of 1776. The colonists destroyed their homes, crops, towns, and granaries, and drove off their cattle and horses. This was the first, but not the last, time the Cherokee were driven into the wilds of the Smokies for refuge by the colonists.

According to Vicki Rozema in *Footsteps of the Cherokees,* after the Revolution, the Federal government adopted a policy of "civilizing" the Cherokee, that is having them learn to read, write, and speak English and become Christians.

Some of the Cherokee reestablished farms that produced corn, beans, and cotton during this period. The more prosperous Cherokee farms south of the mountains were several hundred acres in size and used slave labor.

At about this time, a great change took place within the largely illiterate Cherokee nation as a result of the efforts of one man. Born George Gist (or Guess) in 1776, to Nathaniel Gist (hunting partner of Daniel Boone), a white who abandoned him in infancy, and Wureth of the Paint Clan, this man would be known as Sequoyah.

He was physically crippled from birth and walked with a limp. He enjoyed the reputation among his people of being able and intelligent, but little did they realize that this man who could neither read nor write English would be responsible for developing the means for the Cherokee to read and write in their own language.

Initially, he invented several thousand characters for individual words, but he realized that this system would be too cumbersome for anyone to remember or use. For twelve years, he labored at his task. Success finally came when he changed his approach, using a total of 85 characters to represent the sounds in the Cherokee tongue that form words. Within months, a substantial segment of the Cherokee Nation was literate. There were originally three Cherokee dialects. Kituhwa is presently used at Qualla, Atali is used in Oklahoma, and Elati is now extinct.

In 1824, Sequoyah went to Arkansas to teach the new alphabet to the Cherokee who had already been persuaded to move west to Arkansas between 1819 and 1824. By 1827, the Cherokee had a written constitution and a republican form of government. In 1828, a newspaper called the *Cherokee Phoenix* was being published in both Cherokee and English.

In the same year, Sequoyah was part of a delegation to Washington that ceded Cherokee lands in Arkansas in exchange for land in what is now Oklahoma, and gold was discovered along Duke's Creek on Cherokee lands in present-day Georgia (for more information see the Dahlonega, Georgia, section).

The Georgia legislature proceeded to pass legislation intended to deprive the Cherokee of their land and their rights for protection from gold-hungry Georgians. In 1832, Georgia divided land it had "annexed" from the Cherokee Nation and held lotteries for 160-acre homesteads or 40-acre gold lots in defiance of Supreme Court rulings and public opinion with the backing of Pres. Andrew Jackson.

Cherokee Principal Chief John Ross continued attempts to negotiate with the Federal government for resolution and redress, but factions within the Cherokee Nation signed an illegal treaty agreeing to move the Cherokee westward to join other members of the Cherokee Nation who had moved to Oklahoma earlier.

According to author Horace Kephart, the treaty was rejected formally by the Cherokee in October 1835. Chief Ross had moved to Tennessee to escape persecution by Georgians, but the Georgia militia was sent across state lines to arrest him and prevent him from traveling to Washington on behalf of the Cherokee. The Cherokee newspaper was destroyed. Written protests were sent to Washington representing nearly 16,000 (out of a population of 17,000) Cherokee. Champions like Davy Crockett, Henry Clay, and Daniel Webster were powerless to help the Cherokee, who had been at peace with the United States for forty years. Georgians robbed, attacked, and beat them without reprisal.

General Wool was dispatched to disarm the Cherokee and prepare them for removal. In February 1837, Wool reported, "So determined are they in their opposition that they . . . preferred living upon the roots and sap of trees rather than receive provisions from the United States . . . and thousands . . . had no other food for weeks." Soon after this report, Wool was relieved of his command at his own request and Gen. Winfield Scott assumed his duties. On May 26, 1838, the arrest of the Cherokee began.

James Mooney of the Bureau of American Ethnology wrote about the removal in detail, describing scenes of men seized in their fields, families driven from their dinner tables, and children torn from their parents' arms for the long march west. Nearly 4,000 of the 16,000 died along the way.

Cherokee from the Kituhwa settlement in present-day Swain County on the Tuckasegee and the neighboring mountain settlements at Oconaluftee fled with their chief, Yonaguska, to the high reaches of the Smokies. They were joined by others until they numbered nearly 1,000. Although the remote area saved them from pursuit, many of them starved because it was summer and there was very little to eat except roots, berries, tree bark, toads, snakes, and the occasional squirrel.

General Scott knew the fugitives would be very difficult to drive from their remote mountain hideouts without large numbers of troops moving in simultaneously.

What happened next is a matter of some controversy. The end result was that an old Cherokee named Tsali, who had killed a soldier in defense of his wife, his brother, and two older sons was executed in exchange for calling off the pursuit of the other Cherokee

Crafts, such as basket weaving, are as old as the Cherokee Nation. Today these items are sold to tourists rather than used for carrying and storing food. *(Courtesy of Cherokee Tribal Promotions)*

fugitives in the mountains. This story is told in the powerful outdoor drama, *Unto These Hills.*

Kephart tells us Cherokee prisoners were forced to carry out
the execution when the Cherokee's representative, Col. William
Holland Thomas, returned with the condemned men. Thomas was
a white trader who had been adopted by Chief Yonaguska as a boy.
He would later serve as the agent for the Cherokee, remaining at
Oconaluftee to negotiate with the Federal government on their
behalf. For three years he labored in Washington, requesting permission for them to remain in the east and receive compensation
for the lands that had been seized.

The Oconaluftee Cherokee were eventually paid $53.33 each for
their seized lands. Although he was not Cherokee by birth, Thomas
served as Principal Chief of the Eastern Band of the Cherokee from
1839 to 1867. Because the state of North Carolina did not recognize the rights of Cherokee to own property until 1866, Thomas
purchased the land in his name for the Cherokee and held it in trust.
These scattered properties became the Qualla Boundary. Thomas is
buried at Campground Cemetery off US 441 south of Cherokee.

Today about 9,000 Cherokee are listed on the rolls of the Eastern Band of the Cherokee. Their governing body, the Tribal Council, has twelve members (two from each of the five voting districts),
a chief, and a vice-chief elected by popular vote.

The town of Cherokee and the tribe derive about 70 percent of
their income from tourism. A maze of shops and tourist attractions
line US 441 through Cherokee. Many of them have offerings like
plains Indian warbonnets, tipis, and tomahawks that have little rela-
tion to the Cherokee culture. But remember, these are descendents
of a proud people who would rather starve than relinquish their
mountain homeland. Their survival at the moment depends on
Cherokee's tourism, which creates jobs in an area where unemploy-
ment can reach 50 percent in winter.

The Eastern Band is challenged by the need to create an environment that will encourage the best and brightest to remain
among them or return to tribal life after going away to college.
Among the newer Cherokee enterprises, Tribal Bingo is very popu-

lar, and the two video casinos on the Qualla Boundary are vital sources of revenue for the tribe and entertainment for visitors. It remains to be seen how these funds will be put to use for the Cherokee.

A good place to start your visit is the Cherokee Visitor's Center in downtown Cherokee. It is open daily except Thanksgiving, Christmas, and New Year's Day. The following sites are the best opportunities for sampling the history and culture of the Cherokee.

The Qualla Arts and Crafts Co-op has fine examples of intricately woven baskets, stone and wood carving, beadwork, and low-fired, hand-built pottery from more than 400 Cherokee members of the craft co-op. The co-op is the culmination of an organized arts and crafts program first established in the 1930s. Items are priced from a few dollars to thousands, and it is the best source of quality craftsmanship in Cherokee.

The Oconaluftee Indian Village is a realistic recreation of life in a Cherokee village during the eighteenth century. The Historical Association of the Eastern Band of the Cherokee operates the site, which is a living history museum with traditional craft demonstrations by Cherokee craftsmen. Guides lead visitors through a council house, sweat house, and log cabins as they discuss Cherokee culture. Visitors also see native craftsmen making pottery, canoes, arrowheads, and beaded belts by traditional methods. Cherokee musical instruments, ranging from turtle shells filled with small stones to drums, are demonstrated. There are also displays of fish traps and bear traps of ancient design.

The Museum of the Cherokee Indian has artifacts and exhibits to acquaint you with the history of the proud and once powerful Cherokee Indian Nation, their myths, and culture. Six mini-theaters provide videotape presentations about the prehistoric period to the present. You can read about Sequoyah's syllabary and hear the spoken word of the Cherokee via audiotape presentations. Cherokee Ceremonial Grounds host public powwows several times each year, including Memorial Day and the Fourth of July.

A 20-foot hand-carved statue of Sequoyah greets visitors to the Museum of the Cherokee Indian. Inside the museum visitors can learn of Cherokee history through audiovisual displays, artifacts, and exhibits. *(Courtesy of Cherokee Tribal Promotions)*

Unto These Hills is a musical drama that has told the story of the Cherokee people from the mid-1500s to the time of Tsali and the Cherokee's struggle to survive in the mountains after the removal. It is presented by the nonprofit Cherokee Historical Association, and receives funding from the North Carolina Legislature and the National Endowment for the Arts. Performances are held in a 2,800-seat outdoor amphitheater from June to August. There are provisions for handicapped parking and access.

Mingo Falls in Big Cove is a popular destination. To visit the falls or camp in Big Cove, turn onto Acquoini Road and take the first left onto Big Cove Road. Travel approximately five miles to the Mingo Falls Campground. The trail to Mingo Falls is 0.5 miles round-trip.

There's good fishing in the area at Bunches Creek and Fish Pond in Big Cove, one of the prettiest areas to visit around Cherokee.

There are more than 1,500 rooms and 2,200 campsites for visitors in Cherokee. One of the best choices is Newfound Lodge and Restaurant on US 441 North. Our favorite group of rooms overlooks the banks of the Oconaluftee River. This section of the motel has private decks overlooking the river, and rooms with phones, color television with cable, and queen- or king-sized beds.

The Blue Ridge Parkway begins in Cherokee and quickly climbs to 5,100 feet above sea level as it travels through some of the loftiest peaks to be found along the Parkway.

Unto These Hills is the popular outdoor drama depicting the struggles of the Cherokee with the encroaching white men.

The following are Cherokee, NC 28719 and area code 704 except where noted.

ACCOMMODATIONS

Comfort Inn—POB 132; 800-221-2222, 497-2411.
Days Inn—US 19N, Box 523; 800-325-2525, 497-9171.
Hampton Inn—US 19S, Box 1926; 800-HAMPTON, 497-3115.
Holiday Inn—US 19S, Box 1929; 800-HOLIDAY, 497-9181.
Newfound Lodge and Restaurant—US 441 North, 28719; 497-2746.

ATTRACTIONS

Cherokee Indian Cyclorama Wax Museum—POB 398; 497-4521; April to October.
Cherokee River Trips—#172 Hwy. 19S; 497-2821.
Museum of the Cherokee Indian—US 441 N; 497-3481, Daily.
Oconaluftee Indian Village—US 441 N; 497-2315; 9:00 A.M.-5:30 P.M. daily; Mid-May to October.
Santa's Land—US 19 E; 497-9191.
Smoky Mountain Jamboree—441 N. at Acquoni Rd.; 497-5521.
Tee Pee Village Casino—US 441; 497-3352.
Tribal Bingo—US 441; 800-410-1254, 497-4329; Daily.
Tribal Casino—US 441; 800-659-1115, 497-6835.
Unto These Hills—US 441; 497-2111; Mid-June to late August; 8:30 P.M.

CAMPING

Cherokee KOA—Star Route Box 39; 800-825-8352, 497-9711.
Indian Creek Campground—Star Route Box 75A, Buches Creek Rd., 28719; 497-4361.
Indian Hills Cabins—497-4361.
Mingo Falls Campground—Big Cove Rd.; 497-9944.

DINING

Big Boy Restaurant—497-4590.
Tee Pee Restaurant—Hwy. 441N; 497-5141.

❧ SHOPPING

Qualla Arts and Crafts Mutual, Inc.—POB 310; 497-3103.
The Old Mill—Hwy. 441S; 497-6536.

❧ SPECIAL EVENTS

Memorial Day and July 4—*Pow-wows, Cherokee Ceremonial Grounds (497-3028)*
May—*Western Carolina University; Elderhostel Program has classes on Cherokee culture and history; Accommodations at the Balsam Mtn. Inn; 227-7397, 800-WCU-4YOU.*

❧ FOR MORE INFORMATION

Cherokee Visitor's Center—POB 460, Cherokee, 28719; 800-438-1601, 497-9195.
Cherokee Publications—POB 430; 488-8856.
Fish and Game Management Enterprise—Box 302; 800-438-1601, 497-5201.

❧ DIRECTIONS

From Atlanta—Take I-85 to US 23/441 to Cherokee.
From Greenville/Spartanburg, SC—Take I-26 to the Blue Ridge Parkway. Or continue to Asheville and take exit 27 off I-40 West.
Take I-81 to I-40 and exit to the Great Smoky Mtn. Nat. Park, then follow 441S to Cherokee through the Park.

3 1 *Balsam:*
Comfort Among the Mountains

Leave the Blue Ridge Parkway at milepost 443 onto US 74 west toward Sylva and Dillsboro. You are looking for the small, nearby community of Balsam. You have to be as watchful for the turnoff as you are for the community, as it's smaller than you think.

To reach Balsam Mountain Inn, turn south at the small green sign on US 74 indicating Balsam, make a quick right, cross the railroad track, continue until you cross the tracks again, and then look up—there she is. There is no mistaking the huge three-story, long two-tiered porches of a beautiful lady known as the Balsam Mountain Inn. It occupies three-quarters of the hillside.

Merrily Teasley saved Balsam Mountain Inn from bulldozers to become more than the lovely functioning hotel it was designed to be in the early 1900s. *(Courtesy of Balsam Mountain Inn)*

The inn has an interesting past. Joseph Kenney and Walter Christy of Athens, Georgia, owned a small inn in Balsam but wanted a larger one. They chose a site just up the hill from the Murphy branch of the Southern Railroad. They hired a local builder to begin construction in 1905.

While the owners wintered in Georgia, leaving the construction in the hands of the builder, the inn grew. When they returned in the summer of 1908 to a completed inn, the owners were surprised to see their new inn was much larger than they had planned. The builder had added an unplanned third floor, totaling 100 rooms.

Their fears of not being able to fill these rooms were abated. The inn flourished, as did the economy, until the Depression. After the Depression, the inn changed hands and, because the new owner was not going to operate the inn, he rented it to the Moll family. Thus began the beautiful lady's slow decline.

In 1988, the health department condemned her. Vandalism occurred. The slow decline gained speed. Even though the inn had been on the National Register of Historic Places since 1982, her fate seemed doomed to bulldozers.

While it was slowly disintegrating, even while operating as an inn, Merrily Teasley was renovating an inn in Monteagle, Tennessee. Little did she know that she was wittingly preparing, in 1977, to become the savior of the Balsam Mountain Inn 13 years later. When the time was right, Merrily met the condemned lady and fell in love with her potential. That was in 1990.

Today, the inn is again the beautiful lady of the mountains. She stills looks like the Colonial Revival she always was, but her heart is brighter. One look at the third floor and you will see what we mean.

Merrily said, "As I worked to the third floor, renovating the rooms, I loosened up. I was more conservative downstairs."

We fell in love with the colors! Bold reds, bright yellows, lavenders, greens—all brilliant. It seemed like the heart of the inn was laughing with joy.

The amount of work to bring the inn back from the edge of degeneration seems improbable: a porch that was sliding down the hill; plumbing held together with old rags and duct tape; a dirty, hideous, pink dining room floor; a leaking roof; and an inadequate water supply, and septic system. The list of ailments appeared interminable.

One of Merrily's first obstacles in rejuvenating the inn was finding contractors and journeymen who were knowledgeable about restoring historic buildings. But with her sleeves rolled up, all the money she had and all the banks would lend her, Merrily began. She transformed the 100 small bedrooms and 13 baths into 50 ample rooms with window seats with private baths. She salvaged, cleaned, and installed 157 radiators from Western Carolina University, including the one in the dining room that weighs eight tons. Building codes required a sprinkler system whose pipes are cleverly hidden in the overhead beams.

The monumental tasks are behind her, though while we visited with Merrily, workmen were busy with additional cosmetic touches.

The dining room was restored to perfection. The ambiance was early 1900s. Wait until you see the tile she and her nephew laid in the dining area—gorgeous.

Merrily is a strong supporter of local artisans. The first floor hall has become a gallery for artists rather than a place to store guests' trunks as it once did. Another thoughtful touch to the Balsam Mountain Inn.

Before returning to the Parkway you may want to explore the area. Tucked among these mountains are many summer homes and permanent residences. Recreation abounds in the vicinity (see North Carolina Outdoor Recreation section).

The following are Balsam, NC 28707 and area code 704.

ACCOMMODATIONS

Balsam Mountain Inn—POB 40; 800-224-9498, 456-9498.
Hickory Haven Inn—POB 88; 452-1106; 6 rooms, breakfast.

CAMPING

Moonshine Creek Campground and Resort—POB 10; 586-6666; 72 trailer sites with hook-ups, 20 tent sites, showers, toilets, camp store, fishing.

You must see this room and the main dining room at the Balsam Mountain Inn in person to feel and appreciate their elegance.

32 *Asheville:*

An Uptown Downtown

The Vance Monument and fountain dominate Pack Square in downtown Asheville. Zebulon Vance became known as the "War Governor of the South."

In a 1995 survey, *Southern Living* readers selected Asheville as one of their top three favorite mountain getaways. Several national magazines have ranked Asheville in the top ten US cities for living or visiting. These accolades come as no surprise to Ashevillians. Visitors have been coming to Asheville for the scenery and the climate and remaining to enjoy the culture and lifestyle for more than a century.

William Davidson, his wife, and children are credited with being the first settlers in Asheville-Buncombe County. The area was well known to mountain men like Davy Crockett and Daniel Boone. Even earlier, Cherokee Indians held footraces here.

Enough homesteaders had arrived by 1791 to establish Buncombe County with its small log courthouse in what is now Asheville's downtown Pack Square. The frontier outpost at the confluence of the French Broad and Swannanoa Rivers was originally named Morristown, but was renamed Asheville in 1797 to honor Gov. Samuel Ashe.

Asheville became known as a health resort as early as the 1850s, bringing affluent Southerners by stagecoach. The "boom" began when the railroad penetrated the Blue Ridge Mountains in 1880 and Asheville was transformed into a true resort town. Its population tripled, with nearly 30,000 summer residents in 1886.

Asheville's boom continued until the stock market crashed in 1929. The city's financial institutions were insolvent and Asheville was unable to pay its debts, but it refused to default as many other cities chose to do during this era.

Asheville spurned urban renewal and saved the city's Art Deco architecture.

While the city labored under a debt that was the highest per capita in the country, it was prohibited from undertaking expensive urban renewal projects. When the debt was cleared in 1976, the city found itself in possession of faded architectural gems that have become some of the city's greatest economic assets under an ambitious restoration program. The number of Art Deco buildings found here is second only to Miami Beach.

The Public Square was traditionally the heart of the city's early commerce and was the site of early inns, mercantiles, and markets. George Willis Pack was a lumberman from Cleveland, Ohio, who moved to the area in 1883 to improve the health of his wife, Frances. While living here, he donated the public library building, the Vance monument in Public Square, now known as Pack Square, and various parks around the booming city.

Today, Pack Square is the centerpiece of the revitalized downtown area. It is ringed by shops, outdoor cafes, and coffee houses, as well as Pack Place Arts, Education, and Science center. Models in the lobby show the evolution of Pack Square through the years. Inside the complex, visitors will find the 500-seat, acoustically perfect Diana Wortham Theatre, which hosts performances ranging from Shakespeare and ballet to Ronnie Milsap and modern jazz.

Pack Place is a downtown cultural center and home to a theater and several museums.

The Asheville Art Museum is a three-story modern facility that houses a collection of twentieth-century art and pottery, sculpture, etchings, lead reliefs, and photography. A glass collection features prominent artists from the American Studio Glass movement, including artists from the nearby Penland School.

The Colburn Mineral Museum has also found a home in Pack Place and features dazzling displays of North Carolina riches as well as treasures from around the world, including an 853,000-carat aquamarine crystal that weighs 376 pounds and a 2405.5-carat Boulder Opal Emerald.

The Health Adventure is also a vital part of Pack Place. It teaches children and adults about science, health, and the environment through a series of interesting hands-on exhibits.

In an adjacent building, the Young Men's Institute Cultural Center is also part of Pack Place. It is the site of the African Heritage Center and exhibits artifacts and art of local, regional, and national African-American art, culture, and history.

You'll find downtown Asheville especially inviting if you're interested in antiques, shopping, or delicious food. Lexington Park is an antiques shopper's dream come true. Antiques shops and malls line Lexington and Broadway, offering a tempting array of antiques and collectibles.

Appalachian Craft Center on Spruce Street has handcrafted furniture, jewelry, quilts, pottery, paintings, etchings, rugs, jams and jellies, and more on display.

Wall Street has lots of specialty shops and restaurants. Shoppers may want to browse Bodycare, Folklore, Southern Arts and Crafts, Cobblestone Collectibles, Turtle Creek Gallery, and Celtic Way. One of the most unusual shops is the World Market Place, a nonprofit organization bringing baskets from the Philippines, African and Russian art, musical instruments from Indonesia and South America, and wheat straw carts from Bangladesh to Asheville. The volunteers import items from some of the most impoverished cultures in the world.

We ventured to the Market Place for pepper encrusted steak and trout served with delicious potatoes and steamed julienne vegetables. Other selections include appetizers like smoked chicken and vegetable strudel, watermelon and red onion salad, cedar roasted salmon, and roasted rack of lamb crusted with pistachios, along with a good wine list.

The Laughing Seed Cafe delights vegetarian diners with healthful salads with dressings like creamy tofu tahini and parsley vinaigrette, sandwiches of grilled eggplant with provolone, and Jamaican jerk tempeh.

Our favorite among the downtown restaurants was the Cafe on the Square across from Pack Place. The sidewalk dining offers wonderful entertainment as you sip a glass of wine and enjoy Asheville's street scenes, while you wait for delicious selections like pecan crusted chicken or peppery garlic shrimp linguini. John Tycer, our waiter, explained that the deep melodic rumble we heard was emanating from a digiteedo, a large bamboo wind instrument played by street musicians near Pack Place. It was a real pleasure to enjoy the visual kaleidoscope of an active, thriving downtown.

The Laughing Seed Cafe is one of many reasons Ashevillians visit Wall Street.

Far above Pack Square, diners at Jeffrey's, on the sixteenth floor of the BB&T building, can enjoy a spectacular view and delicious crab cakes for lunch or dinner daily except Sunday. Other classic selections include smoked chicken and fried green tomato salad, Beef Wellington, rainbow trout with a parmesan-lemon crust, poached salmon, and lobster and shrimp thermidor. The lunch menu offers a variety of sandwiches and salads also.

Asheville's native son, Thomas Wolfe, grew up near Pack Square in a typical Asheville boarding house run by his mother, Juila, for middle-class vacationers. The Wolfe boarding house was one of about 100 in the area at the time.

Wes Morrison, our guide at the Thomas Wolfe Memorial, was a history major in college. From him we learned that Wolfe was the baby of the family and his mother insisted that he sleep here with her until he was nine years old, while his seven brothers and sisters lived with his father, who ran a monument company on Pack Avenue.

The tradition in a boarding house at the time was that you rented half the bed, with the owner retaining the right to rent the other half to someone else. So Thomas sometimes slept with a boarder. He never had

You can tour the boyhood home of Thomas Wolfe to hear the story of his life and learn of the significance of certain memorabilia and antiques.

Although Thomas Wolfe's famous novel *Look Homeward, Angel* was once banned from the Asheville library, his home is now a memorial.

his own room until he returned from college at age 19. Without a doubt he used his half of the bed. He was six-foot, six inches tall as an adult. Thomas Wolfe went to University of North Carolina at 16 and earned his master's of theatre degree at Harvard, but wasn't very successful with his plays (one was more than 4 hours long and had 100 characters).

He idolized his older brother, Benjamin, who died in the great influenza epidemic of 1918 while Tom was in college. This was a profound experience for Wolfe, who said, "We can believe in the nothingness of death and of life, but who can believe in the nothingness of Ben . . ." His father moved into the boarding house the same year and died there in 1922, calling it "a bloody, murderous old house."

Wolfe, who said "all serious work in fiction is autobiographical," drew heavily on his experiences in Asheville for his writing. In the preface to the 1929 Scribner's publication of his first and most famous novel, *Look Homeward, Angel*, the statement is made ". . . a novelist may turn over half the people in a town to make a single figure for his novel . . . without rancor or bitter intention." Many unhappy Ashevillians believed they identified themselves in his unflattering fiction. The city fathers felt it painted such an unattractive portrait of life in Asheville that they banned it from the city library.

Wolfe never married, but he dedicated *Look Homeward, Angel* to "A.B.," Aline Bernstein, who was the love of his life. When he briefly returned to Asheville in 1937, he wondered whether it was better to be forgiven or damned. He died of tubercular meningitis on September 15, 1938, just a few weeks before his thirty-eighth birthday. Without a doubt, he has long been forgiven by the city, which proudly directs visitors to his home to learn more of this tragic man who stands tall among America's finest authors. He is buried in Riverside Cemetery on Birch Street, as is the legendary O. Henry.

The Radisson Hotel on Woodfin Street is across the street from the Wolfe home. Other accommodations near the downtown area include the Days Inn and the bed and breakfast district a few blocks away at Historic Montford.

After traveling the world and staying in guest houses and bed and breakfasts in Europe, Caroline Logie began searching for her own bed and breakfast. Her first was in Massachusetts. She came home to Asheville in 1995 after searching for two years for her next property. She came upon the lovely 1897 Queen Ann Victorian home in the midst of the Montford Historic District on Good Friday. It was love at first sight, and a few hours later she made an offer. It was accepted and it all went "like a bed of roses" from there.

She's done a complete restoration of the house. Visitors are welcomed with comfortable lodging and delicious breakfasts that may include fresh fruit bowls, homemade cinnamon rolls, eggs, sausage, and hash browns in the oak and walnut dining room.

A Bed of Roses has roses out front and along the path from the parking lot, as you would expect. Inside, even more roses await guests: in the wallpaper patterns, on the table in the downstairs hallway, and on the wrappers of Caswell Massey soaps Caroline places in each of the private baths. Each of the three guest bedrooms has a television, large comfortable beds, and deep pile carpeting. Caroline offers hospitality, homemade cakes and cookies, gourmet coffee, and English tea in the parlor in the afternoon.

Several other bed and breakfasts are in the immediate vicinity with several of them along Montford Avenue. The Inn on Mont-

The Victorian A Bed of Roses Bed and Breakfast has been lovingly restored by owner Caroline Logie.

Asheville's historic Montford District has several excellent bed and breakfast establishments, such as the Lion and the Rose.

ford has four antiques-filled guest rooms with queen-sized four-poster beds, comfortable reading chairs, and private baths with showers and whirlpool tubs (or a clawfoot tub if you prefer).

The 1898 Lion and the Rose has six rooms and suites and the kind of extras you expect from the Asheville bed and breakfast community like fresh flowers, turn-down service, and a breakfast menu ranging from crepes to creative omelets.

The Black Walnut Inn has four guest rooms and a garden cottage with private baths, and offers bicycles for guests upon request. The Flint Street Inns are side by side and offer eight bedrooms with private baths and a full southern breakfast.

The 1899 Queen-Ann style Wright Inn and Carriage House has eight guest bedrooms with private baths, telephones, and televisions and one suite. The Carriage House welcomes children of all ages to three bedrooms and two baths for family outings.

Richmond Hill Inn and Gabrielle's, the gourmet restaurant operated by the inn, sit on 47 acres overlooking the Asheville skyline near the French Broad River. The 1889 Victorian Mansion has twelve guest rooms that offer private baths, telephones, televisions, antiques, and individual amenities like fireplaces, Jacuzzi, skylights, and views. One of the Croquet Cottages on the property has a handicapped access bathroom, all have furnished porches, telephone, television, and refrigerator with complimentary beverages, in addition to fireplaces, private baths, and queen or double beds.

Edwin Riley Grove made his fortune in patent medicines before coming to Asheville and building the Grove Park Inn. Grove Laboratories, Inc., of St. Louis, Missouri, offered Grove's Tasteless Chill Tonic for $1 for 10 oz. with the boast on the label, "No cure, no pay. Makes children and adults as fat as pigs." One-and-a-half million bottles were sold in a single year despite the warning, "Some people are unusually sensitive to the cinchona antimalarials as they are to certain foods such as strawberries and eggs. If skin rash, slight interference with vision or hearing develop consult your physician as to how the medication should be continued." Hardly the warning the FDA would insist upon today!

Grove was determined to build an inn on his property in Asheville and searched for an architect to design a rustic, yet luxurious, inn suitable for a mountain setting. When his search failed to yield such a man, he settled upon his son-in-law, Atlanta journalist Fred Seely, as his builder. For the inexperienced Seely, it became a labor of love. The results were spectacular, even by Asheville's high standards. Elbert Hubbard, one of the founders of the Arts and Crafts Movement, said of the Grove Park Inn, "This hotel is the manifestation of an idea . . . nursed and loved into being by one man . . . Things made by nature, assisted by artists, carry sentiment."

When the inn opened during the summer of 1913, it was proclaimed to be the finest resort hotel in the world. Seely stayed on as general manager, displaying the same devotion to service that he had shown in construction. Only low tones and whispers were allowed by the staff, who tiptoed through the hallways. They were absolutely forbidden to slam doors.

The famous and near-famous have stayed at the Grove Park Inn, including Enrico Caruso, Thomas Edison, Henry Ford, F. Scott Fitzgerald, Will Rogers, Woodrow Wilson, Mikhail Baryshnikov, Burt Reynolds, and George Bush.

It received the *Southern Living* 1996 Readers' Choice Award for favorite country inn. The view was so incredible that we found it hard to take our eyes off it long enough to eat our lunch at the Terrace Garden Restaurant. We're sure you'll enjoy seeing for yourself.

The interior is a veritable Arts and Crafts living museum, with extensive collections of Stickley, Roycraft, and Limbert furnishings in the Arts and Crafts style. The annual Grove Park Inn Arts and Crafts Conference features speakers, exhibits, and the largest Arts and Crafts antiques show in the United States.

Visitors will find indoor and outdoor pools, 6 outdoor and 3 indoor tennis courts, and an 18-hole par 71 Donald Ross golf course. Activity programs are available for children ages 3 to 12 and range from fully-supervised day camp with lunch and a snack provided from May through Labor Day, to Kid's Night Out on Friday and Saturday nights yearround. The Grove Park Inn is located on the western slope of Sunset Mountain on Macon Avenue north of Pack Square. Take Exit 5B off I-240 or follow Charlotte out of downtown Asheville to Macon Avenue.

The Grove Park Inn has been known for its excellent service, Arts and Crafts furnishings, and unique architectural style since it opened in 1913.

Many of America's wealthy and influential were drawn to this mountain mecca, including George Washington Vanderbilt, the grandson of "Commodore" Cornelius Vanderbilt. The Commodore had made his first fortune parleying a ferry service across the Bay in New York City into a fleet of steamboats that traveled the world during the early 1800s. His second fortune came from investments in railroads, chief among them the New York Central.

George's father, William Henry, being the eldest of the Commodore's 13 children, inherited the bulk of the wealthy industrialist's estate in 1877. William Henry enjoyed fashionable society, travel, the arts, and horse racing. George inherited his father's love of travel, making his first trip to Europe at 10. His first acquaintance with the mountains of Asheville came in 1888 when he journeyed with his mother, Maria Louisa, to the area that was already widely known for its healthful climate. He was 16.

He traveled the world, but he never forgot the beauty of the mountains. Vanderbilt returned to purchase 125,000 North Carolina acres and build his fabulous 250-room Biltmore Mansion here in 1895.

An appreciative public can enjoy a variety of tours of the fabulous Biltmore Home and Gardens, the largest privately owned home in the United States. (© *The Biltmore Co., photo by J. Valentine*)

Richard Morris Hunt, the premier architect of his day with important private and public works like the Metropolitan Museum of Art in New York, was commissioned to build a suitable showcase for Vanderbilt's extensive collections of antiquities and art. A thousand artisans were required to construct the four-story stone house inspired by sixteenth-century French chateaux Vanderbilt had visited. No damp, drafty relic, the house was a showplace of the most advanced technology of the day, including central heating, electricity, fire alarms, mechanical refrigeration, an indoor swimming pool, and elevators.

Frederick Law Olmstead, the designer of New York's Central Park and the man considered to be the founding father of American landscape architecture, was engaged to create the extensive gardens. The results have been hailed among the finest public gardens in the United States. The blooming schedule begins in early April with flowering shrubs like forsythia and spirea and progresses to spring bulbs, flowering dogwoods, and redbuds in mid to late April. Native azaleas generally peak in early May, and fall foliage peaks in mid to late October. But there's always something blooming somewhere at Biltmore.

Popular events include candlelight tours with live performances of turn-of-the-century entertainment, by reservation only on Friday and Saturday evenings during the Festival of Flowers beginning in April, and during the Christmas season. The estate is open daily except Thanksgiving, Christmas, and New Year's Day.

Vanderbilt's vision of a self-supporting estate was the creation of all three men—himself, Hunt, and Olmstead. To this end, Olmstead created a nursery to supply plants for the projects he proposed on a 250-acre pleasure park and a series of gardens around the house. He recommended that the bulk of the property be replanted as a commercial forest. The Biltmore School of Forestry was established here and more than 87,000 acres of the estate would eventually be deeded to the United States government for the creation of the Pisgah National Forest after Vanderbilt's untimely death in 1914.

The Biltmore mansion remains the largest private residence in the United States and, true to its creator's dream, is entirely self-sustaining. In the hands of the present owner, William A. V. Cecil, the grandson of George Washington Vanderbilt, the operation and restoration of the mansion and the maintenance of the remaining 8,000-acre estate is funded entirely by admission fees and proceeds from the garden and gift shops, winery, and eating establishments on the property.

Three restaurants serve visitors on the grounds. Deerpark Restaurant was originally a calving barn but today serves soups, salads, entrées like pork loin, Beef Stroganoff, and spring trout with lemon butter and fresh vegetables.

The Stable Cafe offers casual dining with selections like cashew chicken salad, rotisserie chicken, beefburgers, wine, and beer. The Bistro offers salads, wood fired pizzas, and pastas with sauces like rock shrimp and sweet garlic thyme.

You'll find shopping in the gardener's shop behind the conservatory and the five shops in the Gatehouse Gift Shop near the entrance and at Biltmore Village across the road from the entrance of the estate. The village is where many of the artisans who worked on the house lived. It now is home to shops and restaurants, including the charming Chelsea's Cafe and Tea Room. Don't miss the New Morning Gallery in Biltmore Village. Its selection of art is beyond reproach.

The Biltmore Estate is located off Hendersonville Road (US 25), which can be easily accessed from Broadway/Biltmore Avenue in downtown Asheville, I-26, I-40 or the Blue Ridge Parkway.

For an unusual way to tour the estate, consider Southern Waterways canoe or raft trip down the French Broad River, which passes through the estate. The trips are suitable for adults and children over 2 years of age.

The closest motels are Holiday Inn Express and Howard Johnson. Several bed and breakfasts are located near the Biltmore Estate, including North Lodge, Corner Oak Manor, and Cedar Crest.

You can follow US 25 south from the entrance to the Biltmore Estate to access the Blue Ridge Parkway and visit the Highlands Craft Center. This is the home of the Southern Highland Craft Guild, an assemblage of fine craftsmanship including bobbin lace, wooden bowls, pewter, pottery, quilts, wood carvings, corn shuck dolls, and jewelry.

Weaverville is a short drive north of Asheville via US 25. A look into the next section will help you decide to make this excursion.

The following are Asheville, NC and area code 704 except where noted.

✒ ACCOMMODATIONS

Abbington Green B&B—46 Cumberland Cir., 28801; 251-2454; 5 rooms, breakfast.

A Bed of Roses—135 Cumberland Ave., 28801; 800-471-4182, 258-8700; 3 rooms, private baths, breakfast.

Aberdeen Inn—64 Linden Ave., 28801; 254-9336; 5 rooms, breakfast.

Acorn Cottage B&B—25 St. Dunstan's Cir., 28803; 800-699-0609, 253-0609; 4 rooms, breakfast.

Albemarle Inn—86 Edgemont Rd., 28801; 255-0027; 11 rooms, breakfast.

Applewood Manor B&B—62 Cumberland Cir.; 254-2244; 4 rooms, 1 cottage, breakfast.

Beaufort House Victorian B&B—61 N. Liberty St., 28801; 254-8334; 9 rooms, 1 cottage, breakfast.

Black Mountain Inn—718 W. Old Hwy. 70, Black Mtn., 28711; 669-6528.

Black Walnut B&B—288 Montford Ave., 28801; 254-3878.; 4 rooms, 1 carriage house, breakfast.

Blake House Inn & Pati's Restaurant—150 Royal Pines Dr., 28704; 684-1847; 5 rooms, restaurant.

Bridle Path Inn—30 Lookout Rd., 28804; 252-0035.

Cairn Brae B&B—217 Patton Mtn. Rd., 28804; 252-0035; 8 rooms, breakfast.

Carolina B&B—177 Cumberland Ave., 28801; 254-3608; 5 rooms, breakfast.

Cedar Crest Victorian Inn—674 Biltmore Ave., 28891; 254-3608; 5 rooms, breakfast.

Comfort Inn Black Mountain—Exit 64 off I-40, 28711; 800-221-2222.

Corner Oak Manor—53 St. Dunstan's Cir., 28803; 253-3525; 3 rooms, 1 cottage, breakfast.

Days Inn Downtown—120 Patton Ave., 28801; 254-9661.

Dogwood Cottage Inn—40 Canterbury Rd., 29903; 258-9725; 4 rooms, breakfast.

Freedom Escape Lodge—Upper Flat Creek Rd., Weaverville, 28787; 800-722-8337.

Grove Park Inn Resort—290 Macon Ave., 28804; 800-438-5800, 252-2711;
    Restaurant, 510 rooms.
Howard Johnson Biltmore—190 Hendersonville Rd., US Hwy. 25, 28803;
    800-446-4656.
North Lodge B&B—84 Oakland Ave., 28801; 252-6433; 4 rooms, private
    baths.
Radisson Hotel Asheville—One Thomas Wolfe Plaza, 28801; 800-333-3333.
Old Reynolds Mansion—100 Reynolds Heights, 28804; 254-0496; 1 cottage,
    10 rooms, breakfast.
Reed House—119 Dodge St., 28803; 274-1604; 1 cottage, 3 rooms, break-
    fast.
Richmond Hill Inn—87 Richmond Hill, 28806; 800-545-9238, 252-7313;
    3 suites, 33 rooms, breakfast.
The Inn On Montford—296 Montford Ave., 28801; 254-9569; 4 rooms,
    breakfast.
The Lion and The Rose—276 Montford Ave., 28801; 255-7673; 2 suites, 4
    rooms, breakfast.
Red Rocker Inn—136 N. Dougherty St., Black Mtn., 28711; 669-5991.
The Resting Place—Old Haw Creek Rd., 28805; 298-8500; 2 rooms, break-
    fast.
The Scarlett Inn—315 Pearson Dr., 28801; 353-7888; 1 suite, 3 rooms,
    breakfast.
Wright Inn & Carriage House—235 Pearson Dr., 28801; 800-552-5724,
    251-0789; 1 carriage house, 9 rooms, breakfast.

ATTRACTIONS

Antique Car Museum/Grovewood Gallery—Grove Park Inn; 253-7651; Free.
Asheville Art Museum—Pack Place; 253-3227.
Biltmore Estate—US Hwy. 25; 800-543-2961, 255-1700.
Biltmore Village Historic Museum—7 Biltmore Plaza; 274-9707; Exit 50 from
    I-40, go north one-quarter mile to US 25.
Botanical Gardens—On UNC campus at W.T. Weaver Blvd.; 252-5190.
Colburn Gem and Mineral Museum—Pack Place; 254-7162.
Cradle of Forestry—US 276 4 miles south of Blue Ridge Parkway, Visitor
    Information Center; 877-3130; Exhibits, tours, gift shop; May to
    Oct.
Asheville Historical Tours—Radisson Hotel; Mon. to Sat., 8:00 A.M., 10:30
    A.M., 1:00 P.M. , 3:30 P.M.; Sun., 1:00 P.M., 3:30 P.M.

Diana Wortham Theatre—Pack Place; 257-4530.

Folk Art Center—Blue Ridge Pkwy milepost 382; 298-7928.

Grove Park Inn—290 Macon Ave.; 800-438-5800, 252-2711.

Grovewood Gallery—Next to Grove Park Inn; 253-7651.

Guided Walking Tour of Historic Downtown Asheville—Tour begins at Pack
  Place Arts & Science Center; Mon. to Sat., April to October;
  255-1093.

Health Adventure—Pack Place; 254-6373.

Highlands Craft Center at the Blue Ridge Parkway.

Pack Place Education, Arts, and Science Center—2 South Pack Square; 257-4500;
  Closed Sun. & Mon.

Scottish Touring Service—628-4860.

Southern Waterways—1460 Brevard Rd., 28806; 800-849-1970, 665-1970.

Thomas Wolfe Memorial—Woodfin St.; 253-8304; Closed Mon.

Western North Carolina Nature Center—75 Gashes Creek Rd., 28805; 298-
  5600; Yearround, 10:00 A.M. to 5:00 P.M. daily.

YMI Cultural Center—Pack Place; 252-4614.

⌘ DINING

Barley's Taproom—42 Biltmore Ave.; Lunch and dinner daily.

Cafe on the Square—1 Biltmore Ave., 28801; 251-5565; 11:30 A.M. to 4:00
  P.M., Mon. to Sat., 5:00 to 9:30 P.M. Mon. to Thurs., Fri. to Sat., 5:00
  to 10:00 P.M.; Closed Sun.

Chelsea's Cafe and Tea Room—Six Boston Way, Historic Biltmore Village,
  28803; 274-4400; Lunch 11:30 A.M., afternoon tea at 3:30 P.M.

Flying Frog Cafe—76 Haywood St., 28801; 254-9411.

Horizons at the Grove Park Inn—AAA Four-Diamond dining; 252-2711,
  ext. 1011.

Jeffrey's—16th Floor BB&T Bldg.; Lunch, dinner; Live jazz on weekends.

Laughing Seed Cafe—40 Wall St., 28801; 252-3445.

Sunset Terrace at the Grove Park Inn—252-2711, ext. 1011; Seasonal breakfast,
  lunch, and dinner menus.

The Market Place and Mark's Signature Cafe—20 Wall St., 28801; 252-4162;
  Mon. to Sat., 6:00 to 9:30 P.M., Sun. only 11:00 A.M. to 2:00 P.M.

The Possum Trot Cafe—23 Page; Cajun style po'boys, red beans and rice.

Weaverville Milling Company—½ mile past the Eblen gas station in Weaverville
  (US 25); Chicken with champagne sauce, salad with homemade blue
  cheese dressing, veal Marsala, trout and homemade rolls.

❧ SHOPPING

A Gardener's Place—Biltmore Estate; 274-6236.

Antiques at the Square—Four Biltmore Ave., 28801; 253-3535.

Art For Living—7 Boston Way, Biltmore Village; 274-2831.

Asheville Antiques Mall—43 Rankin Ave., 28801; 253-3634.

B. Barnes Outdoor Outfitters—Fairview Rd.; 274-7301.

Blue Spiral Gallery—38 Biltmore Avenue, 28801; 251-0202 .

Corner Cupboard Antique Mall—49 N. Lexington Ave.; 258-9815.

Fireside Antiques and Interiors—30 All Souls Crescent, Biltmore Village; 274-5977.

Folk Art Center—Blue Ridge Parkway milepost 382; 298-7928.

Gallery of the Mountains—The Grove Park Inn; 254-2068.

Grovewood Gallery—the Grove Park Inn; 253-7651; Yearround.

Lexington Park Antiques—65 Walnut St., 28801; 253-3070; Daily.

Me and My Pals Antiques—24 N. Lexington Ave.; 253-0440.

New Morning Gallery—US 25 N and Boston Way, Biltmore Village; 274-2831; Daily.

Stuf Antiques—52 Broadway; 254-4054.

The Complete Naturalist—2 Biltmore Plaza; 274-5430.

T.S. Morrison—39 N. Lexington; 258-1891.

World Market Place—10 College St.; 254-8374.

❧ SPECIAL EVENTS

February—*Celebration of Black History Month (Diana Wortham Theatre, Pack Place; 254-7046)*

February—*Grove Park Inn Arts & Crafts Conference (Grove Park Inn, 290 Macon Ave., 28804; 800-438-0050)*

March and April—*Rite of Spring Workshops (Dance/clogging, shape note singing, etc.; 298-7928 to register)*

April—*Festival of Flowers Evenings (Biltmore Estate; 800-543-2961, 274-6333)*

June—*Annual Highlands Heritage Art and Craft Show (Asheville Mall; 254-0072)*

July, August, September—*Shindig on the Green (City-County Plaza; 258-6101; Fiddlers, dulcimers, cloggers, bluegrass and old-time bands)*

July, October—*Craft Fair of the Southern Highlands (Asheville Civic Center, I-240 to Haywood St.; 298-7928)*

August—*Annual Village Art and Craft Fair (Biltmore Village; 274-2831)*

August—*Mountain Dance and Folk Festival (Thomas Wolfe Auditorium in the Asheville Civic Center; 800-257-5583, 251-9999, 800-693-8499 for tickets; Show starts "along about sundown")*

August—*North Carolina Shakespeare Festival (Diana Wortham Theatre, Pack Place; 257-4530)*

September—*Kituwah, the American Indian Celebration of Arts, Culture, and Education (Asheville Civic Center; 252-3880)*

December—*Candlelight Evenings at Biltmore Estate (800-543-2961; Reservations)*

❧ CAMPING

Bear Creek RV Park and Campgrounds—81 S. Bear Creek Rd., 28806; 800-833-0798, 253-0798; 90 trailer sites with hook-ups, 20 tent sites, showers, toilets, laundry, camp store.

French Broad River Campgrounds—1030 Old Marshall Hwy., 28804; 658-0772; 18 trailer sites with hook-ups, 18 tent sites, showers, toilets, laundry, camp store.

Taps RV Parks—1327 Tunnel Rd., 28805; 800-831-4385, 299-8277; 46 trailer sites with hook-ups, 15 tent sites, showers, toilets, laundry, camp store.

❧ FOR MORE INFORMATION

Asheville Convention and Visitors Bureau—151 Haywood St., Asheville, NC 28801; 800-257-1300, 258-6111.

North Carolina B&B and Inns—POB 1077, Asheville, NC 28802; 800-849-5392.

North Carolina Campground Owners Assoc.—1418 Aversboro Rd., Garner, NC 26529; 919-779-5709.

❧ DIRECTIONS

Asheville may be accessed from I-40, I-26, and the Blue Ridge Parkway.

33 *Weaverville:*

Rustic and Cozy

This old mill stands at the entrance to the modern Freedom Escape Lodge.

The short drive north from Asheville up Highway 19/23 or 25 is worth it to dine at Weaverville Milling Company Restaurant. We recommend you take Highway 25 if you aren't in a hurry. In addition to a quiet drive by Beaver Lake, you are less likely to miss your turnoff to the "Mill."

Don't be put off by its façade. That is an authentic 1912 mill that ground grain until 1965. When you park, go down the steps and turn right to find the entrance on the right side of the building near the rear. Inside, you will feel like you stepped back in time. Dining is on two rustic floors, much of it original wood. The feel is casual and comfortable, as if sitting down to eat with your neighbors.

From the menu, you may select chicken plum, fresh rainbow trout, prime rib, steak, strawberry rhubarb chicken, or the VIP sandwich that comes with two choices among garden salad, vegetable du jour, herb rice, potato du jour, and fresh baked rolls. The Mill opens at 5 P.M. and is closed on Wednesdays.

North of Weaverville is Freedom Escape Lodge. The new owners plan for it to be a group facility (17 rooms and a cabin) for weddings, business groups, family reunions, and senior and tour groups. Some of the amenities are a one-quarter mile lighted paved trail around the two-acre stocked lake, indoor gym, tennis courts, and outdoor pool.

Lodging for individuals and couples is available for 2- to 3-night minimum, with advance notice of a week to 10 days. Country cooking is available now, but in the future the menu will offer a deluxe menu including steaks and prime rib.

Elkins Antiques has more furniture than you can imagine, including primitive and European antiques. It is open Monday-Saturday from 9 A.M. to 5 P.M. Some examples of what you will find include a twig high chair, banjo made from a candy box, early country pie safes, corner cupboards, beds, handmade guitars, baskets, and folk art.

East of Weaverville via Reems Creek Road is the restored home of Zebulon Baird Vance, the "War Governor Of the South." His birthplace, a two-story pine log cabin built in 1795, was the largest in Buncombe County at the time. Vance was born in 1830 and lived here until 1838.

Vance moved to Asheville, went to UNC, and practiced law in Asheville. In August 1862, he was elected governor while still with his 14th North Carolina Regiment during the Civil War. He was arrested and taken to the Old Capitol Prison in Washington, DC, but eventually released. When he was elected to the US Senate in 1879, however, he was refused admission because he had not been pardoned for his part in the Civil War. He died on April 14, 1894.

A few miles from Weaverville is the birthplace of Zebulon Vance. A tour guide takes you through the home and outbuildings while explaining his life during demanding times.

A tour guide will take you over the grounds and show you the house and outbuildings while explaining its place in history. Among the many things of interest is a Seth Thomas Clock with wooden works and a "Toe-ster," so called because you turned the bread being toasted in the fireplace with your toe. The cabin is complete with items and furniture of the period, some original to the cabin.

There's a small museum and interpretative center near the log structures. Vance is buried in Riverside Cemetery in Asheville, and a monument dedicated to him ascends from the center of Pack Square in downtown Asheville.

Return toward Weaverville on Reems Creek Road until you see a sign directing you to turn (southeast) to the Blue Ridge Parkway. This country road is scenic; in fact, we drove it twice, both times with pleasure. It is almost all uphill. You enter the Parkway just north of the Crafts Center. Turn right to the Crafts Center or left to go northeast to Linville.

The following are Weaverville, NC 28787 and area code 704.

ACCOMMODATIONS

Dry Ridge Inn—26 Brown St.; 800-839-3899; 7 rooms, breakfast, limited
    wheelchair access, game room, horseback riding, jogging/nature trail.
Freedom Escape Lodge—530 Upper Flat Creek Rd.; 658-0814.
Inn on Main Street—88 Main St.; 645-3442; 6 rooms, breakfast, lawn games.
Weaverville Featherbed & Breakfast—3 Perrion Ave.; 645-7594; 5 rooms, break-
    fast, limited wheelchair access.

DINING

Weaverville Milling Company Restaurant—Reems Creek Valley Rd.; 645-4700.

FOR MORE INFORMATION

Asheville Convention and Visitors Bureau—151 Haywood St., Asheville, NC
    28801; 800-257-1300, 258-6111.

DIRECTIONS

Vance's Birthplace—From Weaverville go east on Reems Creek Rd, bear left
    on SR 1103. From Blue Ridge Parkway—Take SR 2109 to SR 1103
    and turn east, look for Vance homeplace on your right. This is a scenic
    drive.
Weaverville—US 19/23 or US 25 north from Asheville.

The Inn on Main Street is one of
Weaverville's three inns. This small
community is growing rapidly because
of its natural rural surroundings and
proximity to Asheville.

34 *Banner Elk, Linville, Little Switzerland, Spruce Pine, Valle Crucis:*
The Higher Highlands

Here in the "higher Highlands" are a number of small communities in Avery, McDowell, and Mitchell Counties that offer varied forms of accommodations, recreation, and attractions.

Leave the Blue Ridge Parkway to the north at milepost 331 onto NC 226 to look in the North Carolina Mineral Museum.

Old Hampton Store and Grist Mill provides tourists and locals with freshly ground meals and flour. Author Cathy Summerlin is looking for whole-wheat pancake mix for breakfast.

The Blue Ridge Parkway operated museum, with exhibits of 300 indigenous rocks, minerals, and gems, explains the local geology and mining history. Admittance is free to this interesting archive that is open yearround.

Going south across the Parkway, stay on NC 226 to Little Switzerland. One of its main attractions is Switzerland Inn and Chalet Restaurant (a taste of Bavaria), open from May to October. The complex has a two-story Main Lodge, Chanticleer Building, Heidi & Alpine Building, and three cottages. Rates include full breakfast, swimming pool, tennis courts, and shuffleboard.

There are small specialty shops around the inn, including the Trillium Gallery, which displays local artists' work of pottery and jewelry, Pine Crossing, The Swiss Shop, Edelweiss Shop, and Busy B's.

In the village of Little Switzerland that is three miles wide and 10 miles long, stands Switzerland Store built in 1927. Originally it was a general store and post office. Now, even with additions, it is much the same.

From the village, return to the Parkway, and drive north to US 221 that takes you to Altamont, Pineola, then Linville. Along this section is the Gardens of the Blue Ridge. For a century they have been shipping native wildflowers around the world.

Pineola Inn & Country Store is about seven minutes from ski areas. The inn has 40 rooms with cable TV. A gift shop, beverage shop, and museum are on the premises. The Pineola Motel has rooms, cabins, and kitchenettes.

At Pineola, US 221 turns north to Linville. Before getting to Linville, you should turn on to NC 181 to see the Old Hampton Store and Grist Mill. This is a fun stop to look at all the eclectic merchandise and buy some freshly ground corn meal, wholewheat, buckwheat pancake mix, or grits. We certainly enjoyed our buckwheat pancakes when we returned home.

Return to US 221 to Linville. Founded in the 1891, this was the site of the first planned mountain golf resort. The Eseeola Lodge built in 1926 (the original lodge built in 1892 burned in 1936) still provides accommodations and golf at this Mobil Four-Star Resort. Eseeola Lodge Restaurant serves gourmet cuisine with a style

Across the road from Mast General Store in Valle Crucis is Country Farmhouse, which offers handiwork for sale.

unchanged in more than 100 years. Call for reservations. Gentlemen, be sure to put on a coat and tie, and ladies, dress appropriately.

From Linville, take NC 184 to Banner Elk. Along the way, you'll pass the road to Sugar Mountain with its ski resort, shops, golf, mountain bike trails, swimming, and tennis. Some of the scenic areas will make you glad you brought your camera.

Banner Elk's first white inhabitant was Samuel (some say Daniel) Hix in 1779. Around 1845, the first of the Banner boys moved to the area. Soon, six more Banner brothers arrived. Two of the brothers shepherded the "underground railroad" between 1863 and 1865, helping escaped Federal prisoners and Union sympathizers get to Tennessee.

The town, surrounded by Beech, Grandfather, and Sugar Mountains, got its name from the many Banner families and the good elk hunting. The elk are gone now, but this area thrives on tourism yearround.

Annual snowfall averages about five feet, and the steep slopes make it a magnet for skiers. Of course, the spring and fall attract their own fans and summer drives the flatlanders to play golf in the cool mountain air (see North Carolina Outdoor Recreation section for golfing).

While in Banner Elk, watch for the Woolly Worm crossings. If you see any, catch them. One good worm can be worth $500 at the Woolly Worm Festival, held the third Saturday in October. More than 800 people with fuzzy brown- and black-striped worms race for the big purse. Then the winning worm is "read" to predict the coming winter weather.

From Banner Elk, take the crooked, meandering downhill drive on NC 194 to Valle Crucis. The view may be spectacular when there are no leaves on the trees, but with them you only see steep uphill banks and foliage as you wind down into the "Vale of the Cross."

The community got its name in the 1800s from the meeting of three creeks that form the shape of a cross. The first Protestant monastery since the Reformation, the Society of Holy Cross, was established here during the 1800s.

Several excellent inns make the valley worth visiting; Mast Farm Inn, the Inn At the Taylor House, and Bluestone Lodge.

Mast Farm Inn, built in 1885, first became an inn the early 1900s, when it was operated by Finley & Josephine Mast. Entered on the Register of Historic Places in 1972, the main house now has nine rooms, seven with private baths and one bath shared by two rooms. Three cottages are available: the Blacksmith Shop, Woodwork Shop, and Loom House. All rooms reflect the feel of the early 1900s.

Innkeepers Sibyl and Francis Pressly were featured on the PBS TV series *Inn Country USA.*

The original Mast General Store is located in Valle Crucis and is open every day. If you've come this far, you certainly will want to visit this old store, established in 1883. W.W. Mast took possession around the turn of the century and developed a reputation of having everything from cradles to caskets. As you enter, you'll see on your left the antique post office boxes still in service.

Behind the store is the Schoolhouse Shop and Museum, built in 1907. There were musicians providing entertainment the Sunday afternoon we passed through. You can catch storytellers there on many weekends. Local crafts, furniture, and souvenirs are in the schoolhouse.

As you enter the original Mast General Store in Valle Crucis, to your left you will see an old but still functioning post office.

The Annex and Candy Store is two-tenths of a mile from the Mast Store. Originally, in 1909, this was a competing general store. Now under the Mast Store umbrella, it offers deli sandwiches, candy, and general Mast Store merchandise.

From Valle Crucis you are only a few miles from Boone via NC 194, then east on US 321, or you can turn west on US 321 to the Watauga Lake area in Tennessee.

The following are area code 704.

❧ ACCOMMODATIONS

Alpine Inn—POB 477, Little Switzerland, 28749; 765-5380; 13 rooms and efficiency apartment; April to November.

Azalea Inn—Box 1151, Banner Elk, NC 28604; 898-8195; 5 rooms with private baths in the heart of town.

Banner Elk Inn B&B—POB 1953, Banner Elk, NC 28694; 898-9004; 2 rooms, 1 suite, full breakfast, cable TV, fireplace.

Big Lynn Lodge—POB 459, Little Switzerland, 28749; 765-6771; 27 rooms, 11 cottages, 4 condos, private bath, breakfast, restaurant, laundry, lawn games, jogging/nature trail; April to November.

Bluestone Lodge—POB 736, Valle Crucis, NC 28691; 963-5177; All accommodations have kitchenette, private bath, sauna, hot tub, outdoor pool.

Eseeola Lodge—Box 99, Linville, NC 28646; 800-742-6717, 733-4311; 29 rooms, private bath, telephone, cable TV, fresh flowers, heated pool, children's day camp, special services; Dress code for dining and golfing.

Hummingbird Lodge B&B—Rt. 4, Box 403, Banner Elk, NC 28604; 963-7210; Full breakfast.

The Inn at the Taylor House—Box 713, Valle Crucis, NC 28691; 963-5581; Open April to December. All rooms with private baths and breakfast, cottages (breakfast extra); Massages available.

Linville Cottage Inn—Box 508, Linville, NC 28646; 733-6551; $65 to $95; Breakfast; No children or pets; Yearround.

Mast Farm Inn—POB 704 Valle Crucis, NC 28691; 963-5857; 9 rooms, 7 with private bath, 3 cabin cottages; Children over 12; Breakfast and dinner included; 1 room has wheelchair access; Closed part of December, January, March, and April.

Pineola Inn and Motel—Box 53, Pineola, NC 28662; 733-4979.

The Pinnacle Inn—POB 1136, Banner Elk, NC 28604; 800-438-2097, 387-4276 (NC); Condos and villas, indoor pool, sauna, steam rooms, hot tubs, tennis, minutes from skiing on Beech Mountain, canoeing, rafting, hiking, horseback riding; Yearround.

Richmond Inn B&B—101 Pine St., Spruce Pine, 28777; 765-6693.

Switzerland Inn—POB 399, Little Switzerland, 28749; 800-654-4026, 765-2153; 6 cottages, 41 rooms, 8 suites, efficiency apartment; Restaurant, pool, golf, tennis, jogging/nature trails; April to November.

ATTRACTIONS

Grandfather Mountain—733-4337; Scenery, swinging bridge, nature museum, shops, restaurant.

North Carolina Mineral Museum—Blue Ridge Parkway (milepost 331) junction with NC 226; 756-2721.

DINING

Cedarcrest—311 Locust Ave., Spruce Pine, 28777; 765-6124.

Banner Elk Cafe—Hwy. 184, Banner Elk, NC 28604; 898-4040; Homestyle cooking; Breakfast, lunch, dinner.

Eseeola Lodge Restaurant—POB 99, Linville, NC 28646; 733-4311; Five-course meal of French and new American cuisine; Coat and tie required; Reservations.

Louisiana Purchase Food & Spirits—Hwy. 184, Banner Elk, NC 28604; 898-5656; Cajun, Creole, and French cuisine for dinner only; Reservations.

Small Town Blues Cafe—Hwy. 184, Banner Elk, NC 28604; 898-8988; Soup, salad, sandwiches, pizza, entrées, desserts; Music on Friday and Saturday nights; Yearround.

The Soda Shop—202 Oak Ave., Spruce Pine, 28777; 765-1125.

SHOPPING

Annex and Candy Store—Hwy. 194, Valle Crucis; 963-6511; Everything from candy to socks.

Alpine Ski Center—Near entrance to Sugar Mt.; 898-9701; Ski equipment, rentals, clothing, accessories.

Edge of the World—Hwy. 184 Banner Elk; 898-9550; Guided outdoor adventures, equipment.

Mast General Store—Hwy. 194, Valle Crucis; 963-6511; Everything from deli sandwiches to sleeping bags.

Mountain Image Photo—Near entrance to Sugar Mt.; 898-6448; Photo supplies and finishing.

The Old Hampton Store—Ruffin St., Linville, NC 28646; 733-5213.

Trillium Gallery—POB 518, Little Switzerland, 28749;765-0024.

Woody's Colonial Design Chairs—110 Dale Rd., Spruce Pine, NC 28777; 765-9277; Fifth-generation craftsman makes chairs and stools the old-fashioned way.

✎ SPECIAL EVENTS

January—*Winter Fest (Beech Mountain)*

June—*Cornbread Cook-off (Old Hampton Store, Linville)*

June—*Storytelling Festival (Beech Mountain)*

July—*Grandfather Mountain Highland Games & Gathering of the Scottish clans (Linville)*

August—*Crafts on the Green (Beech Mountain)*

October—*Blue Ridge Bridge-to-Bridge Centennial Bike Ride (Grandfather Mountain)*

October—*Wooly Worm Festival (Banner Elk)*

✎ CAMPING

Bear Den Campground—Bear Den Mt. Rd., Spruce Pine, 28777; 765-2888.

Blue Ridge Gemstone Mine & Campground—POB 327, Little Switzerland, 28749; 765-5264.

Spruce Pine Campground—Box 354 Dale Rd., Spruce Pine, 28777; 765-4078.

✎ FOR MORE INFORMATION

Avery County Chamber of Commerce—POB 700, Newland, NC 28657; 773-4737.

Banner Elk Chamber of Commerce—POB 355, Banner Elk, NC 28604; 800-972-2183, 898-5605.

Beech Mountain Chamber of Commerce—403-A Beech Mountain Pkwy., Beech Mountain, NC 28604; 800-468-5506, 387-9283.

Mitchell County Chamber of Commerce—Rt. 1, Box 796, Spruce Pine, NC 28777; 800-227-3912, 765-9483; Ask for *Discover Mitchell County* brochure.

35 Boone:

Coolest Town in the South

Boone's downtown is geared to students from Appalachian State University and tourists. This Mast General Store is one of five in North Carolina.

In 1800, Jordan Council established a store at the foot of Howard's Knob that became the center of the community that would later become Boone. There were few inhabitants before then, not even the Cherokee, who claimed the area for their hunting grounds, lived here. Only 100 people lived in Boone in 1850, 80 years after Daniel Boone left the area. Although 13,000 people call the growing city home today, the population doubles when Appalachian State University (ASU) is in session.

Appalachian State University gives Boone youthful vigor that can be readily seen in the restaurants and shops catering to students. Events centered at ASU draw much attention, adding dimensions of culture not normally seen in isolated mountain towns. Appalachian Cultural Museum's exhibits of the area's cultural past is contrasted by the culture of symphonies, dance, theater, and other art forms. There is a monument on campus near the Duck Pond marking one of Daniel Boone's hunting cabins. He lived in Boone between 1706 and 1769.

Horn in the West is a drama of the lives of the first pioneers to the region, including Daniel Boone. Many of them were escaping the tyranny of British rule before the American Revolution. The play was written by Kermit Hunter to tell of the struggles between British soldiers and warring Indians under the leadership of Chief Dragging Canoe against the Mountain Men. The production runs every night except Monday from late June through mid-August.

Daniel Boone Native Gardens is adjacent to Horn in the West and Hickory Ridge Homestead. Eight acres of indigenous flora include a cabin that belonged to Daniel Boone's grandfather and where his father grew up, and a wrought iron gate constructed by Daniel Boone IV, a direct descendant of old Dan'l. You can walk the grounds daily, May through September, and on weekends in October.

The Dan'l Boone Inn Restaurant was built in 1923 and became a restaurant in 1959. Originally a home for Dr. R.K. Bingham, it also served as his office and Boone's first hospital. It does not offer accommodations, but is a preferred place to eat big family-style meals seven days a week, yearround except for two days at Christmas. Three meats, five vegetables, biscuits, preserves, desserts, and beverage are served at supper. Saturday and Sunday breakfasts of country ham, sausage, bacon, scrambled eggs, grits, fresh stewed apples, red-eye and cream gravies, buttermilk biscuits, cinnamon biscuits, preserves, juice, and another beverage will keep you going until lunch.

The most popular place to eat in Boone, the Daniel Boone Inn serves full family-style country meals.

The city of Boone claims to be the coolest spot in the South, with an average summer temperature of 68 degrees. There are more than a thousand rooms available, and plenty of mountains to roam if you want to make Boone one of your stops. Reservations are a good idea on autumn weekends while ASU is in session.

On our way to Blowing Rock via US 221/321, we stopped at an unusual roadside business, Roger's Trading Post. Here you will find twig furniture, birdhouses, garden benches, and a whole lot more. Roger Reedy started his business on a card table across the road. News commentator Paul Harvey said in one of his stories that this was the best place in the United States to go for birdhouses. Indeed, they were stacked up, piled up, and hung up everywhere—thousands of them.

We heard the Tweetsie train whistle echoing through the mountains on our way to Blowing Rock, so we stopped by the Tweetsie Railroad theme park. Number 12 engine steadily hauls several cars of passengers through the mountains on a three-mile journey. You can expect to be held up by train robbers, watch the ensuing gun fight and be saved—just like in the old Western movies. With about 30 different things to do, from exploring shops in the town to patting your foot to mountain music, you are in for a day-long treat.

Just down the hill is Mystery Hill, administering the seemingly impossible through natural phenomena; see water flow uphill, lose

Just south of Boone at Roger's Trading Post is the largest collection of birdhouses for sale in the United States.

Located close together, Tweetsie Railroad Amusement Park, Appalachian Heritage Museum, and Mystery Hill make for a full day of entertainment.

your shadow on a phosphorus wall, witness optical illusions, stand inside a soap bubble, and delight in other things that trick your mind.

The Appalachian Heritage Museum is next door in an old frame house filled with period furnishings and many household items from the early 1900s. Its theme is "History is the keeper of the lessons mankind has learned." The natural and cultural heritage of the Blue Ridge Mountain people from the time of the Native American through the early 1900s is depicted. It's open daily, yearround.

The following are Boone, NC 28607 and area code 704 except where noted.

✍ ACCOMMODATIONS

Grandma Jean's B&B—254 Meadowview Dr.; 262-3670; 4 rooms, breakfast, limited handicapped facility, baby-sitter, dog kennel; April to November.
Lovill House Inn—404 Old Bristol Rd.; 800-849-9466, 264-4204; 5 rooms, breakfast, handicapped facility, lawn games, jogging/nature trail.
The Gragg House—210 Ridge Pt. Dr.; 264-7289; 2 rooms, breakfast, TV, game room, lounge, laundry.
The Lions Den—Rt. 3, Box 832; 800-963-5785; 4 rooms, 1 chalet, breakfast, swimming pool, lounge, tennis, playground, picnic area.

✍ ATTRACTIONS

Appalachian Cultural Museum—Blowing Rock Rd.; 263-3117; Antique quilts, arrowheads, handsewn furniture, Junior Johnson's race car are a few of the things that depict the area's history.
Appalachian Heritage Museum—Blowing Rock Rd. (part of Mystery Hill complex); 264-2792; Located in the historic Dougherty House (circa 1903) displays artifacts, photographs, and mountain culture; Admission fee.
Hickory Ridge Homestead—On *Horn of the West* grounds; 800-852-9506, 264-2225; An eighteenth-century living history museum.

Horn in the West—800-852-9506, 264-2225; The third oldest outdoor drama is set in 1771, a time of British dominance and Colonial unrest. Watch the development of mountain culture as early settlers led by Daniel Boone struggle for independence from the Crown and the Cherokee Fire Dance.

Mystery Hill—Rt. 1, Box, 278; 264-2792; On US 321 south of Tweetsie Railroad; "Plays havoc with Newton's theory!"; Optical illusions, natural phenomena, exploration of science; Fun and interesting.

Tweetsie Railroad—POB 388; 800-526-5740, 264-9061; Between Boone and Blowing Rock on US 321 and at Blue Ridge Parkway milepost 291, Boone exit.

DINING

Boone has many eateries ranging from traditional to trendy.

BeansTalk—400 E. King St.; 262-0999; Coffees and sandwiches.

Blues Barbeque—506 W. King St.; 265-1411; Hickory smoked ribs, vegetarian dishes, live music nightly.

Boone Drug-Old Time Soda Fountain & Grill—617 W. King St.; 264-3766; Short-order grill and fountain.

Dan'l Boone Inn Restaurant—130 Hardin St.; 264-8657; Family-style meals.

Red Onion—227 Hardin St.; 264-5470; Soups, salads, sandwiches, entrées, homemade desserts, beer and wine; Outside dining.

Mom's Country Store & Restaurant—1601 Blowing Rock Rd.; 262-0916; Country cooked meals.

Richmonds Steak House—205 Blowing Rock Rd; 262-1666; Steaks, barbecue ribs, chicken, seafood.

SHOPPING

Antiques Unlimited Mall—Boone Heights Dr.; 265-3622; Country and fine furniture, glassware, collectibles.

Aunt Pymm's Table—Hwy. 421S; 262-1041; Early American country furniture, one-of-a-kind pieces.

Boone Antique Mall—631 W. King St.; 262-0521; 3 floors with over 60 antique dealers.

Doe Ridge Pottery—149 W. King St.; Gallery and studio; Stoneware, dinner ware, lamps.

Old Boone Mercantile (Mast General Store)—630 King St.; 262-0000; Traditional clothing, housewares, gifts, camping gear.

Morning Glory Craft Shop—904 W. King St.; Contemporary crafts, fine art, pottery, wooden boxes.

Old Boone Antique Mall—631 W. King St.; 262-0521.

Roger's Trading Post—US 221/321S.

Watauga Auction Co.—Hwy. 421N; 297-2181; Auctions every Saturday night at 7:00.

Wilcox Emporium Warehouse—Howard St.; 262-1221; Over 150 vendors of antiques, art, collectibles.

SPECIAL EVENTS

July—*An Appalachian Summer (Appalachian State Univ., 800-841-2787, 262-4046; North Carolina Symphony, dance, chamber groups, theater, classes)*

July—*Firefly Festival (Downtown; 800-852-9506, 264-2225)*

August—*Gospel Singing Jubilee (800-852-9506, 264-2225)*

CAMPING

Flintlock Family Campground—Rt. 3, Box 22; 963-5325; 90 trailer sites, 28 tent sites, full hook-ups, toilets, showers, cable TV, dump stations, laundry, ice, picnic areas, games.

KOA Kampground—Rt. 2, Box 205; 264-7250. Over 115 trailer sites, 14 tent sites, full hook-ups, toilets, showers, dump stations, camp store, laundry, ice, picnic areas, games.

FOR MORE INFORMATION

Boone Area Chamber of Commerce—208 W. Howard St., Boone, NC; 800-852-9506, 264-2225.

North Carolina High Country Host—1700 Blowing Rock Rd., Boone, NC 28607; 800-438-7500, 704-264-1299.

DIRECTIONS

Boone is at the junction of US 321, US 421, and NC 105. I-40, I-81, and I-77 are an hour away.

36 *Blowing Rock:*
Crown Jewel of the Blue Ridge

The original name for this mountain resort town was Laurel Ridge. Blowing Rock took its name from the famous outcropping over Johns River Gorge and was incorporated in 1889.

The Blowing Rock attraction is south of the village off US 321 just after you pass Green Park Inn. The cliff is 4,000 feet above sea level and 3,000 feet from the valley below. The phenomenon is called Blowing Rock because the rocky walls of the gorge form a flume through which the northeast wind sweeps with such force that it returns light objects cast over the void.

On the same road to The Blowing Rock is Gideon Ridge Road and a very special bed and breakfast. Gideon Ridge Inn is perched dramatically on a hillside overlooking the Blue Ridge Mountains. It is an agreeable combination of comfortable and chic, rustic and sophisticated much like the village of Blowing Rock itself.

The rambling structure has 10 guest rooms, six with fireplaces. Owners Cobb and Jane Milner were looking for a home in the area in the early 1980s when they found this gem. Jane has a masters degree in history/museum conservation from NYU and her tastes are reflected throughout the house beginning with the gathering room with its cozy fireplace, oriental rugs and book-lined shelves. Cobb is an engineer and was consulting in Hickory when they began their search for a mountain home. Gideon Ridge was built in 1939 by the nephew of Mrs. Moses Cone (see the Blue Ridge Parkway section for more information on the Moses Cone Memorial Park).

No trip to Blowing Rock would be complete without walking out to the Blowing Rock that Ripley found to be a marvel and included in his book *Believe It Or Not.*

The Milners purchased the house in the fall of 1984 and added a roof over the lovely stone terrace and the dining area. The rooms are all comfortable and tastefully decorated but some are especially appealing, like the Sunrise View room, where the beautiful Blue Ridge Mountain sunrise is visible from the bed. Extra touches like robes and hair dryers are just the beginning of the attention to details that makes Gideon Ridge so comfortable.

Gideon Ridge is a family affair with current innkeepers Cobb III and his wife, Cindy, introducing visitors to the charms of Blowing Rock and the inn. It seems rather remote on its hilltop but it's actually less than five minutes from the heart of Blowing Rock. Breakfasts vary but may include fresh fruits, mixed cereals, and steaming hot buckwheat pancakes and sausage.

In the heart of the village, we suggest Maple Lodge Bed & Breakfast. It was built in the mid-1940s as a bed and breakfast and is now the oldest continually operating bed and breakfast in Blowing Rock.

Owner Marilyn Bateman was a school teacher who became a bed and breakfast owner in Annapolis, Maryland, by accident and genetics. Her paternal grandmother and maternal great-grand-

Gideon Ridge, just out of Blowing Rock, combines the epitome of southern hospitality with magnificent views of the Blue Ridge Mountains.

mother ran boarding houses, and another ancestor ran a tavern before the Revolutionary War.

After her husband, David, retired, they moved to Blowing Rock looking for a home, much as the Milners had done. Marilyn had stayed at Maple Lodge in the past and welcomed the surprise to see that it was for sale, so much for David's retirement.

Maple Lodge has eleven rooms, none were wheelchair accessible at the time we visited. There are several suites in an annex behind the main house that we found roomy and comfortable. Knowing Marilyn's hospitality, she'll find a way to make sure all her guests are comfortable.

Breakfasts include blueberry pancakes and sausage, homemade muffins and breads, egg casserole, sausage frittata, assorted cereals and fresh fruit.

There are several excellent restaurants in Blowing Rock that bring haute cuisine to the high country admirably. In 1995, "The Greensboro News & Record" reported that Blowing Rock had the best food in North Carolina, and *Southern Living* gave rave reviews. It was in *Southern Living* that we read Cobb Milner's quote, "Restaurants don't survive long around here unless they're top-notch." Blowing Rock has become the epitome of Darwin's theory on natural selection. Since tourists select the best places to dine, the less popular wither away. We, the tourists, are the beneficiaries of this natural selection—we get to dine where competition is severe, so we get the best. Of all the places we've traveled, we found no other area so rich with excellent dining.

A tip on deciding where to dine: If you are staying at a bed and breakfast, peruse their guest book for comments about restaurants and, of course, ask your innkeeper for suggestions.

The Village Cafe offers something for everyone including great soups and sandwiches for lunch. We knew we were in a special place to eat when we saw chefs from other restaurants having lunch there. That's about as exalted as praise gets. Our salads, sandwiches and select teas met high expectations.

The Village Cafe is half a block off Main Street. Look for the sidewalk leading to the court yard in the middle of the block. They

Marilyn Bateman, owner of Maple Lodge in downtown Blowing Rock, makes you welcome and comfortable— just as if you were coming home.

also serve breakfast. In good weather you can dine in the court yard under shady trees or go inside the three-story renovated home.

The Riverwood is a particular favorite of ours. Chef Rand Plachy features creative salads like grilled apples and leeks with hearts of palm marinated in basil/balsamic vinaigrette over mixed greens or mixed greens topped with red seedless grapes and carrots tossed in a toasted nut/honey vinaigrette and gorgonzola cheese to accompany entrées like stuffed trout, beef tournadoes, pasta with artichokes and sausage and a variety of gourmet vegetarian choices.

The meal that lit us up was the Chef's Five Alarm Dangerously Hot Specialty. The flavors swirled about the palate like orbiting Lasers lighting up taste buds. We look forward to that experience again!

Entrées include house salad, rice pilaf, vegetable and freshly baked rolls. Riverwood serves dinner daily during the tourist season. Call for winter hours.

The Speckled Trout Cafe on Main Street offers appetizers like escargot and smoked trout and entrées including smoked salmon and spinach fettucine, Paul Tate's blackened filet mignon topped with fresh shrimp and snowcrab meat, roasted chicken with artichoke hearts, black olives and celery and trout stuffed with seasoned shrimp, snowcrab meat and herb butter.

The Best Cellar is a traditional favorite with Blowing Rock visitors. Ask for the older section when you arrive and prepare to enjoy fresh fish like tuna, salmon and grouper, lamb, steaks and chicken dishes along with homemade breads.

The newest contender for Blowing Rock's premier dining spot is Crippen's Country Inn which offers an interesting menu, artfully prepared by an award-winning chef. There's no such thing as an intimate corner in the large open dining room but you will find great service and good food.

Above and to the side of the restaurant is a bed and breakfast operated by the present owner. There are nine rooms with private baths and a cottage with one bedroom with a queen-sized bed and a sofa sleeper in the living room.

The Gamekeeper features unusual food, well prepared and presented in a casual atmosphere. Buchanan's has home-style cooking and fresh locally grown vegetables in season and Woodlands serves up a handsome plate of barbecue.

Lots of visitors enjoy the fare at Twigs ranging from blackened seafood bites and crab cakes to trout and chicken.

To work off those extra calories, look in the Blowing Rock Chamber of Commerce building on Main Street for maps and a listing of trails for hiking, biking and leisurely strolls close by. Also look in the North Carolina Outdoor Recreation chapter at the end of this section.

If you think eating is a consuming past-time (pun intended) in Blowing Rock, then you haven't walked down Main Street seeing all the shops. Shopping, shopping shopping! Think of something you would like to have, it's here.

We guess that 90-plus percent of Blowing Rock's shops are within a five-minute walk of each other, that is if you don't stop to shop. Browsing up and down Main Street and Sunset Drive will satisfy most shopaholics. We will provide you with only a sampling of the shops; once you see Main Street Blowing Rock, you'll understand why.

Appalachian Rustic Furnishings with rustic handmade furniture has one-of-a-kind chairs, tables, settees, rockers and porch swings. Many pieces are twig furniture. They ship anywhere from Main Street. At the other end of the street, on South Main, is Back Creek Heirlooms with hand quilted contemporary and folk art wallhangings, quilts, and other handcrafted items. These rustic furnishings exhibit a simple way of life.

My Favorite Things and My Favorite Kitchen Things present you with a cornucopia of items for all rooms in your home and endless gift ideas from antiques to modern gizmos. It's a fun place to browse and ask yourself, "How did they think of that?" You'll find these goodies upstairs in the Historic Martin House on Main Street.

We had been looking for an oriental rug with just the right combination of colors to go in our new home. After searching in four states, there it was near the bottom of a pile in Hanna's Oriental Rugs.

Blowing Rock has become known for its multitude and variety of shops. You'll need to spend at least a day walking, looking, and sampling the different restaurants.

On the corner of Main and Sunset Drive is a sign listing over 20 businesses you'll find down Sunset. Blowing Rock Antiques & Estate Jewelry, DeWolfson's fine linens, The Green Giraffe and Fovea Art Gallery are a few.

That's not all, but we think you have an idea of what Blowing Rock has to offer you. After spending a day on the streets in the throngs, you may want to ride out toward the Blue Ridge Parkway to walk along the quiet, scenic pathways or fish in the lake in the Moses H. Cone Estate. Look in the Blue Ridge Parkway chapter or the North Carolina Outdoor Recreation chapter for directions.

We recommend you drive north on the Parkway for a pleasant surprise, Mount Airy.

The following are Blowing Rock, NC 28605 and area code 704 except where noted.

ᔪ ACCOMMODATIONS

Crippen's Country Inn and Restaurant—239 Sunset Dr.; 295-3487; 8 rooms, I cottage, one meal per day.

Gideon Ridge—6148 Gideon Ridge; 295-3644; See text.

Green Park Inn—US 321 S.; 800-852-2462; Over a century old, accommodations, dining, private golf course.

Hounds Ear Club—POB 188; 963-4321; Golf (18 holes), tennis (4 courts), resort with European and Modified American Plans; special package rates.

Linridge House Inn—Rt. I, Box 767, Blowing Rock; 295-7343; Mountain top inn with rooms and suites, full breakfast, cable TV.

Maple Lodge—Sunset Dr. (POB 1236), Blowing Rock; 295-3331; 10 rooms, I cottage, game room, fire place, breakfast.

Ragged Garden Inn—Sunset Dr., Blowing Rock; 295-9703; 6 rooms, I meal per day, TV.

Rocking Horse Inn B&B—445 Rocking Horse, Blowing Rock; 295-3311; 7 rooms, I cottage, I meal per day, TV, jogging/nature trail.

New River Inn—POB 868; 888-295-0800, 295-0800; 18 country-style rooms on mountain side overlooking the New River.

Stone Pillar B&B—144 Pine St., Blowing Rock; 295-7343; 2 rooms, I suite, I meal per day, handicapped accessible.

Victorian Inn—242 Ransom St.; 295-0034; Cable TV, two of the rooms have garden tubs, coffee and muffin breakfast.

❧ ATTRACTIONS

Adventure Vacations—POB 1376; 295-3644; Luxury vacations of day-trips or 5-day adventures; Hiking, mountain biking, whitewater rafting; geared toward the more mature but will take children over 12.

The Blowing Rock—2 miles south of Blowing Rock on US 321 S; Exceptional natural setting with gardens, unique rock formations; Light objects tossed from the rock are returned by light winds from the gorge 3,000 feet below.

Blowing Rock Stage Company—295-9627; Professional theater featuring a regional cast performing New York musicals and new plays.

❧ DINING

Best Cellar Restaurant—295-3466; Oysters to prime rib in an old English Pub; Reservations requested.

Blowing Rock Cafe at Sunset and Ransom—295-9474; 3 meals, country ham to trout, homemade soups, beer, wine.

Cosmic Coffee House—461 Main St.; 295-4444; 30 gourmet coffees, desserts, light breakfast.

Crippen's—POB 528; 295-3487.

Gamekeeper—Shulls Mill Rd; 800-962-1986, 963-7400; Reservations requested.

The Riverwood—7179 Valley Blvd.; 295-4162; Reservations requested; We highly recommend Riverwood; See text.

The Speckled Trout—922 Main St.; 295-9819; Reservations requested.

Twig's—321 Bypass; 295-5050; Reservations requested.

Vance's Main St. Cafe—295-7737; High-end breakfast, lunch, brunch.

The Village Cafe—Follow the stone walkway beside Kilwins on Main St.; 295-3769; Wonderful food! Dine on the patio or inside the turn-of-the-century home; Homemade breads, Belgian waffles, salads, sandwiches, soups, crepes; See text.

❧ SHOPPING

Appalachian Rustic Furnishings—Main St.; 295-9554.

Back Creek Heirlooms—Main St. in SouthMarket shopping mall; 295-3700.

Basket Boutique—105-2 Sunset Dr.; 295-3799; Baskets for all occasions.

Blowing Rock Antique Center—POB 963; 295-4950; 60 dealers in 10,000-square-foot mall on US 321 Bypass.

Fovea Gallery—Sunset Drive; 295-4705.
Gaines Kiker, Silversmith—4148 Linville Rd; 295-3992; Custom designed
    sterling silver, gold mixed metals, contemporary jewelry, accessories.
Hanna's Oriental Rugs—Main St.; 295-7073.
Happy Apple Farm—POB 1723; 295-7367; 12,000 old, used, and rare
    books, magazines, maps, sheet music.
My Favorite Things & My Favorite Kitchen Things—Main St.; 295-4488; Unique
    home accents, wall art, mirrors, lamps, tabletop accents.
Old World Galleries— Main St.; 800-736-1269, 295-7508.
Shoppes on the Parkway—US 321 Bypass; 295-4248; 34 outlet shops.

❧ SPECIAL EVENTS

July to August—*Annual Blowing Rock Charity Horse Race (POB 650; 800-295-
    7851, 295-7851; Oldest outdoor horse show in the country)*
Concerts in the Park (Some Sunday afternoons, classical to bluegrass)
July—*Tour of Homes (800-295-7851, 295-7851)*

❧ CAMPING

Morgan Mountain Retreat & Campground—Rt. 1, Box 398; 264-2170; 21 RV
    sites and 44 tent sites, hook-ups, showers, toilets, dump station, laun-
    dry, camp store, games, playground, cabins.
Price Park Campground—Rt. 1, Box 565; 963-5911, 264-7591; 14 tent sites,
    116 RV sites, hook-ups, showers, toilets, dump station, laundry, camp
    store, games, playground, pool, miniature golf.

❧ FOR MORE INFORMATION

Blowing Rock Chamber of Commerce—POB 406, Blowing Rock, NC 28605;
    800-295-7851, 704-295-7851; Ask for the *Visitor* that has the Historic
    Walking Tour inside and the *Three Scenic Tours* brochure.
North Carolina Ski Areas Association—POB 106 Blowing Rock, NC 28605;
    704-295-7828.

❧ DIRECTIONS

From Boone—Take US 321.
From the Blue Ridge Parkway—Take US 221/321 into town then turn south
    staying on US 321, which becomes Main Street. US 321 Bypass misses
    downtown.

37 *Mount Airy:*
A Great Place for a Day or a Lifetime

This here's Andy's town. Even if you were born long after the TV series featuring Andy Griffith as Sheriff Taylor of Mayberry ended, you would have to avoid TV altogether not to have seen the reruns. The essence of *The Andy Griffith Show* touches something in all of us—then and now.

We had not originally planned to include Mount Airy because it isn't in the Highlands, but seeing that it was only about 20 miles off the Blue Ridge Parkway from Fancy Gap, we couldn't resist. And we are glad we made the drive.

The name Sheriff Andy Taylor is as well known as Mayberry. Both Andy Griffith and his imaginary town grew up in Mount Airy.

The Mount Airy Visitor's Center includes brochures and tours of the city, an Andy Griffith museum, where you will learn of the real people whose names came to life in the *Andy Griffith Show*, and a Jeb Stuart museum, featuring another local boy.

Our first stop was the Mount Airy Visitor's Center, which is a museum dedicated to Andy Griffith with memorabilia on loan from one of Andy's childhood friends, Emmett Forrest. Although Mount Airy was the inspiration for Mayberry, you have trouble distinguishing fact from fiction.

Snappy Lunch (in business since 1923) at 125 N. Main Street is next door to Floyd's City Barber Shop. Floyd's has been owned by Russell Hiatt for more than 46 years. Behind the Courthouse on Main Street is Andy's old Ford police car and the Mayberry Jail. Emmett, Opie, and Sheriff Taylor are the "real" names of Mount Airy citizens.

Mount Airy was called home by another citizen, James Ewell Brown Stuart, known as "Jeb" Stuart. Born at his parents' home, Laurel Hill, in southwestern Patrick County, Virginia, Stuart was only 5 miles from Mount Airy.

Stuart graduated from the United States Military Academy at West Point, New York, in 1854. By 1861 he attained the rank of captain. When Virginia seceded from the Union in 1861, he went with his native state. He became Major General Stuart to serve under the command of General Lee in the Army of Northern Virginia, commanding all the cavalry forces.

The J.E.B. Stuart Birthplace, Inc., was formed in 1990 to purchase 71 acres of the Laurel Hill Farm. In 1992, the property was secured. Archaeological work is under way to place the site on the National Register of Historic Places. This work has uncovered the original house site and there are plans to reconstruct the home.

Eng and Chang Bunker, the famous Siamese twins, raised their families here. We met several members of the Bunker families while in Mount Airy, who were in town for a family reunion.

Be sure to go by the Visitor's Center to pick up a map with "Mayberry's" landmarks, as well as many other sites of interest in Mount Airy, such as the world's largest open-face granite quarry of 90 acres.

The mass of granite being quarried is 7 miles long by 4 miles wide and well over 6,000 feet deep. The quarry has been in uninterrupted operation since 1889, and the operators claim they "haven't scratched the surface." Geologists contend they have 500 more years of operation before exhausting the supply.

If you are in the Mount Airy area during the summer and fall, you will see many fruit and vegetable stands along the roadside. We found lower prices for the same fruits and vegetables the farther north we went from town. You'll see antiques stores along the highway, many of which are worth a browse.

The following are Mount Airy, NC 27030 and area code 910 except where noted.

Behind the Court House on Main Street you can see Sheriff Andy's police car and the Old Mayberry Jail.

❧ ACCOMMODATIONS

Mayberry B&B—329 Pine St.; 786-2054; 2 rooms, breakfast.
Pine Ridge Inn—2893 W. Pine St.; 789-5034; 6 rooms, breakfast, golf, pool.
The Merritt House B&B (circa 1901)—618 N. Main St.; 800-290-6290, 786-2174; 4 rooms, breakfast.

❧ ATTRACTIONS

Andy Griffith Home Place (c. 1927)—711 Haymore St.

Merritt House B&B is across the street from the Mount Airy Visitor's Center.

Floyd's Barber Shop—Next door to Snappy lunch; Great places to here about young Andy.

Mount Airy Visitor's Center—615 N. Main St., Mount Airy, NC 27030; 800-576-0231; Andy Griffith Museum, including videos, recordings, clothes, photos, a *Matlock* suite.

Snappy Lunch—125 N. Main. St.; 910-786-4931; Built circa 1896.

❧ DINING

Snappy Lunch—125 N. Main. St.; 910-786-4931; Built circa 1896, it's the city's oldest eating establishment (opened in 1923). Breakfast begins at 5:45 A.M. and closes after lunch at 1:45 P.M. Owner Charles Dowell has been making pies and sandwiches there for more than 50 years. A good place to hear Andy Griffith stories.

❧ SHOPPING

Mayberry Antique Mall—880 Hwy. 52N; 786-8187; 30 dealers from 4 states offer country and Victorian furniture, glassware, Civil War memorabilia, Watt Pottery.

M. Sparger Antiques—338 Sparger Rd.; 786-6906; American furniture, primitives, rugs, collectibles.

The Owls Nest—350 Sparger Rd.; 786-7630; American country furniture, sophisticated garden art.

❧ FOR MORE INFORMATION

Mount Airy Visitors Center—615 N. Main St.; 800-576-0231.

❧ DIRECTIONS

From the Blue Ridge Parkway at Fancy Gap, Virginia—Go south on US 52.
From Winston-Salem—Go north on US 52.

38 North Carolina: Outdoor Recreation

The following are area code 704 except where noted.

STATE & FEDERAL PARKS ALONG THE BLUE RIDGE PARKWAY:

Droughton Park (milepost 241) is the largest recreation area on the parkway, offering picnic areas, hiking, fishing, restaurant and gas station.

Moses Cone Memorial Park, north of Blowing Rock (milepost 294), is one of the chief parkway recreation areas. The 3,600-acre park offers bridle paths, hiking trails, trout streams, two lakes, and craft center in the Manor House.

Julian Price Memorial Park south of Blowing Rock (milepost 297), features campgrounds, boat rentals, fishing, interpretive programs, and hiking trails.

Linville Gorge Wilderness Area (milepost 317) has 7,600 acres preserved in a primitive state. The steep walls of the gorge enclose Linville River that descends 2,000 feet in only 12 miles. Access to the gorge is by foot-trails via a Forest Service road off US 221 at the Linville Falls community exit.

Mount Mitchell State Park (milepost 355) contains the highest peak in the eastern United States, at 6,684 feet. There is an observation tower on top, a nature exhibit, hiking trails, picnicking areas, and limited camping.

Mount Jefferson State Park (in Ashe County) offers hiking, picnicking, and nature study among its 539 undeveloped acres.

Pisgah National Forest offers lake and stream fishing, large and small game hunting, camping (tent and RV), and hiking (more than 400 miles). Linville Gorge and Roan Mountain are within the forest.

Sitting and pondering becomes a meaningful experience among these magnificent mountains. *(Courtesy of Buncombe County, NC, Tourism Development Authority)*

Contact: National Forests in NC, POB 2750, Asheville, NC 28802; 704-257-4200, for Pisgah and Nantahala National Forests.

✒ CAMPING

Camping opportunities are abundant in western North Carolina. The following are contacts to get information of what is available in their location or jurisdiction. Be sure to check each section in the back for commercial camping facilities.

Franklin Area Chamber of Commerce—180 Porter St., Franklin, NC 28734; 800-336-7829, 524-3161; Ask for "Franklin Area and Nantahala Recreation Map."

National Forests in NC—POB 2750, Asheville, NC 28802 (704-257-4200) for camping brochures for Pisgah and Nantahala National Forests.

Pisgah National Forest—Ranger Station Visitor's Center located 1.5 miles west of NC 280 and US 276; 704-877-3265. This Cradle Of Forestry in America has exhibits, gift shop, guided walks on 2 trails with 8 historic buildings and restored stationary logging locomotive.

Davidson River— north of Brevard on US 276. 704-877-4910 (gate house), 800-280-CAMP; 161 tent/RV sites, toilets, showers, dumping station, and near fishing, hiking, and tubing; Yearround. 800-280-2267; Fee area.

Camping in North Carolina ranges from primitive to posh, and you can do it all.

Lake Powhatan—southeast of Asheville off NC 191 on Bent Creek Ranch Rd.; 100 tent/RV sites, showers, dumping station, swimming, fishing, hiking; April to November; 800-280-CAMP, 704-667-8429; Fee area.

Nantahala National Forest—Highlands Ranger District, POB 1299, Highlands, NC 28741; 526-3765.

Ammons Branch Primitive Camping Area—10 miles east of Highlands via Horse Cove Rd., turn right on Bull Pen Rd.; No water, vault toilets.

Blue Valley Primitive Camping Area—6 miles south of Highlands on US 64, then 3 miles west on gravel road; No water, vault toilets; Yearround.

Elliott's Rock Wilderness—10 miles east of Highlands via Horse Cove Rd., turn right on Bull Pen Rd.; On North Carolina, South Carolina, and Georgia border; Primitive camping anywhere except within 50 feet of stream or trail.

Vanhook Glade Campground—Four miles west of Highlands on US 64; 21 sites for tents and small trailers and restrooms; Showers may be used at Cliffside Lake adjacent to campgrounds; April to November; Fee area.

Two areas along NC 28 east of Fontana:

Cable Cove on Fontana Lake has 26 tent/RV sites and is favored by anglers; East of Fontana Village, off NC 28 to the north on F.S. 520; 3 miles from AT and entrance to GSMNP; 3 miles to Fontana Dam.

Recreation Area has camping and 38 miles of multiuse trails; East of Cable Cove, off NC 28, on F.S. 521 to the north; A schedule is posted for bikes and horses; Hikers may use the trail anytime. Fee area.

CANOEING/RAFTING

Finding whitewater rafting companies in western North Carolina is as easy as finding mosquitoes in a swamp. Finding canoeing areas is more difficult because, by comparison, there is less flat water. You can challenge some sections of whitewater in canoes. In either case, check with some of the outfitters listed below.

Appalachian Challenge Guide Service—POB 1029, Banner Elk, NC 28604; 898-6484, 898-6795; Rafting French Broad River, Watauga River, and Wilson Creek.

Carolina Wilderness—POB 488, Hot Springs, NC 28743; 800-872-7437; Whitewater rafting on the French Broad and Nolichucky Rivers (Class III & IV), with lunches.

Whitewater rafting has become the most popular water sport in the state. *(Courtesy of Nantahala Outdoor Center, photo by Philip Hart)*

Edge of the World Outfitters—POB 1137, Banner Elk, NC 28604; 800-789-EDGE, 898-9550; Raft Estatoe and Watauga Rivers.

French Broad Rafting Co.—1 Thomas Branch Rd, Marshall, NC 28753; 800-570-7238; Rafting French Broad River; Class I-IV rapids.

High Mountain Expeditions—POB 1099, Blowing Rock, NC 28605; 800-262-9036; Rafting and kayaking down the Nolichucky, Watauga, Watauga Gorge, and Wilson Creek Gorge on rapids ranging from Class I to Class IV; Meals served on trips; Children encouraged; Specialty trips available.

Nantahala Outdoor Center—13077 US 19 W., Bryson City, NC 28713-9114; 800-232-7238; Whitewater rafting the Chattooga, Ocoee, Nantahala, French Broad, and Nolichucky; Lodging, dining, instructions.

Southern Waterways—1460 Brevard Rd., Asheville, NC 28806; 800-849-1970, 665-1970; Canoeing and rafting on French Broad River.

Wahoo's Adventures—800-444-RAFT; Nolichucky, Pigeon, Ocoee, Watauga, and Wilson Creek.

Wildwater Rafting—800-451-9972; Nantahala, Chattooga, Ocoee, and Pigeon.

⅋ FISHING

Stream fishing is superb in North Carolina for trout, smallmouth, walleye, and white bass. You'll also find largemouth, bream, and catfish in the lakes. Licenses and permits are required and varied. Contact NC Wildlife Resources Commission, Raleigh, NC, 800-662-7137 (in NC only) for regulations. Hunters, use the same contact.

Below are some fishing guides and their specialties. If you are going to fish an area for several days or longer, we recommend you hire a guide for your first outing, not only to learn a few good spots but to pick his brains about other streams or lakes to fish for your favorite species. If you are fly-fishing, hiring a guide will help you select patterns for the time of year on different streams. You are paying for expert advice, so be sure you ask all the questions that will make your trip successful.

Blowing Rock Fly Shop—321 Bypass, Blowing Rock, NC 28605, 295-0040; Guided fly-fishing in western North Carolina, southwestern Virginia and east Tennessee; Float trips and wade trips.

County Junction Sporting Goods—POB 635, South Sparta, NC 28675; 910-372-7730; Guide Brady Proffit specializes in float trips down the New River for smallmouth bass; Half-day and full-day trips in his custom-built 16-foot flat bottom boat.

Danny Brower—Rt. I, Box 364, Sylva, NC 28779; 586-9821; Boat or wade for walleye, smallmouth, largemouth, crappie, and trout.

K&L Outfitters—POB 799, Franklin, NC 28734; 524-9390; Trout fishing guides for the Smoky Mountains.

Smoky Mountain Outdoors—3299 Hartford Rd., Hartford, TN 37753; 800-771-7238; Alan Wray guides for trout and other species in the Smokies, North Carolina, and Tennessee; Alan guided Vern on one of the most successful trout trips ever; In one stretch of a stream, Vern landed 5 rainbows in 5 casts; one weighed more than 6 pounds.

Trout guide Alan Wray of Smoky Mountain Outdoors put author Vernon Summerlin in the right spot to catch and release this rainbow trout.

⚜ GOLF

There is more golfing in the Southern Highlands than you can swing a club at. We recommend contacting Great Smoky Mountain Golf Association, POB 18556, Asheville, NC 28814 (800-799-5537) for their golf brochure. It provides detailed information about some of the following.

Beech Mountain Golf Club—Beech Mountain Pkwy., Beech Mountain NC 28604; 800-972-2183; 18 holes, lodging.

Blowing Rock Country Club—Green Park Inn, US 321, Blowing Rock, NC 28607; 295-3141; 18 holes, lodging.

Blue Ridge Country Club—POB 88, Linville Falls, NC 28647; 800-845-8430, 756-7001; 18 holes, lodging.

You can play golf every day for weeks and not play the same round twice in western North Carolina—more courses than you can swing a club at. *(Courtesy of Buncombe County, NC, Tourism Development Authority)*

Boone Golf Club—Fairway Dr., Boone, NC 28607; 264-8760; 18 holes.

Colony Lake Lure Golf Resort—201 Blvd. of the Mountains, Lake Lure, NC 28746; 800-260-1040; 2 courses of 18 holes each.

Crooked Creek Golf Course—Crooked Creek Rd, Hendersonville, NC 28739; 692-2011; 18 holes.

Cummings Cove Golf Club—3000 Cummings Rd., Hendersonville, NC 28739; 891-9412; 18 holes.

Etowah Valley Country Club and Golf Lodge—POB 2150, Hendersonville, NC 28793; 800-451-8174, 891-7022; 27 holes, lodging.

Eseeola Lodge—Box 99, Linville, NC 28646; 733-4311; 18 holes, lodging.

Grassy Creek Country Club—NC 226, Spruce Pine, NC 28777; 828-765-7436; 18 holes.

Grove Park Inn Resort—290 Macon Ave., Asheville, NC 28804; 800-438-5800, 252-2711; 18 holes.

Hawksnest Golf & Ski—Seven Devils, NC 28604; 800-822-HAWK, 963-6561; 18 holes, lodging.

High Hampton Inn & Country Club—POB 338 Cashier, NC 28717;800-334-1551, ext. 114, 743-2411; 18 holes, lodging.

Highland Lake Gold Club—111 Highland Lake Rd., Flat Rock, NC 28731; 692-0143; 9 holes.

Holiday Inn Sunspree Resort—One Hilton Dr., Asheville, NC 28806; 800-733-3211, 254-3211; 18 holes.

Hounds Ear Club—POB 188, Blowing Rock, NC 28607: 963-4321; 27 rooms, restaurant, limited handicapped facility, tennis, 18 holes of golf; April to January.

Linville Golf Club—US 221, Linville, NC 28646; 733-4311; 18 holes, lodging.

Maggie Valley Resort—340 Country Club Rd., Maggie Valley, NC 28751; 800-438-3861; 18 holes, lodging.

Mill Creek Country Club—POB 848, Franklin, NC 28734; 800-533-3916, 524-6453; Championship 18-hole course, lodging.

Mount Mitchell Golf Club—7590 NC 80 S., Burnsville, NC 28714; 675-5454; 18 holes.

Mountaineer Gold Center—Boone, NC 28607; 264-6830; Practice range, sand trap, chipping green.

Orchard Trace Gold Club—942 Sugarloaf Rd., Hendersonville, NC 28792; 685-1006; 18 fully lighted holes.

Parker Meadows Golf Course—1272 Maxwell Home Rd., Franklin, NC 28734; 369-8008; Driving Range, practice traps, 9 holes.

Reems Creek Golf Club—36 Pink Fox Cove Rd, Weaverville, NC 28787; 645-4393, 645-3110; 18 holes.

Sapphire Mountain Golf Club—50 Slicers Ave, Sapphire, NC 28774; 743-1178; 18 holes, lodging.

Springdale Country Club—200 Golfwatch Rd., Canton, NC 28716; 800-553-3027; 18 holes, lodging, restaurant.

Waynesville Country Club Inn—POB 390, Waynesville, NC 28786; 800-311-8230, 452-2258; 27 holes.

Weaverville—36 Pink Fox Cove Rd., Weaverville, NC 28787; 704-645-4393; 18 holes.

Willow Creek Golf Course at Willow Valley Resort—105 S., Boone, NC 28607; 963-6551; 15 cabins, 44 condo units, limited handicapped facility, playground, tennis, 9 holes.

Wolf Laurel Resort—Rt. 3, Mars Hill, NC 28754; 800-221-0409; Full resort, 18 holes.

HORSEBACK RIDING

This sport does not seem as popular in North Carolina as it is in the area of Virginia we covered. The potential is here, but not yet well developed. We have listed a few stables, but you may prefer to strike out into a national forest, which we also list.

Contact National Forests of NC, POB 2750, Asheville, NC 28802 (257-4200) to get *Horse Trails* booklet of trails in Pisgah and Nantahala National Forests.

Blowing Rock Stables—Laurel Lane, Blowing Rock; 295-7847; 27 miles of trails, rent horses by the hour, guided tours on Moses H. Cone Memorial Park.

Cowee Valley Riding Ranch—94 Ruby Mine Rd., Franklin, NC 28734; 369-5779; Horseback guided trail rides; April to October.

Pisgah Forest Stables—POB 435, Cashiers, NC 28717; 883-8258; 4 trails guided daily (one hour to three days); April to end of October. Recreation Area has camping and 38 miles of multiuse trails; East of Fontana off NC 28 on F.S. 521 to the north; A schedule is posted for bikes and horses; Fee area.

BIKING

The bicycle has been legally considered a vehicle in North Carolina since 1937. Bicyclists have full rights and responsibilities on the roadways and are subject to the regulations governing the operation of a motor vehicle (where applicable).

North Carolina traffic laws require the following: Ride on the right, in the same direction as other moving traffic. Obey all traffic signs and signals. Use signals to communicate intended movements. Yield to pedestrians and emergency vehicles. Equip the bicycle with a front lamp visible from 300 feet and a rear reflector or lamp visible from 200 feet at night.

The following are recommended precautions: Always wear a helmet. Use a backpack or bicycle bag to carry goods. Avoid biking at night. Ride in single file when in a group. Wear bright clothing to be easily seen. Be sure your bicycle is in good condition and of the right size for you. Keep traffic flowing by helping motorists pass you in a safe manner.

Contact: Bicycle Program, NC Dept. of Transportation, POB 25201, Raleigh, NC 27611; 919-733-2804.

The Blue Ridge Parkway has 255 miles in North Carolina available for bicyclists. The road is yours for the pedaling.

The following are bike routes in Haywood County (Maggie Valley area): Mountain bikes routes: Graveyard Ridge, Harmon Den and Upper Crabtree. Road bike routes: Fines Creek, Balsam Ridge Breakaway, Waterrock Knob Loop, and more.

Contact: Haywood County Visitors Information, POB 1079, Maggie Valley, NC 28751; 926-5426; Ask for maps of bike trails.

Macon County (Franklin area) has 8 bike routes ranging from easy-to-moderate valley rides to demanding mountain routes. All are marked, including the Mountain-to-Sea Trail, and are centered around Franklin so you can make alterations to the courses for shorter or longer treks. All have been selected to link communities by way of scenic, less traveled, and safer roads. Some do include sections of busy roads and are noted in the *Macon County Bicycle Routes* map.

West Mills Route is 4 miles long from north to south and you pass through what were once the chief towns of the Middle Cherokees that were destroyed during the Revolutionary War.

Lost Bridge Route is 16.5 miles long, following stretches along the Little Tennessee River with one stretch of steep hills.

Cowee Valley is 8 miles long and passes through the "gem mining district" with some steep rolling hills.

Black Mountain Route is 24 miles round-trip, looping west from Franklin.

Little Tennessee River Route runs north to south for four miles along the river.

Mountain and touring biking is gaining prominence in North Carolina. Be sure you are in shape to take on the mountains.

Nikwasi Route is 15 miles long and has occasional stretches of steep hills.

Holly Spring Route runs 8 miles north to south, partially along Lake Emory.

Highlands Spur Route is 19 miles long, contains busy roads during peak tourist seasons.

Contact: Franklin Area Chamber of Commerce, 180 Porter St., Franklin, NC 28737; 704-524-3163; Ask for *Macon County Bike Routes* brochure with maps.

Pisgah National Forest has 400 miles of trails, some for biking. Ranger Station Visitor's Center is located 1.5 miles west of NC 280 and US 276; 877-3265.

Recreation Area has camping and 38 miles of multiuse trails; East of Fontana off NC 28 on F.S. 521 to the north; A schedule is posted for bikes and horses; Hikers may use the trail anytime; Fee area.

You can get bikes, tours, and local information at *Nantahala Outdoor Center*, 13077 US 19 W., Bryson City, NC 488-6737.

HIKING/NATURE TRAILS

There are 43 mountain peaks in North Carolina that exceed 6,000 feet elevation and 82 that exceed 5,000 feet. We're sure you'll want to climb them all, and hike the valleys. Because we can only mention a few here, we included contacts who can provide maps to most of them. Happy hiking!

Appalachian Challenge Guide Service—POB 1029, Banner Elk, NC 28604; 898-6484, 898-6795; Backpacking (overnight) and day hiking in the higher Highlands.

Appalachian Trail Conference—100 Otis St., Asheville, NC 28802; 254-3708; The most primitive section of the AT is through the Great Smoky Mountains National Park, the 70-mile crest-line. Clingman's Dome at 6,643 feet and Mt. Guyot at 6,621 feet are the highest peaks.
From south of Watauga Lake in Tennessee between Laurel Fork Gorge and Roan High Knob (6,285 feet), the AT runs the North Carolina-Tennessee border southeast through Cherokee National Forest and the GSMNP to Cades Cove, where the trail turns south from the state's border toward Stecoah Gap in the Nantahala National Forest heading for Standing Indian (5,499 feet) near the Georgia border.

Bartram Trail ranges from easy to strenuous. The blaze is yellow. The 100-mile trail is close to the original route William Bartram hiked in 1775.

North Carolina could be called "the waterfall state" because of the abundance of water and steep topography. Some falls are along highways, while others require taking a hike in order to take in the view. *(Courtesy of Buncombe County, NC, Tourism Development Authority)*

Contact: Bartram Trail Society, Rt. 3, Box 406, Sylva, NC 28779 for maps and detailed information.

Mountain-to-Sea Trail will run 750 miles from Clingman's Dome to the Outer Banks when completed.

Trails along the Blue Ridge Parkway between mile posts 217.5 and 451.2 number 73, ranging from less than a mile to more than 13 miles. Contact Blue Ridge Parkway, POB 453 BRP, Asheville, NC 28802-0453 for free "Info Pak" and ask for list of hiking trails in North Carolina and Virginia.

Easy Trails: Moses Cone Memorial Park, Julian Price Memorial, Linville Falls & Linville Gorge, the Cascades, the Beacon Heights Trail, Flat Rock Nature Trail, and Crabtree Falls.

Moderate Trails: Linville Gorge, Cloudland Trail, Boone Fork Trail, Grandfather Mountain, and Wilson Creek Trails.

Challenging Trails: Linville Gorge, Grandfather Mountain, Wilson Creek Gorge, and Appalachian Trail.

Pisgah National Forest has 400 miles of trails. Contact National Forests in NC, POB 2750, Asheville. NC 28802; 704-257-4200 for brochure of Forest Trails.

French Broad Rafting Co.—1 Thomas Branch Rd, Marshall, NC 28753; 800-570-7238; Guided hiking treks and Pack & Paddle trips.

Recreation Area has camping and 38 miles of multiuse trails; East of Fontana off NC 28 on F.S. 521 to the north; A schedule is posted for bikes and horses; Hikers may use the trail anytime; Fee area.

JACKSON COUNTY HIKES

Waterrock Knob—1.25 miles round trip, steep hike to 6,292-foot peak at junction of Great Balsam and Plott Balsam Ranges. Trailhead at Waterrock Knob parking area on Blue Ridge Parkway (mile-451.2).

Richland Balsam—Highest peak in Great Balsam Mountains (6,410 feet). Trailhead at Haywood-Jackson overlook on Blue Ridge Parkway (mile-431).

Wet Camp Gap—This short, easy hike is 3 miles round trip. Trailhead at Bear Pen Gap overlook, Blue Ridge Parkway mile-427.6 Be sure to take a sharp left at trail junction about 15 minutes from start to remain on Mountains-to-Sea Trail.

Whiteside Mountain—National Recreation Trail to top of 4,930-foot landmark along the Eastern Continental Divide. Fairly easy two-mile loop. Side trail 1.5 miles round trip near main overlook to Devil's Courthouse. Trailhead: From Cashiers, take US 64 west for 5 miles to Whiteside Mountain Road (NC 1690), turn left on 1690, and go 1 mile to parking area.

Bad Creek—A strenuous 7-mile hike to a spot on the Chattooga River where North Carolina and Georgia meet. Trailhead: From Cashiers take NC 107 south for 7 miles to Bull Pen Road, turn right onto Bull Pen, and go 2.5 miles to Fowler Creek Bridge. Park beyond the bridge, and walk back over bridge to trailhead on opposite side of road from parking lot.

Southwestern North Carolina is overflowing with waterfalls, some require only a short walk and others are more difficult to reach. Remember: Always be careful at the top of falls! Slick rocks and long falls!

Bridal Veil Falls—120 feet; 2.5 miles east of Highlands on US 64.

Courthouse Falls—Take US 64 east from Cashiers, turn north on NC 215 to Balsam Grove and Courthouse Creek.

Cullasaja Falls—250 feet; 11 miles east of Franklin and 9 miles west of Highlands in Cullasaja Gorge. A half-mile foot trail through rough, steep terrain.

Drift Falls—From Cashiers, take US 64 10 miles east to Whitewater Road, go south about 3 miles to Horsepasture River.

Dry Falls—75 feet; Located near US 64, 3.5 miles west from Highlands, 16.5 miles east from Franklin. Paved walkway leads to falls.

Glen Falls—180 feet; From Highlands go 3 miles south on NC 106, turn on US Forest Service Rd. with "Glen Falls" marker. Rough, steep 1-mile trail to set of 3 falls about 60 feet each.

Horsepasture Falls—Near Drift Falls; From Cashiers take US 64 10 miles east to Whitewater Road, go south about 3 miles to Horsepasture River.

Kiesee Falls—From Cashiers, go 16 miles east on US 64 to "Glouchester Rd." Falls on Kiesee Creek near Courthouse Falls.

Indian Creek Falls—60 feet; From Bryson City take Deep Creek Rd. north 3 miles to Deep Creek Campground in GSMNP. Hike 1 easy mile to falls.

Indian Creek Falls—From Bryson City take Deep Creek Rd. north 3 miles to Deep Creek Campground in GSMNP. The 1-mile hike to see the 60-foot falls is easy.

Juneywhank Falls—About one-quarter mile downstream from Indian Falls.

Looking Glass Falls—From Waynesville go about 22 miles south on US 276. From well-marked parking lot, it's a short walk to the falls.

Rainbow Falls—200 feet; On same road as Drift and Horsepasture Falls.

Soco Falls—From Cherokee go 6 miles north on US 19. Falls located on slopes of Soco Bald.

Tom's Branch Falls—A quarter-mile walk from Deep Creek Campground (see Indian Creek Falls).

Toxaway Falls—From Cashiers go about 16 miles east on US 64. Highway passes over the falls.

Whitewater Falls—411 feet; Highest falls in eastern United States. From Cashiers go 10 miles east on US 64, turn on Whitewater Rd. and go about 10 miles near the North Carolina-South Carolina state line. On same road as Rainbow Falls, Drift, and Horsepasture Falls. Also accessible from Cashiers via NC 107 south.

Lower Whitewater Falls—About 3 miles downstream of Whitewater Falls in South Carolina; Drop of about 400 feet; Considered as spectacular as the upper falls.

For a list of more waterfalls contact Visitor's Information, 35 W. Main St., Brevard, NC 28712; 800-648-4523.

Hickory Nut Falls—(404 feet) is on private land but open to the public in Chimney Rock Park. Contact: Chimney Rock Park, POB 39, Chimney Rock, NC 28720; 800-277-9611, 625-9611.

⅛⅛ SNOW SKIING

Some of North Carolina's mountains have been cultivated for downhill skiing. Most resorts don't depend on Mother Nature to provide snow, just cold temperatures to maintain machine-made snow. This part of the tourism industry has been refined for years, even to the point you can go to a ski resort and have all the fun you want without putting on a pair of skis. Resorts have entertainment, shops, and other forms of recreation. Contact North Carolina Ski Areas Association, POB 106 Blowing Rock, NC 28605 (295-7828) for more detailed information.

Appalachian Ski Mountain—POB 106, Blowing Rock, NC 28605; 800-322-2373, 295-7828; 9 slopes.

Cataloochee Ski Area—Rt. 1, Box 502, Maggie Valley, NC 28751; 800-868-1401, 800-768-3588 (report), 926-3588 (report), 800-768-0285 (office), 926-0285 (office), 926-1401; 9 slopes, lodging.

First Tracks—POB 3227, Boone, NC 28607; 264-7368

Hawksnest Golf & Ski Resort—1800 Skyland Dr., Seven Devils, NC 28604; 800-822-4295, 963-6561, 898-5135; Lodging, 14 slopes

Ski Beech—1007 Beech Mountain Pkwy., Beech Mountain, NC 28604; 800-438-2093, 387-2011; Lodging, 14 slopes

Sugar Mountain Resort—POB 369, Banner Elk, NC 28604; 800-784-2768, 898-4521; Lodging, 18 slopes

Sugar Top Resort—303 Sugar Top Dr., Banner Elk, NC 28604; 898-6211

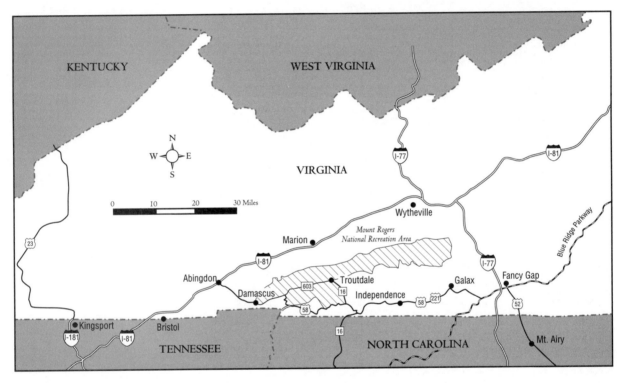

VIRGINIA

Virginia

Virginia

The small area of Virginia we explored for this book is between major routes into the Southern Highlands, Interstates 81 and 77. The Blue Ridge Parkway parallels I-81, offering travelers a choice between a quick jaunt or a restful journey.

Our chapters for each state are arranged so that they progress linearly and make a loop. In Virginia, we take you from Abingdon, the largest city in the area, across the southern Virginia border via US 58 to Damascus, Independence, Galax, and some of the prettiest country you'll ever see. From Galax, you have quick access to the Blue Ridge Parkway or I-77. You can easily make the drive in a day, but take more time if you can, because you have dozens of enjoyable stops ahead of you.

Along this route we take you on a spur to visit a bed and breakfast in the Troutdale area. Nearby is the magnificent Mount Rogers and Grayson Highlands State Park, which is covered in Viriginia Outdoor Recreation. This last chapter samples the abundant outdoor opportunities in this small region. We are sure you'll find Virginia as friendly and majestic as we did.

Flowers are part of Virginia's mountains whether they are indigenous or cultivated like this Cosmos.

39 *Abingdon:*
Living History

In 1584 Sir Walter Raleigh discovered and claimed land, part of which is now Virginia, for England—at some surprise to Native Americans, no doubt. In 1606, 120 colonists arrived under a charter from the Virginia Company of London.

In 1776, 170 years later, Virginia published its Bill of Rights and, as one of the 13 original colonies, was represented on Old Glory by one of the 13 stars and bars.

As white people moved West in search of new lands, in 1748, Dr. Thomas Walker surveyed land for himself west of the Blue Ridge Mountains. In 1760, Col. William Byrd and his men cut the Great Road through what is now Abingdon to present-day Kingsport, Tennessee.

The "Martha," named after Martha Washington, spent its first years as a private home to later become a women's college, then the inn it is today.

That same year Daniel Boone camped in Abingdon with Nathaniel Gist during a hunting trip. While camped, wolves emerged from a cave attacking their dogs. Boone gave Abingdon its first name, "Wolf Hills." Today, Cave House Craft Shop sits on the site of the wolves' den.

Joseph Black, in 1774, built a fort here named "Black's Fort" to protect the whites from the Cherokees, who, from the late 1760s until the early 1770s, lived relatively peacefully. The name Wolf Hills faded from use.

Two years later, in 1776, the General Assembly of Virginia established Washington County, naming Black's Fort as the meeting place of the first county court and county seat. The county, named for George Washington, was the first named for the Father of our Country.

Dr. Thomas Walker, Joseph Black, and Samuel Briggs donated 120 acres of land to be used to establish a town. In 1778, this land received the name of Abingdon, derived from Martha Washington's English home of Abingdon Parrish, and was incorporated.

By 1800, Abingdon was well established and attracted Gen. Francis Preston to the region in 1830. The home he built for himself, at a cost of $15,000 in 1832, later became the Martha Washington Inn it is today, but served as the Martha Washington College for Women from 1858 until 1931. The college paid $21,000 for the property. The "Martha," as the school was called, was visited by Martha Washington, and she presented the college with a tea cup and saucer.

The Martha suffered during the Civil War; her students became nurses, her grounds became training areas for troops, and she became a hospital for Rebs and Yanks. Yet she survived. It was during the war that the Martha "earned" three ghost stories.

One ghost story involves a Reb who loved a Martha girl. The Confederates were about to move out to join Lee's army. This young Southern soldier, trying to see his girlfriend before he left, crept up a secret stairway to kiss her goodbye and was met by Union soldiers. The startled Reb drew his pistol but was killed on the spot. He fell at his sweetheart's feet, staining the floor with his blood.

Through the years, attempts to remove the stain were futile. Even when they were thought to be removed, they reappeared. Eventually they had to be covered with carpet. This happened in what is now the Governor's Suite. (If you stay in the suite, let us know what you find!)

After the war, the Martha returned to educating young women until she fell victim to the Great Depression and typhoid fever. She closed in 1932, but the building revived in 1933 as a theatre. An out-of-work actor, Robert Poterfield, returned from New York City to Abingdon, bringing a troupe in tow. The hungry actors established the idea of "ham for Hamlet" and used the old Preston home as headquarters for two years. Then the theatre moved into a church across the street.

Early in Barter Theatre's history you could swap surplus garden vegetables for a ticket to a play or, as an actor, you could be paid with a ham.

Trading tickets for produce from local farms and gardens earned the theatre its name. Barter Theatre opened June 10, 1933, proclaiming, "With vegetables you cannot sell, you can buy a good laugh." Admission price was 40 cents or 40 cents' worth of produce. At the end of Barter Theatre's first season, it had $4.35 in cash, two barrels of jelly, and more than 300 pounds of grain.

Playwrights, including Noel Coward, Tennessee Williams, and Thorton Wilder, accepted ham as payments for royalties. George Bernard Shaw, a vegetarian, accepted spinach.

It is now the longest running professional equity theatre in the nation. Gregory Peck, Patricia Neal, Ernest Borgnine, Hume Cronyn, Ned Beatty, Gary Collins, and Larry Linville performed here before moving on to stardom.

Barter presents three distinct programs of live theatre: the Main Stage at Barter Theatre, Barter Stage II, and the First Light Theatre. Main Stage productions are in the old Presbyterian Church that seats 400. The Playhouse, across the street, seats 150. First Light is for young actors playing in five youth-oriented plays during the summer months.

Directly across the street from Barter Theatre, Martha Washington Inn was restored in 1984 after a long career housing Barter Theatre actors and functioning as an inn.

Tour historic Abingdon in style on an English double-decker bus. (*Courtesy of Abingdon Convention and Visitors Bureau*)

Today the Martha has 51 guest rooms; 10 suites; salons and parlors for social gatherings, receptions, and meetings; entertainment in the President's Club; and dining.

You will want to spend a few hours delving into the books and antiques in the three-story Abingdon Mercantile.

Hazel, the Love House's "Eclectic Chef," creates foods that tease and caress your tastebuds.

Abingdon is the oldest town west of the Blue Ridge Mountains. You can enjoy the history and charm of Abingdon's 20-block Historic District filled with exceptional examples of Federal and Victorian architecture.

Be sure to pick up a copy of the *Walking Tour of Main Street* at the Abingdon Convention and Visitor's Bureau. It takes you from 1748 to the present. Abingdon retains buildings from each decade of its first 100 years.

A 110-year old hotel on Wall Street is now Abingdon Mercantile. Three floors with 12,000 square feet feature 19 antiques dealers. Enter the door with hours of time to spare; you'll need it. The Starving Artist Restaurant is nearby if you need a nourishing break.

The highlight of our visit to Abingdon was our stay at the Love House. Built in 1850 by John and Remember A. Love, the present owners, Hazel Ramos-Cano and Richard Cano, renovated it in 1995.

Though the home has been brought up to modern standards, including a whirlpool tub in each bathroom, it maintains its original charm with six fireplaces, original hardwood floors, over-sized doors, and hand-blown glass windows. Each of the three guest rooms has a queen-size bed and fireplace with gas logs. The house is centrally heated and cooled.

The rooms are comfortable, but even if you had to sleep on straw mats, Hazel's meals are worth it. She prepares meals only for guests, who may invite a lucky friend or two to join them.

Hazel has more than 30 years of experience in the culinary field as a caterer, restaurant owner, and cooking instructor. In fact, she holds "gourmet weekends" in the inn. She is a fine artist, creating marvelous works of art for you to enjoy. Hazel claims the title of "Eclectic Chef." We rank dining at the Love House "a must!"

The Cave House, a 140-year old building housing the works of 160 members of the Holston Mountain Arts and Crafts organization, merits a look. Originally the home was built by Adam Hickman as a wedding present for his daughter.

This National Trust for Historic Preservation landmark got its name, The Cave House, because it is built a few yards from the cave that you read about earlier in this chapter. Although the cave is covered by a padlocked structure, you can walk behind the Cave House to peer between the slats of lattice to see the old wolf den.

The oldest building in Abingdon, built in 1779, was originally a tavern and inn for stagecoach travelers. Because people like Andrew Jackson, Henry Clay, Pierre Charles L'Enfant (designer of Washington, D.C.) and Louis Phillippe, King of France, slept here, the building has served as a bank, bakery, general store, cabinet shop, barber shop, private residence, post office (first west of the Blue Ridge), antiques shop, and restaurant. During the War it served as a hospital for Confederate and Union soldiers.

The Tavern, now a restaurant, was faithfully restored in 1984. Two-foot-thick brick and stone walls, plaster over wood lath, log beams, hand-forged locks, bolts and hinges, and wood shingles were some of the elements of the reconstruction. Courtyard dining under umbrellas is an added modern touch that patrons like.

The following are Abingdon, VA 24210 and area code 540 except where noted.

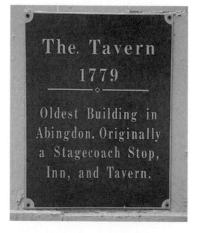

Abingdon's oldest building began as a tavern over 200 years ago. Today, again a tavern, it has a new look with outside dining under umbrellas.

ACCOMMODATIONS

Camberley's Martha Washington Inn—150 W. Main St.; 800-555-8000, 628-3161, FAX 628-8885.

The Gables—153 W. Main St.; 628-1521; Built in 1879, Close to Barter Theatre.

Inn On Town Creek—445 E. Valley St., 24211; 628-4560; A historic creek is the theme of this B&B on 4 acres. Antiques filled, it has 3 rooms and 2 suites; Full breakfast. Children over 10; Smoke-free; no pets,

Litchfield Hall—247 E. Valley St., 24211; 676-2971; 3 rooms with private baths near the historic district.

Maplewood Farm B&B—20004 Cleveland Rd., 24211; 540-628-2640; A 66-acre farm with hiking trails and fishing has 2 rooms and a 2-bedroom suite with private baths; Full breakfast; Equestrian services available, including boarding; Wheelchair accessible.

The Love House—210 E. Valley St., 24211; 623-1281 (see text).

Silversmith Inn—102 E. Main St., 24211; 676-3924; 4 rooms with private baths; Gift shop; Close to Barter Theatre.

Summerfield Inn—101 W. Valley St., 24211; 800-668-5905, 628-5905; Convenient to historic district, this B&B has 4 rooms with private baths; The new cottage addition has 3 rooms with TVs, phones, and whirlpool/shower combination, including a bridal/anniversary suite with double whirlpool bath; I wheelchair accessible room; Full breakfast; Smoking restricted; No pets.

Victoria & Albert Inn—224 Oak Hill St., 24211; 676-2797; Each room has fireplace and whirlpool.

White Birches Inn—268 White's Mill Rd., 24211; 800-BIRCHES, 676-2140; 4 rooms with private baths.

ATTRACTIONS

Arts Depot—314 Depot St.; 628-9091; Co-op featuring studios, exhibits, and classes.

Barter Theatre—POB 867; 800-368-3240, 628-3991; Open yearround.

The Carter Family Memorial Music Center—Maces Springs, VA; 386-9480, 386-6054; Call for map and schedule of performances.

Cumberland Textiles Museum—628-5572; Exhibits turn-of-the-century textiles.

Fields-Penn 1860 House Museum—208 W. Main St.; 800-435-3440, 676-0216; Free; Open to public Wednesday to Saturday 1:00 to 4:00 P.M. or by appointment.

White's Mill (1790)—12291 White's Mill Rd.; 676-0285; The only water-powered, commercially-run mill in Virginia, a historic landmark.

William King Regional Arts Center—415 Academy Dr., Abingdon 24212; 628-5005; An affiliate of the Virginia Museum of Fine Arts and has changing exhibits, studios, a museum store, and classes. Free admission.

DINING

Abingdon General Store & Gallery—301 E. Main St.; 628-8382; Bakery/deli and 2 restaurants with gourmet flair, Dumb Waiter and Plumb Alley Eatery (May to October); Dine in or take out; Special evening events.

The First Lady's Table (Martha Washington Inn)—150 W. Main St.; 628-3161; Elegant dining to guests and visitors; Reservations suggested for lunch and dinner; Sunday brunch from 11:00 A.M. to 3:00 P.M. is a local tradition.

Hardware Company—260 W. Main St.; 628-1111; Once a hardware store, now a unique dining atmosphere for lunch and dinner of beef, seafood, salads, and sandwiches with free snacks in the Main Street Yacht Club Lounge.

Max & Kathy's International Gourmet—130 Pecan St,; 623-1111; Abingdon's newest upscale restaurant.

Thomas B's Restaurant & Lounge—414 E. Main St.; 628-4111; Features a taste of the bayous as well as traditional fare; Enjoy the jazzy atmosphere for lunch, dinner, or cocktails.

Starving Artist Cafe—134 Wall St.; 628-8445; Features gourmet sandwiches, unique entrées for lunch and dinner; The restaurant doubles as an art gallery; Outdoor dining in season.

The Tavern—222 E. Main St.; 628-1118; Abingdon's oldest building, faithfully restored, serves lunch and dinner.

SHOPPING

Abingdon Mercantile—130 Wall St.; 628-2788.

Antiques Etc.—420 E. Main St.; 628-2855.

The Arts Depot—314, Depot Square; 628-9091; Open Thursday to Saturday or by appointment; Studio artists (oil, watercolor, weaving, ceramics), galleries, sales, workshops, lectures, performces, literary arts programs.

Cave House Craft Shop—279 E. Main St.; 628-7721; Home for Holston Mountain Arts and Crafts Co-op.

Dixie Pottery—Claims 100,000 square feet of world class shopping; Off I-81 between exits 10 and 13 on US 11.

Tea & Sympathy—164 E. Valley St.; 628-6465; Behind the Courthouse is a Victorian gift shop and tea room with fine linens, exotic teas, gourmet foods.

SPECIAL EVENTS

May—*Plumb Alley Day welcomes spring with entertainment, food, arts, and crafts annually the last Saturday in May.*

August—*The Carter Family Memorial Music Center, Maces Springs, VA; 386-9480, 386-6054; Call for map and information about their Annual August Festival, first Friday and Saturday in August; Camping available.*

August—*Virginia Highlands Festival gives you a taste of southwest Virginia's Blue Ridge Highlands; Juried arts, crafts, photography, youth events, drama, concerts, hot air balloons, and more held annually the last two weeks of August.*

September—*Washington County Fair & Burley Tobacco Festival exhibits farm equipment, crops, tobacco, livestock, food, and flowers, and features live music, talent show, beauty pageants, and a parade. Held annually the second week of September.*

November—*Christmas Parade along Main Street is held the third Friday in November.*

December—*Community Christmas Tree Lighting features music of the season and a holiday party in the heart of Abingdon the second Tuesday of December.*

December—*Candlelight Christmas in Historic Abingdon held each second Sunday in December.*

CAMPING

Lake Shore Campgrounds—540-628-5394; On South Holston Lake; 200 campsites, sanitation facilities, and swimming, plus use of Washington County Pool, boat ramp boat storage, game room, fishing; April to November.

Riverside Campground—18496 N. Fork River Rd., Abingdon 24210;540-628-5333; Overlooks South Holston River with 126 campsites, 96 full hook-ups, 30 tent sites, and self-contained units, sanitation facilities, laundry, convenience store, game room, pool, children's pool; April to November.

Washington County Park near South Holston Lake—540-628-9677, 676-6215; 140 campsites with electricity, water, sanitation facilities, 10 tent sites, playground picnic shelters, swimming pool, fishing, boat ramp; April to October.

FOR MORE INFORMATION

Abingdon CVB—335 Cummings St., Abingdon, VA 24210; 800-435-3440, 540-676-2282, FAX 676-3076; e-mail: ACVB@ naxs.com, http://www.naxs.com/abingdon/tourism.

DIRECTIONS

Three exits from I-81 lead to Abingdon. Exit 17, west on Cummings Street, takes you to Main Street near the Martha Washington Inn and Barter Theatre.

40 *Damascus:*

Friendliest Town on the Applachian Trail

Not many more than a thousand souls live in Damascus, but many more pass through, usually involved in the abundance of outdoor opportunities or sightseeing.

The Appalachian Trail (AT) runs through downtown, then crosses the Virginia Creeper Trail just down the street. The Transcontinental Bicycle Trail, on its way from Oregon to Yorktown, Virginia, and the historical Daniel Boone Trail run through town also. The meeting of these four trails paints a picture of people on the move.

Part of downtown, on the AT, is a section of brick paved sidewalk. The community leaders said they couldn't afford to repair or replace the sidewalk, so some inventive minds came up with the idea to sell bricks to pave the sidewalk, now called Friendship Path.

The path is composed of colorful, hand-painted bricks, glazed and fired, then set in the path between plain bricks. Anyone can buy a brick for the path for $50. For $75, you get a brick in the path and a full-sized replica to keep. For an order form, write Friendship Path/Good Earth, P.O. Box 340, Damascus, Virginia, 24236.

We visited with John and Gwen Wright at Briar Patch Antiques, who were store-sitting for their daughter Sara. They have furniture, Blue Ridge plates, blanket chests, china cupboards, an 1850 Eastlake bookcase, and much more. They recommended Dunburn Farms as the best B&B in the area. It has three Scottish motif rooms, a hot tub, and provides a full Scottish breakfast. Nearby trout fishing is an added bonus.

Here is the intersection of the Appalachian Trail and the Virginia Creeper Trail in Damascus.

You can have your name baked into a brick to support Friendship Path on the Appalachian Trail that runs through downtown Damascus.

Downtown Damascus is compact and you can visit all the shops within a few hours. We found Damascus to be like most of the small towns in southwestern Virginia, full of exceptionally friendly people with ready smiles.

The following are Damascus, VA 24236 and area code 540 except where noted.

ACCOMMODATIONS

Appalachian Inn—628-3882; accommodates hikers.
Dunburn Farms—33175 Mast Rd., Glade Spring, VA 24340; 475-5667; 3 rooms, hot tub, full breakfast, trout fishing nearby; Open Friday to Sunday.
Four Trails Inn—POB 579, Damascus, VA 24236; 475-6026, 475-5363.
Mountain Laurel Inn Christian B&B (circa 1901)—POB 1015, Damascus, VA 24236; 475-5956; 4 rooms, Continental breakfast.
The White House—Cottage; 475-5811.

DINING

Cowboy's—On Greenway Ave.; 475-5444.
CJ's Market and Deli—On Douglas Dr.; 475-5500.

Dot's Inn—On Greenway Ave.
T.K.'s Deli—On Greenway Ave.
Trails Restaurant—2 miles west of town on US 58N; 475-3380.

SHOPPING

Briar Patch Antiques—Downtown; 475-5014.
School House Antiques—VA 708 off US 58.
Laurel Creek Cottage Collectibles—Downtown.
Nell's Place—Downtown; 475-5438.
In the Country—1 mile west of town on Hollyfield Rd.; 475-5376.

SPECIAL EVENTS

April to May—*Appalachian Trail Days.*
May—*Ramp Festival.*
August—*Virginia Highlands Festival; 16-day event in August with more than 90 antiques dealers; 800-435-3440, 623-5266 for dates.*
October—*Fall Festival.*
Live music on Saturday nights at Trails Restaurant.
Mike's Friday Night Auctions, downtown Damascus.

CAMPING

Backbone Rock—4 miles out Backbone Rd.
Bear Tree Lake—7 miles east on US 58.
Jefferson National Forest—540-783-5196.

FOR MORE INFORMATION

Damascus Chamber of Commerce—POB 609, Damascus, VA 24236; 540-628-8141.

DIRECTIONS

At the crossroads of US 58 and VA 91, 10 miles southeast of Abingdon.

41 Troutdale:
In the Shadow of Mount Rogers

Fox Hill Inn, a few miles off the Appalachian Trail, is a favorite resting spot for hikers. As you can see, the view from the top of the hill is heavenly.

We entered the drive to Fox Hill Inn at sunset off VA 16. We stopped several times to take photos of the stunning mountains as we drove up the hill. The mountains appeared to change as we climbed the drive to the inn, which seemed like a mile long. We slowed to let sheep move from our path. At the inn the view was more stunning than from below. Now we were at eye level with the peaks many miles away.

Fox Hill Inn was designed with a large entry hall, living room, dining room, and kitchen on the first floor. Six guest rooms were upstairs. Located among 70 secluded acres, you are invited to stroll in the fields or hike through the woods.

Innkeepers Mark and Janet Holmes are experienced Appalachian Trail (AT) hikers. They met the owner of the inn when hiking through the area and were offered the position of innkeepers when they completed their hike up the AT. An accident cut their trip short and they later returned to Fox Hill. Get Mark to tell you about his "slipping on the grass."

Although Fox Hill has guests of all ages and interests, many hikers take a few days off to rest here. On the library table in the foyer are notebooks with comments from the many visiting hikers.

Mark and Janet can give you directions to many outdoor recreation spots in the area including hiking, bicycling, horseback riding, canoeing, camping, skiing, fishing, and hunting.

Also ask them about Shatley Springs Inn. It has family-style dining and shops about 30 minutes away in Crumpler, North Carolina. We had a more-than-filling dinner there one evening.

In 1890, Martin Shatley stopped to bathe his blistered skin in a mountain stream. He had been plagued by a skin disease for seven years. A few hours after bathing in the stream, his skin disease began to disappear. Martin bought the springs feeding the stream and in time people came from all over to partake. The land changed hands several times over the years, and a resort grew where a crude bath house and tent sites once were.

Even now, people come to the springs to drink and take home some of the "healing waters." Since Lee McMillan bought the springs in 1958, visitors can sit down for a bite to eat. Sample country fried ham, fried chicken, buttermilk biscuits, a variety of vegetables, and homemade dessert. Shatley Springs healing water is served with your meal.

Fox Hill Inn recommends Shatley Springs over the state line in North Carolina to its guests. The healing springs are only part of its enticement—all-you-can-eat family-style dining is the main attraction.

The following are VA locations and area code 540 except where noted.

ACCOMMODATIONS

Fox Hill Inn—Rt. 2, Box 1A1, Troutdale, 24378; 800-874-3313 or 677-3313; At this new B&B with 6 rooms and private baths, you are centrally located for the AT, Mount Rogers, and the New River; Full breakfast and, with notice, dinner; Children welcome; Smoking restricted; No pets.

DINING

Shatley Springs Inn—Rt. 1, Box 64, Crumpler, NC 28617; 910-982-2236.

DIRECTIONS

Troutdale—From Marion, take VA 16.
From Damascus—Go east on US 58, at Volney go north on VA 16 (US 58 turns south).

42 Independence:
Legacy Preserved

Independence, a small, warm, and friendly town, is the county seat of Grayson County. And, like a handful of other towns in the Southern Highlands, it's on the brink of a booming tourist trade.

At the intersection of US 59 and US 21 is a Richardsonian-style courthouse built in 1908. This architecture was common among pubic buildings built between 1865 and 1915. The Byzantine decorations, Flemish gables, octagonal towers, hip roof, elaborate dentil work and arched windows of this massive stone-and-brick construction make this historic building unique in this area.

Court is no longer held here, but it is now home to the Vault Museum, exhibiting early mountain home, barn, and blacksmith shop

The old Independence Court House is the predominant landmark in this rural community.

tools and implements. Formerly the clerk's vault room, it is now the centerpiece of several heritage projects for preserving Grayson County's history. The history of the courthouse is displayed in the lobby.

The Treasury, also in the courthouse, is a fine art and crafts gallery. Local artists create pottery, stained glass, paintings, prints, woodwork, and more. The Treasury is worth a look.

Independence has two bed and breakfasts, the Virginia House and the Davis-Bourne Inn. The Davis-Bourne Inn, constructed c. 1864 by Confederate Col. Alexander Davis (and later a congressman) is an example of Queen Anne architecture. J. Simeon Bourne purchased the property in the 1930s and named it *Journey's End.* Today Eddie and Lucy Copenhaver own the inn.

All guestrooms have functioning fireplaces and private baths on the second floor. The Copenhavers serve breakfast and light afternoon refreshments in their carefully restored Victorian period inn. You will enjoy the dining room's period antiques, and you may take your coffee to the wraparound porch for a relaxing morning view of the mountains.

The Virginia House is three miles east of Independence on VA 58. The guestrooms have private baths, telephones, televisions, and hair dryers. A continental breakfast is served in the sunroom or in the dining room from eight until ten.

Both bed and breakfasts allow smoking outside but no pets.

From Independence you have access to the New River, the Blue Ridge Parkway, Grayson Highlands State Park, Mount Rogers National Recreation Area, the Appalachian Trail, the Virginia Creeper Trail, Lake Hale, and Shately Springs.

South of Independence on US 21 at the North Carolina border is New River Canoe & Campgrounds. Owner Bobby Catron is an encyclopedia of outdoor recreation, and he has a grabbag of tales about people floating on the New River.

Bobby took us way back in the boonies before turning us loose on the New River in our canoe, Wave Dancer. The easy float trip was a pleasure because the scenery was enchanting and the current was just right.

New River Canoe & Campgrounds has tent and RV sites, apartments, cabins, a fully stocked camp store, a playground for children, pedal boats, picnic areas for families or groups, shuttle service, and canoe rentals. You can rent a tube and float by the campgrounds or get on the shuttle to make a longer float trip.

The following are Independence, VA 24348 and area code 540 except where noted.

ACCOMMODATIONS

Davis-Bourne Inn—119 Journey's End; 773-9384; Private baths and fire places.
Virginia House B&B—3529 Grayson Parkway; 773-2970; Continental breakfast.

ATTRACTIONS

1908 Courthouse Foundation—107 E. Main St.; 773-3711.
Vault Museum—107 E. Main St.; 773-3711; Free admission.

DINING

Ogle's Sandwich Shop—Turn south at the traffic light and it's on your right; Pizza, sandwiches, soups.

SHOPPING

Hoffman Pottery—Rt. 3, Box 848; 773-3546; David and Sherry make stoneware suitable for eating, drinking, cooking (oven, microwave, and dishwasher safe); Decorative pottery available; Call ahead for appointment and directions.
The Treasury—1908 Courthouse; 773-3711; Fine art, pottery, woodwork, baskets, stained glass, paintings, etchings, prints, dolls.

CAMPING

New River Canoe & Campgrounds—Rt. 2, Box 221; 773-3905; see Virginia Recreation section.

FOR MORE INFORMATION

Tourist Information Center—107 E. Main St., Independence, 24348; 773-3711.

DIRECTIONS

Independence is on US 58 11 miles west of Galax and about 50 miles east of Abingdon via US 58.

43 Galax:
Virginia's Rising Star

Our drive to Galax via US 58 from Abingdon was as scenic as any we've driven. In a word, awesome.

Galax, settled primarily by Quakers, gets it name from the galax plant common in the southwestern Virginia mountains. The galax plant derives its name from the Greek word *gala,* meaning milk. The white spire produced by the plant in spring resembles a stream of milk. The city sends the plant leaves to florists around the world.

Kathy Price, director of the Galax-Carroll-Grayson Chamber of Commerce, made us feel right at home in this friendly town with a 250-year-old culture. She pointed out the things that would interest most tourists, including the Fiddle Festival. One of the things we knew before we arrived was that Galax held the largest and oldest fiddling contest in the world.

The Old Fiddlers Convention is held the second weekend in August each year. The music is reminiscent of the area's early Scottish and Irish settlers. You can hear the bag pipes in the twang of the fiddle.

Many of the musicians have played in most of the conventions since they began in 1935. The convention is dedicated to "Keeping alive the memories and sentiments of days gone by, and making it possible for people of today to hear and enjoy the tunes of yesterday."

Often times the stage isn't the place for some carrying on. Musicians and dancers take their fun to the parking lot where they perform what they "would not dare do on stage."

Fiddles, fiddles, fiddles; the Old Fiddlers Convention in Galax draws more "sawers" than any musical contest in the world. Rosin up your bow for this annual event in August.

Every B&B, motel, spare room, and camping spot is taken for miles around come the second weekend in August. Keep this in mind when making your plans. Contact Kathy Price or Rebecca Ogle at Galax-Carroll-Grayson Chamber of Commerce in Galax (address and number below) for more information.

Speaking of campsites, Felts Park at the south end of town becomes a huge campground with RVs and tents bumping one another in August.

To go along with the hoopla, Fiddlefest is a street festival with arts, crafts, food, and childrens' activities that coincide with the Old Fiddlers Convention.

The Galax Mountain Music Jamboree, featuring old-time and bluegrass music, is held outside in June, July, August, and September. From October through May it is held downtown in the historic Rex Theatre.

Barr's Fiddle Shop on Main Street has a large selection of fiddles. This is a focal point in Galax during the Fiddle Festival, with musicians trying out the feel and sound of different instruments.

We walked up and down Main Street looking in the shops and, of course, taking advantage of the "good deals."

Put Rooftop of Virginia on your list if you are interested in antiques and mountains crafts; it's loaded—and the prices are great!

Rooftop of Virginia, once a church, now houses divine crafts and antiques.

To get a seat in the County Line Cafe you have to be early. It's the best place to eat in Galax, with family dining and country cooking. We had flounder and crab cakes with vegetables. It was interesting to see rice pudding listed as a vegetable (and it was good!).

We found Galax to be a special town for its friendliness, mountain crafts, and music.

The following are Galax, VA 24333 and area code 540 except where noted.

ACCOMMODATIONS

Blue Ridge Motel & Restaurant—Hwy. at Blue Ridge Pkwy. (Milepost 177.7), Meadows of Dan, VA; 952-2244.
Lakeview Motel & Restaurant—Hwy. 52 at Blue Ridge Pkwy., Fancy Gap, VA; 728-7841.
Travel Host Inn—303 N. Main St.; 236-5127.

ATTRACTIONS

Levering Orchard—Rt. 2 Box 310, Ararat, VA 24503; 775-4837; Levering Orchard is the largest pick-your-own cherry orchard in the South.
Jeff Mathews Memorial Museum—606 W. Stuart Dr.; 540-236-7874; The home of John Austin consists of 2 cabins, one built in 1834 and the other in the 1860s, when John returned from the Civil War; Originally built on the New River, they were moved to Galax to house Jeff Mathews' collection of Indian artifacts, more than 200 photos of Civil War veterans, and more.

DINING

Alley Oop's Sandwich & Ice Cream—104 Oldtown; 238-2419.
County Line Cafe—956 E. Stuart Dr.; 236-3201; Home cooked meals of meat, vegetables.
Fiddler's Family Restaurant—101 N. Main St.; 236-2543.
Roy's Underground—101½ E. Oldtown; 236-7452

SHOPPING

The Antique Apple—118 S. Main St.; 236-0881.
Barr's Fiddle Shop—105 S. Main St.; 236-2411.

Cherry Creek Cyclery—107 S. Main St.; 236- 4013.

Framer's Daughter—121 N. Main St,; 236-4920; Civil War art, local and
national artists.

Galax Flea Market—211 W. Oldtown; 238-1337.

Long & Short Tales Books—112 S. Main St.; 236-9683.

Rooftop of Virginia—206 N. Main St.; 236-7131.

Vintage Gallery—109 S, Main St,; 800-806-4725 and 236-1849.

✌ SPECIAL EVENTS

August—*Annual Old Fiddlers Convention; Second weekend in August; POB 655,
Galax, VA 24333; 540-236-8541.*

August—*Fiddlefest Street Festival; Arts, crafts, food, childrens' activities; Second weekend in
August.*

November—*Galax Art Guild Art Festival; Third and fourth weeks in November.*

✌ CAMPING

Felts Park is open to camping during the Fiddle Festival. Contact Galax-
Carroll-Grayson Chamber of Commerce (see below).

✌ FOR MORE INFORMATION

Galax-Carroll-Grayson Chamber of Commerce—405 N. Main St., Galax, VA
24333; 540-236-2184.

Galax Downtown Association—POB 544, Galax, VA 24333; 540-236-0668.

✌ DIRECTIONS

From the Blue Ridge Parkway—Take VA 89 (near NC state line); US 58 west
from I-77 exit 14

From Abingdon (I-81)—Take US 58 east

From Marion—Take VA 16 to US 58, then go east.

44 *Virginia Outdoor Recreation*

Although we are covering only a small part of Virginia, roughly under the "umbrella" shaped area of I-81 and I-77 in the southwest, there are a tremendous number of outdoor recreation opportunities worth noting.

CAMPING

Mount Rogers National Recreation Area—Rt. 1, Box 303, Marion, VA 24354; 540-783-5196; Reserve campsites by calling 800-280-CAMP, 540-783-5196; Reserve picnic areas by calling 540-783-5196 only; There are 12 recreation areas, but the following have camping for a fee:

Grindstone Campground on VA 603 between Troutdale and Konnarock; 100 sites, warm showers, toilets, water, dump stations; Some sites are first-come, first served.

Fox Creek Horse Camp at junction of VA 603 and 741 between Troutdale and Konnarock; primitive facility for horse campers, no water for human consumption or showers, hitching posts and access to Fox Creek for watering horses and portable toilets; For a fee, water and showers are available at Grindstone Campground.

Hurricane Campground is about 2 miles off VA 16 on VA 650 and is popular with trout anglers who fish Hurricane and Comers Creeks; 29 campsites, warm showers, drinking water, toilets.

Raccoon Branch Campground is 3 miles south of Sugar Grove on VA 16; 20 paved campsites, toilets in summer (vaults in winter), drinking water, dumping station, no showers; Fishing in season. Virginia Highlands Horse Trail nearby.

Bri Money shows us what you can expect to catch in Virginia's New River and the South Holston Lake. Trout, stripers, walleye, largemouth bass, crappie, bream, and catfish keep company with fish like this smallmouth bass.

Comers Rock Campground and Picnic Area is on F.S. Road 57, four miles west of US 21. Ten campsites, drinking water, and vault toilets. Five-acre Hale Lake for trout fishing in season two miles west.

Hussy Mountain Horse Camp on F.S. Road 14, two miles east of US 21. Hitching rails, horse trailer parking, chemical toilets. Access to Virginia Highlands Horse Trail.

Raven Cliff Campground and Picnic Area off VA 619, two miles east of Cripple Creek in Wythe County. Twenty campsites, chemical toilets, and fishing (trout and smallmouth bass).

Raven Cliff Horse Camp a mile east of Raven Cliff Campground just south of VA 642. Hitching rails, horse trailer parking, and chemical toilets. Access to Virginia Highlands Horse Trail.

New River Campground and Picnic Area is a few hundred feet from New River State Park. The East End where the New River Campground has been constructed is not as well known as other areas, such as the High Country, and therefore offers you more solitude.

Canoeing, tubing, and fishing are but a few choices for recreation; you may be more adventuresome and want to try climbing the steep bluffs along the river. The New River Trail State Park is accessible from the campground where you can hike or pedal a bike.

From I-81 east of Wytheville, go south on VA 94 until you see a sign for Byllesby Dam and VA 602, turn left on 602, go until you see Appalachian Power Station, and turn left. You'll find the campground on your right.

New River Canoe & Campground—Rt. 2, Box 221, Independence, VA 24348; 540-773-3905; or Rt. 2, Box 238-A, Sparta, NC; 910-372-8793; On the Virginia-North Carolina border is a one-stop destination with tent sites, complete RV hook-ups, efficiency apartments, camp store, picnic areas, New River Restaurant, playgrounds, fishing, tubing, pedal boats, canoeing.

Grayson Highlands State Park—540-579-7092; Dumping station, showers, toilets, mountain bike trails, hiking trails, bridle trails, groceries, visitors center, programs; Some handicapped facilities; Parking fee.

Contact the following for more camping details.

Virginia Division of State Parks—203 Governor St., Suite 306, Richmond, VA 23219; For general information, call 804-786-1712; phone 804-490-3939 for reservations.

National Forest Service (Southern Region)—1720 Peachtree Rd NW, Atlanta, GA 303047; 404-347-4191.

✤ CANOEING

New River Canoe & Campground—Rt. 2, Box 221, Independence, VA 24348; 540-773-3905; or Rt. 2, Box 238-A, Sparta, NC; 910-372-8793; See above, and Independence, VA section.

✤ FISHING

Contact Virginia Department of Game and Inland Fisheries (VDGIF), P.O. Box 11104, Richmond, VA 23230 (804-367-1000) for the *Freshwater Fishing Guide* and more information. The fishing guide has detailed information for the entire state, divided into regions.

The longest of the Holston River's three forks, the North Fork is under health advisory for mercury contamination. Fish elsewhere for food or practice catch-and-release. The North Fork has an exceptional smallmouth fishery downstream from Saltville. Catfishing is considered good also.

The Middle Fork is also a good smallmouth bass stream, but is not easily accessible. Near Marion you can catch trout. The stream roughly parallels I-81. Public access is from highway right-of-ways.

The best fishing is in the South Fork, the shortest of the three forks. It has excellent trout fishing in the upper region near Damascus, and you'll snag some walleye there, too. Both species run the river from South Holston Lake to the headwaters. As you go downstream, you will catch more walleye and white bass.

None of the forks has much swift water and all the upper reaches are wadable. Below the wading stretches, try a canoe or light johnboat, keeping in mind summer dry periods affect the water level. During periods of plenty of water, float-fishing is ideal. Access may be your most difficult problem because you will have to get permission from riparian owners (exception noted below). Public access is available from highway right-of-ways and Jefferson National Forest.

The South Fork (Smyth County) has trophy trout sections where only artificial lures with single hooks are required. The first section is within the property boundaries of VDGIF's Buller Hatchery where catch-and-release is in effect. The second section is south of Marion and west of the com-

Author Vernon Summerlin displays a crappie, one of the most popular fish for catching in large numbers and for the skillet.

munity of Sugar Grove off VA 16. Two miles of the stream extend from just below the confluence of Comer's Creek upstream, and flows through the National Forest and private land. Permission is not required within the privately owned sections. You may keep two trophy trout (minimum of 16 inches). Rainbows and browns between 10 and 14 inches are abundant.

South Holston Lake lies in Virginia and Tennessee and contains 7,580 surface-acres in its 24-mile length. Smallmouth bass, largemouth bass, muskie, northern pike, white bass, walleye, crappie, catfish, and bluegill round out the game fish species. From I-81 at Abingdon, take VA 75 south to the lake. From I-81 at Bristol, take US 421 southeast to the lake.

New River is very popular with anglers, canoeists and tubers (floating on inner tubes). We fished a five-mile section near Independence for smallies, but rain the previous night made the river too muddy for a good fishing trip. However, the float-trip was outstanding.

New River contains muskie, smallmouth (dominate bass species), largemouth, spotted bass, walleye, stripers, hybrids and white bass, and catfish. The best muskie, stripers, walleye, and catfish fishing is below Claytor Dam.

Virginia and North Carolina fishing licenses and permits are honored on the mainstream portion lying between the confluence of the North and South Forks of the New River in North Carolina, downstream to the confluence to the New and Little Rivers in Grayson County Virginia. We found Virginia's nonresident fishing licenses to be less expensive than North Carolina's.

Wild trout streams are Big and Little Wilson Creeks (in Grayson County) and their tributaries within the boundaries of Grayson Highlands State Park and the Mount Rogers National Recreation Area. You get a chance to outsmart wily brookies and 'bows. Brook trout stay in the higher elevations, while rainbows can be caught throughout the area.

Access to the stream is through Grayson Highlands State Park or VA 806 and 817 off US 58. Hiking is required.

Whitetop Laurel and Green Cove Creeks (Washington County) have wild rainbow trout. The special regulation area includes the lower mile of Green Creek, plus Whitetop Laurel Creek from the mouth of Green Cove to the first bridge above the village of Taylors Valley. Whitetop Laurel is one of Virginia's largest and most beautiful wild trout streams.

A few wild brown trout are present in Whitetop Laurel providing occasional trophy sized fish. VDGIF's *Freshwater Fishing Guide* lists all fishing waters including trout streams and locations. It's a must for the serious angler.

Northfork Guide Service—Barry Loupe, POB 139, Saltville, VA 24370; 800-889-0139, 540-496-4874, 496-5121; Float or wade for smallmouth bass and trout; Hunting also.

⤷ GOLF

Deer Field Golf Course—540-475-5649; 9 holes; Take VA 91 northeast of Damascus, turn east on VA 605 and look for signs.

Olde Mill Golf Resort—Rt. 1, Box 84, Laurel Fork, VA 24352; 540-398-2211; Just off the Blue Ridge Parkway and I-77 on US 58, this 4-star resort offers golf packages; 9 holes, pro shop.

Skyland Lakes and Golf Corse and Resort is a golf and residential community on the Blue Ridge Parkway (milepost 202.2). It has 18 holes, with an abundance of water and sand traps. *Skyland Lakes*—Rt. 1, Box 178, Fancy Gap, VA 24328; 703-728-4923.

For more information contact Golf Virginia Resorts Association, POB 358, Nellyford, VA 22958; 800-93-BACK9.

⤷ HORSEBACK

Southwest Virginia is being discovered by more and more equestrians. The best trails for beginners and experts are in the Mount Rogers area. We were amazed at the number of horse camps along VA 603 from Troutdale to Damascus. *Warning:* Meeting long horse trailers on a curve can send you into the relative safety of a ditch.

Hungry Horse Farm Mountain Trail Excursions—Rt. 1 Box 316, Ivanhoe, VA 24350; 540-744-3210. From the farm, you can ride on more than 60 miles of trails from US 94 to Mount Rogers on the Virginia Highlands Horse Trail, or you can take the 57-mile New River Trail (abandoned railroad). These trails can be challenging. Changes in elevation range from 2,000 feet to 5,700 feet with flats and steep grades. Hungry Horse has campgrounds and evening meal in the Trading Post.

Horse Heaven and Iron Mountain Loops in Jefferson National Forest—5162 Valley-pointe Parkway, Roanoke, VA 24019. Horse Heaven Ridge area is full of spectacular horse trails to explore. Depending on your needs and desires, you are sure to find a trail that suits you well. To the north, Horse Heaven Loop offers a wider trail mostly along a moderate road-like grade. Along the ridge top on the Virginia Highland Horse Trail, you will encounter several small clearings, which present inviting vistas. You may see some wildlife. This loop is 8.75 miles long and is used by hikers and bicyclists. Highest elevation is 3,870 feet.

To the south, Iron Mountain Loop offers a more challenging ride, with steeper grades and mostly a single-track path. You will also see grand vistas. This loop is 8.5 miles long and is used by hikers and bicyclists. Highest elevation is 3,800 feet.

To get there from Wytheville, go south 32 miles to Speedwell on US 21, stay on 21 through Speedwell to F.S. 14, turn left, and go about 2 miles to the Hussy Horse Camp on right. Expect a parking fee.

Virginia Creeper Trail—208 W. Main St., Abingdon, VA 24210; 540-676-2282: This public access, multiuse trail 34.3 miles long, connects Abingdon with Damascus and Whitetop Station (1.1 miles east of Whitetop Station, Virginia). It was created by converting an old railroad bed of the Virginia-Carolina Railroad (known as the Virginia Creeper because of its slow pace up the steep grades) that made its last run March 31, 1977.

This trail began as an Indian footpath and was subsequently used by European pioneers. Shortly after 1900, the railroad connected Abingdon with Damascus. Five years later it was extended to Konnarock, Virginia, and Elkland, North Carolina. The old engine and tender are on display at the Abingdon Trailhead.

Virginia Creeper Trail has 100 trestles and bridges, sharp curves, and steep grades. Bicyclists and pedestrians should yield to equestrians, and equestrians should move over to allow bicyclists to overtake them. Equestrians should dismount and walk horses across bridges and trestles, and bicyclists should use caution.

The list of "do nots" includes littering, hunting, carrying firearms (hunting is allowed in the Forest Service portion but no target shooting), blocking gates, possessing fireworks, and leaving your common sense at home. Dogs and cats on leashes are OK.

Some landmarks along the trail: Mile-0, trailhead at Black's Fort (Abingdon); mile-15.5, entrance to Damascus and Appalachian Trail junction; mile-17.5, Iron Bridge and enter Mt. Rogers National Recreation Area; mile-23.0, Taylor's Valley, Daniel Boone campsite; mile-33.4, Whitetop Station and highest point in on the trail.

For $10/year you can join the Virginia Creeper Trail Assoc., POB 2382, Abingdon, VA 24210.

Horseback riding in the Mount Rogers area rivals hiking as an outdoor interest. The many horse trails and horse "B&Bs" attract equestrians from all over the South.

Mount Rogers High Country—POB 151, Troutdale, VA 24378; 540-677-
3900. Wilderness day rides, covered-wagon day trips, overnight horse
and pack mules, overnight backpacking trips.

New River Trail State Park—A 57-mile linear park follows an old railroad bed,
paralleling the New River for 29 miles; The gently sloping trail is used
by hikers, bicyclists, and equestrians; Fishing and picnicking are two
outdoor opportunities. Accesses are at Ivanhoe, Fries, Galax, Draper,
Pulaski, and Shot Tower Historic State Park.

Mount Rogers National Recreation Area—Rt. 1, Marion, VA 24354; 540-783-
5196; Many horse camps and liveries in the area.

For more information contact:

Grayson Highlands State Park—Rt. 2, Box 141, Mouth of Wilson, VA 24363;
540-579-7092

Jefferson National Forest Supervisor—5162 Valleypointe Parkway, Roanoke, VA
24019; 800-446-9670.

⤳ BIKING

Mountain biking popularity has soared in the last decade. Trails now
abound, especially in the Mount Rogers area. See "Horseback," above, for
Virginia Creeper and Iron Mountain Trails.

Blue Blaze Bike & Shuttle Service—227 W. Laurel Ave., Damascus, VA 24336;
800-475-5095, 540-475-5095; They offer reserved shuttle service for
Virginia Creeper and Iron Mountain Trails; Also you can rent a bike, go
on a moonlit night ride, rent tubes for tubing, and get a box lunch.

Creeper Trail Mountain Bike Rental and Shuttle Service—Mt. Rogers Outfitters,
110 Laurel Ave., Damascus, VA 24236; 540-475-5416; You can rent
bikes and/or take a shuttle to the Whitetop Mountain Station.

For more information contact:

Blue Ridge Parkway—2551 Mountain View Rd., Vinton, VA 24179; 703-
857-2490; There are 214 hilly miles in Virginia.

Virginia Creeper Trail—Abingdon CVB, 335 Cummings St., Abingdon, VA
24210; 800-435-3440, 540-676-2282.

Virginia Dept. of Motor Vehicles—Bicycle Safety, 2300, W. Broad St., Richmond,
VA 23269; 804-257-6620.

Virginia Dept. of Transportation—State Bicycle Coordinator, 1401 E. Broad St.,
Richmond, VA 23219; 804-786-2964.

The Virginia Creeper Trail lures bikers
and hikers to travel the old railroad
bed. The increased number of bikers
taking advantage of new trails has
created a need for outfitters that rent
equipment and provide shuttle services
in Damascus.

❧ HUNTING

For more information contact:

Northfork Guide Service—Barry Loupe, POB 139, Saltville, VA 24370; 800-889-0139, 540-496-4874, 496-5121; Hunting and fishing guide.

❧ HIKING/NATURE TRAILS

Appalachian Trail (AT)—One of the longest hiking trails in the world, it is 2,100 miles long, connecting Georgia to Maine with 534 miles in Virginia. This is the single longest section.

"Damascus Dave," at Mount Rogers Outfitters in downtown Damascus, is an experienced AT hiker. This should be your first stop for information and supplies when heading out. There we learned that the average cost of completing the AT is one dollar per day for food on the trail, from $700 to $1,000 for gear, and your transportation to the trail and back home.

In addition to the financial burden, it takes about six months to carry yourself with gear the 2,100 miles. Of that six months, you can reasonably expect to spend one month resting, or as one hiker put it, "taking days off."

Many hikers of the AT are "section hikers," as they call themselves, who hike a portion at a time. Some we've talked with have spent years completing the trail.

This young man took time out from college to hike the esteemed Appalachian Trail. Going straight through or taking it in sections, it requires about 6 months and a dollar a mile to complete the task.

The first part of the AT completed was in New Jersey back in 1922. Thousands of hiking clubs picked up the banner after that and completed marking the trail in 1951. The AT is marked by a white blaze.

We were interested to learn that, just as in society, there are niches filled with different personalities. We encountered "Pirate," who spends his life on the trail. In the spring he walks from Miami, Florida, up a trail to Georgia, where he picks up the AT. He is in Maine by fall, where he then rides a train back to Miami to start all over. Pirate has lived his last six years on the two trails.

Another niche is filled by what we call "angels of the trail." They prepare food and show up where the AT meets a highway to serve the hikers. These angels are also hikers. We met Pirate at such a place, as well as collegiate hikers.

We were told of "scavenger" hikers, who collect discarded gear. Some ask for unwanted items from other hikers or pick up discarded gear at rest stations along the trail.

We met more of the collegiate and adult couples. All we met were friendly, and most were tired and curious about weather reports.

Appalachian Trail Conference—Box 236, Harpers Ferry, WV 25425; 304-535-6331; The 534 miles of the AT in Virginia run roughly parallel to the Blue Ridge Parkway, crossing it twice. Jefferson National Forest has several AT crossings; The highest point of the AT in Virginia is at Mount Rogers (5,729 feet).

Grayson Highlands State Park—Rt. 2 Box 1411, Mouth of Wilson, VA 24363; 540-579-7092; This park has access to the AT, 2 horse trails, and 8 color-marked hiking trails ranging from 1 to 2 miles long. For a map, order the *Grayson Highlands State Park Guide.*

Mount Rogers National Recreation Area—Rt. 1, Marion, VA 24354; 540-783-5196; There 123 miles of hiking trails broken into named trails; The West End Circuit is 44.2 miles long and begins where VA 603 crosses the AT near Troutdale. Travel the AT and Pine Mountain Trail cutoff on foot for 27 miles along the southern side of the circuit. Return on the northern side of the loop along Feathercamp Trail and Iron Mountain Trail.

Horses and Mountain bikes are allowed on the Virginia Creeper and Iron Mountain Trails.

The West End Circuit is moderate to strenuous with mountain top views and spectacular scenery, which may include wild ponies.

Blazes: AT, white; Feathercamp, blue; Iron Mountain, yellow. Highest elevation is at Rhododendron Gap of 5,400 feet and the lowest elevation is 2,300 feet at Whitetop Laurel Creek.

For the experienced camper-hiker, the Lewis Fork Wilderness may be of interest. It is one of the most used wilderness areas in the Southeast, but you can find solitude during off-season and on weekdays. Grassy Branch, Helton Creel and Sugar Maple Trails are used much less than the AT, Mount Rogers, Virginia Highlands, and Mount Rogers Spur Trails.

These are No-Trace Trails, if you take it in, take it out, and use your stove rather than make a fire. Small fires are allowed.

For maps and information: Jefferson National Forest Supervisor; 5162 Valleypointe Parkway, Roanoke, VA 24019; 703-265-60545.

New River Trail State Park—Rt. I, Box 81X, Austinville, VA 24312; 703-236-8889; This "Rails to Trails" program uses abandoned railroad beds of the Norfolk and Western line from Pulaski to Fries and Galax. Currently there are 456 rail-trails in the United States, with 400 more projects underway.

The trail surface is a nearly level cinder bed, making it ideal for walkers, joggers, hikers, bicyclists, and horseback riders. Camping is being developed along the New River Trail.

North from Galax (milepost 51.8) it is 11.9 miles to Fries Junction and another five miles to Fries to the southwest and 38.6 miles to Pulaski to the northeast. Between Galax and Fries Junction is a 195-foot long tunnel (milepost 40.6) cut through rock, and at milepost 45.1 is the remains of the Old Chestnut Yard turntable, where engines were switched from one set of tracks to another by a giant Lazy Susan. There are more than two dozen historic and/or points of interest along the trail, and much of the trail is wheelchair accessible.

For more information, brochures, and maps contact: Grayson County Tourist Information Center; 1908 Courthouse, Independence, VA 24348; 540-773-3711.

Suggested Readings

Footsteps of the Cherokee, Vicki Rozema, John F. Blair, Winston-Salem, NC, 1995.

Mountain Roads and Quiet Places, Jerry Delaughter, Great Smoky Mountains Natural History Association, Gatlinburg, TN, 1989.

Our Restless Earth, The Geologic Regions of Tennessee, Edward T. Luther, Tennessee Historical Commission, U of Tenn Press, 1977.

Tennessee Angler Magazine, 5550 Boy Scout Rd., Franklin, TN 37064.

Tennessee Historical Markers, Tennessee Historical Commission, 1980.

The Blue Ridge Parkway Guide, William G. Lord, the Stephens Press, Inc., Asheville, 1965.

The Cherokee of the Smoky Mountains, Horace Kephart, 1936.

The Great Smokies and the Blue Ridge, ed., Roderick Peattie, the Vanguard Press, New York, 1943.

The Hiking Trails of North Georgia, Tim Holman, Peachtree Publishers, 1981.

The Southern Colonial Frontier, 1607–1763, W. Stitt Robinson, University of New Mexico Press, Albuquerque, 1979.

The Tennessee, Frontier to Secession, Donald Davidson, Rinehart and Company, New York, 1946.

Time Well Spent: Family Hiking in the Smokies, Hal Hubbs, Charles Maynard, and David Morris, Panther Press, Seymour, Tennessee, 1991.

TroutSouth Newsletter, POB 344, Andersonville, TN 37705.

Trout Streams of Southern Appalachia, Jimmy Jacobs, Backcountry Publications, Woodstock, Vermont, 1994.

Whistle Over the Mountain, Ronald G. Schmidt & William S. Hooks, Graphian Press, Yellow Springs, Ohio, 1994.

Index

Cathy and Vernon Summerlin live quietly in the country near Leipers Fork, Tennessee.

Cathy, when she gets time away from performing duties as a registered nurse at Vanderbilt Medical Center, loves to travel and garden. She is a regular contributor to the travel sections of newspapers throughout the southeast. Her first book, *Traveling the Trace*, was coauthored with Vernon.

Vernon is an award-winning outdoor writer, columnist, and photographer. He is the publisher and editor of *Tennessee Angler* magazine, producer of *Tennessee Angler Radio*, cohost of *Volunteer Sportsman Radio*, a freelance writer and photographer, and a television field host. His articles have appeared in many outdoor magazines, including *Field & Stream*, *Outdoor Life*, and *Bassmaster*. His first book was *Two Dozen Fishing Holes—A Guide to Middle Tennessee*.

Notes

Notes

Notes